DEEP CURRENTS
AND
RISING TIDES

DEEP CURRENTS
AND
RISING TIDES

The Indian Ocean and International Security

EDITED BY
JOHN GAROFANO AND
ANDREA J. DEW

Georgetown University Press
Washington, DC

FOUNDATION®
BOOKS

Delhi • Bengaluru • Mumbai • Kolkata • Chennai • Hyderabad
Pune • Thiruvananthapuram

Published by
Cambridge University Press India Pvt. Ltd.
under the imprint of Foundation Books
Cambridge House, 4381/4 Ansari Road, Daryaganj, **New Delhi** 110 002

Cambridge University Press India Pvt. Ltd.
C-22, C-Block, Brigade M.M., K.R. Road, Jayanagar, **Bengaluru** 560 070
Plot No. 80, Service Industries, Shirvane, Sector-1, Nerul, **Navi Mumbai** 400 706
10 Raja Subodh Mullick Square, 2nd Floor, **Kolkata** 700 013
21/1 (New No. 49), 1st Floor, Model School Road, Thousand Lights, **Chennai** 600 006
House No. 3-5-874/6/4, (Near Apollo Hospital), Hyderguda, **Hyderabad** 500 029
Agarwal Pride, 'A' Wing, 1308 Kasba Peth, Near Surya Hospital, **Pune** 411 011
T.C. 25/ 2731 Lukes Lane, Ambujavilasam Road, **Thiruvananthapuram** 695 001

This edition is published by Cambridge University Press India Pvt. Ltd. by arrangement with Georgetown University Press, Washington DC, USA

First South Asia Edition 2013

ISBN 978-93-82993-14-8

Published by Manas Saikia for Cambridge University Press India Pvt. Ltd. and
Printed at Bhavish Graphics, Chennai

CONTENTS

ILLUSTRATIONS

TABLES

FIGURES

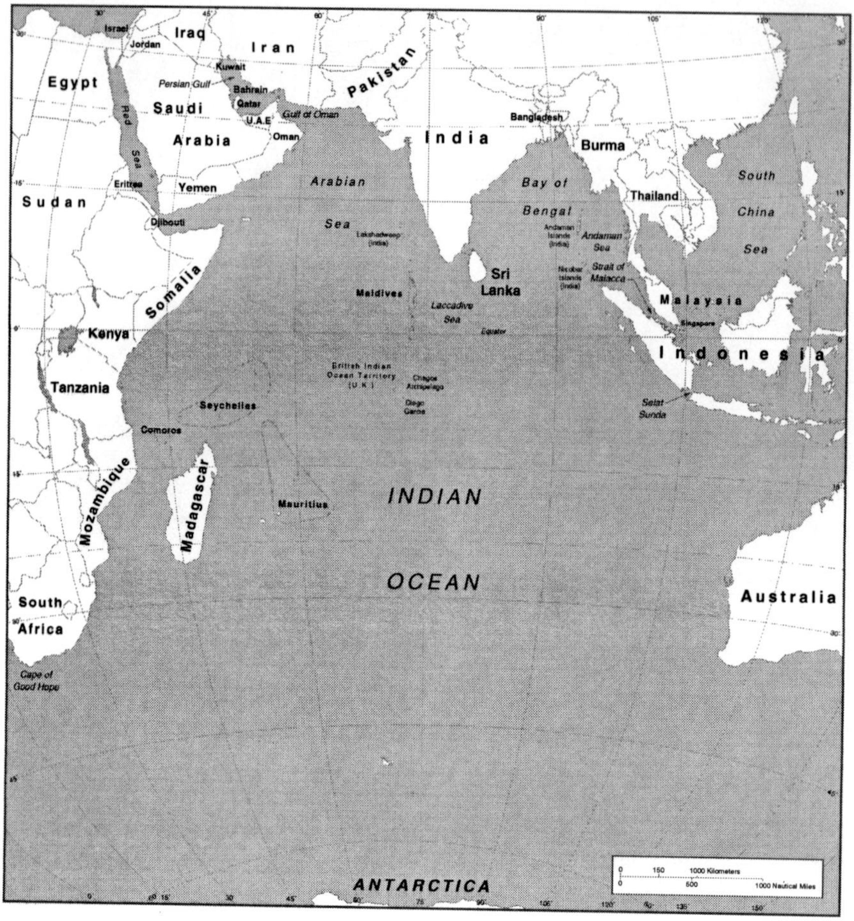
Israel
Jordan
Iraq
Iran
Egypt
Kuwait
Persian Gulf
Bahrain
Qatar
Pakistan
Saudi
Arabia
U.A.E.
Gulf of Oman
Oman
Red Sea
Bangladesh
India
Burma
Eritrea
Yemen
Arabian
Sea
Bay of
Bengal
South
China
Sea
Thailand
Sudan
Djibouti
Andaman Islands (India)
Andaman
Sea
Lakshadweep (India)
Somalia
Sri
Lanka
Nicobar Islands (India)
Strait of
Malacca
Maldives
Laccadive
Sea
Malaysia
Singapore
Kenya
Equator
Indonesia
British Indian
Ocean Territory
(U.K.)
Chagos
Archipelago
Tanzania
Seychelles
Diego
Garcia
Selat
Sunda
Comoros
Mozambique
Madagascar
Mauritius
INDIAN
OCEAN
South
Africa
Australia
Cape of
Good Hope
ANTARCTICA
1000 Kilometers
1000 Nautical Miles

INTRODUCTION

JOHN GAROFANO AND ANDREA J. DEW

In the waning years of the twentieth century, pundits and policymakers alike argued that the new century would be a Pacific Century, one in which the rising economic powers around the Pacific Rim would dominate economic, military, information, and diplomatic spheres of power. In this new century the axis of influence in the world would shift to a new center of gravity centered on a far distant ocean: the Pacific Ocean. The Pacific Rim countries—from China and Japan in the north to the ASEAN (Association of Southeast Asian Nations) trading blocs in the south, from the western coastal states of the United States to Chile, Australia, and New Zealand—so the argument went, would emerge from the shadow of the Atlantic Century, the twentieth century.

The argument in this book is that the security, economic, cultural, and diplomatic spheres of influence in the twenty-first century have indeed begun to shift from the northern Atlantic to far distant oceans, but not just to the Pacific. Rather, it is also to the Indian Ocean where we must turn our strategic attention. The Indian Ocean region has rapidly emerged as the geographic nexus of vital economic and security issues that have global consequences. As such, we argue, it is the Indian Ocean region that deserves urgent renewed strategic and diplomatic attention. Indeed, Robert Kaplan argues that "the Indian Ocean is an environment in which the United States will have to keep the peace and help guard the global commons—interdicting terrorists, pirates, and smugglers; providing humanitarian assistance; managing the competition between India and China. It will have to do so . . . as a sea-based balancer lurking just over the horizon."[1]

This raises the question, of course, of what exactly constitutes the Indian Ocean; where are its boundaries and what issues—competition and cooperation—must we understand in order to help guard the global maritime commons? The Indian subcontinent divides the Arabian Sea in the west and the Bay of Bengal in the east, and these regional seas are part of the Indian Ocean, the world's second largest. The two subregions of the Arabian Sea and the Bay of Bengal—each vast and, except for Oman and Yemen in the west, each densely populated—separate the volatile mix of Arab politics and Islamic extremism in the west from the Confucian and Buddhist societies and booming economies of Southeast Asia in the east. India is the dominant geographic feature of the region, and the nation possesses several large island chains extending throughout the Indian Ocean.

As a global thoroughfare, the Indian Ocean is anchored by some of the most important geographic infrastructure and choke points on the planet. Traffic entering the Arabian Sea from the north must pass through two strategic choke points. From the Mediterranean, ships bound for the Indian Ocean must travel through the Suez Canal, Red Sea, Strait of Bab el-Mandeb, and Gulf of Aden; farther to the northeast, vessels may enter the Arabian Sea from the Persian Gulf via the Strait of Hormuz and Gulf of Oman.

From East Asia, vessels entering the Indian Ocean do so through the Straits of Malacca and Singapore, or farther south, through the Sunda or Lombok Straits. These key strategic straits are important for commercial and naval shipping, and the rules set forth in the international law of the sea control their use. Submarines, for example, are entitled to transit through straits while submerged, and warships can launch and recover aircraft during a strait transit, even in close proximity to the coastal state. Thus, the experience of state practice and sense of legal obligation that form customary international law, and the application of the codified international law of the sea pertaining to transit through straits used for international navigation, colors Indian Ocean security.

In the western Indian Ocean, abutted by East Africa and the Somali Basin, warlords rule the land and pirates roam the seas. An international coalition of naval forces has had mixed success in suppressing maritime piracy. The threat of piracy and the fractured nation of Somalia serve as a reminder that the problems in East Africa are greater than those of any of the continent's five geographic regions. It is no wonder that only the Africa Bureau at the US Department of State has a security affairs component.

As John Martin, Clive Schofield, and Robin Warner discuss in chapters in this book, Somali piracy has also been a boon for the region's naval forces, and for developing new collective security mechanisms and legal measures to promote maritime security. India, for example, has been a leader in counterpiracy operations and in capacity-building in the region, since Indian dhows are frequent victims of Somali pirates. India is assisting Mauritius in installing shipborne sensors on Mauritius patrol ships and constructing coastal surveillance networks on shore. Delhi also helped the small island nation create a marine commando force to combat piracy. Seychelles and Comoros have also benefited from Indian support. Similarly, South Africa has expanded the mission set for the frigate SAS *Mendi* to conduct counterpiracy operations in the Mozambique Channel. The antipiracy mission is being used to improve interoperability with Mozambique's forces, and to advance maritime law enforcement training. Similarly, the SAS *Drakensberg* has routinely exercised with French Indian Ocean forces.

Although the Indian Ocean security complex is dominated by India, the northern tier of the Indian Ocean sweeps across an "Islamic arc" of instability that includes Yemen, Iran, and Pakistan. The Islamic nations of Bangladesh and Indonesia, which also have an extensive shoreline along the Indian Ocean, are more stable but are also subject to recurring natural disasters and potential humanitarian crises. Military spending in the Middle East and Asia is booming, and India is in between these two dynamic regions, which is increasingly associated with a budding strategic alignment with the United States; the expansion of Chinese naval power into the region and a stronger Chinese–Pakistani axis may introduce an additional geopolitical fulcrum and unpredictable legal dimension to regional security.

Robert Kaplan also argues that the rise of the Chinese and Indian navies, an intense increase in seaborne trade, threats to shipping and ports, and the spread of Mahanian "big navy" thinking in the East, even as it disappears in the West, are evidence that it is in the Indian Ocean that global struggles will play out in the twenty-first century. Indeed, it is the Indian Ocean that has seen waves of high-profile piracy cases that have caught the attention of not only the US public but also the navies of regional powers; it is the Indian Ocean region (IOR) in which the conjunction of increased energy transports traffic; and it is the Indian Ocean in which the possible spread of terrorist tactics has prompted a concern for the safety of global, not just regional, oil and gas supplies.

Since 2009 China has joined the fight against Somali piracy, ostensibly to protect Chinese shipping but with the added benefit of exercising distant water operations for the first time. The move has not gone unnoticed in Delhi. In 1962, the brief Sino-Indian War was fought at high altitudes over the issue of the Himalayan border. China occupies thousands of square kilometers of India, and lays claim to an even greater area of India along the border—depicted on some Chinese maps as already part of China. Today China is making forays into the Indian Ocean, and Beijing has strong relationships with Pakistan, Bangladesh, and Burma—nations not entirely friendly to India. China also has heavily courted the Maldives, Sri Lanka, Mauritius, and Seychelles in an effort to offset India's positional advantage. In December 2011 the government of the Seychelles announced that it had invited China to develop a counterpiracy base at Mahe.

The Chinese base would be only the second foreign military outpost in the small country; the other installation is a US drone base used to conduct counterpiracy surveillance.

The strategic position of India and its large and industrious population, expanding economy, and growing military will combine to make the country the dominant player in South Asia and the Middle East. India, a democracy and the world's second-largest population (but destined to overtake China in as few as ten years), is expected to quadruple its national wealth over the next two decades. In addition to a large and young population and a booming economy, India is rapidly expanding its military forces—including its navy, which is already one of the largest in the world.

India's acquisition of military hardware and increasing defense budgets stands in contrast to impending cuts in Western armed forces. The United Kingdom adopted severe austerity cuts in the Royal Navy, and few believe the US Navy can maintain its current force structure, let alone achieve the 313-ship fleet recommended by the service. The Japan Maritime Self-Defense Force is also not programmed to grow. As a result, China could reach parity with US naval power in ten to fifteen years, fueling military spending among its nervous neighbors in Asia. Likewise, Iran's military investments are growing rapidly, setting off a corresponding arms buildup among Arab Gulf states. Even South Africa, located on the periphery of Indian Ocean politics and presumably unconcerned with threats from either China or Iran, is increasing its defense budget by 11 percent during 2011–12. Finally, along the southeastern edge of the Indian Ocean, Australia is gearing up for its largest naval expansion since World War II.

Given this background and this new interest and focus on the IOR, the purpose of this volume is to survey and analyze current security and political arrangements in the IOR and to identify areas for potential cooperation in which the United States can take a lead. To that end, there are three overarching themes in this volume:

- First, conventional wisdom insufficiently appreciates the extent to which the energy market has and will continue to grow in the region, the extent to which the maritime domain is used by armed groups, and the effect of land-based instability on maritime stability.
- Second, great power confrontation in the IOR, while in no way inevitable, is a real danger and springs from the views, policies, and to some extent misunderstandings of India and China.
- And third, the Indian Ocean provides a vast drawing board for international cooperation on lower-level threat issues while the great power challenges are significant and will require more imagination.

We conclude that the region deserves a much higher level of policy, strategic, and scholarly attention, and that there is much work to be done in properly understanding sources of conflict and instability throughout the region to develop policies and strategies that enhance cooperation across the Indian Ocean in this new oceanic century.

PART I: ENERGY, PIRACY, TERROR, AND ACCESS

The first part of this edited volume, "Energy, Piracy, Terror, and Access," explores each of these dangers as a backdrop to the real challenges for the United States and for regional security in the IOR—great power security and military policies and the initiatives necessary to reconcile them peacefully. Rising energy demand and the increasing number of ships transiting the Indian Ocean and its straits are said to be a new emerging threat to international security. As Kaplan writes in *Monsoon*, "global energy needs will rise by 45% by 2030, with half of this emanating from India and China, while China's demand for crude will double by 2020, and 85% of its supplies will pass through the Indian Ocean."[2] Constantly rising energy demand is often cited as a potential source of friction and conflict; the question arises, however, of to what extent this is an accurate assessment of current and future trends.

In chapter 1, "The Indian Ocean: Geographic Center of the Global Oil Market," Sarah Emerson and Vivek Mathur of Energy Security Analysis, Inc. (ESAI) focus on the issue of energy flows in the region and their increasingly critical role in the global economy. They note that, although the use of larger vessels may keep the actual number of ships transiting the Indian Ocean and the Strait of Malacca close to current numbers, the direction of those flows has significantly shifted. Drawing on twenty-five years' experience forecasting trends, including analysis of transportation and refinery technology, sophisticated economic modeling, and up- and downstream exploration trends, the authors argue that since 1997 the emergence of China as a net importer of oil has shifted the locus of the global oil trade to the IOR. Coupled with ongoing investment in refining capabilities, Emerson and Mathur argue, there will be more rather than less waterborne trade across the Indian Ocean, and the security of those flows will be vital to the global energy markets.

Picking up on this theme of security on the high seas, the other chapters in part I examine the threat, both real and imagined, from pirates and terror groups at sea. The hijacking of the US-owned *Maersk Alabama* container ship in 2009 spurred both the US Navy and other navies to focus on the issue of piracy. In addition, news agencies worldwide have commented that piracy is an immediate and growing threat that major powers have failed to take seriously. The International

Maritime Bureau, the US Navy, and other institutions have reinforced this belief with reports and new initiatives. John Martin argues in chapter 2, "Maritime Piracy in the Indian Ocean: A Statistical Analysis of Reported Incidents, 1994–2011," that despite recent successes at capturing the public's imagination, pirates do not pose the kinds of extreme problems commonly discussed, that the phenomenon has not expanded in scope, and that the trend line is not in their favor. Martin, an investigator and researcher on the subject for some three decades, provides the first concrete and rigorously disaggregated quantitative analysis of piracy events over the fifteen-year history for which we have data. He convincingly demonstrates that the vast majority of piracy events should hardly be characterized as such, that they are easily deterrable, and that the private industries involved recognize this fully even if academics, reporters, and policy analysts do not. Martin does set the scene, however, for a discussion of how the attention-grabbing Somali pirates buck this trend and are in fact a dangerous and deadly phenomenon to be reckoned with.

In chapter 3, "Horn of Troubles: Understanding and Addressing the Somali 'Piracy' Problem," Clive Schofield and Robin Warner of the Australian National Centre for Ocean Resources and Security pick up this discussion of Somali piracy and provide a qualitative analysis of the piracy phenomenon in Somalia. Schofield and Warner address the commonly understood problems of poverty and the role of the failed state but also describe the organizational sources of Somali piracy. Such an understanding suggests solutions to the immediate problem even if the underlying, state-based causes are not immediately soluble. The authors describe how each level of the causes of Somali piracy can be addressed by regional and outside powers.

Michael Richardson, based in Singapore, and Andrea Dew from the US Naval War College collaborate to tackle the problem of international terrorism rather than piracy in the IOR in chapter 4, "Armed Groups at Sea: Maritime Terrorism in the Indian Ocean Region." They provide a counterpoint to the conventional wisdom that it is too complicated or expensive for terror groups to launch attacks from the sea or even take advantage of maritime trading networks. Using unclassified source material from around the world that lists incidents and developments relating to the possible spread of terrorist tactics, techniques, and know-how from land-based organizations to potentially seaborne ones, Richardson and Dew argue that terror groups are exploiting seams in state and coalition coverage of the Indian Ocean to their benefit.

PART II: EMERGING RIVALRIES AND POSSIBLE TRIGGERS

The second theme of this volume is that great power confrontation in the IOR is a real danger that springs from the views, policies, and to some extent misunderstandings of India and China. Great power confrontation does constitute the crux of the strategic significance of the Indian Ocean and environs. Thus, the second part, "Emerging Rivalries and Possible Triggers," examines the foreign and security policies of India, Pakistan, and China.

This discussion begins in chapter 5, "India: Dominance, Balance, or Predominance in the Indian Ocean?" by Andrew Winner of the US Naval War College, in which he explains the dominant characteristics of India's own view of its near- and medium-term role in Indian Ocean security. Winner describes the steps taken to secure this role and assesses their feasibility and practicality. It is fair to say that Delhi has a confident view of its place in the hierarchy of middle powers and is somewhat determined to procure the ability to effect this view. India will be one of the two or three predominant naval powers in the ocean before long, with a vision suggesting an activist presence.

In chapter 6, "Pakistan's View of Security in the Indian Ocean," Moeed Yusuf of Boston University discusses Pakistan's spotty maritime policy and the political and economic implications of the development of the new Pakistan port of Gwadar. He is skeptical of the significance of the bases that Beijing seeks along the Indian Ocean littoral but stresses that the growth of Chinese power will lead nonetheless to a new and major presence over the long term. Ideally, he argues, Pakistan would want to maintain excessive Chinese interest in keeping India's hegemonic designs at bay while retaining an amenable relationship with the United States. Equally important is the need to thwart any Indo-Iranian-Afghan alliance that could be pitted against the Sino-Pakistani relationship. Only with those two conditions will Pakistan be able to satisfy its twin objectives of extracting maximum economic gains from Gwadar and keeping the Indian naval threat at bay. The stakes are extremely high. A failure to achieve this could lead Pakistan to fall prey to power politics, and the interested parties could end up vying for supremacy in the littoral at Pakistan's expense.

Chapters 7 and 8 assess China's policies and agree that Beijing conceives of the IOR as a new arena of competition for which it must prepare diplomatically and militarily. Jingdong Yuan of the Monterey Institute for International Studies describes in chapter 7, "China and the Indian Ocean: New Departures in Regional Balancing," possible internal material constraints on Beijing's ability to flex its muscles and discusses the diplomatic compromises that may result. James Holmes and Toshi Yoshihara from the US Naval War College raise the stakes further in chapter 8, "Redlines for Sino-Indian Naval Rivalry," with their discussion of the "redlines," or possible trigger points, for conflict in the region. Delhi has been fairly clear about developments from outside powers that it would deem threatening. The authors consider whether China would cross these lines and how India might respond, how India might be promoting a self-fulfilling prophecy, and how the United States or other powers might manage such emerging conflict.

PART III: THIRD POWERS AND THE WAY FORWARD

This volume's third theme is that the Indian Ocean provides a vast drawing board for international cooperation on the lower-level threat issues, whereas the great power challenges are significant and will require more imagination. Thus, the final part, "Third Powers and the Way Forward," explores the role of the United States in greater detail and, ultimately, what steps the United States may take to preclude the kinds of rivalries described in part II from developing into full-blown conflicts or arms races and to prevent the issues covered in part I from escalating.

In chapter 9, "International Law and the Future of Indian Ocean Security," James Kraska from the international law department of the US Naval War College discusses the range of legal perspectives that these rivalries generate across the IOR. His focus on the use of the Indian Ocean as a great thoroughfare and on the value of legal frameworks for providing rules for resolving resource and maritime boundary disputes, navigational rights and freedoms, and flag state and coastal state authorities adds a vital perspective to this volume's assessment of the areas for competition and cooperation in the Indian Ocean.

Singapore may play a unique role in regional developments. As an economic powerhouse in ASEAN, Singapore is keenly aware of the Indian-Pakistani-Chinese rivalries, but it also sits on a key strategic choke point that brings its own challenges. In chapter 10, "A Merlion at the Edge of an Afrasian Sea: Singapore's Strategic Involvement in the Indian Ocean," Emrys Chew of Nanyang Technical University, Singapore, addresses the multifaceted influences shaping Singapore's outlook toward the IOR before describing its realistic approach to the region's ills, which combine "internal balancing" or capabilities development and arms purchases with hedging with external powers. Chew includes a discussion of Singapore's recent proposals regarding multilateral security solutions and possible future moves.

Timothy Hoyt of the US Naval War College writes about US interests in Indian Ocean security in chapter 11, "The Indian Ocean and US National Security Interests." The rise of Chinese maritime ambitions, the protracted wars in Afghanistan and Iraq, US relations with India, US naval presence in the Indian Ocean, and US relations with Iran and China all affect vital American interests in the region. However, argues Hoyt, while current US efforts to engage Indian Ocean partners are still inadequate, bilateral and regional efforts at engagement, which can include as well as exclude the United States, may be strengthening regional security and helping to safeguard US national interests in the region.

In the conclusion, chapter 12, "Access and Security in the Indian Ocean Region," editors John Garofano and Andrea Dew assess US policy toward the major challenges described in parts I and II and argue that Washington must act on the spread of antiaccess perspectives, taking a hard line with some of our friends no less than with our competitors. Failure on this score will transform the sea-lane/transport and piracy issues into dramatically larger problems, which will further exacerbate some of these trends. But it is in the arena of major power competition that the United States must exert the greater proportion of its energies in the IOR. Garofano and Dew argue that there are two approaches to precluding major power conflict: a confidence-building approach using military-to-military exercises, information sharing, and similar measures; and a bolder approach including diplomatic and legal initiatives to confront antiaccess perspectives. Finally, the book also concludes that in order to manage the challenges that cooperation and competition generate, it is vital to continue to encourage further scholarly and policy-oriented research that adds to our understanding of the key geostrategic and political issues across the vast IOR.

NOTES

1. Robert Kaplan, "Center Stage for the 21st Century: Power Plays in the Indian Ocean," *Foreign Affairs*, March/April 2009; www.foreignaffairs.com/articles/64832/robert-d-kaplan/center-stage-for-the-21st-century.
2. Robert Kaplan, *Monsoon: The Indian Ocean and the Future of American Power* (New York: Random House, 2010).

PART I

ENERGY, PIRACY, TERROR, AND ACCESS

CHAPTER 1

The Indian Ocean

Geographic Center of the Global Oil Market

SARAH A. EMERSON AND
VIVEK S. MATHUR

INTRODUCTION

As oil prices marched from $30 per barrel (bbl) in 2003 to a historic peak of $147 in mid-2008, the issue of energy security moved back to the top of the US policy agenda.[1] Concerns over the adequacy of spare production capacity in a rising market underscored the potential for a damaging supply disruption and brought a new sense of urgency to ensuring the free flow of oil. The ensuing recession and financial crisis, however, triggered a dramatic contraction in oil demand and pulled oil prices back to $33/bbl by the end of 2008. The Organization of the Petroleum Exporting Countries' (OPEC) impressive reduction in crude oil output, intended to match the decline in demand, pushed oil prices back to the $60–$70/bbl range in 2009, and led to the sudden return of surplus production capacity. The global oil market, which had been woefully short of capacity, was suddenly carrying a substantial supply buffer.

Since the end of 2009 oil prices have crept up to $100/bbl (in late 2011), helped first by expectations that the uprisings of the Arab Spring would lead to oil disruptions and then later by the fulfillment of those expectations when the uprising in Libya led to the cessation of Libya's oil exports and eventually the overthrow and death of Libyan leader Muammar Gaddafi. Ironically, this latest oil price rally has taken place in spite of very weak global oil demand, limited by anemic economic growth in the United States, anti-inflation policies in China, and the Eurozone crisis.

One might expect the resumption of surplus production capacity to lessen the sense of urgency over energy security, but it may have done just the opposite. The entire volume of unused oil production capacity is located in OPEC-member countries, and almost all of it is in Persian Gulf countries. In addition, the financial crisis initially tightened credit markets to the point where many capacity expansion projects in non-OPEC countries were delayed or canceled. Moreover, with the dramatic price decline in 2008 and unsteady economic growth since then, uncertainty over high cost or marginal oil developments such as Canadian oil sands has endured. Given the capital requirements and lead time of these projects, delays and cancellations will have a significant impact on oil supplies in the future. This means that as global oil demand grows, the global oil market will shift focus from a situation of weak demand and ample spare capacity in the short run to stronger demand and declining spare capacity in the long run. Furthermore, Persian Gulf supplies will meet more and more of global oil demand in the future. This is true in spite of impending climate policies that are likely to temper oil demand in most developed countries and some developing countries.

Despite efforts to combat climate change, improve conservation, and develop alternative fuels, there is no doubt that the global oil market will continue to grow in the next twenty to thirty years, especially in terms of supply in the Middle East and demand in Asia. The free flow of oil, especially between these two regions, will remain central to the evolution of oil prices, which in turn will determine global economic prosperity. The second section of this chapter presents an analysis of oil flows and the growing importance of the Indian Ocean as the geographic center of the global oil market. The analysis begins with a description of the global oil market and the evolution of spot and futures pricing, which drive

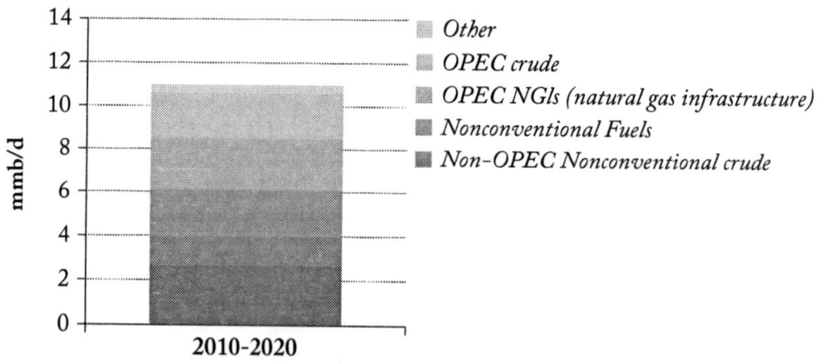

FIGURE 1.1 Sources of Supply to Meet Oil Demand Growth

price arbitrage between regions and thus international trade in oil. We also discuss the dramatic increase in oil prices since the early 2000s and the departure from the low-demand, high-spare-capacity, low-oil-price environment of the 1980s and 1990s. The second section of this chapter concludes with an overview of how the locus of international trade has moved from the Atlantic Ocean to the Indian Ocean as Persian Gulf oil supplies comprise a larger and larger portion of global oil output and the countries of Asia comprise a larger and larger portion of global oil demand. The third section then describes the demand patterns and oil flows through the Indian Ocean over the period from 2010 to 2020. The chapter concludes with a discussion of trade flow volumes for specific petroleum products that will cross the Indian Ocean.

THE EMERGENCE OF THE GLOBAL OIL "MARKET"

During the 1950s, 1960s, and the early 1970s, oil prices were "posted" or set each month by the major integrated oil companies, which managed most of the global flow of oil. As a result, the volume of trade in crude oil spot markets accounted for only about 15 percent of international crude oil transactions. Moreover, spot transactions were possible only because the major oil companies needed to balance their own supply and demand, unloading small surpluses and covering minor deficits in the spot markets. The oil crises of 1973–74 and 1979–80, however, led to fundamental changes in the structure of the oil market and the nature of pricing. The second oil crisis led to a threefold increase in prices, the adoption of fixed prices by OPEC, and the abandonment of fixed-volume contracts between OPEC-member countries and their customers. In the early 1980s, these sharply higher fixed prices for oil stimulated non-OPEC production and cut global oil demand. As a result, in the market for the marginal barrel of crude (the spot market), prices fell below OPEC's elevated and fixed price. Not surprisingly, independent refiners, traders, and even the integrated majors bought more and more crude oil in the spot market. By the mid-1980s crude oil transactions at spot prices or prices tied to the spot market accounted for more than 50 percent of total international crude oil transactions.

Within OPEC, Saudi Arabia had undertaken the role of swing producer, periodically reducing production to defend the higher fixed price. By 1985 the loss of market share had become untenable for Saudi Arabia, leading it to abandon this role. A market-share war ensued and prices collapsed in 1986. Since then almost all of the world's oil has been sold bilaterally, with transactions linked to some kind of market-based pricing, such as netbacks or formulas tied to spot and, more recently, futures prices.[2]

The emergence of spot and futures markets in oil led to more than two decades of market forces as the organizing principle of the global oil sector and price as the driver of trade flows. The deregulation of domestic oil industries and the liberalization of petroleum product pricing proceeded all over the world as countries opted to integrate into the large, transparent, and relatively low-priced global oil market. The view that market forces and industry deregulation were best suited to allocate resources and spur growth was mirrored by policies of the World Bank, the International Monetary Fund (IMF), and the Washington Consensus.[3] This view dovetailed with the rise of Reagan–Thatcher laissez-faire conservatism of the 1980s and the eventual collapse of the Soviet bloc by the early 1990s. The devaluation of the Russian ruble and the Asian financial crisis later in the 1990s showed the folly of policies that ran counter to market forces in global capital markets.

Impact of Paper Markets

The orthodoxy of market forces had laid bare the link between the financial markets and commodity pricing. Financial institutions became important participants in the futures markets, buying and selling paper barrels of oil. Futures markets and the liquidity provided by traders transformed the global oil market from one dominated by month-to-month pricing to one driven by minute-to-minute pricing. In turn, this real-time, well-publicized pricing provided remarkable market transparency and instruments for hedging price risk.

By the 2000s, in an effort to diversify their portfolios, hedge against inflation, and capitalize on Chinese economic growth, which was lifting raw material prices, institutional investors (i.e., pension funds, college endowments) started buying energy-indexed investment instruments. The futures and the related over-the-counter markets increasingly became vehicles for "investment" in oil. This encouraged the price increase after 2003 by tacking a premium onto the price of oil due to fast Chinese growth, dwindling OPEC spare capacity, and the rising cost of marginal non-OPEC production.

The Threat of Limited Spare Capacity

Two decades of lean regulation and free markets encouraged low oil prices (mid-1980s to mid-2000) and supported oil demand. Oil grew not only in the transportation sectors of the industrialized countries but also in the power generation, industrial, and eventually the chemical and transportation sectors of the developing world. Global oil demand caught up with the capacity to produce oil. The spare capacity held by OPEC was reduced to a bare minimum. An enormous increase in oil demand in 2004 led to a commensurate increase in crude oil production, especially in OPEC countries. That jump in output eliminated a significant volume of spare capacity.

In the meantime, with low consumer prices for much of the last two decades, refining has been a fairly low-margin business, discouraging investment except in countries where refiners were partially protected by government policies such as price subsidies or import controls. In sum, both global crude oil production and global refining had become capacity constrained relative to the previous two decades.

But there is more to the physical market story. The market impact of the capacity crunch was intensified by government efforts to protect the environment. Policies to cut polluting emissions led to expensive fuel specification changes that chipped away at the profitability of refining by forcing refiners to focus on investments to refine predominantly medium sour crude into clean low-sulfur transportation fuels rather than investments to expand capacity. These refining investments barely kept pace with demand for cleaner products, so the global market for clean products was supported not only by tight distillation capacity but also by limits on the upgrading and desulphurization capacity available to make cleaner and lighter fuels.

The paradigm of a capacity-constrained industry and hefty reliance on market forces came undone in the fall of 2008 when the recession and financial crisis exposed the drawbacks of unregulated financial markets that had developed exotic derivatives in every market including the troubled US housing market. Moreover, these markets were built on a foundation of stunning capital leverage, so when the foundation began to crumble there was wholesale liquidation of positions in every market as traders and investors rushed to grab capital and cover losses.

Since the financial crisis, there is newfound skepticism regarding unregulated markets, and some modicum of regulation is inevitable. In sum, oil markets have come through a long period of transition that has culminated in a global reappraisal of markets as an organizing principle for energy. The implication is that there will be more government decision making in both the producing and consuming sides of the oil sector. Unless governments can collaborate effectively, competing governmental objectives may lead to international conflict that gets played out in energy. Energy security will remain at the center of international relations.

In the meantime, the US elected a new president, Barack Obama, who campaigned on a platform that promised to combat climate change. The economic crisis, however, has trumped climate; as of this writing, the pace at which the US will enact climate policy remains unclear even as the Environment Protection Agency (EPA) is obligated to address CO_2 emissions and as California tries to develop a low-carbon economy.

Notwithstanding the slow pace of climate policy in the United States, government intervention, largely in the name of climate policy, is under way around the world, and one of the main implications for oil demand will be slower long-term growth. In spite of slower growth, as mentioned earlier, the spare production capacity created by the OPEC production cut in 2009 will gradually diminish. Oil consumers around the world will rely increasingly on Persian Gulf oil. But that reliance will not be geographically uniform across consumers. The United States and Europe are likely to become less dependent on Persian Gulf supplies while Asia becomes more dependent. The demand for and flow of oil will continue to move to the east.

Locus of Oil Trade Moving

For years the primary flow of oil was from the Persian Gulf to the Atlantic Basin. That meant securing the Strait of Hormuz as well as the route around the Cape of Good Hope and through the Atlantic Ocean. Starting about fifteen years ago, however, that all changed with the emergence of China as a net oil importer. In the intervening years China's demand has pulled oil from many locations, especially the Middle East. A comparison of oil flows in 2000 and 2010 shows how the geography of the oil market is changing, and gradually moving east.[4]

In 2000 approximately 18.9 million b/d of oil (crude and products) was exported out of the Middle East to other geographic regions. By 2008 that volume had reached 20.1 million b/d. In less than a decade the volume of oil exported from the Middle East rose by 1.9 million b/d, or 170,000 b/d, on average, each year. That is roughly equivalent to one additional tanker sailing per day by the end of the period. Middle Eastern oil exports still averaged a healthy 18.8 million b/d in 2010 despite a recession-led drop in demand. As it becomes harder to develop oil resources in non-OPEC countries, the countries of OPEC, especially those in the Persian Gulf, will account for a larger and larger portion of the world's supply. Thus, greater flows out of the Strait of Hormuz (as well as through pipeline to the Mediterranean) are inevitable.

But far more impressive than the net increase in flows out of the Middle East is the direction of those flows. Oil trade from the Middle East to Europe has fallen by about 1.5 million b/d over the last ten years, and oil from the Middle East to the United States has also decreased by about 700,000 b/d. The big winner has been Asia. Oil flows from the Middle East to Asia have risen by 3.0 million b/d. More than half of that increase (1.6 million b/d) has flowed to China. The implications for the Indian Ocean are striking. The decreasing flow of oil from the Persian Gulf to Europe has had little impact on tanker traffic crossing the Indian Ocean, whereas the flow of oil from the Persian Gulf to the United States has barely affected tanker traffic around the Cape of Good Hope. Meanwhile, exports to Asia have significantly increased tanker traffic by about one to two cargoes per day going east through the Indian Ocean.

TABLE 1.1 Oil Trade Flows to China by Geographic Region

	2000 (b/d)	2010 (b/d)	Increase 2000–2010 (b/d)
From Mideast	770,000	2,383,000	1,613,000
From West Africa	268,000	878,000	610,000
From East Africa	66,000	254,000	188,000
From FSU	96,000	676,000	580,000
Total	1,783,000	5,963,000	4,180,000

Source: BP Statistical Review of World Energy.

Exports entering the Indian Ocean through the Strait of Hormuz are only part of the story. Over the same period (2000–2010) oil flows from West Africa to Asia have risen by 400,000 b/d. Exports from East (or Southern) Africa to Asia have grown from nothing to 330,000 b/d. Exports from the Former Soviet Union (FSU) to Asia have increased by more than 1.0 million b/d, although some of that volume travels over land.

China has been the driver of these oil flows. China's oil import requirements have pulled barrels from several geographic sources, many of which have required transit across the Indian Ocean to reach China. In sum, between 2000 and 2010, China's imports from the Middle East have risen by 1.6 million b/d; from West Africa, by 610,000 b/d; from East Africa, by nearly 200,000 b/d; and from the FSU, by 580,000 b/d (see table 1.1).

Today almost all of the barrels going to China are crude oil and represent about two tankers sailings per day. More broadly for the entire region, of the 14 million b/d that Asia imported from the Middle East, at least 12 million b/d of that flow is crude oil, or five to six tankers per day, with another tanker or so per day from Africa.

These relatively recent crude oil flows into China, which have swelled the transport of oil to Asia, are in addition to the established crude flows from the Persian Gulf to the United States and Europe. Some of the Atlantic Basin trade goes via pipeline or the Red Sea and Suez Canal into the Mediterranean, so not all of the Atlantic Basin imports transit the Indian Ocean. Even so, the United States and Europe account for more than 5.0 million b/d of oil imports from the Persian Gulf and at least one tanker sailing per day crosses the Indian Ocean en route to the Atlantic Basin.[5]

There is little doubt the volume of oil crossing the Indian Ocean will grow over the next ten years. To quantify the projected oil flows by 2020, we present a view on the demand patterns that will add to the flow of oil through the Indian Ocean over the next ten years.

DEMAND PATTERNS AND OIL FLOWS THROUGH THE INDIAN OCEAN

According to the Energy Security Analysis, Inc.'s (ESAI) 2010 forecast, policies pushing alternative fuels and conservation coupled with consumer preference for more fuel-efficient vehicles will slow annual average global oil demand growth through 2020. After averaging approximately 1.8 percent from 1995 to 2005, global growth had already slowed significantly by 2007, turning negative in 2008 and 2009. Then in 2010 and expected in 2011, the economic recovery has lifted demand to 2 percent per annum. Following this postrecession recovery, ESAI forecasts a significant slowdown in oil demand growth, yielding an annual average growth of just 1.4 percent for the entire period from 2010 to 2020.

China's growth will account for at least 30 percent of global oil demand growth during the next ten years. Moreover, China's net import requirement could rise from 4.0 million b/d in 2009 to more than 8.0 million b/d in 2020. Assuming that most of the additional imports will come from Africa and the Middle East, this increase in import requirement could add at least two more tanker voyages per day across the Indian Ocean. The rest of Asia could add another 2 million b/d, or yet another tanker per day, of additional imports by 2020. Because it takes as much as six weeks to sail from the Persian Gulf to Asia, this increase in tanker sailings could theoretically add well over one hundred ships to the sea-lanes between the two regions.

In the meantime, ESAI projects North America's net crude oil imports to rise by about 800,000 b/d over the same period. While this will be sourced from many geographic regions, some of that additional supply is sure to come from the Persian Gulf, especially Iraq and Saudi Arabia. This change in net import requirement is small enough that it is unlikely to affect tanker movements in the period to 2020. The expected increase in daily tanker sailings across the Indian Ocean is summarized in table 1.2.

TABLE 1.2 Approximate Number of Daily Crude Oil Tanker Voyages across the Indian Ocean

	No. of Voyages	
	2010	**2020**
Middle East to Asia	5–6	7–8
Africa to Asia	1–2	2–3
Middle East to Atlantic Basin	1–2	1–2
Total	7–10	10–13

Source: Data from Energy Security Analysis, Inc.

Refining and Product Trade

The next few years will also see a significant increase in global refining capacity despite weak demand growth and tight credit markets. Even with project delays and cancellations, ESAI expects the refining industry to add more than 1.1 million b/d of distillation capacity on an annual average basis over the course of the next decade. This capacity growth is located largely in Asia and the Middle East, and to a lesser extent North America, Latin America, and Europe. The expansions in Asia will facilitate the increase in crude imports mentioned earlier. Moreover, there is certainly evidence that projects in the Persian Gulf countries, India, and other countries in Asia are targeting exports of petroleum products.

As a result, ESAI does anticipate more interregional petroleum product trade. ESAI expects the primary Indian Ocean petroleum product flows that will grow or emerge will be Middle Eastern and Indian diesel flows to Europe, jet and fuel oil flows from the Middle East to Asia, and selected product flows from India to Africa. Refinery construction around the perimeter of the Indian Ocean will encourage some of these flows.

YEMEN To meet growing domestic demand for refined products and to curb imports, Yemen is encouraging refining investment. Private firm Hood Oil is expected to begin work on a 60,000 b/d refinery at Ras Isa with Indian refiner Reliance.

AFRICA In South Africa state-owned refiner PetroSA is planning a 200,000 b/d plant at Coega, outside Port Elizabeth, with a potential start date of 2016. Further along the eastern coast, the government of Mozambique is also keen to revive its refining sector and recently announced plans to establish two refineries in Maputo and Nacala provinces by 2015; however, without adequate information on financial backing, these projects are uncertain.

ASIA Refining capacity investment in Asia is spearheaded by China and India, compelled by their need to match growing oil demand and, in the case of India, also partly driven by ambitions of establishing itself as a regional refining hub. China has attracted substantial foreign investment in its refining sector with prominent large-scale projects developed as symbiotic joint ventures, providing access to its domestic market for oil majors such as Exxon Mobil, Saudi Aramco, and Kuwait's KPC while ensuring crude oil supply and technical know-how. India has been less successful in finding foreign partners, but its private sector is driving substantial growth in the refining sector. Prominent among these are Reliance and Essar Oil, which have set up export refineries in West India. Together these companies will add nearly 1.0 million b/d of refining capacity before the end of the decade. India's public sector refiners are also undertaking several greenfield projects, such as Indian Oil's 300,000 b/d Paradip refinery on the east coast, scheduled to come online by 2014. Altogether, China's primary distillation capacity will grow by 3.5 million b/d between 2010 and 2020 while India's grows by 2.2 million b/d in the same decade.

Elsewhere in the region, Pakistan's Indus refinery project in Karachi is expected to increase the country's primary distillation capacity by 90,000 b/d. Ceypetco, Sri Lanka's state refiner, also has plans to build a 100,000 b/d oil refinery in the southern part of the island at Hambantota. The refinery expansions expected in the vicinity of the Indian Ocean are summarized in table 1.3.

Individual Petroleum Product Flows

Although crude oil accounts for the lion's share of petroleum flows through the Indian Ocean, there will continue to be growth in the flow of petroleum products. The following analysis provides trade flow projections of both transport and industrial fuels in the Indian Ocean in the coming years.

DIESEL Diesel is by far the most important petroleum product market. Its many uses include transportation (personal automobiles), long-haul freight, agriculture, and industrial applications. Diesel is the fastest-growing petroleum product, and Asia is expected to remain the center of global diesel demand growth for the foreseeable future. Much of the incremental demand growth for diesel will come from China and India. China will increase its share of diesel demand to nearly 47 percent of Asia's total demand by 2020.[6] China and India will together command

TABLE 1.3 Growth in Refining Capacity around the Indian Ocean

	CDU Capacity (b/d)		
Country/Region	2010	2020	Growth
South Africa	539,000	739,000	200,000
Oman	222,000	222,000	0
Yemen	90,000	135,000	45,000
Pakistan	280,000	487,000	207,000
India	4,000,000	5,310,000	1,310,000
Sri Lanka	50,000	150,000	100,000
Indonesia	1,065,000	1,215,000	150,000
China	8,491,000	11,031,000	2,540,000
Total	14,738,000	19,289,000	4,551,000

Source: Data from Energy Security Analysis, Inc.

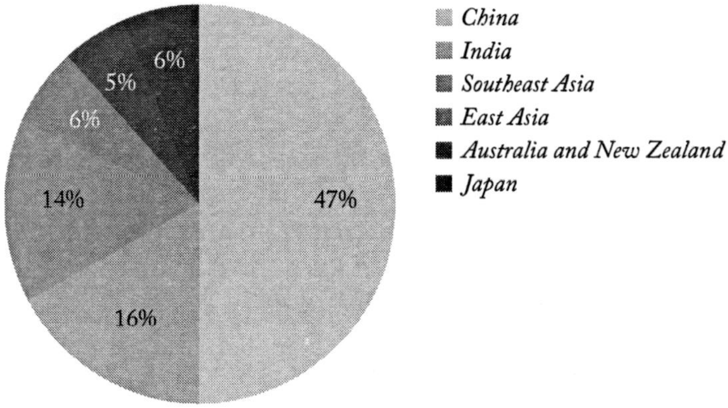

FIGURE 1.2 Asia Diesel Demand, 2020

more than 60 percent of Asian diesel demand by the end of the next decade. Diesel demand in OECD Asia will decline for reasons of fuel efficiency, environmental standards, and slowing population growth. At the same time, however, rapidly expanding refinery capacity will boost regional production of diesel. ESAI estimates the regional diesel supply/demand balance to reach a surplus averaging 150,000 b/d between 2010 and 2020; this will lead to product flows from Asia to other diesel-deficit regions of the world.

Because the global diesel market is fragmented by the quality of fuel consumed (mostly by the level of sulfur content), interregional trade flows will depend heavily on fuel specifications. For example, in India Reliance Petroleum already exports roughly 185,000 b/d of medium- to low-sulfur diesel to various regions of the world, mostly within Asia, but also to Europe and South America. Its new 580,000 b/d refinery is specifically targeting the low-sulfur diesel markets of Europe, which are structurally short of high-quality diesel.[7] Reliance Petroleum continues to export about 200,000 b/d from the refinery, displacing exports from refiners in north Asia and Singapore.

Overall, Asian net product exports are likely to increase with growth in refining capacity; the bulk of this trade will certainly be Indian exports heading westward to Europe, Africa, and the Middle East. Overall, net diesel trade will grow from roughly 800,000 b/d in 2010 to 1,010,000 b/d by 2020. Assuming trade is carried on in medium-range vessels, this trade flow will require six to seven tanker sailings per day by 2020, up from about five daily loadings today.[8]

GASOLINE After years of running a supply/demand deficit, the combination of expanding supply and slowing demand will also push the Asian gasoline balance into surplus. On the demand side, automotive efficiency and fuel switching to diesel and alternative fuels will slow demand growth in many parts of the region.

Japan, for example, will continue its trend of shrinking consumption, with demand falling by an average of 1.2 percent, or 15,000 b/d per year between 2010 and 2020. Demand growth in smaller Asian countries, such as Indonesia, is likely to slow as governments roll back expensive subsidy regimes.

Demand is not falling in the entire region, however. Consumption in India and China, concurrent with their economic growth, will offset declines in other countries. In India demand will grow at an average of 5 percent per year, or 25,000 b/d, coming from a relatively small base. Chinese demand will also grow at an extraordinary rate, 5.5 percent per year, or roughly 90,000 b/d per year between 2010 and 2020.

Along with their healthy demand growth, China and India will also add significant supply to regional markets. Of these additions, the most notable will be the contribution by Reliance's Jamnagar refinery, adding nearly 85,000 b/d in supply. Much of this gasoline will be exported to Africa and other parts of Asia, although Reliance also plans to export its gasoline to the United States. Likewise, China will also add significant capacity, with refineries pumping approximately 90,000 b/d of new gasoline supply into markets on average between 2010 and 2020.

Overall, gasoline trade will be mostly inter-Asian trade, primarily between exporters such as China, Singapore, and India to importers such as Indonesia and Vietnam. Japan and Australia are likely to slow down their imports of clean gasoline grades. In terms of interregional trade, Indian exports will likely move west to East Africa and the Atlantic Basin, bringing net trade from relatively insignificant volumes at present to roughly 200,000 b/d by 2020, and requiring additional carrying capacity equal to one medium-range tanker crossing the Indian Ocean daily.

LIQUEFIED PETROLEUM GAS Liquefied petroleum gas (LPG) demand will continue to rise slowly in the Asian region due to its appeal as a portable clean fuel.[9] The Middle East will continue to be the predominant supplier of LPG into Asia for the foreseeable future, sending most of its waterborne LPG into north Asia. Within Asia, Japan and China are the largest consumers, and although Chinese demand for LPG will continue to grow, its growth will be at a much slower pace in the next ten years. Japanese LPG demand will actually remain flat or decline slightly in the forecast period, due to increased competition from liquefied natural gas (LNG). However, some demand growth in Southeast Asia and India may occur due to governmental policies aimed at boosting auto gas use to cut down on vehicle emissions, or to attempts to replace household fuels such as kerosene with LPG, as recently mandated by the Indonesian government.[10]

Regional demand will also come from the petrochemical sector, but only when LPG prices fall significantly in comparison with the petrochemical industry's most popular feedstock, naphtha. Overall, LPG flow through the Indian Ocean will rise from roughly 900,000 b/d in 2010 to 1,010,000 b/d by 2020. Carrying capacity will stay relatively constant at approximately two tankers daily.

NAPHTHA Naphtha is used in the petrochemical industry as feedstock for steam cracking to produce ethylene and other basic petrochemicals.[11] Ethylene and its derivatives (such as polyethylene) are used in making simple and specialized plastics ranging from packaging materials to consumer goods and toys.

Unlike in the Middle East or North America, where resource endowments favor natural gas as feedstock for petrochemical manufacture, nearly 70 percent of Asia's ethylene crackers use naphtha as feedstock. Apart from its use as feedstock in petrochemical plants, naphtha is also an input to catalytic reforming to produce reformate for gasoline blending.[12]

The main driver of naphtha demand growth in Asia has been Asia's strong economic performance. Several regional governments have also encouraged petrochemical growth as a "value-added" industry. The biggest challenge facing Asian petrochemical operators in the coming years, however, is the imminent start-up of major export-oriented petrochemical capacity built at low feedstock-cost locations in the Middle East that have the potential to depress Asian petrochemical plant operating rates. Although Chinese demand will continue to support regional demand in Asia, for the most part there will be a moderation of demand in Asia's high-growth markets.[13] Critically, the Middle East's export potential of ethylene derivatives into Asia is expected to surge in the next few years as Saudi Arabia, Iran, Qatar, and the United Arab Emirates (UAE) expand petrochemical production.

Nearly all of Asian naphtha demand is currently met by exports from the Middle East, with Japan and South Korea being the largest importers of naphtha in Asia.[14] The preeminent naphtha trade flows will continue to be from the Middle East into north Asia. However, the naphtha market will also be subject to significant arbitrage trade between the Arab gulf and Europe, and between Europe and Asia. The frequency of these trades will affect total trade volumes in the Indian Ocean. Interregional naphtha trade will also be influenced by higher naphtha exports from India, where the availability of natural gas is slowly reducing naphtha consumption in its power and fertilizer sectors. Overall, ESAI estimates current net flows through the Indian Ocean to be roughly 750,000 b/d, which is expected to grow to 1,300,000 b/d in the next ten years. Assuming use of long-range vessels, that flow requires an increase in one additional long-range cargo by 2020 from current levels of two tankers daily. However, smaller product tankers (medium range) imply growth in carrying capacity from eighteen tankers daily in 2010 to nearly twenty-six by 2020.

RESIDUAL FUEL OIL Residual fuel oil flows are likely to decline in coming years.[15] Fuel oil demand continues to diminish as environmental issues play a greater part in energy policy worldwide, capping sulfur limits for fuels used in power generation, industrial manufacture, and marine transport. Expanding natural gas, hydroelectric, and coal use in these sectors have significantly displaced fuel oil demand as well.

In the Asian region, China's economic growth will lend some support to the growth of inland fuel oil demand, but only to a limited extent. Beijing's determination to curb oil imports is already hitting fuel oil-powered utilities hard—burdensome tax rules and low state-controlled electricity tariffs are resulting in exit strategies from this sector or are inducing a switch to coal-fired power generation. Moreover, new policy guidelines actively encourage units that use coal, gas, or hydroelectric power while discouraging new oil-fired power projects. Natural gas use is expected to increase as state-subsidized gas pipelines extend supply reach within the country, thus limiting electricity shortfalls that necessitated the revival of oil-powered utilities in the first place.

Demand in the region's largest consumers of fuel oil—Japan and Korea—will continue to decline, a trend brought about by energy conservation efforts and tightening environmental legislation. In Japan the power sector's share in fuel oil use for thermal generation is fast giving way to LNG and nuclear power. In South Korea as well, gas use has overtaken oil in electricity generation. Fuel oil's last redoubt, however, seems to be in the bunker fuel sector, where demand is still robust.

The majority of fuel oil flowing across the Indian Ocean will continue to come from the Middle East (nearly 70 percent) to Asia while the remaining flows will be intra-Asian trade. Overall, net trade in fuel oil is projected to decline from 990,000 b/d in 2010 to roughly 760,000 b/d by 2020, implying that only two to three fuel oil tankers will be plying the Indian Ocean daily by the next decade.

LIQUEFIED NATURAL GAS Seaborne transportation of large volumes of natural gas requires the gas to be converted into LNG.[16] Developments in technology, reduced costs of liquefaction and regasification, and discovery of new sources of LNG supply have opened up the LNG market to a greater number of consumers. In coming years LNG demand is expected to rise because of its attractiveness as a cleaner-burning fuel compared to coal or liquid petroleum products.[17] The primary driver for demand growth will be the Asian region, where LNG is expected to meet rapidly growing power-generation demand.

Much of this demand will be from established consumers of LNG such as Japan and South Korea but also from China and India. Both China and India want to bring LNG into their energy mix, motivated by concerns of energy security and the need for a sustainable solution to meet long-term power-generation

TABLE 1.4 Increase in Daily Oil Tanker Voyages across the Indian Ocean (2010–20)

Type of Oil Product Transferred	Additional Voyages / Day (2010–20)
Crude Oil	3
Diesel	1–2
Gasoline	1
LPG	no change
Naphtha	1
Fuel oil	–1
LNG	1–2
Total additional voyages per day	6–8
Approximate increase in number of tankers at sea in Indian Ocean (based on 3-week transit time)	125–170

Source: Data from Energy Security Analysis, Inc.

growth. As such, they view LNG as a cleaner fuel for electricity generation.[18] Within the decade, China plans to build at least twelve new LNG terminals on its eastern coast, with Iran emerging as a likely supplier. India started importing LNG in 2004 and has plans to expand existing capacity and build three more terminals by the next decade.

Seaborne LNG flows will expand in coming years. Export streams from Southeast Asia will almost double to 60 million tons per year by 2020. Export flows from Australia are projected to grow from 8 million tons per year to nearly 30 million tons per year by 2020. The UAE, Iran, Oman, Qatar, Australia, Malaysia, Brunei, and Indonesia will be the primary exporters while Japan, South Korea, Taiwan, China, and India will be the region's main LNG importers. Overall, total LNG imports into Asia will nearly double from roughly 90 million tons per year to more than 150 million tons per year by 2020. In terms of carrying capacity, this means LNG cargoes will grow from roughly 1.5 tankers per month today to about 2 to 3 tankers per month in the next ten years.

In sum, the growth in Asian demand for oil and the concentration of spare production capacity in the Persian Gulf countries will expand the number of tankers crossing the Indian Ocean. That expansion is summarized in table 1.4.

CONCLUSIONS

Over the last twenty years, the emergence of spot (and, by extension, futures and forward) markets has encouraged worldwide trade in crude oil and petroleum products as the price mechanism has sent the signals needed to move crude and product within and between geographic markets. For much of that history most of the trade has consisted either of crude flows going from the Middle East to the United States, Europe, and OECD Asia or of crude and product trade in the Atlantic Basin. Starting in 1997 the emergence of China as a net importer of oil shifted the locus of global oil trade into the Indian Ocean. Today the importance of the Indian Ocean in oil trade is encouraged by several factors:

- Continued strong oil demand growth in Asia, especially in China, and slow or declining oil demand in the United States and Europe;
- The increasing reliance of Asian consuming countries on Persian Gulf production;
- The ongoing integration of regional petroleum product markets into global petroleum product markets through the investment in export refining capacity and the gradual harmonization of product specifications; and
- The increase in oil production and refining capacity investment in Asia and the Middle East.

These factors, operating in the transparent and liquid global oil market with its international pricing, will encourage even more waterborne trade crossing the Indian Ocean in the next ten years. This expanding tanker-borne traffic will take place against the backdrop of gradually dwindling spare crude production capacity, which means that the price impact of accidental or deliberate supply disruptions could be dramatic. Securing the trans–Indian Ocean oil flows will be essential to the economic well-being of producers and consumers, especially those in the Middle East, Asia, and Africa, and will be critical to minimizing and managing a supply disruption.

NOTES

1. All energy trade and production data in this chapter are from Energy Security Analysis, Inc.'s proprietary database on global oil and liquid fuels unless otherwise noted.
2. "Netback" refers to the pricing of crude oil that is tied to the net product worth of the petroleum products manufactured from that crude oil. "Price formula" refers to crude pricing that ties a specific crude oil to a benchmark crude oil price through an arithmetic formula that accounts for the geographic and quality differences of the crude oil and the benchmark crude oil. "Spot market" refers to the daily oil transactions that result in a tally of prices at which deals were done. The average of those transaction prices becomes the spot price for that day in that location.
3. The Washington Consensus refers to the idea that there was a consensus in official Washington circles in the late 1980s and early 1990s that developing

countries should undertake market-liberalizing reforms such as deregulation of their markets, privatization of industries, and liberalization of trade in order to achieve sustainable economic growth. The term was originally used in a paper by John Williamson from the Institute of International Economics published in 1990 and titled *Latin American Adjustment: How Much Has Happened.*

4. These data comparing 2000 and 2010 trade flows come from the BP Statistical Review of World Energy, published in 2001 and 2011.
5. Most of the tankers that flow out of the Persian Gulf to consuming countries are very large crude carriers. They can carry between 2 million and 3 million barrels of crude oil. Tankers that leave the region through the Suez Canal are Suezmax and carry less oil, between 850,000 and 1,200,000 barrels.
6. In figure 1.2, Southeast Asia comprises Indonesia, Philippines, Thailand, Myanmar, and Malaysia, and East Asia includes South Korea, Taiwan, Singapore, and Hong Kong. Six percent is accorded to the remainder of Asian demand.
7. Europe has a structural deficit in diesel due to tax regulations, which favor diesel consumption and a refining sector originally configured to manufacture gasoline rather than diesel. Currently Europe gets most of its imported diesel from the FSU and some from the United States.
8. For long-haul voyages (Asia to the Atlantic Basin, for example), it is conceivable that long-range vessels (with a capacity of 500,000 bbls) may be used. As such, tanker traffic will be lower.
9. LPGs are usually two types, propane and butane. Butane has the lower vapor pressure at equivalent temperatures and is suitable for interior use or outside during the summer. Propane is widely used as a fuel source for domestic and commercial heating, hot water, and cooking. It also has a wide range of uses in industry and agriculture. Some LPG is also used as feedstock in petrochemical plants.
10. The Indonesian government hopes to replace kerosene with LPG in all households. The "zero-kero" program commenced in 2007 and originally planned for a complete conversion of kerosene to LPG in household use by 2011.
11. Steam cracking is the basic process in which hydrocarbon feedstocks such as naphtha and ethane are converted to light olefins. Olefins (such as ethylene and propylene) are the subgroup of petrochemical manufacture that produce plastics. In the steam cracking process, naphtha is mixed with superheated steam, which "cracks" it into smaller molecules and leads to the formation of light olefins in the gaseous state.
12. Typically, depending upon the type of crude processed, naphthas can be rich in paraffins or aromatics. Naphthas rich in paraffin content are usually more suited to petrochemical processes while those with a higher cut of aromatics are more in demand as reformer feedstock in refineries to make high-octane gasoline components. It can also be directly blended with higher-octane components to make finished gasoline.
13. To meet domestic demand for consumer goods and plastics, and to overcome the limitations of currently installed ethylene capacity, the Chinese government

has embarked on a program to build several competitive world-scale crackers, most of them integrated with upcoming refineries to ensure domestic naphtha availability.

14. In 2010, for example, 52 percent of Japan's and Korea's petrochemical naphtha demand was met by imports.
15. Residual fuel oil is the high-boiling fraction residue that remains after the distillation of crude oil, used primarily as a feedstock in electricity generation or as marine bunker fuel.
16. At roughly –160 degrees Celsius, natural gas (a mixture of methane, ethane, propane, and butane) becomes liquid. Because of the significant volume reduction in the conversion from gas to liquid, it can be transported over long distances. However, because of the low temperatures involved, LNG is transported in dedicated vessels and through pipelines that are made of very high-quality steel, nickel, and aluminum.
17. Although burning natural gas certainly results in low carbon dioxide, sulfur oxide, and nitrogen oxide emissions, LNG plants are not without their failings in producing vapor emissions or liquid effluents. However, considerable technological progress is being made to increase plant efficiency by using combined cycle power, and in developing different methods to liquefy natural gas to minimize the environmental impact.
18. Both nations are also actively pursuing nuclear power to meet their growing energy needs.

CHAPTER 2

MARITIME PIRACY IN THE INDIAN OCEAN

A Statistical Analysis of Reported Incidents, 1994–2011

JOHN MARTIN

INTRODUCTION

While several militaries, including the US Navy, have been aware of piracy on the high seas since the late 1990s, it wasn't until June 2007 that President George W. Bush went so far as to issue a statement claiming that piracy "threatens US national security interests."[1] Indeed, the summer of 2008 marked a watershed for piracy in the Indian Ocean. At least twenty ships were hijacked off the north coast of Somalia over the course of a few months, effectively catapulting piracy to the forefront of the international community's attention.[2] However, although many seafaring nations have focused their attention on the phenomenon of piracy, there has been little scholarly investigation into the precise nature of this threat. Although there is a large amount of information available on acts of piracy, most of this is raw data presented in the guise of analysis. Given the current interest in the topic and given the current context, this chapter asks three key questions: What are the characteristics of piracy acts in the greater Indian Ocean area and elsewhere around the globe? How and why is piracy off the coast of Somalia different from piracy elsewhere in the Indian Ocean? And what is the nature of the threat posed by piracy?

This chapter examines the publicly available information to discover whether it supports the notion that piracy in the Indian Ocean is a national security concern to the United States or a challenge to maritime security itself: in short, is it a problem, and if so, for whom? The chapter first examines the definition of piracy and that definition's effects on what the sources of information include as piracy. What that information reveals about the size of the problem as a whole and within regions is illustrated by breaking down reported incidents into their constituent elements. The purpose is to describe more accurately what is happening, not to propose a more fitting definition or solution to piracy.

Analysis of incidents reported as piracy shows that most incidents are minor, occurring within ports, while the most serious are terrorist attacks off Sri Lanka, attacks against fishermen, and hijacks by Somali pirates. Wherever piracy occurs, a majority of attacks are effectively resisted or completely foiled by the crew. Pirates elsewhere in the Indian Ocean are mostly interested in stealing from the vessel because even when they commit a hijack they do so to steal the cargo. Off Somalia, however, pirates are only interested in capturing the entire vessel and crew for ransom. Until 2008 piracy posed a threat to its immediate victims, the unfortunate crew. Since 2008 only pirates operating from Somalia pose a wider threat.

DEFINITIONS OF PIRACY SINCE 1982

The definition of piracy used since 1982 by the United Nations Convention on the Law of the Sea (UNCLOS) restricted it to acts on the high seas.[3] In 2001 the International Maritime Organization (IMO) defined armed robbery against ships as acts against ships or persons and property on board within a state's jurisdiction, that is, within territorial waters.[4]

The International Maritime Bureau (IMB) used its own definition of piracy in 1992 to include incidents within territorial waters and has since modified that definition twice, but these changes did not alter the type of incident included in its reports on piracy, which include armed robbery.[5] By including thefts that fell outside its own definition, the IMB was simply doing what it always said it would do: collect and distribute information to help mariners navigate safely.

However, ignoring the UNCLOS definition and expanding its own to cover thefts, no matter how petty, allowed almost any attack on a ship to be called piracy, including the following: "D/O [duty officer] on an oil tanker at anchorage raised the alarm and alerted the crew when he noticed one robber on board and another attempting to board. The robbers jumped overboard and escaped."[6] Lumping such events together with hijackings and the massacre of entire crews has made understanding the scope of the piracy problem even more difficult.

SOURCES, METHOD, AND PURPOSE OF THIS ANALYSIS

One of the most difficult aspects of assessing the threat from acts of piracy lies in how data are collected and reported. Data for this chapter come from the IMO, IMB, the International Chamber of Shipping (ICS), and the Information Sharing Centre (ISC), which was set up in Singapore by the Regional Co-operation Agreement on Combating Piracy and Armed Robbery against Ships (ReCAAP). These organizations describe 6,032 incidents that occurred worldwide between 1994 and 2011. Lloyd's World Fleet Statistics supplied the number, size, and age of vessels of various types since 1994.

The IMO collected reports from the IMB, ICS, ReCAAP, and a variety of other sources, such as the Baltic International Maritime Company (BIMCO), police, and state coastal authorities. It published descriptions of 5,703 incidents in its monthly reports. These incidents are not restricted to the UN definition of piracy but include thefts (stealing without violence) and other incidents. The IMB, ICS, and ReCAAP have all followed the IMO's lead regarding how to code the type of incidents to be included.

The IMB set up its Piracy Reporting Centre (IMB-PRC) in Malaysia in 1992; it issues quarterly and annual reports. As mentioned, these reports do not deal only with piracy but include data on all types of attacks against ships and seafarers. In a press statement in 1993, the IMB declared that it was "helping mariners to navigate safely through the South East Asian waters, where incidents of piracy and armed robbery have occurred."[7] The IMB did not claim it was studying piracy but that it was collecting and distributing information that would help seafarers avoid being the victims of crime.

This is where data collection and interpretation become problematic. The IMB acknowledges that most reported attacks occurred within territorial waters, so it used its own definition of piracy to include them in its data collection. Calling every incident "piracy," regardless of location or what actually happened, implies that they are all equally violent. The IMB did so because of its belief, stated on pages 4–5 of its 1996 annual piracy report, that only by making people aware "is there any hope of containing this serious problem."

Given those caveats, however, the IMB performs a major service. Its piracy reports are compiled from the primary and best source of information: accounts of attacks written by victims and sent directly from their ships—information no organization had previously sought. They also include information from secondary sources, making IMB reports a comprehensive, publicly available source of information rivaled only by the IMO. It has described 5,491 separate attacks in its annual reports from 1994 to 2011.

ICS and ReCAAP in Singapore have both also collected and published information on piracy. The ICS published "Reported Attacks on Vessels" annually from 1998 until 2002, describing 344 attacks. ReCAAP established ISC in Singapore in November of 2006, which has described 525 attacks from 2006 to 2011.

Although the IMO monthly reports contain details of 5,703 attacks from 1994 to 2011, more than any other organization, IMO has not collected and published a complete list of attacks. Consolidating all the descriptions from IMO, IMB, ReCAAP, and ICS and eliminating duplication produces a list of 6,032 attacks. Of these attacks 2,126 occurred within the Indian Ocean, Persian Gulf, and Red Sea.

One further issue must be considered before analyzing the data: whether there were attacks that were kept secret and, therefore, whether there is a significant invisible data set that may skew any analysis. It is of course possible that there have been attacks on vessels that have been kept secret from the public. There are certainly a number of reasons for doing so, including financial and security issues. However, it is difficult to see how any significant number could be kept hidden unless they were minor attacks. The reporting process involves people distributed throughout the globe. The crews and their families, the ship and cargo owners, the ship and cargo brokers, the main agents, the banks that financed the ships and the underwriters that insured those shipping loans, the protection and indemnity clubs, the hull and machinery underwriters, the cargo underwriters and all their key staff would all have to keep the secret. Further, the hull and machinery and cargo underwriters may be syndicates in the Lloyd's insurance market in London. These syndicates would have reinsured their risks to several more syndicates. This extensive list does not include anyone hearing a distress signal. It thus seems unlikely that there have been a significant number of attacks that have been kept secret, and unlikely that there is a significant amount of invisible data that would skew the analysis in this chapter.

In analyzing the data used in this chapter, each attack is broken down into separate elements including the crime committed, crew reaction, and whether the victim vessel was under way, berthed, or at anchor. The type, age, and size measured in dead weight tons (dwt) of each victim vessel was also added to the database.

Several crimes are often committed during an attack because pirates may kill, wound, or otherwise assault crew in order to steal property or the vessel itself. In order to limit the number of acts in the most reasonable and rigorous way possible, a combination of factors was considered: the intention of those attacking the vessel; the result of their action; and the most serious crime committed. For example, whatever their intention may have been, if the attackers failed to take anything and did not wound or kill any crew, then we classify the incident as "foiled" rather than as an attempted theft.

Because both the intention and the result are usually property theft, most attacks are classified as theft or robbery. If no violence was used, threatened, or implied, then the incident is classified as theft. If the pirates assaulted or threatened the crew, or even if the pirates were seen to be armed, thereby implying that violence would be used if necessary, then the incident is classified as robbery. Regardless of whether the pirates took anything, if crew were killed or wounded, then the attack is classified as murder or wounding. But if the intention and result were to hijack the vessel and a crew member was murdered, then the attack is classified as murder because it is the more serious crime.

A subset of these classifications occurs when the crew effectively resists the pirates. For example, pirates may board a vessel and steal a can of paint but then be quickly detected and immediately chased or thrown off the vessel by the crew. Theft has been committed and the attack is classified as such, but it was effectively resisted because the pirates were thwarted in their purpose. Effective resistance has occurred in most classifications, even when pirates have killed or wounded crew members, but it occurs mostly in theft cases.

The suffering of crews is not ignored. The number killed, injured, and assaulted has been published by the IMB in all their annual reports since 1997 and will be referred to in this chapter. However, the total suffering of the crew cannot be accurately measured or coded because the numbers of crew members on each victim vessel are not available. It is thus impossible to count the number of thefts, robberies, or assaults when, for instance, pirates ransack the whole vessel, assault the whole crew, and steal everything from them.

This methodology reveals the main event of each attack, allowing attacks to be classified by these different types of events so that each type of event can be counted. The number of each type of event can then be compared to the whole context of world shipping rather than highlighting the few, dramatic, and tragic incidents.

THE SIZE OF THE PROBLEM IN THE WORLD AND INDIAN OCEAN

For this analysis, reported attacks in the Straits of Malacca will be excluded because attacks there are so numerous and have attracted so much attention and controversy that they warrant a separate study.

As stated, there were 6,032 reported attacks from 1994 to 2011 worldwide, of which 2,126 occurred in the Indian Ocean. Figure 2.1 shows the number of reported pirate attacks in the world and in the Indian Ocean. The year-on-year trend in the world attacks and in the Indian Ocean attacks largely correspond, with the exception of 2004 and 2005, as discussed in the following.

Figure 2.1 illustrates the number of all reported attacks using the IMB definition, which includes attacks within territorial waters. However, if the UN definition is used, the magnitude of the problem is much reduced. Of the total of 6,032

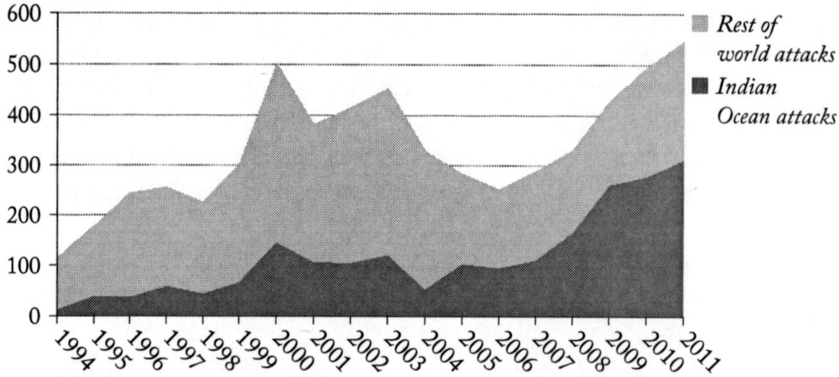

FIGURE 2.1 Number of Reported Pirate Attacks in the Indian Ocean vs. the Rest of the World

reported attacks worldwide, 2,842 were on vessels under way. From 1994 to 2007, there were 1,652 attacks on vessels under way worldwide, an average of 118 per year, while in the four years to 2011, there were 1,190 attacks on vessels under way worldwide, an average of just over 297. The exact location of these attacks is rarely available, so most cannot be classified as occurring inside or outside territorial waters. However, many of these attacks occur as vessels approach or depart from port, so they would fall outside the UN definition. It has been assumed that vessels anchored and berthed are in port and within territorial waters.

Figure 2.2 illustrates the effect of the IMB definition of piracy on the size of the problem. Ignoring the possibility of many of these vessels being within territorial waters, this definition has more than doubled the number of attacks termed

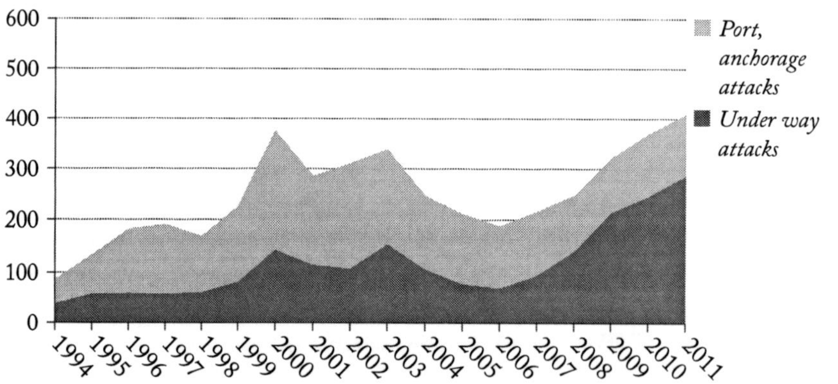

FIGURE 2.2 Worldwide Attacks Under Way and in Port

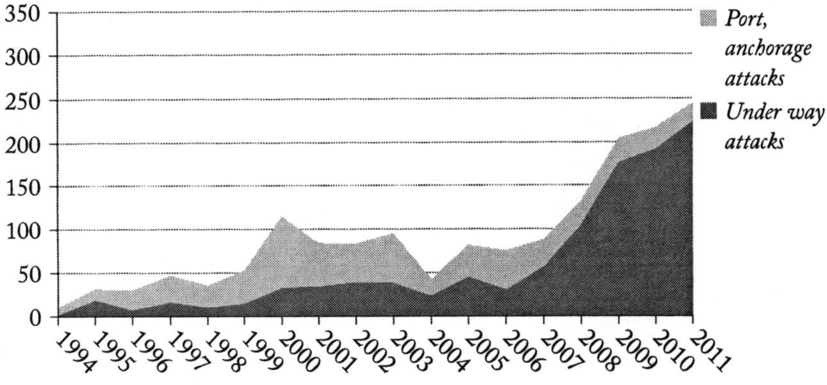

FIGURE 2.3 Attacks in the Indian Ocean Under Way vs. in Port

as piracy. Under this broader definition, the proportion of attacks in port prior to 2007 increased as the number of reported attacks increased. If attacks in port are omitted and only attacks under way considered, the graph would be much flatter, with peaks of about two hundred rather than more than five hundred. However, attacks on vessels under way since 2007 have increased so that they represent 66 percent of the total number of attacks on vessels in the years 2008–11.

The Indian Ocean had the same proportion of attacks on vessels under way as in the world until 2007, about 40 percent, but it rose sharply afterward. Of the 1,017 attacks occurring in the Indian Ocean from 2008 to 2011, 891 were on vessels under way, more than 87 percent. From 1994 to 2007, about a quarter of all reported attacks in the world occurred within the Indian Ocean (1,109 of 4,229), and about a quarter of attacks on vessels under way occurred there, too (473 of 1,652). However, in the four years between 2007 and 2011, more than half of reported attacks in the world occurred in the Indian Ocean (1017 of 1803, or 56.4 percent) and three-quarters of all reported attacks on vessels under way occurred there, too (891 of 1190, or 74.9 percent).

From 1994 to 2007, the same inflation of the numbers by the broader definition can be seen with reported pirate attacks in the Indian Ocean. Instead of peaks of 121 and 146 for all attacks, attacks under way peak at 58 and 73. However, attacks under way in the Indian Ocean have been growing as a proportion of all reported attacks there, from about 38 percent from 1994 to 2004 to more than 54 percent from 2005 to 2007 and to nearly 86 percent from 2008 to 2010. In 2011 more than 91 percent of all attacks in the Indian Ocean were on vessels under way, a peak of 286.

The data in figures 2.1, 2.2, and 2.3 do not distinguish between successful and unsuccessful attacks. Worldwide, crews completely foiled and effectively resisted

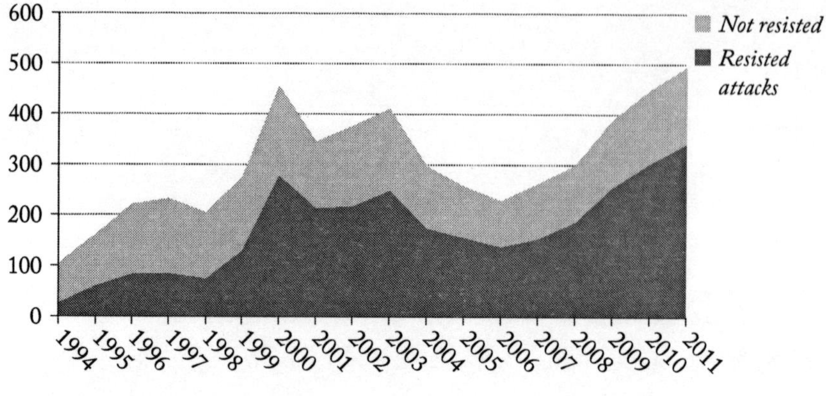

FIGURE 2.4 Attacks Worldwide, Resisted vs. Not Resisted

3,461 out of a total of 6,032 attacks, a combined rate of resistance of more than 57 percent over the whole period (see figure 2.4). The rate of resistance in the Indian Ocean from 1994 to 2007 is nearly 59 percent, with crews foiling and effectively resisting 653 out of 1,109 attacks. However, from 2008 to 2010, the resistance rate rose to more than 74 percent (523 of 705), and in 2011 it rose to nearly 84 percent (262 of 312). The rising rate of resistance in the Indian Ocean from 2008 onward has driven the worldwide rate of resistance up in the same period.

If only attacks under way in the Indian Ocean are considered, then the rate of resistance is higher still, 62 percent (294 of 473) for 1994–2007, nearly 76 percent (459 of 605) for 2008–10, and more than 90 percent (259 of 286) in 2011. Crews in the Indian Ocean resisted pirates more effectively than crews in the rest of

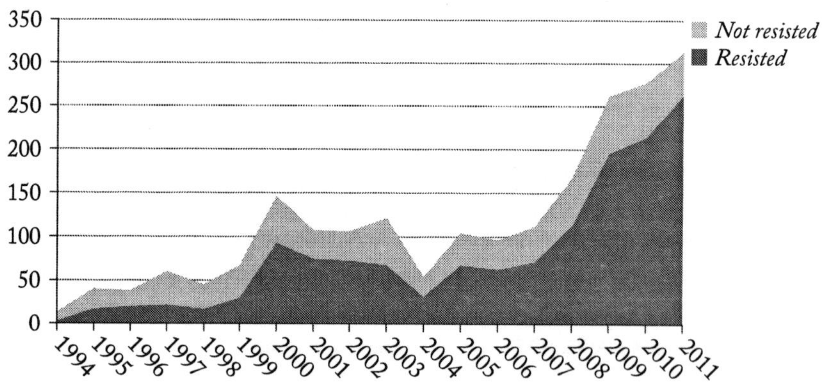

FIGURE 2.5 Indian Ocean Attacks

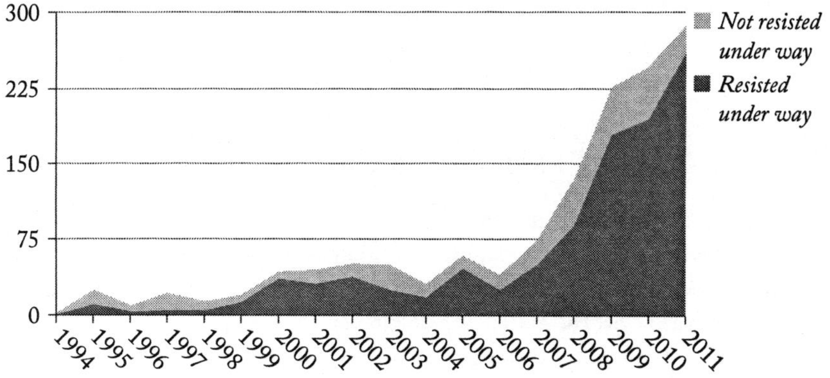

FIGURE 2.6 Attacks Under Way in the Indian Ocean

the world from 1994 to 2007, when they suffered the same proportion of attacks under way (about 40 percent), and from 2008 to 2011, when they suffered a much larger proportion of attacks under way. This is due to the very high resistance rate achieved off Somalia, discussed separately later.

Whether all attacks in the Indian Ocean or just attacks under way there are considered, the rate of resistance by crews in the Indian Ocean is rising. Figure 2.7 shows the inflation of numbers. According to the broader definition, there were 2,126 attacks in the Indian Ocean from 1994 to 2011, but only 352 were successful attacks on vessels under way. From 1994 to 2011, the numbers for all attacks in the Indian Ocean peak in 2000 and again 2011, at 146 and 312, respectively, while successful attacks on vessels under way peak at 25 in 2003 and 52 in 2010 and

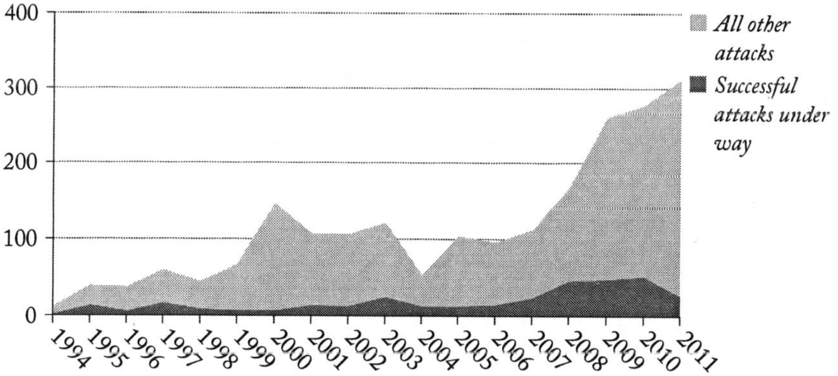

FIGURE 2.7 Indian Ocean Attacks, Successful vs. All Others

fall back to 27 in 2011. After 2007 the numbers for all attacks and for successful attacks rise steeply, but successful attacks still form a small proportion of the total number of attacks called "piracy" and fall back in 2011.

THE PROBLEM IS GROWING

Piracy undoubtedly exists in the world and the Indian Ocean, but its extent has been magnified by the broader definition. Figure 2.1 appears to show that the problem is growing both in the world and in the Indian Ocean. The number of attacks in the world start the period at 115 and end the period at 547, while number of attacks in the Indian Ocean starts at 13 and ends at 312. Figures 2.2 and 2.3 confirm that trend, regardless of the definition used, both in the world and in the Indian Ocean, where the growth is from 2 attacks under way in the Indian Ocean in 1994 to 286 attacks under way there in 2011. There would thus appear to be a massive increase in attacks in the Indian Ocean according to the UN definition.

Figures 2.4 and 2.5 show that the number of unresisted attacks under way and in port is not growing worldwide over the whole period but does grow slightly in the Indian Ocean until 2008, when it rises from an average of more than 32 per year to almost 60 per year thereafter. Figure 2.6 confirms this trend by showing that the number of unresisted attacks on vessels under way in the Indian Ocean is also growing, from an average of nearly 13 per year until 2007 to nearly 50 per year for 2008–10, dropping back to 27 in 2011. This increase is despite crews resisting a greater proportion of attacks in the Indian Ocean than crews in the world as a whole, and despite the rate of resistance by crews improving over the whole period. This can be explained in part by crews being more willing to report all attacks under way, whether completely foiled or not. However, the best explanation is the increase in the number of attempted hijacks by Somali pirates. Attacks under way in the Indian Ocean rose from 34 per year between 1994 and 2007 to 223 per year between 2008 and 2011. More attempts have resulted in more successes by the pirates.

CRIMES AGAINST VESSELS, YEAR BY YEAR

Figure 2.8 uses the IMB definition and illustrates the number of each type of crime committed by year. Robberies and thefts peaked in 2000 and 2003 before falling away. Note that the largest category of attack is "foiled" every year from 1998, and note the growth of hijackings, although erratic, since 1999. The "violence" category is made up of assault, wounding, kidnap, and murder. Although robbery is a violent crime, it has its own category because it is so common. Theft means robbery without violence.

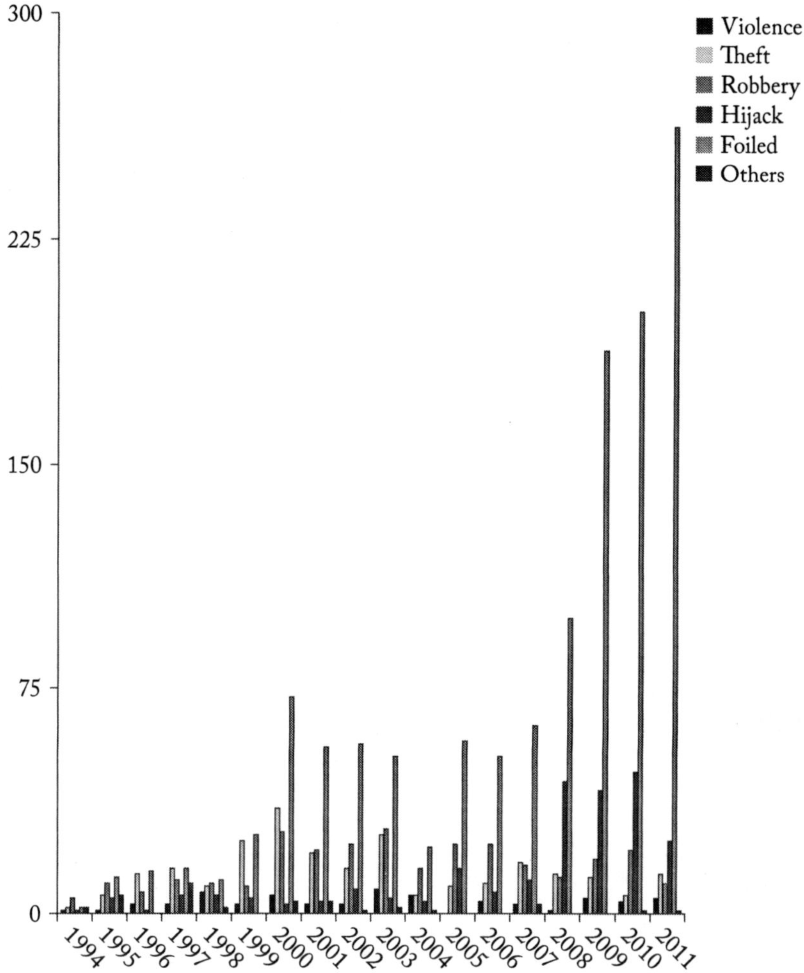

FIGURE 2.8 Number of Each Type of Attack in the Indian Ocean

CRIMES AGAINST VESSELS, REGION BY REGION

Piracy in the Indian Ocean is concentrated on ports, fishermen, terrorism, and Somalia. Ports have always attracted criminals, but only recently have those activities been termed "piracy." If crimes in port are excluded, piracy almost disappears from Bangladesh, except for attacks against fishermen.

Table 2.1 shows the breakdown of attacks by region within the Indian Ocean. The numbers in bold and parentheses are the number that crews effectively

TABLE 2.1 Crimes against Vessels, January 1, 1994, to December 31, 2011

	Area								
Event	Bangladesh	India	Sri Lanka	East Africa	Persian Gulf	Red Sea	Somalia	Elsewhere	Total
Arson	—	1	1	—	—	—	—	—	2
Assault	3	—	—	—	—	—	1 **(1)**	—	4 **(1)**
Boarding	—	4	1	4	—	—	1	—	10
Bombing	3	—	7 **(1)**	—	—	—	—	—	10 **(1)**
Detention	—	—	1	—	8	—	—	—	9
Foiled	126	104	21	39	9	116	805	26	1,246
Hijack	5	3	3	—	3	4	213	6	237
Kidnap	8	1	—	1	—	—	3	—	13
Murder	5	—	3	—	3	—	18 **(2)**	1	30 **(2)**
Robbery	150 **(71)**	53 **(17)**	2	41 **(13)**	23 **(2)**	2	13 **(1)**	5 **(1)**	289 **(105)**
Theft	94 **(20)**	92 **(30)**	15 **(5)**	38 **(17)**	7 **(2)**	—	1	4 **(2)**	251 **(76)**
Wounding	10 **(3)**	1 **(1)**	—	5	—	—	6 **(3)**	1	23 **(7)**
Others	1	—	—	—	—	1	—	—	2
Total	405 **(94)**	259 **(48)**	54 **(6)**	128 **(30)**	53 **(4)**	123	1,061 **(7)**	43 **(3)**	2,126 **(192)**
Resisted	220	152	27	69	13	116	812	29	1,438
%	54.3	58.7	50	53.9	24.5	94.3	76.5	67.4	67.6

Note: Numbers in bold indicate resisted attempts.

resisted. For example, in Bangladesh there were 150 robberies, but crews effectively resisted the robbers 71 times. The second most numerous event is theft, which was committed 251 times. However, crews did not notice any thieves on board during 80 thefts, and they chased thieves off their vessels a further 76 times. Out of 2,126 reported pirate attacks in the Indian Ocean, 606 involved violence against the crew. Furthermore, crews were able to effectively resist 105 robberies (theft with violence) by chasing the robbers off their vessels. "Resisted" refers to attacks that were foiled, plus those effectively resisted. Table 2.2 shows the number of attacks in port and under way by country.

Incidents in the Red Sea and the Persian Gulf are considered individually in the following. Additionally, six regions within the Indian Ocean are considered separately because they have different characteristics. This section, therefore, discusses Bangladesh, India, Sri Lanka, East Africa south of Somalia, and elsewhere. The southeast coast of Somalia and Somalia's north coast (including Gulf of Aden and Arabian Sea) are discussed later.

Red Sea

Almost all reported attacks in the Red Sea were on vessels under way, and almost all were foiled. This may be due to a combination of lack of reporting from the small ports on its coast and the fact that it is easier to defend a large vessel under way than a small vessel in port. The vessels attacked ranged from yachts up to a tanker of 302,000 dwt. The average age and size of vessels that foiled attack was 11.9 years and 52,622 dwt.

TABLE 2.2 Attacks in Port and Under Way, January 1, 1994, to December 31, 2010

	Attacks			
Area	Total Attacks	Port/Anchorage	Under Way	% Under Way
Bangladesh	405	342	63	15.6
India	259	229	30	11.6
Sri Lanka	54	32	22	40.7
East Africa	128	96	32	25
Persian Gulf	53	29	24	45.3
Red Sea	123	2	121	98.4
Somalia	1,061	23	1,038	97.8
Elsewhere	43	9	34	79.1
Total	2,126	762	1,364	

Persian Gulf

Of the twenty-four vessels attacked under way, nine attacks were carried out by Iranian officials who detained eight vessels and hijacked one. Pirates murdered crew members on two fishing boats and one special-purpose vessel. All the thefts and twenty of the robberies occurred on vessels at anchor.

Bangladesh

Of the 405 attacks in or near Bangladesh, 337 occurred in Chittagong and 30 in Mongla. There were 384 attacks on cargo vessels, whose crews foiled or resisted 219, a resistance rate of 57 percent. However, cargo crews did not even notice the thieves during 32 of the 94 thefts. More than 147 fishing boats and 2 ferries were attacked in 21 incidents, mostly in Bangladesh's rivers, with multiple attacks occurring in the same reported incidents. All but one attack were on vessels under way, and only one was foiled or resisted. Fishing vessels suffered four murders, six kidnappings, and three hijacks. Since 2007 there have been no more reported attacks against fishing vessels. This is probably due to underreporting, considering the number of such attacks reported previously.

India

Only two fishing vessels were reported attacked by pirates. Of the other 257 attacks, 63 occurred in Chennai, 53 in Kandla, 37 in Cochin, and 21 in Kakinada. Crews did not notice thieves during 29 thefts. The only hijacks and kidnaps were suffered by fishing and passenger vessels.

Sri Lanka

Terrorists carried out eight bombings of vessels and another six attacks of various types, including one attack that left 33 dead and 17 wounded. Sri Lankan officials detained one vessel. The lower rate of resistance in Sri Lanka can be explained by the difficulty for merchant mariners to resist terrorists, many of whom were suicide bombers. However, crews did not notice thieves during five thefts. In 2008 there were two foiled attempts to board the same yacht but no more reported attacks since. This is probably due to the increased security leading up to and after the final defeat of the Tamil Tigers in early 2009.

East Africa South of Somalia

Of the 128 attacks south of Somalia, 82 occurred in Dar es Salaam, Tanzania, and 22 in Mombasa, Kenya. Only three fishing vessels reported attacks. Nine thefts were committed without the crew noticing thieves on board. There were 32 attacks on vessels under way. It might be expected that these would be the inevitable result of southbound vessels having to sail closer to the notorious Somali coast in order to reach the ports of Mombasa and Dar es Salaam. However, 269 of these attacks on vessels under way occurred just off Dar es Salaam.

Elsewhere

"Elsewhere" consists of everywhere other than the specifically named regions and includes the Andaman Sea (seventeen attacks), the Bay of Bengal (nine attacks), and the coast of Myanmar (nine attacks), where thirty-seven fishing vessels were attacked in five incidents. There were six incidents involving hijack. In one, seven fishing boats were hijacked; one other fishing boat was hijacked in a separate incident. A ferry and three cargo vessels were also hijacked.

One of those cargo vessels was the *Marine Master*. The owners, but not the crew, of this vessel almost certainly colluded with the pirates. Among a host of other suspicious circumstances, its cargo was of low value, the bills of lading were completed before the hijack and deliberately obscured the supplier of that cargo, and the bills of lading contained a false address.[8]

Somalia versus the Rest of the Indian Ocean

From 1994 to 2011 in the Indian Ocean, Persian Gulf and Red Sea, 1,364 attacks took place against vessels under way. Somali pirates committed 1,038 attacks on vessels under way in the Indian Ocean and another 121 in the Red Sea, a total of 1,159 (85 percent). Without Somali pirates, "piracy" as defined by the UN would almost disappear from the Indian Ocean. Attacks by Somali pirates on vessels under way constitute more than half (54 percent) of all attacks on vessels in the Indian Ocean (see table 2.2).

The problem of reported piracy in the Indian Ocean, excluding Somalia, exists mainly in port. Outside Somalia, crews in the Indian Ocean resist pirates effectively more than 54 percent of the time, slightly lower than the world resistance rate of over 57 percent. In contrast, crews effectively resist more than 78 percent of all attacks by Somali pirates and more than 79 percent of attacks by Somali pirates on vessels under way. The proportion of attacks under way is next highest "elsewhere" in the Indian Ocean, where crews effectively resist more than 67 percent of attacks.

There were 171 attacks on vessels under way in the Persian Gulf or near Bangladesh, India, Sri Lanka, and East Africa, of which crews foiled or effectively resisted 63 (36.8 percent). In these regions, vessels under way are near ports, while off Somalia and elsewhere in the Indian Ocean, vessels under way are truly on the high seas, which is the UN definition of piracy. Crews on vessels under way near port are able to resist attacks at a much lower rate than crews on vessels attacked on the high seas.

SOMALIA

Somali pirates deserve their own section; with increasingly bold and high-profile hijackings and rescues such as of the *Maersk Alabama*, Somali pirates seem to grab headlines every month. The question is how and why Somali pirate attacks are different from other attacks in the Indian Ocean.

Somalia and Its Differences

The data discussed here show that both the type of attacks and the frequency present a very different pattern compared to the rest of the world. Theft is the most common crime committed in the Indian Ocean; it was committed only once by Somali pirates. In contrast, Somali pirates committed almost all the hijacks in the Indian Ocean. Analysis of the data also shows that pirates off the coast of Somalia are not interested in robbing crews of their personal belongings, or looting their victim vessels, or even in stealing cargoes; they have grander ambitions: stealing the entire vessel and kidnapping the crew for ransom.

Hijackings illustrate the greatest difference between piracy off Somalia and piracy in the rest of the Indian Ocean and the world. When a freighter is hijacked in Asia, for example, the pirates will detain the crew or put them ashore in a remote place to prevent them from reporting the hijack quickly. Then the vessel is renamed, repainted, and sailed to a port where a buyer for the cargo has been arranged before the hijack, for example, the *Anna Sierra* in 1995, the *Marine Master* in 1999, and the *Global Mars* in 2000. The cargo can thus be sold and the hijacked vessel can effectively vanish before the hijack is reported. The pirates make great efforts to avoid detection by the authorities.

In contrast, pirates in Somalia detain the crew along with the vessel and cargo to ransom them back for cash. There is a very small local market in Somalia for the hijacked cargoes, and most pirates are unwilling to transport cargoes out of the area, break them apart, and find buyers. They focus on ransoming the vessel and cargo, and they openly advertise the plight of the "human cargo" (the crew) to extract a higher ransom. From 1994 to September 2011 Somali pirates reportedly hijacked 217 vessels without murdering crew during the hijack and hijacked another 8 vessels when they did, for a total of 225 vessels. Twelve vessels were subsequently rescued by the authorities or recaptured by their crew. In four cases, crew members were rescued but not their vessels. Two vessels were recovered without their crew. In one attack, Somali pirates abandoned the vessel and released the crew. Ransoms have been reportedly paid for many of these vessels and have probably been paid for all that have been released.

Most attacks outside of Somalia occur in port or near the coast. The Asian coastline and archipelagoes provide thousands of islands, bays, and navigable creeks in which to hide. Somalia, however, provides a lawless coast, and pirates there range hundreds of miles out to sea. Somali pirates are unconcerned with hiding from powerless local authorities.

The degree of violence used in attacks elsewhere in the Indian Ocean compared to off the coast of Somalia is also worth noting. Somali pirates are heavily armed, motivated to take the entire vessel and crew for ransom, and largely unconcerned about intervention by Somali authorities, who are not effective. After the Somali pirates had boarded, crews were able to resist them effectively only 33 times. In contrast, crews were able to effectively resist 339 attacks by non-Somali pirates after they had boarded the vessels. In those attacks, the pirates were frequently not armed with guns; they were usually only motivated to take equipment, stores, and crew belongings; and they feared intervention by the authorities.

Zones of Attack: North versus Southeast Somali Coast, 1994–2007

Given this background, it is also important to understand the differences between attacks off the north coast and southeast coast of Somalia because these reveal further nuances that are vital for understanding the scale and scope of the piracy issue off the Somali coast.

NORTH SOMALI COAST 1994–2007 Attacks off the north coast include those from the Red Sea, past the north coast of Somalia to Cape Guardafui on the tip of the Horn of Africa, and north of Socotra Island. This north sector forms part of the major trade route between Asia and Europe and passes through the Suez Canal, which carries around 7 percent of global seaborne trade. In 2002 the IMO estimated that twenty thousand vessels annually passed through the Strait of Bab el-Mandeb at the southern end of the Red Sea. This estimate came from the fourteen thousand vessels transiting the Suez Canal each year, most of which also went through the Straits of Bab el-Mandeb, as well as ships trading between the Gulf of Aden and ports in the southern Red Sea; deep-sea ships trading between the Red Sea, Indian Ocean, and the Far East; and fishing vessels and dhows.[9]

Here, from 1994 to 2007, twelve vessels were hijacked. Five were cargo vessels with an average size and age of 10,861 dwt and 18.75 years, and three were fishing vessels. Off the southeast coast, fourteen fishing boats were hijacked.

SOUTHEAST SOMALI COAST 1994–2007 Attacks off the southeast coast of Somalia include those south of Cape Guardafui and Socotra Island. The trade route past the southeast Somali coast is used by vessels mainly from the Persian Gulf to East Africa and West Africa, and to the east coast of the Americas. Despite this trade route being less busy than the north, fifty-three vessels were hijacked here between 1994 and 2007, compared to only twelve in the north.

Among those fifty-three victims, thirty-six were cargo vessels with an average size and age of 6,935 dwt and 28.9 years.

Fourteen fishing boats were also hijacked here, compared to three in the north. Because there is no functioning central government in Somalia, it is difficult to see how these foreign fishing vessels could be paying a license fee for fishing off the Somalia coast. It is even more difficult to see why they would want to pay such fees. They run the risk of hijack in return for "free fishing rights."

The thirty-six cargo vessels hijacked in the south sector were small, old freighters within two hundred miles of the coast. They choose not to sail farther out to sea either because of ignorance of the risk or because the savings in fuel cost by sailing closer to shore more than compensates for the risk of hijack and potential cost of ransom. This does not justify the hijack and kidnap of crews for ransom, but it does offer an explanation for the continued presence of such vessels in waters described by the BBC as "the most dangerous for pirate activities in the world."[10]

Somalia: 1994–2007 versus 2008–2011

Since 2007 Somali pirates have been ranging ever deeper into the Indian Ocean, so it is not realistic to divide the problem into two sectors. Before 2008 the real story about reported piracy off Somalia was one of failure—by the pirates. Most hijacks occurred in the south, and pirates were only successful against fishing vessels and small, old freighters. In the fourteen years before 2008, Somali pirates attacked 314 vessels and managed to hijack 64 of them, but in the four years from 2008 to 2011, they attacked 870 vessels, hijacking 161 of them. In 2008 Somali pirates attacked 122 vessels, resulting in 44 hijacks; in 2009 they nearly doubled their attacks, 222, resulting in the same number of hijacks, 44, as in 2008. During the next year, 2010, they attacked 241 vessels to hijack 46. Their success rate dropped from about 36 percent in 2008 to about 19 percent for 2009 and 2010. This low success rate is made completely irrelevant by the rise in the number of attempted hijacks. Somali pirates will keep on trying to hijack a vessel until they get one; then they can go home, extort the ransom, and enjoy themselves. It matters little whether they have to make one attempt or ten. What matters is the number of successful hijacks. In 2011 they attacked 285 vessels but only hijacked 27. This drop in the total number of successful hijacks and in the pirate success rate to less than 10 percent is due to the increase in vessels carrying armed guards and the increased activity of coalition warships. The hijacked vessels consisted of 25 fishing boats, 11 yachts, 4 tugs, 1 passenger vessel, 10 dhows, and 110 freighters. Those freighters have an average age of just over fifteen years and an average size of 36,554 dwt. More hijacks are described here than appear in table 2.1 because some of the events described as murder also involved the hijack of a vessel.

THE SCALE OF THE PROBLEM

To understand the size of the problem, it is not good enough to consider the number of reported pirate attacks in isolation or to compare only the number in, say, one year with the number in the year before. It also is necessary to put the numbers in context by comparing them, for example, to the number of ships and seafarers.

Base Rate Error

Many press reports on maritime piracy result from the quarterly and annual reports from the IMB-PRC. A typical claim is that violence, kidnapping, and murder on the high seas continue to rise out of control.[11] The number of attacks and the percentage rise over the previous period are cited to support this notion. Such a report will often then claim that Somalia or Indonesia or the Straits of Malacca have the highest pirate activity in the world.

Although the numbers reported are correct, they are stated in isolation and not compared to the number of ships sailing in the world. Neither is the number of murders compared to the number of seafarers or to the number of deaths at sea from other causes. This well-known statistical abuse is called the base rate error, which occurs when the absolute numbers and percentage changes are reported but the base rate against which they should be compared is ignored. It makes good press but poor analysis. The fact that a very low number is up a significant percentage does not elevate it to a large figure or to a severe problem.

Attacks versus World Fleet

From 1994 to 2010, the number of cargo vessels in the world of 100 gross tons (gt) or more rose from less than 43,000 to nearly 56,000, an average of 47,893 with an average age of nineteen years.[12] In those seventeen years, there were 716 reported attacks on cargo vessels under way that were successful—that is, neither foiled nor effectively resisted—an average of 42.1 per year. So, of all the cargo vessels of more than 100 gt, one out of sixty can expect to suffer an unresisted attack while under way on average only once in its entire lifetime.[13]

The same calculation can be made for reported attacks in port and under way. During the last fourteen years, there were 2,040 successful reported attacks on cargo vessels in port and under way, an average of 120 per year. So, of all cargo vessels of more than 100 gt, 1 out of 21 can expect to suffer an unresisted attack in port or under way on average only once in its entire lifetime.[14]

And for all vessels in port and under way, there were 2,403 successful reported attacks during those seventeen years, an average of 141.3 per year, when the world fleet numbered an average of about 90,600 vessels of more than 100 gt, with an average age of twenty years. So, of all vessels of more than 100 gt, 1 out of 32 can expect to suffer an unresisted attack in port or under way on average only once in its entire lifetime.[15]

The variations in the number of attacks per year do not follow the steady rise in the number of ships or the rise in seaborne trade. Crew resistance cannot be said to follow a general increase in the number of larger vessels, which are more easily defended, because the number of reported attacks remains so low compared to the number of smaller ships, which are more easily attacked. The variations could be due to random reporting patterns. Despite the efforts of the IMB to publicize the problem and urge seafarers to report all incidents, there is no way of knowing how many seafarers are even aware of the IMB's Piracy Reporting Centre, how many bother to report, or whether they do so consistently. The number of attacks is so small when compared to the world fleet that any variation from year to year has little impact on the whole. If the maximum number of attacks in one year was taken as the average, it is difficult to see how that would alter the situation significantly.

Attacks versus Vessel Movements in the Indian Ocean

It has not been possible to calculate how much of the world fleet sails in the Indian Ocean, but it is possible to make some estimates. The Marine Department of Malaysia stated that 63,636 ships of 300 gt or more passed through the Straits of Malacca in 2004, based on the mandatory reports from transiting ships.[16] Thus, it would be reasonable to estimate that more than one million vessels passed through the straits in the seventeen years from 1994 to 2010.

Not all vessels in the Straits of Malacca would come from or go to the Indian Ocean. They might enter from the South China Sea to visit a port and then return east to, say, China or Japan. Conversely, there would be many vessels in the Indian Ocean that would not enter the Straits of Malacca because they might sail from, say, ports in India to Africa. Those vessels that remained in the Indian Ocean could well compensate for those that sailed in the Straits of Malacca but did not enter the Indian Ocean.

An oceangoing vessel could not make only one movement per day throughout its life; only a ferry or coastal vessel could do so. An oceangoing vessel would spend at least one day in port at either end of its voyage and at least one day sailing between ports, although probably more than just one day in port and in sailing. So the maximum number of movements an oceangoing vessel could make per year is 120. It could therefore expect to suffer one successful attack every twenty-four years.[17] The number of vessel movements in the Indian Ocean at more than one million is only a rough estimate, but even if it is an overstatement, the likelihood of an unresisted attack on any vessel is remote because the number of movements per year per vessel is probably also overstated.

Attacks versus Vessel Movements Past the North Somali Coast

From 1994 to 2007 there were 89 attacks on vessels by Somali pirates in the Indian Ocean and Red Sea that were not foiled or effectively resisted. In 2002 the IMO estimated that more than 20,000 vessels a year passed through the Strait of Bab el-Mandeb at the southern end of the Red Sea. It is therefore reasonable to say that there cannot have been fewer than 280,000 vessel movements in the Red Sea and past both the north and southeast coast of Somalia during the fourteen years from 1994 to 2007.[18] This is an underestimate because it does not include movements of vessels between East Africa to the Persian Gulf, India, Pakistan, and so forth.

But things changed in 2008. In the years from 2008 to 2010, Somali pirates perpetrated 167 attacks successfully throughout the Indian Ocean and Red Sea, where it is reasonable to say that there were at least 80,000 vessel movements, or 1 successful attack for every 479 vessel movements. Most of these attacks were hijacks. The growth in their number is relevant, not the base rate error. Figures 2.5, 2.6, and 2.7 show the increase in activity leading to greater pirate success.

A PROBLEM FOR WHOM?

To understand whether reported piracy is a problem and to understand its nature, it is necessary to consider who might be troubled by it and why. It is also necessary to put this problem into proper context by comparing it to the number of potential victims and the effect upon them.

Crew Casualties

The International Shipping Federation (ISF) and the BIMCO "Manpower Update" for 2000 estimated there were 1,003,000 seafarers employed worldwide.[19] If fishermen are included, there are many, many more.

The IMB-PRC reported that 427 crew were murdered from 1994 to 2011, an average of just under 24 per year.[20] If the host of uncounted, small-time fishermen are included, who suffer disproportionately from the most serious attacks, then the reported murder rate is much less, especially among cargo crews.

Seafaring is one of the most dangerous occupations in the world. Detlef Nilsen estimated that there were 2,354 deaths per year among seafarers from 1990 to 1994.[21] Over that five-year period there were 11,770 estimated deaths on ships from accidents. Compare this to the 427 reported murders by pirates over a period of eighteen years. Those injured by equipment at sea or experiencing severe illness without access to medical assistance have not been counted, but these injuries and illnesses must be many times the number of deaths.

Keeping these statistics in mind, death by reported piracy is a tiny fraction of death by accident at sea. Moreover, entire crews aboard vessels hijacked off Somalia have not been murdered thus far. However, this depends on the pirates obtaining the ransoms they demand. As the number of vessels hijacked for ransom rises, so does the possibility of a ransom not being paid and the crew being murdered in retaliation.

Thousands of crew on hijacked vessels have been held for ransom, especially by Somali pirates. Although most returned home within a few weeks, some have been held for months, and all have suffered the trauma of violent capture and detention. That detention had to be endured without knowing when they might be released, if at all. However, with the reduced number of hijacks by Somali pirates in 2011, this problem is shrinking.

Property Loss

Serious attacks do occur, but they are rare. From 1994 to 2011 pirates got nothing in 1,246 foiled attacks, very little in the additional 192 attacks that crews effectively resisted, and not very much during the 175 thefts that were not effectively resisted (see table 2.1). Most of the other attacks are akin to pilfering, a maritime version of shoplifting. This can really only be verified by reading all the descriptions of attacks reported from 1994 to 2010 because it has not been possible to obtain a complete list of stolen property or to reduce it to a manageable size.

The value of cargo stolen by pirates should be compared to the total value of all cargoes transported by sea within the Indian Ocean. A minimum figure can be guessed by considering the percent of the world's trade transported between Singapore and the Suez Canal. In 2002 the IMO estimated that 7 percent of the world's trade passed through the Strait of Bab el-Mandeb, which included 85 million tons of oil or 680 million barrels from the Persian Gulf. The trade in oil has increased greatly since 2002, and the current price of oil has been hovering around \$100 per barrel. Thus, the value of cargo passing the north coast of Somalia each year cannot be less than \$68 billion, the rough current value of oil at 2002 quantities. The total value of cargoes passing through the Indian Ocean, from outside the Indian Ocean to ports within it, and from those ports to the world outside must be even greater.

The property reported as stolen by pirates both off the north and southeast coasts of Somalia and within the Indian Ocean as a whole simply cannot be anything more than a trifle compared to that gigantic figure. In addition to insuring its hull and machinery, a vessel will also join a protection and indemnity club to cover other risks, which will include losses due to crime. Unless the whole vessel has been lost, hull and machinery underwriters and protection and indemnity clubs in London do not bother to collect information on the value of claims due to piracy.[22]

The majority of attacks involve relatively small amounts of property, with relatively few serious cases. It is obvious from the kinds of things lost in attacks—rope, paint, tools, and so forth—that this kind of petty attack is vastly underreported. But this loss must be compared to the running costs of vessels. The 2002 IMO estimate of more than twenty thousand vessels passing through the Strait of Bab el-Mandeb each year is the minimum number of vessels in the Indian Ocean. Those vessels must cost at least $1,000 per day to run, and probably cost much more. So the annual running cost of the fleet in the Indian Ocean cannot be less than $1,000 × 365 × 20,000 = $7.3 billion. A vast number of ropes and cans of paint and other bosun's stores would have to be pilfered in port to make up a significant fraction of this gross underestimate of the fleet running cost.

All crime is underreported, but the more serious crime is less so. It is most unlikely that the hijack of a bulk carrier, or the total ransacking of a vessel, or the theft of large quantities of valuable equipment would not be reported, if only to underwriters. The majority of the losses are relatively minor.

Trade Disruption

Throughout the Indian Ocean, Red Sea, and Persian Gulf, there were 1,919 reported attacks on cargo vessels (of which the crew completely foiled 1,162) in eighteen years, when there could not have been fewer than 360,000 vessel movements in the Indian Ocean. Of the 757 remaining attacks, 247 were thefts, in which the thieves did not use, threaten, or imply violence to the crew. The property stolen could not have been significant during these attacks. There were 337 other attacks that were more serious (robbery, murder, wounding, and assault directed against crew members) and 173 hijacks that were directed primarily against the crew and vessels.

Pirates do not yet inflict significant casualties on crews to dissuade them from sailing, and they do not steal sufficient quantities of equipment and stores to deter owners operating their vessels. What will disrupt trade is vessel hijack. However, until 2008 it has been fishing boats in Bangladesh and the Bay of Bengal that suffered most from hijack, not cargo vessels in the Indian Ocean, with the exception of off the Somali coasts.

Until 2008 the cargo vessels hijacked off Somalia were few, small, old, and nearing the end of their life.[23] In 2008 the situation changed dramatically. Pirates succeeded in obtaining millions of US dollars in ransom for each vessel in 2008 and then increased their activity to nearly fifty hijacks per year thereafter. They will undoubtedly be tempted to increase their activity further until it becomes intolerable or is stopped. However outrageous, those fifty hijacks per year are tolerable. However, if crews on board hijacked vessels are not returned home safely, the impact on crew morale in general will be great because the fear of crime is far greater than its actual frequency. This may pose a threat to trade.

CONCLUSIONS

Until 2008 reported piracy was so low that it was a problem for those who suffered from it but not for anyone else. These include small-time fishermen in Asia, larger foreign trawlers off Somalia risking hijack in return for license-free fishing, and small, old freighters risking hijack in order to save fuel.

Despite the number of attacks reported and the severity of some attacks, it is important to put piracy in perspective. It is not a threat to seafarers as a whole. The few murders each year, however tragic, should be compared to the thousands of deaths seafarers suffer every year from accidents. Neither is a threat to shipping as a whole. Although the number of attacks is rising, it is doing so from a very low base, which should be compared to the size of the world fleet. Comparing the increase in attacks in one year to the number in a previous year commits the base rate error, gives a false picture, and is of use only to journalists writing exciting copy.[24] Furthermore, some of that increase can be explained by the growth in the world fleet and the increased willingness of crews to report attacks that they effectively resist, and as the proportion of resisted attacks also grows.

Moreover, the reported loss of property is insignificant when compared to the total value of cargoes or the total running costs of the fleet. Examining the reports of property stolen makes it obvious that its value is a tiny proportion of fleet running costs. It is less likely that significant losses will not be reported, although they may be underreported. However underreported, losses from piracy are too small for protection and indemnity clubs to bother to record under its own category. Since 2008 and the increase in hijacks for ransom by Somali pirates, that may have changed. Before 2008 piracy was not a threat to trade through the Indian Ocean, and since then the number of hijacks has not yet risen to an intolerable level. However, the situation in Somalia means that there is no ceiling to the number of attempts that Somali pirates could make in future; thus, the number of hijacks could in theory rise to an intolerable level. Although murders at sea are few, the possibility that Somali pirates would kill the kidnapped crew if ransoms are not paid remains a threat. Even if murders do not increase, and even if the number of vessels hijacked by Somali pirates remains at the 2011 level, hundreds of seafarers would be subjected to the trauma of kidnap every year.

Reported piracy has not been a national security concern for the United States and should not have impacted the national military and security strategy.

This may have been unclear in 1993, but the information collected by the IMO, IMB, ICS, and ReCAAP since then confirms it. Since the compilation of this analysis, there should be no illusion about the impact or challenge that piracy poses to national or global issues.

Adopting a definition to include ships in port more than doubled the number of events that could be called piracy. Expanding that definition to include theft along with almost any attack on a ship, however petty or unsuccessful, meant that essentially all crime on ships was called piracy.[25] When compiling reports of all crime on land, most of which is minor, the police do not call them all murder and mayhem. It is just as inappropriate for reports of all crime aboard ships to be called piracy. The fact that some of those crimes are very serious is no excuse because on ships, just as on land, most crimes are not serious. Claiming that such minor events are vastly underreported only emphasizes the abuse of labeling all such crime by the most emotive term. Such a tactic draws attention to the problem but does not make it serious.

Although the number of incidents called piracy has been inflated by the definition, that definition needs no refinement once its effects are known. The abuse of the term "piracy" by the popular press is of no greater concern than the abuse by the popular press of the private lives of celebrities. Such abuse is squalid entertainment of the masses, nothing more.

However, since 2008 the hijacks off the north coast of Somalia threaten a major sea trade route that is important to world trade and to trade within the Indian Ocean. It is not piracy in the world or in the Indian Ocean that is a problem, or even piracy off Somalia, but piracy off the north coast of Somalia that has become a problem. Piracy in this one corner of the world, albeit astride an important choke point, should not be used to justify the notion that piracy anywhere else is a problem—except, of course, to its unfortunate immediate victims.

NOTES

1. See, for example, Kevin M. Tokarski, "A Modern Day Response to Piracy in the Straits of Malacca and Singapore" (Newport, RI: US Naval War College, June 18, 1993), www.dtic.mil/cgi-bin/GetTRDoc?AD=ADA266681&Location=U2&doc=GetTRDoc.pdf; Adm. Thomas Fargo, commander of US forces in the Pacific, asserted in May 2004 that "transnational threats like . . . piracy . . . challenge maritime security itself." See Thomas Fargo, "Remarks" (Military Operations and Law Conference, Victoria, British Columbia, May 3, 2004), www.pacom.mil/speeches/sst2004/040331housearmedsvcscomm.shtml. For President Bush's statement see "Memorandum from the President to the Vice President," June 14, 2007; http://georgewbush-whitehouse.archives.gov/news/releases/2007/06/20070614-3.html.

2. United Nations Office on Drugs and Crime, "The Globalisation of Crime—A Transnational Organised Crime Threat Assessment." www.unodc.org/unodc/en/data-and-analysis/tocta-2010.html; 195.
3. Article 101 UNCLOS defines piracy as:
   "a) any illegal acts of violence or detention, or any acts of depredation, committed for private ends by the crew or the passengers of a private ship or a private aircraft, and directed
      i) on the high seas, against another ship or aircraft, or against persons or property on board such ship or aircraft;
      ii) against a ship, aircraft, persons or property in a place outside the jurisdiction of any State;
   b) any act of voluntary participation in the operation of a ship or of an aircraft with knowledge of facts making it a pirate ship or aircraft;
   c) any act of inciting or of intentionally facilitating an act described in subparagraph (a) or (b)."

   See "Legal Framework for the Repression of Piracy under UNCLOS," *United Nations, Division for Ocean Affairs and the Law of the Sea*, September 9, 2010, www.un.org/Depts/los/piracy/piracy_legal_framework.htm.
4. MSC circular 984 defines armed robbery as: "any unlawful act of violence or detention or any act of depredation, or threat thereof, other than an act of 'piracy,' directed against a ship or against persons or property on board such ship, within a State's jurisdiction over such offences." See IMO, *Draft Code of Practice for the Investigation of the Crimes of Piracy and Armed Robbery against Ships*, MSC/Circ. 984 (London: International Maritime Organization, Dec. 20, 2000), www.imo.org/blast/blastDataHelper.asp?data_id=1880&filename=984.pdf.
5. "Piracy is an act of boarding any vessel with the intent to commit theft or other crime and with the capability to use force in the furtherance of the act." *IMB Annual Piracy Report 92* (Kuala Lampur, Malaysia: IMP Regional Piracy Centre, February 1993), 2. In 2000 and 2001, the IMB added "attempted boarding" and "an act of boarding or attempting to board any ship with the intent to commit theft or any other crime and with the intent or capability to use force in the furtherance of the act." See ICC, "Piracy and Armed Robbery against Ships Annual Report," January 1–December 31, 2000 (London: ICC–International Maritime Bureau, January 2001), 1. From 2002 to 2007, the IMB added "apparent" to the intent (Piracy and Armed Robbery against Ships Annual Reports 2002 through 2007, p. 3): "act of boarding or attempting to board any ship with the apparent intent to commit theft or any other crime and with the apparent intent or capability to use force in the furtherance of the act." The IMB currently follows the UNCLOS definition: "The IMB Piracy Reporting Centre (IMB PRC) follows the definition of Piracy as laid down in Article 101 of the 1982 United Nations Convention on the Law of the Sea (UNCLOS) and Armed Robbery as laid down in Resolution A.1025 (26) adopted on 2 December 2009 at the 26th Assembly Session of the International Maritime Organisation (IMO)." See

"Live Piracy and Armed Robbery Report," *ICC Commercial Crime Services*, www.icc-ccs.org/piracy-reporting-centre/live-piracy-report.

6. IMB 2007 Report on Piracy against Ships (London: ICC Commercial Crime Services), 42.
7. IMB 1992 Report on Piracy against Ships (London: ICC Commercial Crime Services).
8. In 1999 the author investigated this hijack and examined the bills of lading.
9. IMO Sub-Committee on Safety of Navigation, *Routeing of Ships, Ship Reporting, and Related Matters*, 48th session, agenda item 3, NAV 48/3/4 (London: International Maritime Organization, April 11, 2002), www.nmri.go.jp/safe/imo/nav48/3/NAV48-3-4.pdf.
10. Mark Doyle, "Somali Piracy Is Worst in the World," *BBC*, January 5, 2006, http://news.bbc.co.uk/2/hi/africa/4584878.stm.
11. See, for example, "High Sea Pirate Attacks Soar," *CNN*, Feb. 6, 2002, www.cnn.com/2002/WORLD/sailing/02/06/piracy.ppl/index.html (last visited March 17, 2004).
12. Lloyd's *World Fleet Statistics*, 1994–2010 (Miami: IHS-Fairplay, 2011), available at www.ihs.com/products/maritime-information/statistics-forecasts/world-fleet.aspx.
13. Total world cargo fleet of more than 100 gt: 47,893; average number of successful attacks on cargo vessels under way worldwide per year: 42.1; average number of cargo vessels for each successful attack per year: 1,138; average age of cargo vessels (in years): 19; average number of cargo vessels for each unresisted attack per vessel lifetime: 60.
14. Total world cargo fleet of more than 100 gt: 47,893; average number of successful attacks on cargo vessels, both in port and under way, per year: 120; average number of vessels for each unresisted attack per year: 399; average age of vessels (in years): 19; average number of vessels for each unresisted attack per vessel lifetime: 21.
15. Total world fleet of all vessels over 100 gt; 90,600; average number of successful attacks on all vessels, in port and under way, per year: 141.3; average number of vessels for each unresisted attack per year: 641; average age of vessels (in years): 20; average number of vessels for each unresisted attack per vessel lifetime: 32.
16. The current English-language site for the Marine Department of Malaysia is found at www.marine.gov.my/indexBI.htm.
17. Possible number of vessel movements in the Indian Ocean 1994–2010: 1,000,000; number of successful attacks on vessels under way: 352; average number of vessel movements for each successful attack: 2,840.
18. Number of vessel movements past Somalia, 1994–2007: 280,000; number of unresisted attacks past Somalia: 89; average number of vessel movements for each unresisted attack: 3,146.
19. *BIMCO/ISF Manpower Update* (Bagsvaerd, Denmark: BIMCO; and London: International Shipping Federation, 2000); and *BIMCO/ISF Manpower Update*

(Bagsvaerd, Denmark: BIMCO; and London: International Shipping Federation, 2005). The worldwide supply of seafarers in 2000 was estimated at 404,000 officers and 823,000 ratings, for a total supply of 1,227,000. Worldwide demand was estimated at 420,000 officers and 599,000 ratings, for a total demand of 1,019,000. Therefore the estimated number of seafarers working in 2000 was estimated at 404,000 officers (supply lower than demand) and 599,000 ratings (demand lower than supply), for a total employment of 1,003,000.

20. IMB, *Annual Piracy Report 2004* (London: International Maritime Organization, 2005), 9; and IMB, *Annual Piracy Report 2007* (London: International Maritime Organization, 2007), 12
21. See Detlef Nielsen, *The Acquisition and Analysis of Global Statistics on Injuries and Fatalities of Seafarers as a Result of Accidents on Board Ship* (Cardiff, Wales: Seafarers' International Research Centre for Safety and Occupational Health, 1997), 13.
22. Author's interviews with protection and indemnity clubs: Willy Tan, UK P&I Club, 2000; Graham Edmiston, Bilborough, 2002; and South of England P&I (SEPIA), 2008.
23. See Lloyd's *World Fleet Statistics* 1994–2007 for the average age of vessels leaving the world fleet.
24. Examples include John Grissim, "Sea Wolves Feasting," *World Paper Online*, May 1997; "Yo Ho Ho and a Bottle of Rice Wine," *Economist*, January 30, 1991, 40–41; Jack Hitt, "Bandits of the Global Shipping Lanes," *New York Times Magazine*, August 20, 2000, 6–37; and "Buccaneers Raking in the Bucks," *Newsday*, May 1998.
25. See the first and third narration of *Piracy and Armed Robbery against Ships 2007*, 41: "Several unlit fishing boats approached the ship underway. Master, suspecting piracy, increased speed and started taking evasive action. One of the boats was hit on the stbd [starboard] bow. Emergency alarm was raised and a search carried out. Two persons were found on board. No one was injured. No arms were found on them however they were carrying mobile phones. Fearing further attacks and repercussions, the master continued his passage towards Singapore. The owners/agents are making arrangements to hand over the two persons to authorities for investigations"; and "D/O on a container ship under way saw the beams of flashlights on deck. As no crew were on deck at that time the D/O suspected piracy and raised the alarm, the deck lights were switched on. As the crew were mustered, they saw a small boat on the port quarter moving away from the ship."

CHAPTER 3

HORN OF TROUBLES

Understanding and Addressing the Somali "Piracy" Phenomenon

CLIVE SCHOFIELD AND ROBIN WARNER

INTRODUCTION

Recent years have witnessed an unprecedented surge in piratical attacks off the Horn of Africa. While attacks against shipping in the northwestern Indian Ocean are by no means a new phenomenon, the scale and scope of recent attacks, predominantly attributed to Somali "pirates," has made these waters comfortably the most dangerous in the world and has imperiled key sea-lanes vital to global maritime commerce.[1] Although these developments have spurred the international community to respond through a range of measures, including most saliently the deployment of warships to the region from a diverse array of navies in order to conduct counterpiracy patrols, piratical attacks have persisted and now pose a major threat to shipping across a broad swath of the Indian Ocean.

In this chapter we provide a critical assessment of recent developments off the Horn of Africa. We outline the rise in maritime insecurity off the Horn of Africa and assess a number of the key drivers associated with the rise of Somali piracy. We then examine international responses to the problem, including relevant UN Security Council resolutions and military responses as well as preventative measures on the part of the shipping industry. In the latter part of the chapter we provide an analysis of the international legal framework for dealing with piracy and criminal justice cooperation issues arising from Somali piracy as well as some of the emerging legal developments designed to address deficiencies in bringing the pirates to justice and tackling the problem of maritime insecurity off the Horn of Africa. Finally, we offer concluding thoughts and suggest that without addressing fundamental root causes on land in Somalia, piracy off the Horn of Africa is likely to prove an enduring concern.

THE RISE AND RISE OF THE SOMALI PIRATES

The problem of attacks against shipping off the Horn of Africa is longstanding with in excess of seven hundred piracy-style attacks recorded in the region during 1993–2005.[2] Although there was a noticeable dip in attacks on shipping off the Somali coast in the second half of 2006, attacks rose rapidly thereafter and especially from 2008, which witnessed a 200 percent increase in attacks over the previous year.[3] Overall in 2008 there were 111 attacks against ships and 42 successful hijackings.[4] Despite concerted and multifaceted efforts on the part of the international community to address the issue, the number of attacks attributed to Somali pirates—far from being reduced, let alone eradicated—almost redoubled in 2009 with 217 attacks and 47 successful hijackings recorded.[5] Somali pirates were therefore responsible for more than half of the attacks recorded globally (406). In 2010 the number of attacks off the Horn of Africa held steady at 219 attacks (of 445 globally), with 49 successful hijackings. In 2010 hijackings off the coast of Somalia accounted for 92 percent of all ship seizures.[6] The most recent figures for 2011 (at the time of writing, February 2012) suggest that the problem of Somali pirates shows no sign of diminishing, with 237 recorded incidents (of 439 globally). If some positive news can be gleaned from the statistics, though, it is notable that the number of successful hijackings in 2011 (28) declined sharply from previous years.[7] Nonetheless, piratical attacks off the Horn of Africa still accounted for 54 percent of such attacks worldwide, which underscores both the scale and sustained nature of the problem.

Distinctive to Somali piracy is the high rate of vessel hijackings with a view to securing a ransom payment in exchange for the release of the captured vessel, cargo, and crew. This type of practice runs contrary to the experience of other areas prone to attacks against shipping such as the Gulf of Guinea, Bay of Bengal, and some parts of Southeast Asia, where many attacks tend to be maritime hit-and-run robberies under cover of darkness. In contrast, attacks by Somali pirates often take place in broad daylight with the objective of capturing entire vessels. Once hijacked, captured vessels are generally taken back to the Somali coast, near the pirates' safe havens ashore, and ransom negotiations are initiated. Piracy has proved to be hugely lucrative for the successful pirates. Perhaps inevitably, ransoms have increased sharply over time with multimillion-dollar sums paid for the release of hijacked ships, especially high-value ones such as very large crude carriers. The largest ransom reportedly paid for the release of a ship was $13.5 million paid to secure the release of the Greek-flagged *Irene SL.*[8] Overall, ransoms have increased substantially, from around $150,000 per vessel in 2005 to approximately $5 million in 2011, with an estimated $238 million in ransoms being paid in 2010 and an additional $160 million in 2011.[9]

Although the payment of ransoms is entirely understandable where the lives of crew members are under threat, the willingness of ship owners and insurers to pay hefty sums for the release of hijacked vessels, crews, and cargoes nonetheless represents a major incentive and thus a key factor in sustaining the Somali piracy "business." In this context it could be argued that piracy attacks on shipping in fact only affect a small proportion of the shipping traversing the waters off the Horn of Africa (under 1 percent). Moreover, ransom payments, increased insurance costs, and the costs of counterpiracy measures for merchant shipping arguably represent an unwelcome but, to date at least, manageable financial penalty associated with using sea-lanes off the Horn of Africa. However, the escalating nature of these costs is also becoming unsustainable. Indeed, it has been estimated that maritime piracy cost the global economy between $7–10 billion in 2010 alone, while the cost of Somali piracy in 2011 has been estimated at $6.6–6.9 billion.[10]

These hijacking, kidnap, and ransom activities play on the general reluctance of naval forces engaged in counterpiracy efforts in the region to intervene when hostages are involved. This reluctance to act, which thereby puts the lives of hostages at risk, varies from navy to navy and also seems to be changing over time.

The methods and means needed to engage in piracy off Somalia are relatively simple. Small skiffs equipped with powerful engines—nicknamed "Volvos"—are used to approach vessels. Ladders adapted to hook over the target ship's railing or grapnels are then used to board the vessel. Multiple small boats are often used in concert to try to "swarm" a target vessel or to act as decoys.[11] It has been suggested that former fishermen, disenfranchised largely as a consequence of the actions of foreign poachers, offer valuable maritime skills in terms of handling the small boats used in attacks against ships. The pirates are generally armed with small arms such as the ubiquitous Kalashnikov automatic rifle (AK-47) and rocket-propelled grenade launchers (RPG), which are readily available in Somalia. These are frequently fired to force a particular ship to heave to.[12]

There is evidence, however, of pirates becoming better equipped and organized, more flexible and responsive to counterpiracy efforts, and, regrettably, more violent. Pirate gangs have developed into more cohesive and better organized criminal syndicates and increasingly have access to more sophisticated equipment such as satellite phones and navigation gear such as global positioning systems.[13] The employment of "mother ships" (a larger vessel used as a base by smaller craft) or "brother ships" (a larger skiff, filled with fuel and towing other skiffs) has also been used to great effect, radically extending the pirates' range spatially and temporally. Pirates have been able to use mother ships as bases from which to attack shipping far from the Somali coastline. For example, the first supertanker to be captured by Somali pirates, the *Sirius Star*, was hijacked on November 15, 2008, 450 nautical miles offshore. The seizure of such a large (330 m and 318,000 dwt), modern vessel (launched in April 2008 at an estimated cost to build of $150 million and carrying a cargo of 2 million barrels of oil valued at more than $100 million) with such apparent ease and so far offshore grabbed headlines around the world.[14] Adm. Mike Mullen, then chairman of the US Joint Chiefs of Staff, commented on November 18, 2008: "I'm stunned by the range of it."[15] This was only the first of many long-range attacks on the part of the Somali pirates, however. Indeed, numerous attacks have now occurred more than 1,000 nautical miles (nm) from Somalia's shores, east into the Arabian Sea off the coast of Oman and as far east as the west coast of India and the Maldives, and south off the coasts of Kenya and Tanzania and as far as the Mozambique Channel and Seychelles.[16] Consequently, the International Maritime Bureau (IMB) has warned that the Somali pirate threat extends over an expanse of the Indian Ocean, from 76° E, as far south as 22° S, and as far north as 22° N.[17] This extended range for attacks has allowed pirates to shift the geographical focus of their attacks, adapting to the counter-piracy efforts of the international community and, particularly, to the increased naval patrols of the Gulf of Aden, the initial focus for pirate attacks by Somali pirates. Accordingly, although attacks in the Gulf of Aden halved to 53 in 2010 from 117 in 2009, the pirates were arguably venturing further afield to evade the international naval presence in the region.

The use of mother ships has also allowed pirates to lengthen the period during which attacks can take place. In the past, piracy attacks were generally dependent on favorable weather conditions, which tended to cause a lull in attacks during monsoon periods (from the northwest in winter and the southwest in summer); the use of mother ships means that this is no longer necessarily the case, and attacks have now been reported in the monsoon season in adverse weather conditions. In 2010 no piracy incidents were reported in the Indian Ocean in June–August 2010, that is, during the summer monsoon season. However, the IMB reported that three attacks had taken place in June 2011 approximately 450 nm east of Socotra in the Indian Ocean, despite strong winds (Beaufort force 7, around 34 mph) and rough seas with swells of around 4.5 m.[18] This suggests that monsoon weather conditions no longer represent a guarantee against attack. That said, the likelihood of pirates successfully boarding a target vessel from small boats in wind and sea conditions such as those prevailing when the June 2011 attacks occurred must be considered as slim and it is worth noting that the June 2011 attacks were unsuccessful.

Unfortunately, there are also signs that the Somali pirates are becoming more violent. The number of fatalities has risen, and the IMB reports that eight seafarers were killed in 2011.[19] While Somali pirates have often fired their arms indiscriminately to force ships to halt, since their primary objective has been to secure a ransom for the release of the vessel, cargo, and crew intact, hostages have tended to be viewed as an asset and consequently are treated relatively well. The killing of four American hostages on the hijacked yacht the M/V *Quest* in February 2011 represents a major departure from past practice on the part of the pirates.[20] Although it is questionable whether this event marks a distinct shift in the practice of the pirates, it clearly illustrated the potential threat of pirates to seafarers and led a US State Department official to state that it would force the US to "recalibrate."[21] Even if the deaths of the crew of the *Quest*, the first Americans to die as a result of pirate attack off Somalia, are an exception to the rule, the preventative measures adopted by seafarers, together with more robust counterpiracy measures on the part of international forces, appear to have directly led to greater violence against mariners. This has stemmed from pirates using additional force in attempting to hijack better-protected ships. For example, where "citadels" or safe rooms are used on ships, RPGs have been fired and high explosives have been used to try to breach citadel doors, or fires have been set to try to force the crew to evacuate the safe room. There have also been indications of increasing abuse of seafarers held hostage, including their use as human shields and as enforced participants in further attacks against shipping and allegations of torture.[22] It is certainly the case that seafarers held hostage are facing long periods in captivity as pirates seek to extract maximum ransom payments for their release. Furthermore, in a particularly worrying development, some pirates have responded to increasing pressure on their activities as a result of the efforts of international naval forces by adapting their tactics and changing the implicit rules of the game by holding some hostages back despite the payment of a ransom so the retained hostages can act as human shields or bargaining chips. For example, in April 2011 a $3.5 million ransom was paid to secure the release of a hijacked Panamanian-flagged merchant vessel, the *Asphalt Venture*. The pirates, however, released only eight of the fifteen-strong crew, opting to carry on holding the Indian nationals among the hostages in order to ward off reprisals on the part of Indian naval forces and, apparently, to try to exchange the hostages for pirate comrades captured by the Indian authorities.[23] Overall, these developments led the operational commander of EU NAVFOR, Maj. Gen. Buster Howes, to comment in February 2011 that "there have been regular manifestations of systematic torture" and that whereas in the past pirates "were very constrained and much more respectful" to hostages, they now "showed a willingness to use violence much more quickly and much more violence."[24]

THE TROUBLED HORN: KEY FACTORS DRIVING SOMALI PIRACY

A combination of factors serves to explain how piracy and attacks against shipping have become such a significant and enduring challenge to freedom of navigation in the Indian Ocean. One fundamental consideration is that the Horn of Africa borders key shipping lanes linking the Mediterranean to the Indian Ocean by way of the Suez Canal and the Red Sea. This represents a key route for international navigation carrying an estimated 8 percent of global maritime trade.[25] The alternative route between Europe and East and Southeast Asia, by way of the Cape of Good Hope at the southern tip of the African continent, would add an additional 4,850 nm to a vessel's passage. About 22,000 ships transit through the Red Sea "choke point" of the Strait of Bab el-Mandeb annually, predominantly en route to or from the Suez Canal.[26] In 2009 it was estimated that about 3.2 million barrels of oil a day passed through the strait.[27] At approximately 3,300 km, the Somali coastline is the longest on the African continent and encompasses the majority of the coast of the Horn of Africa. If ships opt to use the Suez–Red Sea route, they are inevitably forced within close proximity to the Somali coastline, which brings multiple tempting targets within easy reach of the Somali pirates. In this context it is worth noting that although Somalia is a party to the UN Convention on the Law of the Sea (UNCLOS[28]) it retains a claim to a 200-nm territorial sea dating from 1972.[29] This excessive territorial sea claim has resulted in an international protest on the part of the United States but has yet to be "rolled back," largely as a consequence of Somalia's internal civil and political strife.[30] Somalia's 200-nm territorial sea claim and lack of a claim to an exclusive economic zone has consequences for the safeguarding of Somalia's offshore resources and in terms of the definition of piracy.

Geopolitical factors in particular are critical to the rise in acts of piracy in the northwestern Indian Ocean. The Horn of Africa region as a whole has been beset by geopolitical instability and conflict in recent decades. Interstate disputes and conflicts have included a territorial and maritime dispute between Eritrea and Yemen over the Hanish Islands and the maritime boundary delimitation in the southern Red Sea, a two-and-half-year-long border war between Eritrea and Ethiopia, and, more recently, border disputes between Djibouti and Eritrea as well as longstanding conflict in western and southern Sudan.[31] Additionally, the region features multiple weak and failing states as well as armed insurgent groups seeking to overthrow these states.

Somalia itself has now lacked a functioning central government for more than two decades since the fall of the Siad Barre dictatorship in 1991. The Somali piracy problem has in large part emerged from and is fundamentally sustained by the resultant breakdown in law and order in Somalia, which has provided the essential platform for the growth in piratical attacks off the Somali coast. Indeed, Somalia is perhaps the epitome of a failed state, renowned for chronic political instability, anarchic factional violence, grinding poverty, and humanitarian crisis.[32]

That said, parts of Somalia boast a degree of stability and security thanks to the fragmentation of the country. Of particular note in this context is the Republic of Somaliland in the northwest of the country, based on former British Somaliland (as opposed to the remainder of Somalia, which constituted Italian Somaliland), which declared its independence from Somalia on May 18, 1991. Arguably, the Republic of Somaliland fulfils the requirements for statehood considerably better than Somalia itself.[33] What Somaliland lacks is recognition for its independence and statehood from any government. Additionally, the region of Puntland in the northeast of Somalia, which seeks autonomy rather than full independence, is an important factor in the Somali piracy equation. Despite protestations from the Puntland authorities that they are actively combating piracy, together with calls for international support toward that end, it is nonetheless the case that a number of pirate groups operate from and find safe haven in Puntland, which is strategically located at the tip of the Horn of Africa.[34]

Despite the failure of international efforts to intervene and reestablish the Somali government in the early to mid-1990s, notably through two UN missions to Somalia (UNOSOM I and II), the international community has predominantly opposed formal recognition of the de facto reality of the fragmentation of Somalia.[35] Consequently, Somaliland remains an unrecognized state, the independence of Eritrea in 1991 and, more recently, South Sudan in 2011 notwithstanding. Instead, the international community has largely backed efforts to essentially reconstitute Somalia as a functioning state through the formation of the Transitional Federal Government (TFG), formed under UN auspices in August 2000. This resolve to recreate Somalia may be wavering to some extent, however, because there have been suggestions that some states, such as Kenya, may break ranks and recognize Somaliland.[36] For its part, the United States indicated in September 2011 that it would pursue a "dual-track" policy of supporting the TFG and engaging with regions such as Somaliland and Puntland.[37]

This change can be attributed in large part to the failures of the TFG, which has proved to be a weak and unstable entity with little influence on the ground in Somalia. Indeed, up to mid-2011, the TFG controlled only a few key locations in Mogadishu and around 35 percent of the city overall.[38] Moreover, the TFG is heavily reliant on the troops of the African Union peacekeeping mission (AMISOM). The AMISOM contingent was dispatched to Somalia in 2009 to relieve Ethiopian forces that had intervened in late 2006 in order to oust the Union of Islamic Courts (UIC), a loose coalition of both moderate and radical Islamic forces that had succeeded in taking control over much of southern Somalia from mid-2006.[39] The imposition of sharia law by the UIC had a strong influence on the law and order situation in those areas under the UIC's control.[40] This development extended to piracy, leading to a noticeable dip in attacks against shipping in this period.[41] The Ethiopian intervention, apparently backed and prompted by the United States, alarmed at possible linkages between the UIC and radical Islamic groups, led to the toppling of the UIC. Unfortunately, the law-and-order situation in southern Somalia deteriorated once again as a result, with the ironic side effect of clearing the way for piratical attacks to escalate.[42] With the fall and fragmentation of the UIC, numerous Islamic insurgent groups, notably the al-Qaeda-aligned al-Shabaab group, emerged to oppose the TFG and their Ethiopian and AMISOM allies. The conflict between the insurgent groups and the TFG has increasingly drawn in AMISOM forces as combatants rather than peacekeepers, resulting in sustained conflict. In particular, an insurgent offensive against the TFG from May 2010 led to escalating fighting, which led to an estimated 170,000 persons displaced from Mogadishu. An attempt by al-Shabaab to launch what it termed a "final offensive" against the TFG during the Islamic holy month of Ramadan in August to September 2010 proved unsuccessful, however.[43]

Some qualified progress was achieved in 2011 and into 2012, partly a result of developments relating to AMISOM as well as TFG-aligned forces. AMISOM, perennially undermanned, underresourced, and ill equipped for the challenging operating environment offered by Somalia, had progressively been built up.[44] From a force of only 3,400 in February 2009, by mid-2011 AMISOM boasted around 9,000 troops with a further 3,000 troops pledged.[45] Further, in February 2012 the United Nations Security Council voted unanimously to lift AMISOM's mandated troop strength from 12,000 to 17,731.[46] Additionally, AMISOM's mandate was amended and expanded to allow it to undertake peace enforcement operations including "all necessary measures" in order to "reduce the threat" posed by al-Shabaab and other armed opposition groups with the objective of establishing conditions for "effective and legitimate governance across Somalia."[47] Moreover, support from the United States, for example, has addressed some of the equipment and training concerns identified, enhancing AMISOM's capabilities.[48] These developments, together with similar support for TFG-aligned forces as well as limited cross-border interventions on the part of Ethiopian and Kenyan forces, put considerable pressure on insurgent forces such that al-Shabaab was forced to withdraw from Mogadishu entirely in August 2011, even if al-Shabaab itself characterized this withdrawal as purely "tactical."[49] These successes have been followed up by further progress on the ground with al-Shabaab strongholds including Baidoa, Afgoye, Merca, and Kismayo falling to AMISOM and Somali government–aligned or Ethiopian or Kenyan forces in the period February to October 2012.[50]

Although these advances are to be welcomed, Islamist forces remain in control of large areas of southern Somalia, and it remains unclear whether they can be sustained in the absence of a clear postconflict strategy to provide security, stability, and—critically—enhanced governance in "liberated" areas. Based on past performance, the TFG would appear to be ill equipped for such a task. Progress has, however, been made in this context as well. In particular, a major international conference on Somalia took place in London in February 2012, bringing together representatives from fifty-five nations and international organisations, with the UN-backed TFG, leaders of Somalia's breakaway regions, US Secretary of State Hillary Clinton, and UN Secretary-General Ban Ki-moon.[51] Recognizing the failure of the TFG, the joint communiqué issued at the end of the conference maps out a plan to replace the TFG on the expiry of its mandate in August 2012 with a broad-based, inclusive constituent assembly.[52] Accordingly, Somalia's first formal Parliament in more than two decades was sworn in in August 2012 and duly voted Hassan Sheikh Mohamud as president with Abdi Farah Shirdon appointed prime minister in September 2012.[53] Nonetheless, overall, the situation within Somalia remains unstable and the future uncertain despite some undeniably promising developments. Fundamentally, without stability and security being reestablished ashore, and without the economic, developmental, and humanitarian concerns of ordinary Somalis addressed, insecurity will continue offshore.

The Somali piracy phenomenon is also fundamentally motivated by the dire humanitarian situation in Somalia itself. Widespread poverty, famine, and profound dislocation resulting from the violence and conflict that have been key features in large parts of Somalia over most of the last two decades are notable contributory factors. Indeed, according to the United Nations in mid-2011, the Horn of Africa was experiencing its worst drought in sixty years, with more than 10 million people affected across Djibouti, Ethiopia, Kenya, Somalia, and Uganda.[54] As a result of this situation, coupled with the potent lure of the vast financial rewards offered by ransoming even a single vessel, pirate groups have little trouble recruiting. Given the horrific conditions on shore, it is little wonder that even the sternest of penalties, up to and including capital punishment, do not serve as a compelling deterrent. In fact, since the majority of captured pirates have been released, the incentives to take up piracy appear to far outweigh the disincentives to doing so.[55]

A further contributing, though often underreported, factor is the fact that, in the past at least, foreign fishing vessels routinely engage in illegal fishing in Somalia's waters.[56] It is also alleged that the Somali coast has been used as a site for the dumping of toxic waste, including radioactive waste, from abroad.[57] The scale of foreign poaching of Somalia's marine resources as well as allegations of the dumping of toxic waste on Somalia's shores are difficult to verify in the absence of adequate monitoring and reporting mechanisms, as the 2011 report of the UN secretary-general indicated.[58] For example, in 2005 the Food and Agriculture Organization estimated "700 foreign-owned vessels that are fully engaged in unlicensed fishing in Somali waters."[59] While it is likely that the surge in piracy off Somali shores, coupled with the increasing reach of the pirates, has resulted in a sharp decline in these activities because the risks have outstripped the potential rewards, it has also been suggested that enhanced naval patrols have inadvertently allowed for a resurgence in illegal foreign fishing off Somalia.[60] Such accusations have led to a perception on the part of many Somalis that their country has been exploited by foreign powers. This in turn has provided some pirates with a fig-leaf justification of their actions, with pirates styling themselves as "coast guards" and characterizing ransom demands as "fines."[61] How the illegal fishing or the toxic waste dumping justifies, for example, the hijacking of a supertanker remains unclear. In any case, it is highly likely that even if illegal fishing and dumping were eradicated from Somali waters overnight, the piracy problem off Somalia would remain because increasingly sophisticated transnational pirate syndicates are now engaged in this practice. The strong perception of disenfranchisement and exploitation inspired by suspected illegal fishing in Somali waters and alleged toxic waste dumping in Somalia nevertheless remain potent underlying drivers for Somali piracy. In response, the UN secretary-general's report noted International Maritime Organization (IMO) guidance to governments to ensure that fishing vessels flying their flag not engage in fishing activities within two hundred miles of Somalia's coast and raised the possibility of expanding the mandates of international naval forces operating off Somalia to include "monitoring and deterrence of illegal fishing and the illegal dumping of waste."[62]

INTERNATIONAL RESPONSES

The primary responses of the international community to the rise in piracy-style attacks off the Horn of Africa have included international legal and diplomatic ones, principally through the United Nations, and military responses that have in large part taken place under the auspices of numerous UN Security Council resolutions. Additionally, the shipping industry itself has taken concerted steps to counter the increased level of threat to vessels transiting piracy-prone waters, for instance, through implementing preventative measures designed to evade or thwart attacks on shipping. These responses are considered in the following.

United Nations Resolutions

The UN Security Council has provided the overarching authority for the naval operations in a series of resolutions under chapter VII of the UN Charter. Initially, Resolution 1816 (of June 2, 2008) authorized states cooperating with the Somali TFG to enter the territorial waters of Somalia and to use "all necessary means" to repress acts of piracy and armed robbery at sea in a manner "consistent with the relevant provisions of international law for a period of six months."[63] In passing this resolution, the Security Council was clearly recognizing the fact that Somalia was unable to provide its own maritime security and law enforcement in waters under its jurisdiction. To avoid any allegation of intrusion into the domestic affairs and sovereignty of Somalia, the resolution was passed with the consent of the Somali TFG following a request for international assistance. Resolution 1816 was renewed with the adoption of Resolution 1846 on December 2, 2008, which extended the international community's mandate for another twelve months and added authorization for regional organizations such as the European Union to participate in the fight against piracy.[64]

In Resolution 1851 on December 16, 2008, the Security Council extended the international community's mandate even further by allowing states and regional organizations to undertake "all necessary measures that are appropriate in Somalia for the purpose of suppressing acts of piracy and armed robbery at sea." The words "in Somalia" are understood as including the land territory and the territorial airspace of Somalia. This resolution also invited all states and regional organizations participating in the antipiracy patrols off Somalia to conclude special agreements or arrangements, known as "shiprider agreements," with countries willing to take custody of the pirates in order to embark law enforcement officials from those countries to facilitate the investigation and prosecution of persons detained as a result of the antipiracy operations.[65] States were also encouraged to establish an international cooperation mechanism to act as a common point of contact among them all on aspects of the fight against piracy off Somalia. In accordance with Resolution 1851, the Contact Group on Piracy off the Coast of Somalia, which held its inaugural meeting on January 14, 2009, was established as the principal contact point between states and regional and international organizations on combating piracy. It is supported by four working groups that cover

- Military and operational coordination;
- The establishment of a regional coordination center;
- Legal issues including the prosecution of suspected pirates and strengthening of shipping awareness; and
- Diplomatic and public information.

On September 10, 2009, the contact group approved the terms of reference of an international trust fund to help defray prosecution expenses.[66] Expressing its concerns with the ad hoc and inconsistent nature of criminal justice outcomes for Somali pirates, the Security Council passed Resolution 1918, sponsored by Russia, on April 27, 2010.[67] This resolution expressed continuing concern about the threat posed by piracy and armed robbery for Somalia, nearby states, and international shipping, and it reiterated the need to address problems caused by the limited capacity of the judicial systems in Somalia and neighboring states to effectively prosecute piracy suspects. The resolution called upon member states to criminalize piracy in their national laws and to detain and prosecute suspected pirates off the coast of Somalia in accordance with international human rights law. The UN secretary-general was requested to report within three months on options for prosecuting and imprisoning those responsible for piracy and armed robbery at sea.

The viability and implementation of some of the options considered in the UN secretary-general's report of July 26, 2010, are discussed in a later section of this chapter on the legal challenges and capacity-building efforts associated with combating piracy off the Horn of Africa. Following this examination of the legal options available to the international legal community in combating the Somali piracy phenomenon, the Security Council passed Resolution 1950 on November 23, 2010, which reauthorizes states to intervene in acts of piracy by Somali pirates at sea for an additional period of twelve months.[68] The council expressed its ongoing concern at the threat of piracy and armed robbery at sea and noted that this threat now extended beyond Somalia to the Western Indian Ocean and that children were involved. It referred to the report of a group monitoring the situation in Somalia, which found that there was a lack of enforcement of the arms embargo imposed by UN Security Council Resolution 733 in 1992 and found that increased ransom payments were fueling the growth of piracy off the coast of Somalia. Member states were urged to improve the capacity of authorities in Somalia to prosecute those planning and undertaking attacks, to determine jurisdiction, and to criminalize piracy under their domestic laws. The council also directed Interpol and Europol to investigate criminal networks involved in piracy off the coast of Somalia, and the secretary-general was instructed to report within eleven months concerning the implementation of Resolution 1950.

During 2011 the Security Council passed three more resolutions on the piracy situation off the Horn of Africa. The first of these, Security Council Resolution 1976 of April 11, 2011, is a very comprehensive resolution focusing primarily on the capacity-building needs of Somalia and the surrounding region to combat the piracy problem.[69] It requests states, the UN Office on Drugs and Crime (UNODC), the UN Development Programme, the UN Political Office for Somalia, and regional organizations to assist the TFG in Somalia in establishing a system of governance, rule of law, and police control in lawless areas where land-based activities related to piracy are taking place, and it requests the TFG to increase its efforts in this regard. It encourages states and regional organizations cooperating with the TFG to assist Somalia in strengthening its coast guard capacity by supporting the development of land-based coastal monitoring and increasing their cooperation with the Somali regional authorities in this regard. In addition to the legal issues, Resolution 1976 urges states individually or within the framework of competent international organizations to positively consider investigating allegations of illegal fishing and illegal dumping of toxic substances with a view to prosecuting such offences when committed by persons under their jurisdiction, and it emphasizes the importance of the earliest possible delimitation of Somalia's maritime spaces in accordance with the UNCLOS. In this connection, it requests that the secretary-general report within six months on the protection of Somali natural resources and waters and on alleged illegal fishing and illegal dumping, including of toxic substances off the coast of Somalia.

UN Security Council Resolution 2015 of October 24, 2011, continues the consideration of establishing specialized antipiracy courts in Somalia and other states in the region with substantial international participation and support and to investigate the kind of international assistance needed to establish such courts.[70] Finally, UN Security Council Resolution 2020 of November 22, 2011, renews the authorizations contained in earlier resolutions for states and regional organizations to cooperate with the Somali TFG in fighting piracy off the coast of Somalia for another twelve months.[71]

Military Responses

A salient element of the international response to piracy off Somalia has been a military one in the shape of an enhanced naval presence and increased patrols off the Somali coast. Naval vessels from a diverse array of interested states including the United States, a number of European states (notably Britain, Germany, France, and Spain), Australia, Canada, India, Iran, South Korea, Malaysia, Turkey, and Russia have been active in the fight against piracy over the past four years. This has led to remarkable and unprecedented international naval cooperation designed to counter piracy. Within the region, antipiracy efforts are coordinated, and information is shared under the "Code of Conduct Concerning the Repression of Piracy and Armed Robbery Against Ships in the Western Indian Ocean," concluded in Djibouti on January 29, 2009.[72] Several interlocking naval operations now exist in the region. In October 2008 NATO established a counterpiracy operation called Allied Provider, renamed Ocean Shield in August 2009, and in December 2008 the European Union initiated Operation Atalanta, which included warships from ten countries. In January 2009 the United States established Combined Task Force 151. Overall, between thirty and forty naval vessels from a variety of states have been deployed to the region at any one time.

The naval vessels that rushed to the region started by providing escorts for World Food Programme–chartered cargo ships that were delivering sorely needed humanitarian aid shipments to Somalia.[73] To better protect shipping in the perilous Gulf of Aden area, a Maritime Security Patrol Area (MSPA), or "corridor" for safe passage, was established.[74] However, even this did not guarantee security because, notwithstanding the significantly enhanced naval presence now in the region, there were simply not enough warships to provide comprehensive patrols. Indeed, if four naval vessels were tasked with patrolling the MSPA, only 24 percent of the corridor and 4 percent of the overall area would be covered.[75] The gaps in the system were most starkly illustrated by the fact that vessels were hijacked while passing through the supposedly safe corridor.[76]

A key practical difficulty for the commanders of the naval vessels involved has been the brief window that they have to catch pirates in the act—an extremely difficult task. Commonly as little as fifteen minutes may elapse from attack detection to hijacking.[77] As we have seen, the reach of the pirates has expanded considerably, largely through the use of mother ships, so the scale of the challenge is staggering. Pirates now pose a threat to shipping across a vast expanse—around 2 million square kilometers—of the Indian Ocean. Even with more warships operating off the Horn, patrols cannot be everywhere at once. This is why measures such as escorts, safe corridors, and the embarking of special forces on board merchant ships are proving attractive. A further problem concerns how to distinguish between, for example, pirates and innocent (albeit heavily armed) fishermen. The mere possession of arms is not proof of piratical intent or guilt (almost every small vessel operating in these waters carries arms for self-protection). As a result, international naval forces operating in the region have developed "tripwires," or indicators of piratical intent, backed by surveillance footage from maritime patrol aircraft, helicopters, or drones.[78]

Once the pirates are in control of a vessel and have hostages at their disposal, the problem becomes significantly more complicated. Although many navies have been reticent to intervene under such circumstances for fear of endangering the lives of hostages, this varies from navy to navy, and there are indications of a growing trend toward increasingly aggressive approaches to dealing with the Somali pirate threat. The Indian Navy, in particular, has been involved in a series of confrontations with pirate mother ships, and has sunk or recaptured them, earning praise from the IMB.[79] The French authorities have also responded to the Somali piracy threat in a robust manner. A series of French yachts have been seized off the Horn of Africa, and France has sometimes intervened on land once a ransom has been paid and hostages have been released.[80] More daringly, France has also used special forces to storm pirate-controlled vessels.[81] However, the dangers inherent in this approach are illustrated by the storming of the yacht *Tanit* in April 2009. While this intervention was successful in that four hostages were freed, one hostage and two pirates lost their lives in the action.[82]

The Russian authorities have responded in similarly forthright fashion in dispatching special forces based on their warship *Marshal Shaposhnikov* to successfully regain control of a Russian tanker, the MV *Moscow University*, on May 6, 2010, the day after its hijacking—an action that left one pirate dead with the remaining ten captive pirates then reportedly set adrift in an inflatable boat lacking navigational gear and presumed to have subsequently drowned.[83] Early 2011 witnessed several assertive actions on the part of international naval forces, including a commando raid by South Korean forces that resulted in the recapture of a Korean-owned cargo vessel, the MV *Samho Jewelry*, the release of all twenty-one crew members unharmed, the deaths of eight pirates, and the capturing of five pirates.[84] The Royal Malaysian Navy commandos were also involved in a gun battle while preventing an attempted hijacking of a Malaysian-flagged chemical tanker, the M/T *Bunga Laurel*, in January 2011.[85] Dutch marines killed two suspected pirates and captured sixteen others while freeing an Iranian fishing boat in April 2011.[86]

For its part, the US Navy has also been involved in incidents leading to loss of life, notably in April 2009 when US Navy SEAL snipers killed three of the pirates holding the master of the US-flagged MV *Maersk Alabama*.[87] In early 2012 the United States went a step further with a raid on a camp on land in Somalia to free two aid workers held hostage since their capture in October 2011. Nine suspected pirates were killed in the operation.[88]

Preventative Measures by the Shipping Industry

Two options for avoiding attacks by pirates present themselves to the shipping industry: first, to avoid the affected area altogether, or, second, to try to minimize the hazards posed by pirates when sailing through such dangerous waters. The IMB recommends that all vessels "keep as far away as possible from the Somali coast, ideally more than 600 nautical miles" offshore.[89] This option necessarily precludes use of the Suez Canal–Red Sea–Bab el-Mandeb route, and it therefore significantly lengthens and adds to the costs of voyages. In any case, given the extended range of piracy attacks, even staying 600 nm off the Somali coast no longer guarantees avoiding the pirates given their extended range of operations.

The alternative option, and one that appears to be the favored one, is for seafarers to do all they can to minimize the risk of a successful pirate attack. The IMB urges all vessels transiting the pirate attack-prone waters off the Horn of Africa to follow the industry Best Management Practice designed to avoid, deter, or delay piracy attacks on commercial shipping in the region.[90] IMB also advises vessels traversing pirate-threatened waters to maintain a strict twenty-four-hour radar and antipiracy watch (something that is difficult to achieve given the scale of some vessels and the small crews on board) and, in particular, to watch for "small suspicious boats converging on the vessel."[91] Coordination with the international naval forces present in the region is also highly recommended.[92] Vigilance and early detection enables the master of the threatened vessel maximum opportunity to engage in counterpiracy measures. In addition to taking evasive action, increasing speed is often critical because vessels traveling at 18 knots and above are generally considered to be immune to boarding from small boats, largely because of the bow wave and wake that they generate.[93]

Antipiracy measures may involve the use of high-pressure water hoses and foam. They may also include the use of barbed or razor wire to make boarding more difficult. More low-tech measures include the use of mannequins or dummy sailors to give the appearance that more crew/guards are on board the vessel than there actually are. New technologies are increasingly being introduced, such as electric fencing for shipping (although this is not suitable in all cases as electricity and flammable vapor make for an explosive mix) and the use of "sonic weapons" such as long-range acoustic devices that generate noises at painful but nonlethal decibel levels to disorient and deter pirates.[94] Such devices were used as part of the response to the first recorded piracy incident involving a cruise liner, the attack on the *Seabourn Spirit*, on November 5, 2005.[95]

The option of arming nonmilitary vessels has not generally been greeted with much enthusiasm from authorities and mariners alike.[96] Nonetheless, the shipping industry is increasingly countering the piracy threat by employing armed guards. For example, the presence of armed security guards on board the cruise ship *Melody* proved influential.[97] In the past vessels such as those carrying humanitarian aid shipments have used security guards recruited from local Somali militia to provide protection.[98] Shipping companies are opting, albeit reluctantly, to provide their vessels transiting the piracy-prone waters off the Horn of Africa with private armed security personnel. The IMB has acknowledged the "deterrent effect" of private contracted armed security personnel (PCASP) in the reduced number of successful hijackings in 2011 while observing that the "regulation and vetting" of such personnel "still needs to be adequately addressed."[99] The IMO has issued revised interim guidance to shipowners, ship operators, and shipmasters on the use of PCASP on board ships as well as recommendations to flag states on their use in the "high risk area" off Somalia.[100] There have even been suggestions that the shipping industry and insurance firms could fund their own "private navy."[101] Alternatively, in certain circumstances states have embarked teams of special forces personnel on merchant vessels, usually of their own flag, to provide shipborne security.[102]

INTERNATIONAL LEGAL CHALLENGES AND RESPONSES

Piracy is the oldest of the limited crimes subject to universal jurisdiction that are punishable by any state regardless of the nationality of the victim or perpetrator. Universal jurisdiction is generally reserved for crimes of an exceptionally serious and heinous nature, and the placing of piracy in this category illustrates the extent to which piratical activities are seen as a widespread scourge.[103]

A customary international law regime was developed to respond to the threat of piracy in the nineteenth century.[104] In the twentieth century this was codified in the 1958 Convention on the High Seas (HSC) and the 1982 UNCLOS, both of which contain provisions recognizing the universal jurisdiction of states to repress piracy and investigate and prosecute its perpetrators.[105] Article 100 of the UNCLOS commits state's parties to cooperate in the suppression of piracy on the high seas. Piracy is defined in Article 101 of the UNCLOS as:

> (a) any illegal acts of violence or detention, or any act of depredation, committed for private ends by the crew or the passengers of a private ship or a private aircraft, and directed:
>
> (i) on the high seas, against another ship or aircraft, or against persons or property on board such ship or aircraft;
>
> (ii) against a ship, aircraft, persons or property in a place outside the jurisdiction of any State;
>
> (b) any act of voluntary participation in the operation of a ship or of an aircraft with knowledge of facts making it a pirate ship or aircraft;
>
> (c) any act of inciting or of intentionally facilitating an act described in subparagraph (a) or (b).

Important elements in the definition are the requirement for two ships or aircraft; the criminal intent; the use of force; the taking over of a vessel against the wishes of its master; and the robbery of cargo, the possessions of those on board, or even the vessel itself as the ultimate objective.[106] Piracy can only be committed for private ends, so any acts committed for political motives are excluded from the definition.[107] Somali-style piracy differs from the traditional concept of piracy reflected in the UNCLOS provisions since robbery does not appear to be the major objective of some contemporary Somali pirates because vessel, crew, and cargo are released after the payment of ransom. However, the taking over of the vessel by force with the intent of obtaining financial gain can be regarded as falling within the definition of piracy. Piracy also extends to the operation of a ship or boat used to commit piratical acts.[108] In the Somali context, this ancillary provision may cover the operations of mother and brother ships.

A point to note is that the term "piracy" as defined under international law is often applied to piratical type activities that do not strictly fit that definition of piracy. Piracy within the meaning of Articles 100 and 101 of UNCLOS only applies to acts taking place within the exclusive economic zone or on the high seas—not analogous acts within the territorial sea that are subject to the criminal jurisdiction of the relevant coast state rather than the universal jurisdiction of all states.[109] The vast majority of attacks on shipping around the world, including many off the Horn of Africa, tend to take place relatively close to shore and thus within the territorial seas or archipelagic waters of coastal states. Technically, therefore, the vast majority of piracy-style attacks are not deemed piracy under the UNCLOS definition. Of note in this context is Somalia's aforementioned claim to a 200-nm territorial sea. The IMO instead uses the term "armed robbery against ships" to cover piracy-style attacks taking place within the territorial sea.[110] In contrast, the IMB has adopted a more all-encompassing definition of piracy as "an act of boarding any vessel with the intent to commit theft or any other crime and with the intent or capability to use force in the furtherance thereof."[111]

DEFICIENCIES IN THE CURRENT INTERNATIONAL LAW REGIME FOR PIRACY

The initial approach of the United Nations and navies around the world primarily addressed the symptoms of piracy rather than the practical measures necessary to bring the pirates to justice. In many cases the navies deployed to combat the piracy off the Horn of Africa were dependent on the willingness of other states in the region, particularly Kenya, to accept transfer of the pirates for investigation and prosecution. Where this was not available, some navies adopted a catch-and-release policy.[112] The ability of a state to apply and enforce its own laws against piracy will depend on applicable provisions criminalizing the relevant piratical acts in the domestic law of the state and its political will to take jurisdiction.[113] Some domestic laws on piracy only provide jurisdiction to the state concerned, where the pirate ship or the pirates have the nationality of that state or are in the territory of that state. Not all national laws make piracy a universal crime that can be subject to arrest and prosecution anywhere in the world. Initial responses to questionnaires by the IMO-sponsored Contact Group on Piracy off the Coast of Somalia indicated that the criminalization of piracy in national legislation is far from comprehensive.[114]

Some acts of violence at sea against ships may potentially also be investigated and prosecuted under national laws implementing the 1988 Convention for the Suppression of Unlawful Acts against the Safety of Maritime Navigation (SUA Convention). Maritime violence, including piracy, became an issue of increasingly greater concern to the international community during the 1980s following the *Achille Lauro* hijacking in 1985 off Egypt by terrorists representing the Palestine Liberation Front. As a consequence of this attack, the United States submitted a proposal to the IMO Assembly that further measures should be required, and a regime dealing with all aspects of suppression of acts of maritime violence should be drafted.[115] As a result the SUA Convention was adopted on March 10, 1988, and entered into force on March 1, 1994. The convention makes it an offense for a person to seize or exercise control over a ship by threat or use of force or any other form of intimidation.[116] Under the convention, state's parties must create criminal offenses, establish jurisdiction, and accept into their custody persons responsible for such acts.[117] The convention was accompanied by the "Protocol for the Suppression of Unlawful Acts against the Safety of Fixed Platforms located on the Continental Shelf."[118] Measures to amend both were adopted in 2005 and entered into force on July 28, 2010, although the 2005 protocol only has seventeen parties to date, representing 29.52 percent of global shipping tonnage.[119] These amendments are more related to the unlawful use of a ship to intimidate governments or international organizations, or the use of a ship or any of its cargo, fuel, or other equipment in a manner likely to cause serious injury, death, or destruction; the amendments are therefore not directly relevant to the suppression of piracy.[120] In addition, many countries in piracy-ridden countries such as Somalia have opted to stay outside the SUA Convention and its protocols.

The criminal justice response to Somali pirates after their capture has become a focal point in the UN response over the last two years. The lack of a stable and effective central government in Somalia has made handing the pirates over to Somali authorities difficult. Although the pirates can be tried under the capturing state's laws (such as the individuals captured in the course of the French and US actions discussed earlier), dealing with and imprisoning pirates in the capturing state represents a considerable burden to that state. In addition, there have been significant disparities in the sentences imposed on convicted Somali pirates across national jurisdictions. The UNODC reports that sentences by prosecuting countries have generally ranged from five to twenty years but that sentences of more than thirty-three years have also been handed down.[121] Moreover, even when such individuals have served their time, it may be difficult to return them to Somalia on human rights grounds as there is a legitimate concern that they may be subject to torture or execution on their return.[122]

BUILDING THE CAPACITY OF THE INTERNATIONAL COMMUNITY TO BRING PIRATES TO JUSTICE

Combating the effects of the piratical activity off Somalia requires a more effective and comprehensive global and regional regime that is capable of bringing the pirates to justice in a more efficient and timely manner. A range of options have been considered by the United Nations in the context of the special report to the UN Secretary-General of July 26, 2010:

- Option 1 The enhancement of United Nations Assistance to build capacity of regional States to prosecute and imprison persons responsible for acts of piracy and armed robbery at sea off the coast of Somalia
- Option 2 The establishment of a Somali court sitting in the territory of a third State in the region either with or without United Nations participation

- Option 3 The establishment of a special chamber within the national jurisdiction of a State or States in the region without United Nations participation
- Option 4 The establishment of a special chamber within the national jurisdiction of a State or States with United Nations participation
- Option 5 The establishment of a regional tribunal on the basis of a multilateral agreement among regional States with United Nations participation
- Option 6 The establishment of an international tribunal on the basis of an agreement between a State in the region and the United Nations
- Option 7 The establishment of an international tribunal by Security Council resolution under Chapter VII of the United Nations Charter.[123]

The response of the UN Security Council to the report of the special adviser to the UN secretary-general on legal options to combat the piracy off the coast of Somalia in Resolutions 1976 and 2015, mentioned earlier, has largely debunked the costly option of establishing a specialist international tribunal, preferring instead to strengthen the capacity of Somali- and regional-based antipiracy courts through international assistance. Resolution 1976 emphasizes the need for a multifaceted response to the criminal justice issues associated with the piracy off the Horn of Africa, again urging all states to criminalize piracy in their domestic legislation including ancillary offenses such as incitement, facilitation, conspiracy, and attempt to commit acts of piracy. It underlines the need to investigate and prosecute those who illicitly finance, plan, organize, or unlawfully profit from pirate attacks off the coast of Somalia, and it invites states in conjunction with UNODC and Interpol to assist Somalia and other states in the region to strengthen their counterpiracy law enforcement capacities, including implementing anti–money laundering laws, establishing financial intelligence units, and strengthening forensic capabilities. In relation to specialist antipiracy tribunals, the resolution supports the ongoing efforts by regional states for the development of antipiracy courts or chambers in the region and urges consideration for the establishment of specialized Somali courts to try suspected pirates both in Somalia and the region including an extraterritorial Somali specialized antipiracy court, an option referred to in the report of the special adviser to the secretary-general on legal issues related to piracy off the coast of Somalia. Resolution 2015 continues to consider establishing specialized antipiracy courts in Somalia and other states in the region with substantial international participation and support, and continues to investigate the kind of international assistance needed to establish such courts.

The criminal justice capacity-building efforts of the international community in Somalia and the surrounding region have been spearheaded by the UNODC counterpiracy program. This program initially operated in Kenya and now works in six countries in the Somali Basin region. A range of assistance has been provided to Somalia, Kenya, the Seychelles, Mauritius, Tanzania, and the Maldives to support fair and efficient trials and humane and secure imprisonment in all these states. The types of assistance provided span judicial, prosecutorial, and police capacity-building programs as well as building prisons and supplying office equipment, law texts, and coast guard equipment. A new prison has now been built in Hargeisa, the capital of Somaliland, to strengthen the capacity of Somalia to imprison piracy and other offenders.[124]

DEVELOPING CRIMINAL JUSTICE COOPERATION NETWORKS

In addition to criminal justice capacity-building within regional states, there is also a need to forge closer criminal justice cooperation links between all states involved in combating the Somali piracy. The IMO-sponsored soft law instrument, the Djibouti Code of Conduct Concerning the Repression of Piracy and Armed Robbery against Ships, adopted by seventeen states from the western Indian Ocean in January 2009, represents a political and moral commitment by those states to cooperate in the arrest, investigation, and prosecution of persons who have committed or are suspected of having committed piracy.[125] This could form the basis of a regional agreement to spread the burden of criminal justice action relating to the Somali pirates among states in the immediate region.

Establishing more fully fledged criminal justice cooperation mechanisms between states for piracy offences and promoting widespread criminalization of piracy in the domestic legislation of all states are integral steps in the effective repression of piracy. A durable solution to bringing the Somali pirates and future piracy offenders to justice, which is consistent with human rights prescriptions and distributes the burden of investigation, prosecution, and punishment of alleged offenders more equitably among states, will depend on further development of the international law framework and its domestic implementation. The duty to cooperate to the fullest possible extent in the repression of piracy in Article 100 of the UNCLOS could form the basis for an implementing agreement to the UNCLOS that obligates states' parties to criminalize piracy in their domestic law, and that contains provisions on the transfer of pirates to face justice in situations where the seizing state is unable or unwilling to investigate and prosecute the alleged offenders. A global antipiracy agreement of this nature could contain similar provisions to other crime suppression treaties such as the UN Convention against Transnational Organized Crime and the SUA Convention obligating states' parties to cooperate with each other in providing evidence for the investigation and prosecution of pirates and to accept transfer of alleged pirates for investigation and prosecution subject to prescribed criteria. States whose flag vessels are attacked could be obliged to accept transfer of the alleged offenders, as could states of the same nationality as the pirates. Transfer of alleged offenders to receiving states could be made dependent on human rights safeguards common in extradition agreements that the death penalty would not be imposed or, if imposed, would not be carried out, and that transfer would be prohibited if there is evidence of the likelihood of torture or discrimination on the basis of race, religion, nationality, or political opinion during investigation or trial. Tightening the net around the perpetrators of this egregious crime goes beyond apprehension of the culprits and requires further expansion and strengthening of criminal justice links between seizing states and others who are able and willing to investigate and prosecute the offences.

CONCLUDING THOUGHTS: AN ENDURING PROBLEM?

That there has been a surge in piratical attacks against shipping off the Horn of Africa over recent years is abundantly clear. It is also evident that these attacks and the threat to freedom of navigation that they pose have provoked substantial and multifaceted reactions from the international community. While the recent efforts to combat piracy off the Horn of Africa have most notably yielded unprecedented international naval cooperation, it is clear from the continued large number of attacks against shipping that international counterpiracy efforts have failed to eradicate the threat to freedom of navigation in the northwestern Indian Ocean.

This is not to suggest that the international naval patrols off the Horn of Africa, allied to preventive measures on the part of shipowners and seafarers, have been without impact. Attacks against shipping off Somalia would be considerably worse if it were not for the international naval presence. Indeed, preemptive attacks against pirate action groups have been credited with disrupting at least twenty "pirate action groups" in the last quarter of 2011 alone.[126] It is also notable that although the overall number of attacks has increased year by year, the number of successful hijackings in the Gulf of Aden has been reduced substantially, and 2011 saw an arguably significant reduction in the number of successful hijackings attributed to Somali pirates from forty-seven and forty-nine in 2009 and 2010, respectively, to twenty-eight in 2011.

Nonetheless, international responses to the Somali piracy threat have tended to address the symptoms rather than the underlying causes of the problem. It is now well recognized that the fundamental causes of the Somali piracy phenomenon lie ashore in unstable and conflict-beset Somalia, and are directly linked to the failure of the central government of that state. Military responses offshore in the shape of naval flotillas and convoys therefore do not begin to address the roots of the Somali piracy problem—how pirates are able to operate from secure safe havens on land and why individuals are driven to become pirates in the first place. Indeed, it is likely that naval actions are likely to result in only ephemeral victories. These military responses may result in some short-term successes but do not go to the roots of the problem. Driven by poverty and the perceived theft of Somali offshore resources, in the absence of governmental control on land to restrain criminal activities, and allied to ready access to maritime skills and military hardware plus proximity to busy shipping lanes replete with tempting targets, it is little wonder that piracy has flourished off Somalia. Until peace, stable political governance, and the rule of law are restored in Somalia—things that, despite some promising signs, unfortunately, still seem to be far over the horizon—piracy seems set to continue off the Horn of Africa.

While there have been some promising recent developments within Somalia, with the TFG, supported by AMISOM and in concert with regional allies making gains against insurgent groups, it remains uncertain whether these advances can be sustained and the law and order as well as the developmental and humanitarian situation in Somalia can be substantially improved over the long term.

There are also positive developments in terms of greater acknowledgment and understanding of the complex and fractured geopolitics of Somalia, which has resulted in the adoption of a more nuanced approach. This is illustrated by the US announcement of a "dual-track" approach including engagement with some of the more stable parts of Somalia, notably Somaliland and, to a lesser extent, Puntland, with the objective of enhancing and underpinning the rule of law, thus combating piracy. Criminal justice capacity-building activities both within and beyond the borders of Somalia also accord with this type of approach, as does the call to member states in UN Security Council Resolution 1976 of April 2011 to assist Somali authorities in strengthening their coast guard capabilities.

There also appears to be scope for the international community to address some of the less-well-acknowledged underlying factors that contribute to Somali piracy—notably, illegal foreign fishing in Somali waters and the alleged dumping of toxic waste within Somalia. While it is the case that eliminating illegal fishing off Somalia would in all likelihood not lead to an end to piracy, addressing this issue would remove one of the main arguments that the pirates use to legitimize their actions—something that is arguably vital to the pirates' continued access to safe havens within Somalia.

A further key contributing factor that could be addressed is the willingness of the international shipping industry and insurers to pay out huge ransoms. The payment of multimillion-dollar ransoms for the release of hijacked vessels, cargos, and kidnapped crew members is a key incentive for piratical attacks. This is, however, a delicate issue where the lives of crew members are under threat.

Piracy off the Horn of Africa represents a real, present, and ongoing threat to freedom of navigation in the Indian Ocean. The range of pirate attacks has increased dramatically, and the number of attacks has increased every year to record levels. Some solace can be gleaned from the recent drop in the number of successful hijackings, but the pirates have proved themselves to be adept at reacting to and adapting to the counterpiracy efforts of the international community. There are also alarming indications that the pirates are becoming substantially more violent in their methods, at least partially in response to more robust counterpiracy efforts on the part of patrolling naval forces and better protection measures for targeted ships transiting the region. This raises the possibility of a spiraling cycle of violence and significantly enhanced threats to seafarers. The associated costs of piracy—whether from ransoms, increased insurance costs, the cost of deploying warships to the region, rerouting costs, and investments in counterpiracy measures for shipping, which are already measured in the billions—are also likely to persist and in all probability will rise.[127]

At present it appears that the challenge posed by Somali piracy is highly likely to persist and become more virulent over time, akin to other forms of corruption such as bribery. If Somali piracy initially emerged from disgruntled and disenfranchised fishermen seeking restitution, it has now evolved into a multimillion-dollar business that has spawned relatively sophisticated, organized, and well-equipped transnational criminal syndicates. The pirates have strong motives, great opportunity, ready means, and limited disincentives to engage in piracy. Consequently, piracy off the Horn of Africa is likely to remain an enduring threat.

NOTES

1. Technically, many of the attacks against shipping off the shores of the Horn of Africa are not piracy in the strict legal sense, so the perpetrators are not "pirates" as such (as we discuss later). A more inclusive understanding of the term "piracy" that encompasses both acts of piracy under the law of the sea and armed robbery against ships is used here.
2. Karsten von Hoesslin, "Making Sense of Somalia's Anarchic Waters," *Philippine Star Online*, March 25, 2006.
3. International Maritime Bureau (IMB), *Piracy and Armed Robbery against Ships, Annual Report 1 January–31 December 2006* (London: ICC International Maritime Bureau, 2007), 17, 24–25.
4. Alison Bevege, "NATO Warship Hunts Somali Pirates, Escorts Food Aid," *Reuters*, June 12, 2009; www.reuters.com/article/latestCrisis/idUSLC801321.
5. IMB, "2009 Worldwide Piracy Figures Surpass 400," January 14, 2010; www.icc-ccs.org/news/385-2009-worldwide-piracy-figures-surpass-400.
6. IMB, "Hostage-taking at Sea Rises to Record Levels, Says IMB," January 17, 2011; www.icc-ccs.org/news/429-hostage-taking-at-sea-rises-to-record-levels-says-imb.
7. IMB, *Piracy and Armed Robbery against Ships, Annual Report 1 January–31 December 2011* (London: ICC International Maritime Bureau, 2012), 5–6, 20.

8. Anna Bowden and Basnet Shikha, "The Economic Cost of Maritime Piracy 2011," One Earth Future Working Paper; http://oceansbeyondpiracy.org/sites/default/files/economic_cost_of_piracy_2011.pdf, 11.
9. Anna Bowden, "The Economic Cost of Maritime Piracy 2010," One Earth Future Working Paper, December 2010; http://oceansbeyondpiracy.org/sites/default/files/documents_old/The_Economic_Cost_of_Piracy_Full_Report.pdf, 9–10; and Bowden and Basnet, "Economic Cost of Maritime Piracy 2011," 12.
10. Bowden, "Economic Cost of Maritime Piracy 2010," 25; and Bowden and Basnet, "Economic Cost of Maritime Piracy 2011," 39. The apparent decline in the estimated economic cost of piracy between 2010 and 2011 in large part reflects refinements in the assumptions and methodology used in the two reports. See ibid., 9.
11. Clive Schofield, "Plaguing the Waves: Rising Piracy Threat Off the Horn of Africa," *Jane's Intelligence Review* 19, no. 7 (July 2007), 45–47.
12. Clive Schofield and Robin Warner, "Scuppering Somali Piracy: Global Responses and Paths to Justice," in *Australia's Response to Piracy: A Legal Perspective*, edited by Andrew Forbes, 45–74, Papers in Australian Maritime Affairs, No. 31 (Canberra: Sea Power Centre, Australia, 2011), 51.
13. Ibid.
14. "Seized Tanker Anchors Off Somalia," *BBC News Online*, November 19, 2008; http://news.bbc.co.uk/2/hi/africa/7735507.stm.
15. "Admiral Stunned by 'Very Good' Pirates," *Sydney Morning Herald*, November 18, 2009; www.smh.com.au/news/world/admiral-stunned-by-very-good-pirates/2008/11/18/1226770413138.html.
16. "Pirates Expand to Oman's Waters," *BBC News Online*, June 13, 2009; http://news.bbc.co.uk/2/hi/africa/8098365.stm; and "US Navy Says Pirates Extend Activity into Red Sea," *Reuters*, June 10, 2009, available at http://af.reuters.com/article/somaliaNews/idAFL9104173220090609.
17. IMB, *Piracy and Armed Robbery against Ships* (2012), 22.
18. "New Dynamic to Indian Ocean Piracy despite Monsoon Conditions," IMB, June 16, 2011; www.icc-ccs.org/news/446-new-dynamic-to-indian-ocean-piracy-despite-monsoon-conditions-.
19. IMB, *Piracy and Armed Robbery against Ships* (2012), 20.
20. See, for example, "Hijacked Americans 'Killed by Captors' Off Somalia," *BBC*, February 22, 2011, available at www.bbc.co.uk/news/world-us-canada-12541297.
21. Jeffrey Gettleman, "Suddenly, a Rise in Piracy's Price," *New York Times*, February 26, 2011; www.nytimes.com/2011/02/27/weekinreview/27pirates.html?_r=2&ref=global-home&pagewanted=all.
22. Kaija Hurlburt, "The Human Cost of Piracy, Oceans beyond Piracy," One Earth Foundation, June 6, 2011; http://oceansbeyondpiracy.org/sites/default/files/human_cost_of_somali_piracy.pdf, 15.
23. "UN Agency Deplores Pirates' Use of Seafarers as Human Shields," *UN News Centre*, April 19, 2011; www.un.org/apps/news/story.asp?NewsID=38147&Cr=somali&Cr1=; see also Adam Rawnsley, "Pirates to India: This Time It's Personal,"

Wired, April 20, 2011, available at www.wired.com/dangerroom/2011/04/pirates-to-india-this-time-its-personal/.

24. Katherine Hourfield, "Somali Pirates Torturing Hostages," *Associated Press*, February 1, 2011; www2.tbo.com/news/nation-world/2011/feb/02/T2NEWSO4-somali-pirates-torturing-hostages-eu-gene-ar-10960/.
25. "Piracy in the Waters Off the Coast of Somalia," *International Maritime Organization*; www.imo.org/blast/mainframe.asp?topic_id=1178.
26. Estimates of the number of ships passing through the Strait of Bab el-Mandeb and Gulf of Aden vary, but the IMO suggests a figure of 22,000. See ibid.
27. "World Oil Transit Chokepoints," *Energy Information Administration*, August 22, 2012; www.eia.gov/cabs/world_oil_transit_chokepoints/Full.html.
28. United Nations, *United Nations Convention on the Law of the Sea*, Publication no. E97.V10 (New York: United Nations, 1983). See 1833 United Nations Treaty Series (UNTS) 3, opened for signature December 10, 1982, Montego Bay, Jamaica (entered into force November 16, 1994); www.un.org/Depts/los/convention_agreements/convention_overview_convention.htm (hereinafter "UNCLOS" or "the Convention").
29. Republic of Somalia, "Law No. 57 on the Territorial Sea and Ports, 10 September 1972," *United Nations*, www.un.org/Depts/los/LEGISLATIONANDTREATIES/PDFFILES/SOM_1972_Law.pdf, at Article 1(1).
30. J. Ashley Roach and Robert W. Smith, *United States Responses to Excessive Maritime Claims* (The Hague: Martinus Nijhoff, 1996), 158–61.
31. The maritime boundary delimitation in the southern Red Sea was resolved through international arbitrations. See *Arbitration between Eritrea and Yemen, Award of the Arbitral Tribunal in the First Stage (Territorial Sovereignty and Scope of Dispute)*, October 9, 1988; and *Award of the Arbitral Tribunal in the Second Stage of the Proceedings (Maritime Delimitation)*, December 17, 1999; www.pca-cpa.org/showpage.asp?pag_id=1160.
32. Schofield and Warner, "Scuppering Somali Piracy," 45–48.
33. Peggy Hoyle, "Somaliland: Passing the Statehood Test?," *Boundary and Security Bulletin* 8, no. 3 (Autumn 2000): 80–91, at 88.
34. Peter Greste, "Puntland Turns against Somali Pirates," *BBC News Online*, May 31, 2009; http://news.bbc.co.uk/2/hi/africa/8072188.stm.
35. T. Jennings, "Controlling Access in the Absence of a Central Government: The Somali Dilemma," in *Ocean Yearbook*, vol. 15, 403–27 (Chicago: Chicago University Press, 2001), 401. See also, Thean Potgieter and Clive Schofield, "Poverty, Poaching and Pirates: Geopolitical Instability and Maritime Insecurity Off the Horn of Africa," *Journal of the Indian Ocean Region* 6, no. 1 (2010): 89–90.
36. Eric Kulisch, "Will Terrorists Turn to Piracy?," *MaritimeSecurity.Asia*, available at http://maritimesecurity.asia/free-2/piracy-update/will-terrorists-turn-to-piracy/.
37. Michael Onyeino, "Renewed Mandate in Doubt as Puntland Breaks Away from Somali Government," *Voice of America*, January 17, 2011, available at www.voanews.com/english/news/africa/east/Renewed-Mandate-in-Doubt-as-Puntland-Breaks-Away-From-Somali-Government-114136594.html.

38. Clive Schofield, "Plundered Waters: Somalia's Maritime Resource Insecurity," in *Crucible for Survival: Environmental Security in the Indian Ocean Region*, edited by Timothy Doyle and Melissa Risely, 215–41 (New Brunswick, NJ: Rutgers University Press, 2008), 103–4.
39. Atle Mesoy, "Somalia on the Verge of War," *Protocol Strategic Insights*, no. 5 (November/December 2006):18–25, at 19; Schofield, "Plundered Waters," 104; and "Ethiopia Completes Somali Pullout," *BBC News Online*, January 25, 2009; http://news.bbc.co.uk/2/hi/africa/7849900.stm.
40. S. Healy, "Courts in Charge," *World Today* 62, no. 8/9 (August/September, 2006): 16.
41. Schofield, "Plundered Waters," 107–8; and Schofield and Warner, "Scuppering Somali Piracy," 49.
42. Potgieter and Schofield, "Poverty, Poaching and Pirates," 96.
43. Human Rights Watch, "Somalia: Stop War Crimes in Mogadishu," February 14, 2011; www.hrw.org/news/2011/02/14/somalia-stop-war-crimes-mogadishu.
44. Potgieter and Schofield, "Poverty, Poaching and Pirates," 92.
45. United Nations Security Council Resolution 1964 (2010), S/RES/1964, of December 22, 2010, authorized an increase in AMISOM's force strength from eight thousand to twelve thousand troops. See www.un.org/ga/search/view_doc.asp?symbol=S/RES/1964%282010%29.
46. United Nations Security Council Resolution 2036 (2012), S/RES/2036, of February 22, 2012. See www.un.org/Docs/sc/unsc_resolutions12.htm.
47. Ibid.
48. Jeffrey Gettleman, Mark Mazetti, and Eric Schmitt, "US Relies on Contractors in Somalia Conflict," *New York Times*, August 10, 2011, available at www.nytimes.com/2011/08/11/world/africa/11somalia.html?pagewanted=all.
49. A. K. Mohamed Odowa, "Al-Shabaab Quits Mogadishu," *Somalia Report*, August 6, 2011; www.somaliareport.com/index.php/post/1303.
50. See, for example, "Somalia Profile," *BBC News Online*, October 8, 2012, www.bbc.com/news/world-africa-14094503.
51. See United Kingdom, Foreign and Commonwealth Office (FCO), "London Conference on Somalia," available at www.fco.gov.uk/en/global-issues/london-conference-somalia/.
52. London Conference on Somalia: Communique, Lancaster House, February 23, 2012, available at www.fco.gov.uk/en/news/latest-news/?id=727627582&view=PressS.
53. See, for example, ibid.; Mary Harper, "Will President Mohamud Be Able to Tame Somalia?," *BBC News Online*, September 11, 2012, www.bbc.com/news/world-africa-19556377; and "Somalia MPs Approve Shirdon as the New Prime Minister," *BBC News Online*, October 17, 2012; www.bbc.com/news/world-africa-19979371.
54. "Worst Drought in 60 Years Hitting Horn of Africa-UN," *Reuters*, June 28, 2011, available at http://af.reuters.com/article/ethiopiaNews/idAFLDE75R0IR20110628?sp=true.

55. See "Report of the Secretary-General on Possible Options to Further the Aim of Prosecuting and Imprisoning Persons Responsible for Acts of Piracy and Armed Robbery at Sea Off the Coast of Somalia, Including, in Particular, Options for Creating Special Domestic Chambers Possibly with International Components, a Regional Tribunal or an International Tribunal and Corresponding Imprisonment Arrangements, Taking into Account the Work of the Contact Group on Piracy Off the Coast of Somalia, the Existing Practice in Establishing International and Mixed Tribunals, and the Time and Resources Necessary to Achieve and Sustain Substantive Results." S/2010/394, July 26, 2010; www.un.org/ga/search/view_doc.asp?symbol=S/2010/394.
56. Jennings, "Controlling Access," 403–27; S. Coffen-Smout, "Pirates, Warlords and Rogue Fishing Vessels in Somalia's Unruly Seas," www.chebucto.ns.ca/~ar120/somalia.html; and Schofield, "Plundered Waters," 108–9.
57. United Nations Environment Programme (UNEP), "National Rapid Environmental Desk Assessment—Somalia," UN Environmental Programme, 2006; www.unep.org/tsunami/reports/TSUNAMI_SOMALIA_LAYOUT.pdf.
58. See "Report of the Secretary-General on the Protection of Somali Natural Resources and Waters," A/2011/661, 25 October 2011, pp. 10–13 and 17, available at http://daccess-dds-ny.un.org/doc/UNDOC/GEN/N11/540/51/PDF/N1154051.pdf?OpenElement.
59. Food and Agriculture Organization of the United Nations, "The Somali Republic," Fishery Country Profile, January 2005; www.fao.org/fi/oldsite/FCP/en/SOM/profile.htm.
60. See United Nations Security Council, "Report of the Secretary-General on the Protection of Somali Natural Resources and Waters" S/2011/661, October 25, 2011; http://unpos.unmissions.org/Portals/UNPOS/Repository%20UNPOS/S-2011-661%20(25Oct).pdf, 12.
61. Coffen-Smout, "Pirates, Warlords"; and Schofield, "Plundered Waters," 109–10.
62. "Report of the Secretary-General on the Protection of Somali Natural Resources and Waters," 11, 18.
63. UN Security Council Resolution 1816, S/RES/1816 (2008), June 2, 2008; www.un.org/Docs/sc/unsc_resolutions08.htm.
64. UN Security Council Resolution 1838, S/RES/1838 (2008), October 7, 2008; www.un.org/Docs/sc/unsc_resolutions08.htm.
65. UN Security Council Resolution 1846, S/RES/1846 (2008), December 2, 2008; www.un.org/Docs/sc/unsc_resolutions08.htm.
66. UN Security Council, 6221st Meeting, "Piracy Off Somali Coast Not Only Criminal but Very Successful, Security Council Hears, Cautioned There Could Be No Peace at Sea without Stability on Land," *ReliefWeb*, November 18, 2009; www.un.org/News/Press/docs/2009/sc9793.doc.htm.
67. UN Security Council Resolution 1918, S/RES/1918 (2010), April 27, 2010; www.un.org/Docs/sc/unsc_resolutions10.htm.
68. UN Security Council Resolution 1950, S/RES/1976 (2010), November 23, 2010; www.un.org/Docs/sc/unsc_resolutions10.htm.

69. UN Security Council Resolution 1976, S/RES/2020 (2011), April 11, 2011; www.un.org/Docs/sc/unsc_resolutions11.htm.
70. UN Security Council Resolution 2015, S/RES/2020 (2011), October 24, 2011; www.un.org/Docs/sc/unsc_resolutions11.htm.
71. UN Security Council Resolution 2020, S/RES/2020 (2011), November 22, 2011; www.un.org/Docs/sc/unsc_resolutions11.htm.
72. "Piracy in the Waters Off the Coast of Somalia."
73. More than 90 percent of the World Food Programme's aid to Somalia arrived by sea. See Bevege, "NATO Warship Hunts Somali Pirates."
74. "Coalition Warships Set up Maritime Security Patrol Area in the Gulf of Aden," *International Chamber of Commerce*, August 26, 2009; www.iccwbo.org/News/Articles/2008/Coalition-warships-set-up-Maritime-Security-Patrol-area-in-the-Gulf-of-Aden/.
75. Pierre-Emmanuel Augey, "Indian Ocean Maritime Security Cooperation: The Fight against Piracy Off the Somali Coast," Paper presented at the Indian Ocean Maritime Security Symposium, Australian Defence College, Canberra, April 15–17, 2009.
76. For example, the *Malaspina Castle* was seized while transiting the MSPA. See Mark Tran, "Somali Pirates Seize British-Owned Ship," *Guardian*, April 6, 2009; www.guardian.co.uk/world/2009/apr/06/somali-pirates-hijack.
77. Augey, "Indian Ocean Maritime Security Cooperation."
78. Such tripwires include the presence of boarding equipment, the presence of additional fuel supplies on board the suspect vessel, and the absence of fishing gear. See Schofield and Warner, "Scuppering Somali Piracy," 55–56.
79. See, for example, Xan Rice, "Indian Navy Destroys Pirate Ship after Coming under Fire," *Guardian*, November 19, 2008; www.guardian.co.uk/world/2008/nov/19/somalia-pirates; and IMB, "IMB Commends Robust Action by Indian Navy," March 18, 2011; www.icc-ccs.org/news/438-imb-commends-robust-action-by-indian-navy.
80. This occurred in the case of the hijacked yacht *Le Ponant* in 2008. See "France Raid Ship after Crew Freed," *BBC News Online*, April 12, 2008; http://news.bbc.co.uk/2/hi/africa/7342292.stm.
81. For example, the yacht *Carre d'As* was successfully retaken and two hostages were freed on September 18, 2008. See Augey, "Indian Ocean Maritime Security Cooperation."
82. "Frenchman Dies in Somali Rescue," *BBC News Online*, April 11, 2009, available at http://news.bbc.co.uk/2/hi/7994201.stm.
83. Danilova Ludmila, "Hijacked Russian Tanker Freed, Crew Safe, Pirate Dead," *Reuters*, May 6, 2010; http://af.reuters.com/article/topNews/idAFJOE64500820100506?sp=true; and "Freed Somali Pirates 'Probably Died'—Russian Source," *BBC News Online*, May 11, 2010; http://news.bbc.co.uk/2/hi/africa/8675978.stm.
84. "South Korea Rescues Samho Jewelry Crew from Pirates," *BBC News Online*, January 21, 2011: www.bbc.co.uk/news/world-africa-12248096.

85. "Malaysian Navy Foils Ship Hijack Attempt, Seizes Pirates," *BBC News Online*, January 22, 2011; www.bbc.co.uk/news/world-asia-pacific-12258442.
86. "Dutch Marines Kill Pirates, Iranian Boat Freed," *BBC News Online*, April 4, 2011; www.bbc.co.uk/news/world-africa-12962900.
87. Xan Rice, "US Navy Commandoes Free Hostage Captain in Dramatic Raid on Somali Pirate Boat," *Guardian*, April 13, 2009; www.guardian.co.uk/world/2009/apr/12/hostage-captain-freed-somali-pirates.
88. Abdi Guled, Kimberly Dozier, and Katharine Houfeld, "Raid in Somalia: US Navy SEALs Free Hostages Held since October," *Huffington Post*, January 25, 2012; www.huffingtonpost.com/2012/01/25/raid-in-somalia_n_1230062.html?ref=daily-brief?utm_source=DailyBrief&utm_campaign=012512&utm_medium=email&utm_content=NewsEntry&utm_term=Daily%20Brief.
89. IMB, "Piracy Prone Areas and Warnings," www.icc-ccs.org/piracy-reporting-centre/prone-areas-and-warnings.
90. See IMO Maritime Safety Committee circular, MSC.1/Circ.1339, "Best Management Practices for Protection against Somalia Based Piracy" (BMP 4); www.imo.org/MediaCentre/HotTopics/piracy/Pages/default.aspx.
91. IMB, "Piracy Prone Areas and Warnings."
92. Ibid.
93. Schofield and Warner, "Scuppering Somali Piracy," 57.
94. Ibid.
95. Schofield, "Plaguing the Waves," 47.
96. Jonathan Saul, "Shippers Weigh Armed Response to Somali Piracy," *Reuters*, June 3, 2009; www.reuters.com/article/2009/06/03/idUSL31024866; and Schofield, "Plaguing the Waves." See also, Adam Blenford, "Cruise Lines Turn to Sonic Weapon," *BBC News Online*, August 11, 2005; http://news.bbc.co.uk/go/pr/fr/-/2/hi/africa/4418748.stm.
97. "Cruise Ship Evades Pirate Attack," *BBC News Online*, December 2, 2008; http://news.bbc.co.uk/2/hi/africa/7760216.stm; "Italian Cruise Ship Foils Pirates," *BBC News Online*, April 26, 2009; http://news.bbc.co.uk/2/hi/africa/8019084.stm. On the following day it was reported that a number of the would-be pirates were apprehended. See "Spanish Capture 'Somali Pirates,'" *BBC News Online*, April 27, 2009; http://news.bbc.co.uk/2/hi/africa/8021795.stm.
98. Schofield and Warner, "Scuppering Somali Piracy," 57.
99. IMB, *Piracy and Armed Robbery against Ships* (2011), 24; www.denizticaretodasi.org/DetoPortal/Portals/Documents/2011_imb_p_report.pdf.
100. IMO, Maritime Safety Committee circulars MSC.1/Circ.1405/Rev.1 and MSC.1/Circ.1406/Rev.1; www.imo.org/MediaCentre/HotTopics/piracy/Pages/default.aspx.
101. Cahal Milmo, "Insurance Firms Plan Private Navy to Take on Somali Pirates," *Independent*, September 28, 2010; www.independent.co.uk/news/world/africa/insurance-firms-plan-private-navy-to-take-on-somali-pirates-2091298.html.
102. Augey, "Indian Ocean Maritime Security Cooperation."

103. Daniel Patrick O'Connell, *The International Law of the Sea*, vol. 2 (Oxford: Clarendon Press, 1984), 966.
104. Donald R. Rothwell, "Maritime Piracy and International Law," *Crimes of War*, February 24, 2009; www.crimesofwar.org/commentary/maritime-piracy-and-international-law/.
105. HSC, Arts. 14-19; LOSC, Arts. 100-107.
106. O'Connell, *International Law of the Sea*, 968–70.
107. Robin R. Churchill and A. V. Lowe, *The Law of the Sea*, 3rd ed. (Manchester, UK: Manchester University Press, 1999), 210; and Rothwell, "Maritime Piracy and International Law."
108. HSC, Art. 17, LOSC, Art. 103.
109. Rothwell, "Maritime Piracy and International Law."
110. Robert C. Beckmann, "Combating Piracy and Armed Robbery against Ships in Southeast Asia: The Way Forward," *Ocean Development and International Law* 33, no. 3 (2002): 319.
111. Ibid.
112. Kathryn Westcott, "Pirates in the Dock," *BBC News*, May 21, 2009; http://news.bbc.co.uk/2/hi/africa/8059345.stm.
113. Churchill and Lowe, *Law of the Sea*, 210; O'Connell, *International Law of the Sea*, 967; and Rothwell, "Maritime Piracy and International Law."
114. Contact Group on Piracy Off the Coast Off Somalia (CGPCS) Working Group on Legal Issues, "Chairman's Conclusions," March 5, 2009; www.marad.dot.gov/documents/wg2-Vienna_Meeting-chair-summary-March_5-2009.pdf.
115. Churchill and Lowe, *Law of the Sea*, 210–11; and Rothwell, "Maritime Piracy and International Law."
116. SUA Convention, Art. 3.
117. SUA Convention, Arts. 5–7, 10.
118. Churchill and Lowe, *Law of the Sea*, 211.
119. Status of ratifications for the 2005 SUA protocol can be found at International Maritime Organization (IMO), Status of Conventions; www.imo.org/About/Conventions/StatusOfConventions/Pages/Default.aspx.
120. Rothwell, "Maritime Piracy and International Law."
121. UNODC, *UNODC and Piracy*, www.unodc.org/easternafrica/en/piracy/index.html.
122. Michael H. Passman, "Protections Afforded to Captured Pirates under the Law of War and International Law," *Tulane Maritime Law Journal* 33, no. 1 (2008): 36.
123. "Report of the secretary-general, S/2010/394."
124. UNODC, *UNODC and Piracy*, www.unodc.org/easternafrica/en/piracy/index.html.
125. "High-Level Meeting in Dijbouti Adopts a Code of Conduct to Repress Acts of Piracy and Armed Robbery against Ships," *International Maritime Organization*, January 30, 2009; www.imo.org/blast/mainframe.asp?topic_id=1773&doc_id=10933.

126. IMB, *Piracy and Armed Robbery against Ships* (2011), 24.
127. See, in particular, Bowden, "Economic Cost of Maritime Piracy"; and Bowden and Basnet, "The Economic Cost of Maritime Piracy 2011."

CHAPTER 4

ARMED GROUPS AT SEA

Maritime Terrorism in the Indian Ocean Region

MICHAEL RICHARDSON
AND ANDREA J. DEW

INTRODUCTION

This chapter explores the phenomenon of armed groups at sea. With the exception of pirates, discussed in previous chapters, we tend to think of armed groups as landlocked threats who take to the water temporarily for mobility or perhaps smuggling, but who are ultimately landlubbers. While terrorists, militia groups, antigovernment rebel networks, and even pirates are based on land, the use of the littorals, coastal waters, and high seas by a range of armed groups has become increasingly sophisticated. Indeed, this chapter argues that increasingly sophisticated weapons and maritime operating techniques have been used by an array of nonstate actors in the Indian Ocean region (IOR) with varying degrees of seaborne capability to strike against adversaries, including governments, their navies, and merchant shipping. This development is being watched with concern by both regional and extraregional navies and coast guards, as well as by intelligence agencies.

Navies and coast guards are responsible for maintaining law and order at sea and for ensuring that the huge volume of international trade, most of which is carried along busy and well-defined sea-lanes, continues to flow without threat of attack or disruption by nonstate actors. The energy-rich Persian Gulf, the Arabian and Red Seas, and the Suez Canal, as well as the Indian Ocean are all vital links in sea trade between Asia and the West. Moreover, the Gulf, the Arabian Sea, and the Indian Ocean are vital links in energy and other trade exchanges between Asia and the Middle East. Referring in part to developments in the IOR, Lt. Gen. Michael Maples, head of the US Defense Intelligence Agency (DIA), has warned that as the proliferation of weapons and information technology accelerates, non-state actors "will have more opportunities to develop very capable conventional and asymmetric military, intelligence and counterintelligence abilities, perhaps matching or even exceeding those of some advanced nations, including US allies." This, he added, "could further destabilize regions critical to US interests."[1]

This chapter focuses on an assessment of three armed groups: the decentralized al-Qaeda movement; the Liberation Tigers of Tamil Eelam (LTTE, also known as the Tamil Tigers) based in northern Sri Lanka, which was defeated by Sri Lankan forces in spring 2009; and the Lebanese Hezbollah in the Middle East.[2] All three groups have used well-honed techniques of political violence and have extensive networks of external financial and material support. Further, all three groups have a deep understanding of the importance of sea transport and have experience disrupting it. While we may think of terrorism as primarily a land-based phenomenon, these groups demonstrate that as long as armed groups use the sea to reach their targets or choose seaborne targets, it is only a matter of time until global sea trade feels its impact. This chapter explores the evolving tactics and strategies of these different armed groups and discusses the extent to which both they and the continuing arms proliferation in the Gulf region present significant security challenges.

STRATEGIC SETTING

Because this book focuses on the vast IOR, it is worthwhile taking a moment to place the groups and the area of operations discussed in this chapter in geographical context. This section discusses the Persian Gulf and Southeast Asia, which each have their own specific challenges.

The Persian Gulf

The first focus is the Persian Gulf (Arabian Gulf), which is a huge source of energy for the world and is predicted to become even more important in the future. As Emerson and Mathur discuss in chapter 1 of this book, although about 16 percent of Gulf oil exports are shipped to Europe and 11 percent to the United States, fully 66 percent of Gulf oil exports go to Asia. This relationship is expected to strengthen as Asian oil production plateaus and demand rises. Moreover, the Gulf is a geopolitical cockpit where the interests of many major outside powers, including the United States, Europe, Russia, China, India, and Japan, are deeply engaged. As US and allied forces strive to stabilize Iraq and counter the resurgence of the Taliban and al-Qaeda in Afghanistan and Pakistan, Iran's rise and its program to enrich uranium on an industrial scale are pressing US national security issues. Enrichment can make fuel for reactors to generate electricity or fissile material for nuclear bombs. Iran says its intent is peaceful, but the United States and other Western powers as well as Israel suspect that Teheran is seeking nuclear weapons capability.

Finally, at the Persian Gulf end of the Indian Ocean, it is worth noting the repercussions of Iran's rise as a regional power led by a militant Shiite theocracy, which challenges the primacy of long-established Sunni-Arab regimes in and around the Gulf. As the Stuxnet incident in 2010 and diplomatic posturing following that incident demonstrate, the United States and Israel are determined to try to stop Iran from following North Korea in developing nuclear weapons. US officials are seeking to tighten financial sanctions on Iran, and have accused Iranian paramilitary forces of siding with Shiite militia factions in Iraq to attack US troops. US warships deployed in or close to the Gulf are seen as a warning to Iran not to underestimate America's power and resolve despite its troubles in Iraq, Afghanistan, and Pakistan. All of this provides a backdrop for Hezbollah's use of the maritime domain to disrupt and destroy maritime- and land-based targets in the region.

Southeast Asia

At the other end of the Indian Ocean, the international shipping straits of Southeast Asia are closely connected by maritime trade to the Strait of Hormuz, the only way into and out of the Gulf by sea. As chapter 1 discusses, these straits are integral parts of the same vast conveyor belt of seaborne commerce that runs between the Indian and Pacific Oceans carrying huge quantities of oil and other cargo. The Hormuz strait, bounded by Iran in the north and Oman and United Arab Emirates in the south and about twenty-one miles wide at its narrowest point, is described by the US Department of Energy as the world's most important oil choke point: more than 90 percent of all the oil exported from the Gulf moves via this strait.[3]

At the eastern entrance to the Indian Ocean, the adjacent Malacca and Singapore Straits, which run between Indonesia on one side and Malaysia and Singapore on the other, provide the shortest sea passage for ships traveling between the Gulf and East Asia. They are part of a lifeline for the export-oriented but oil-short economies of East Asia. With its rapidly growing economy and rising demand for imported oil and gas, India is also locked into this maritime highway. More than half of India's trade goes through the Malacca and Singapore Straits, which link the Indian and Pacific Oceans via the Andaman and South China Seas.[4] More than 60,000 vessels involved in international commerce, an average of about 170 a day, transit the straits. The waterway carries about 30 percent of global trade and a substantial part of the world's energy shipments. The traffic is growing, and this is increasing the strategic significance of Southeast Asia's main maritime choke point.[5]

The United States has important military and alliance interests in the Malacca and Singapore Straits. Although relatively little of America's oil imports come through the waterway, the overwhelming proportion of oil reaching its Northeast Asian allies, Japan and South Korea, is carried by tankers that traverse the Southeast Asian straits. An average of more than 15 million barrels of oil per day (b/d) passed through the Malacca and Singapore Straits in 2007. This figure rose from 11 million b/d in 2004 and is expected to double to 22 million b/d by 2030. If the tankers carrying this oil had to take the longer way round through Indonesia via the Sunda or Lombok Straits, they would travel an extra 1,600 kilometers from the Gulf, adding approximately one and a half days to the shipping time. According to the International Energy Agency, this would effectively remove 17 million barrels of oil—about 20 percent of global consumption—from the market.[6]

The United States also sends warships, including aircraft carriers, from its Pacific Fleet through the Malacca and Singapore Straits to reinforce its military presence in the Indian Ocean, the Arabian Sea, and the Persian Gulf. This naval "surge" capacity through the straits is especially important to Washington at times of crisis in the Gulf or IOR. The US Navy's Fifth Fleet is based at Bahrain in the Gulf, operating under the US Central Command. Drawing ships as needed from the Pacific and Atlantic Fleets to augment its force, the Fifth Fleet's mission includes keeping the Persian Gulf and the Strait of Hormuz open to international shipping.

Since the collapse of the Soviet Union and the end of the Cold War in the early 1990s, US and allied military power has become both preponderant and pervasive. This has been underscored by the US-led invasions of Afghanistan and Iraq, the increased mobility of Western forces, and the enhanced strike capability of those forces. This has provided an incentive for terrorists and other armed groups to look for ways of countering superior force on land and at sea, just as Communist insurgents in Southeast Asia during the Cold War adopted different tactics and strategies for fighting numerically superior and better-armed local government forces and their foreign allies. Fortunately, the irregular strategies used by nonstate actors so far have been relatively unsuccessful in exploiting these developments and disrupting maritime trade. But this may change in the future. The activities of al-Qaeda, Hezbollah, and the LTTE all suggest a continuing interest in seaborne operations coupled with significant arms proliferation.

TRENDSETTERS: THE LTTE AND HEZBOLLAH AT SEA

This section considers two trendsetting groups, the LTTE and Hezbollah, whose mastery of the maritime domain suggests possible patterns for future use of the maritime domain by armed groups. Although both cases are interesting in their own right, they also raise the question of what inspiration a global terror group such as al-Qaeda might take from their activities, especially in a post–bin Laden world.

The Sea Tigers

The Liberation Tigers of Tamil Eelam (LTTE) were pioneers in showing how nonstate actors can use ships in support of political violence. Although their areas of operations were mostly limited to Sri Lanka and the southern Indian Ocean, their value in an examination of the use of the sea by terror groups is twofold. First, they proved that an armed group not only can use the maritime domain but also can master all of the functions of a modern navy. The LTTE used small boats to land elite troops for attacks, ran extensive cross-channel shipping routes for resupply between Sri Lanka and India, and maintained a network of "mother ships" hundreds of miles away in the Indian Ocean for resupply. Second, the Sri Lankan response to this armed group's use of the water was to rethink how an island or coastal power uses its naval capabilities, which provides a useful blueprint for other small navies faced with maritime terrorism threats.

Before Norway brokered a cease-fire between the government and the LTTE in February 2002, the LTTE had developed into a prototypical terrorist organization with a potentially global reach.[7] Founded in 1976, the LTTE claimed to represent the Tamil minority (which is mainly Hindu) in Sri Lanka, a country with a Sinhalese and predominantly Buddhist majority. At the peak of its power, the LTTE's ethnonationalist organization was estimated to have a ten-thousand-strong armed force. After 1983 it used both overt and illegal methods to raise funds; acquire weapons, ammunition, and explosives; and publicize its cause in fighting for a separate state for Tamils in the northeast of the island. The conflict between government troops and LTTE fighters has cost more than seventy thousand lives over the past twenty-five years. The LTTE frequently used suicide bombers in operations against the government and has exploited commercial maritime shipping, both to make money and to bring in arms, ammunition, and other war-related material for attacks in Sri Lanka.

The LTTE is the only group to have successfully assassinated two national leaders—Rajiv Gandhi of India in 1991 and Ranasinghe Premadasa of Sri Lanka in 1993. Both were well-orchestrated suicide operations that evaded tight official security cordons. Sri Lanka's former president Chandrika Kumaratunga narrowly survived a LTTE suicide bomb attack in 1999. Underlining its pioneer role, the LTTE had conducted 155 battlefield and civilian suicide attacks through July 1998, compared to the 50 carried out by all other groups worldwide to that date, including Hamas and Hezbollah in the Middle East, the Kurdish Worker's Party in Turkey, and the Sikh Babbar Khalsa in South Asia.

Moreover, some analysts believe that the LTTE and al-Qaeda have learned from each other, that Tamil guerillas trained in al-Qaeda camps in Afghanistan, and that the attack on the USS *Cole* and the French tanker *Limburg* in 2002 copied LTTE strikes against shipping. The Sea Tigers, the naval arm of the LTTE, developed a range of naval capabilities, including rapid-attack fiberglass boats used to attack the Sri Lanka Navy (SLN), deploy frogmen, insert land-attack teams, and mount suicide attacks. They also developed semisubmersible craft used for suicide attacks and a small flotilla of offshore warehouse ships located southeast of Sri Lanka.[8] The "Black" Sea Tigers, the specially trained suicide attackers, frequently used high-speed boats filled with explosives to ram naval vessels, and have sank dozens both in harbor and at sea. Moreover, there have been reports that members of Jemaah Islamiyah, the Southeast Asian terrorist group linked to al-Qaeda, have been trained in the seaborne guerrilla tactics developed by the LTTE.[9]

The key to the LTTE's fighting strength was its international support network. It collected money from large Tamil communities in North America, Europe, and Australia. There is also some evidence that the LTTE officially sanctioned drug smuggling as well as arms smuggling to support its independence struggle.[10] Starting in the mid-1980s the LTTE controlled an extensive and profitable network of freight forwarders and up to a dozen or so cargo ships that were not registered in Sri Lanka. To help disguise their ownership, they flew Panamanian, Honduran, or Liberian flags. The heart of the LTTE's military procurement was its secretive shipping network, which included at least ten freighters by 1999.

Most of the time, the LTTE ships made money carrying legitimate cargo such as timber, tea, rice, cement, and fertilizer. But in some cases the LTTE carried weapons and ammunition for other paying terrorist groups, including the Harkat-ul-Mujahideen of Pakistan, which is a member of the al-Qaeda-linked International Islamic Front. When needed, their ships and traders also played a vital role in supplying explosives, weapons, ammunition, and other war-related material to the LTTE in Sri Lanka.[11]

In one of the largest such shipments, in August 1994, an LTTE freighter, the *Swene*, loaded sixty tons of the explosives RDX and TNT bought from a factory in Ukraine. The transaction was arranged through an LTTE front company in Dhaka that had produced a forged end-user certificate showing the Bangladesh armed forces as the approved recipient. However, the shipment landed on the northeast Sri Lankan coast controlled by the LTTE and transferred to jungle bases. Between 300 kg and 400 kg of the explosives would be used in the massive truck-bomb attack against the Central Bank building in Colombo, Sri Lanka, in January 1996, which killed sixty people and injured as many as fifteen hundred.[12]

The LTTE was also able to disrupt vital Sri Lankan sea lines of communication. On May 23, 1997, for example, a Greek-registered freighter, the *Stillus Limassul,* left the port Beira in Mozambique for Sri Lanka carrying more than thirty-two thousand 8-MM mortar bombs intended for the Sri Lankan army. The deal, worth $3 million, had been arranged between officials of the Sri Lankan Ministry of Defence and the state-owned Zimbabwe Defence Industries. The munitions were shipped by train to the Mozambique port of Beira. But the Sri Lankan military never received them. This was the result of a well-organized and well-concealed "sting" operation by the LTTE that deeply embarrassed the Sri Lankan government.

The LTTE claimed that on July 11, 1997, they had hijacked the *Stillus Limassul* while it was on its way to Colombo. However, subsequent investigations revealed that the *Stillus Limassul* was owned by the LTTE. Further inquiries uncovered a paper trail that led to Ben Tsoi, an Israeli arms dealer who had arranged the mortar supply and apparently had been bribed by the LTTE to let one of their own freighters collect the consignment. Tsoi's company, LBJ Military Supplies, reportedly persuaded some officials of the Zimbabwe Defence Industries to provide false information to the authorities in Sri Lanka, claiming that the shipment had been loaded in Beira, as scheduled. The Sri Lankan government was then informed that the munitions were on their way to Sri Lanka via Namibia and Madagascar. This gave the LTTE time to complete the sting. By the time Colombo learned the full extent of what had happened, the mortars had been unloaded and transshipped by smaller LTTE vessels to LTTE jungle bases in Sri Lanka. Within weeks, the weapons were being used by the LTTE to cause serious setbacks to government troops.[13]

A major turning point in the battle between the Sri Lankan government and the LTTE came in spring 2009 as Sri Lankan troops captured LTTE strongholds and regained control of LTTE-held territory. The success of the Sri Lankan offensive against LTTE culminated in May 2009 with the death of the LTTE leader Velupillai Prabhakaran. Subsequently, Selvarasa Pathmanathan, the head of LTTE's International Diplomatic Relations and alleged head of the LTTE's weapon procurement division, stated that the LTTE had decided to "silence our guns to save our people."[14]

After nearly thirty years of conflict, it is worth considering how the Sri Lankan government and armed forces were able to drive the LTTE to this point and to the maritime transformation that supported this final campaign. First, it should be noted that Sri Lankan success against the LTTE was the result of a prolonged, multiphase strategy that combined diplomatic, economic, legal, and military dimensions and focused not just on the domestic and regional dimensions but also on undermining the LTTE in the international environment. The operating environment for the LTTE, both in and outside Sri Lanka, became more constrained from the late 1990s on, especially after the United States and other countries launched their global campaign against terrorism following 9/11; indeed, the LTTE was proscribed in the United States, Canada, Britain, and India, as well as in twenty-eight other countries.

As part of the international crackdown, four Indonesians, a Sri Lankan, and a Singaporean were arrested in September 2006 and charged in US courts in 2007 with involvement in two arms-dealing conspiracies, one to export arms to Indonesia illegally and the other to funnel weapons to the LTTE in Sri Lanka. The six had tried to buy sophisticated weapons, including shoulder-fired, heat-seeking antiaircraft missiles; night vision devices; sniper rifles; machine guns; grenade launchers; and ammunition. According to the US Justice Department, two down payments totaling more than $700,000 were made from a Malaysian bank account controlled by the LTTE to an account in the US set up by FBI agents.[15]

Although both Canada and Britain launched new crackdowns on LTTE fundraising and arms procurement, the campaign had mixed results. While it failed to net the LTTE's head of arms procurement based in Thailand, some analysts believe that it disrupted at least 75 percent of the rebel group's supply chain.[16] However, LTTE attempts to secure training guides and weapons continued throughout 2009 despite intensified international scrutiny. For example, the *Telegraph* (UK) newspaper reported that a British-based Sri Lankan was jailed for helping secure guides to underwater warfare systems, explosive ordnance disposal, and mine clearance for the LTTE.[17]

One of the most clear-cut success stories in the defeat of the LTTE is the transformation and operational success of the SLN in disrupting the LTTE's sea lines of communication. In conjunction with the use of legal and law enforcement strategies to interdict financial resources to the LTTE, the SLN focused on developing its ability to interdict material resources and interrupt LTTE sea-based operations.

Beginning in 2006 the revamped and revitalized SLN has used these capabilities with great success to attrite LTTE sea-based capabilities. In addition to disrupting LTTE use of coastal waters and their sea lines of communication and resupply, the SLN destroyed eight Sea Tiger oceangoing cargo vessels and eleven of the fishing trawlers used to offload and ferry clandestine shipments to shore.

The SLN also destroyed a number of Sea Tiger floating warehouses containing arms and ammunition.[18] Between March and October 2007, the SLN announced that six Sea Tiger cargo ships were intercepted and destroyed in international waters up to 3,000 km southeast of Sri Lanka, off the coasts of Australia and Indonesia; an additional eight were destroyed in 2008. The SLN reported that more than 10,000 tons of munitions and military equipment were destroyed in these attacks, including three aircraft in ready-to-assemble condition, torpedoes, jet skis, diver-delivery vehicles, outboard motors, radar, and night vision goggles.[19]

These long-range strikes by the SLN appear to have been part of a counterterrorist operation that spanned a number of countries, including the United States. Coupled with improved naval intelligence and cooperation with the Indian Navy, they led to Sri Lanka regaining control of the sea lines of communication and limiting the movement of the LTTE and its ability to resupply from India across the Palk Strait.

The timing of these successes was also particularly important; they left Prabhakaran without the ability to resupply his embattled LTTE land forces, which created an opportunity for the Sri Lankan army to press forward into LTTE strongholds in the northeast of the island.[20] This advantage was further enhanced by the SLN's transformation of its naval capabilities and doctrine as part of a small boats concept. The SLN used more than 150 inshore patrol craft to create a flexible mesh capable of monitoring Sri Lanka's coast around the port area of Trincombolee, where Prabhakaran made his last stand in 2009. The four-layer defense barrier, which involved the innovative use of ground-based sensors, was maintained for several months by swapping out crews to keep the pressure on the LTTE. The net consisted of fast-attack craft, offshore patrol vessels, and gunboats in addition to the SLN's rapid-action boat squadron and special boat squadron.[21] Both independent analysts and the SLN credit these strategic and doctrinal innovations and operational successes to the SLN's ability to successfully conduct irregular warfare at sea and irreparably damage LTTE naval capabilities.[22]

However, despite Sri Lankan successes against the LTTE at sea and on land, it would be premature to assume that the LTTE capabilities and infrastructure no longer remain a threat to peace and stability in the region. After thirty years of bitter ethnic armed conflict and numerous broken peace accords, the root causes of conflict remain, and both the LTTE and Sri Lankan government face a rocky reintegration process. In addition, despite the setbacks discussed earlier, the LTTE's overseas fundraising, arms procurement, and smuggling network reportedly raised between $200 million and $300 million in 2008 from among at least six hundred thousand Sri Lankan Tamils living abroad, mainly in Canada, the United States, Britain, Western Europe, and Australia. Some of the donations were voluntary while others were coerced. The LTTE used the money to buy arms from legitimate weapons manufacturers in Europe and Asia via front companies and middlemen.[23]

The SLN's repeated assaults on the LTTE sea-based capabilities from 2006 to 2009 may have decimated much of their hardware, but the fact remains that Black Sea Tigers ran a successful and sophisticated irregular warfare campaign at sea and from the sea. In particular, their use of external funding, legal knowledge, and suicide swarming tactics at sea made them a very difficult adversary to defeat. This may be of particular concern to Indian, Indonesian, Philippine, and Thai governments, all of which have their own domestic security challenges from armed groups that may look to the LTTE for maritime inspiration.

Hezbollah

In contrast to the LTTE, Hezbollah's use of the maritime environment has been more sporadic and less sophisticated, although it includes some alarming developments. Their primary use of the sea is for arms shipments, but in the 2006 cross-border conflict with Israel, Hezbollah's use of antiship missiles against the Israeli navy shocked regional security analysts and changed perceptions about the threat state navies face from armed groups at sea.

The Lebanon-based Hezbollah is not widely branded as a terrorist organization. It has a well-developed political arm in Lebanon with substantial representation in Parliament and a social welfare program that is reputed to be more effective than the Lebanese government's counterpart services. Indeed, only a small number of states, among them the United States, Israel, and the Netherlands, have proscribed Hezbollah as a whole. Australia and Britain treat Hezbollah's paramilitary wing, Al-Muqawama al-Islamiyya ("The Islamic Resistance"), as a terrorist organization. Hezbollah cells, front organizations, and support groups have been involved in fundraising, recruitment, and intelligence gathering as well as criminal activity and money laundering.

The collapse of the 2008 Doha Agreement between Hezbollah's political wing and political rivals has resulted in a political deadlock, however, and coupled with the 2006 cross-border conflict with Israel, the paramilitary wing of Hezbollah remains an ongoing concern. Indeed, Hezbollah's leader, Hassan Nasrallah, has rebutted calls to disarm Hezbollah, claiming that they are the buffer between Israel and Lebanon.[24] With some 3,500 fighters, an infantry brigade-size force, Hezbollah's military wing proved to be very well organized, equipped, and armed. As Hezbollah tightens its grip on political power in Beirut and more resources become available to it, the question becomes what other military resources it may add to its arsenal.

In addition to internal Lebanese activities, Hezbollah also gives predominantly Shiite Iran an international capability for retaliation against US and Israeli interests on several continents.[25] Indeed, Iran's supreme leader, Ayatollah Ali Khamenei, has warned that Iran would strike at US and allied interests worldwide with all its capabilities if attacked, and many analysts in the region consider Iran's "capabilities" to include Hezbollah. Moreover, Hezbollah has become increasingly involved in the Palestinian struggle against Israel in recent years, providing arms and other assistance to fighters of Hamas and other units.

Given this increasing involvement in regional politics, it is probably no surprise that Hezbollah has been arming itself via sea routes. Israeli forces have intercepted at least three major weapons shipments by sea since 2001.[26] In May 2001 Israeli naval forces intercepted the *Santorini*, a 65-foot wooden boat laden with a large shipment of munitions including SA-7 Strela man-portable antiaircraft missiles. The shipment, smuggled from Libya, was arranged by the Popular Front for the Liberation of Palestine—General Command for delivery to Palestinian National Authority representatives.

Israel has thwarted many other more recent attempts to smuggle explosives, weapons, and terrorists by sea into Gaza.[27] In May 2003, for example, Israeli naval commandos boarded an Egyptian fishing boat, the *Abu Hassan*. Of the eight people aboard, at least one was a Hezbollah operative. Hidden in the vessel were fuses for Katyusha rockets, electronic bomb-making components, materials used to make explosive vests for suicide bombers, and Hezbollah compact discs containing instructions.[28]

The biggest arms haul was taken from a 4,000-ton freighter, the *Karine A*, in January 2002. When boarded off the Israeli Red Sea port of Eilat, it was found to be carrying 50 tons of rockets, mines, antitank missiles, guns, and C-4 plastic explosives from Iran for Palestinian terrorists. The *Karine A*'s captain was a longtime Fatah activist and adviser to the Palestinian National Authority's naval police. The freighter went from the Jordanian port of Aqaba to an Iranian island in the Persian Gulf, where its military cargo was loaded. Further investigation revealed that the arms were purchased through Iran's so-called Export Committee of the Islamic Revolution for $15 million. Payment was made through Lebanon via Hezbollah agents. Senior US intelligence officers in Iraq have said that the Iranian government spent millions of dollars to train and equip Shiite extremist groups in Iraq, and that Iranian C-4 captured in Baghdad in 2006 is identical to the C-4 taken by the Israelis from the *Karine A* in 2002.[29]

Hezbollah's maritime activities are not limited to supply routes—it has demonstrated offensive naval ambitions. In June 2002, for example, Singapore's Internal Security Department disclosed that Hezbollah had planned several years earlier to attack US naval vessels and Israeli commercial ships in Singapore as they approached, using small boats packed with explosives.[30] The minister for home affairs said that the Hezbollah members had been expelled, but not before they had tried to recruit Singaporeans and establish a cell similar to those Hezbollah has across the world.[31]

Moreover, the cross-border conflicts with Israel in 2006 and 2008 revealed Hezbollah to be one of the best-equipped guerrilla forces in the world. Hezbollah is a militia trained like an army and equipped like a state, according to an Israeli soldier who returned from combat against the group in southern Lebanon in August 2006.[32] Its weapons included some that have previously been out of the reach of nonstate actors: advanced antitank missiles and rocket-propelled grenades such as the Russian-designed RPG-29, which proved to be effective against Israeli tanks and armored vehicles. The RPG-29, which Russia had sold to Syria, has a tandem warhead. The first explosion is designed to blow away the target's protective armor while the second penetrates it.[33] Another weapon they possessed was the Ababil unmanned aerial vehicle (UAV), a drone with a self-guidance system that is capable of carrying an 88-pound warhead for up to 150 miles. Iran builds the Ababil and supplied it to Hezbollah. Three were launched against Israel but were shot down, one carrying an explosive charge.[34] The UAVs and the armor-piercing missiles are potentially new weapons in the hands of nonstate actors for use against ships.

More alarmingly, however, on July 14, 2006, two days into the 2006 cross-border conflict, Hezbollah opened a new chapter in armed group maritime exploits: it fired two C-802 radar-guided cruise missiles at the Israeli navy. One killed four sailors and seriously damaged an Israeli corvette about 16 km off the coast that was helping to enforce Israel's blockade of Lebanon. The second C-802 narrowly missed another Israeli corvette. Instead, it hit a Cambodian-registered freighter, sinking the vessel and killing eleven Egyptian crewmen.[35]

The C-802 is rated as one of the most lethal antiship missiles in the world. It has a range of around 120 km and a warhead packed with 165 kg of high explosives. Neither Israel nor the United States knew that Hezbollah fighters had such sophisticated weapons in their arsenal; accordingly, the Israeli vessel did not have its missile-defense system on. Even if it had, the system would probably have been unable to protect it from the sea-skimming missile, which travels at just under the speed of sound.[36]

How did Hezbollah get such an advanced weapon, and what does this mean for state navies around the world? Most analysts point to Iran as the supplier and the supply route as via sea or perhaps overland through Syria, another Hezbollah ally. Iran bought at least seventy-five of the missiles from China in the mid-1990s and reportedly received help from China and North Korea to extend their range and improve their accuracy. With its own product line, it appears that Teheran felt it had enough of the C-802s to send some to Hezbollah in Lebanon and provide the training needed to operate them successfully.[37] While these weapons may be out of the reach of most armed groups, tension between Iran and Israel continues to escalate in 2012, and with it the temptation to supply Hezbollah or another proxy group with similar capabilities. Moreover, together with the LTTE small-boat suicide swarming tactics and innovative use of mother ships as floating warehouses, this tactic also raises the stakes for navies not just at sea but in coastal waters as well. It reinforces that armed groups continue to push the tactical envelope at sea and continue to surprise states with their innovation and ambitions.

AL-QAEDA AT SEA?

In a post–bin Laden world, there has been much speculation on how al-Qaeda will evolve and adapt to its tactical, operational, and strategic challenges. Since its inception, the al-Qaeda network's plans and attacks against ships and their cargo have been far less numerous than its strikes on land-based targets. Al-Qaeda's maritime-related activities have also been overshadowed by its aircraft hijackings. The most spectacular, of course, was the 9/11 plot in which al-Qaeda operatives seized four civilian jet airliners in the United States and crashed three of them into landmark buildings in New York and Washington, DC, on September 11, 2001, killing nearly three thousand people from at least eighty nations. The fourth crashed into a field in Pennsylvania.

As of 2012 the refocusing of al-Qaeda's leadership on the Arabian peninsula, Egypt, Yemen, and Somalia emphasizes the importance of the maritime domain for transportation, resupply, access, evasion, and income. Although less is known about its maritime-related activities, they have been and will likely remain important to al-Qaeda's strategic and tactical planning.[38] The list of their foiled, failed, and successful attempts at maritime-related terrorism over the last decade is significant; indeed, the terrorist network associated with al-Qaeda understands the vital role of sea transport and has exploited it since the 1990s.

This section provides two perspectives on the issues. First, it outlines the known incidents in which al-Qaeda and its associated movements have used the maritime trading system, and its land links through the cargo container supply chain, to conceal weapons or agents for attack purposes or to provide funding or support for their operations. Table 4.1 summarizes several operations from the 1990s to the present, which leads to the second issue in this section: Why have there been relatively few such large-scale attacks? If LTTE and Hezbollah have demonstrated what armed groups can achieve in the maritime domain, why haven't al-Qaeda's leaders better exploited its potential?

TABLE 4.1 Al-Qaeda's Use of the Maritime Domain, 1998 Onward

Where	When	Event	Success?	Outcome
East Africa[a]	August 1998	Al-Qaeda-controlled cargo ship delivered explosives used to bomb two US embassies	yes	224 killed; over 5,000 injured
Yemen	January 2000	Attempted attack on US destroyer *The Sullivans*	no	The overloaded attack boat sank; it was salvaged and used to strike the *Cole*

(continues)

TABLE 4.1 Al-Qaeda's Use of the Maritime Domain, 1998 Onward *(Cont.)*

Where	When	Event	Success?	Outcome
Yemen[b]	October 2000	US destroyer *Cole* rammed and seriously damaged by an explosive-packed boat	yes	17 US soldiers killed and 40 wounded; two al-Qaeda operatives sentenced to death and four others jailed
Yemen[c]	October 2002	French-registered oil tanker *Limburg* crippled and set ablaze by an explosive-laden small boat	yes	Al-Qaeda claimed responsibility
Iraq[d]	April 2004	Attempted attack on laden tankers and pumping and storage facilities in the main oil export terminal by suicide terrorists in explosive-packed small boats	no	Attack boats either blew up or were blown up before they reached their targets; restoring normal output took several days; assault ordered by Abu Musab al-Zarqawi
Jordan[e]	August 2005	Three Katyusha rockets fired at two docked US warships	no	Rockets missed their targets; one Jordanian soldier killed; a taxi driver wounded
Turkey[f]	August 2005	Plan to ram an explosive-laden yacht into a cruise ship carrying Israelis as it approached the port to discharge passengers; US soldiers on rest and recreation were thought to be aboard the cruise ship	no	Louai Sakka, longtime associate of Zarqawi, arrested after the one-ton bomb he was making exploded prematurely; Sakka later said he was prepared to attack NATO warships if he couldn't find Israeli passenger vessels
Morocco[g]	March and April 2007	Multiple suspects arrested on suspicion of planning attacks on a range of targets, including foreign ships in Casablanca and facilities in main tourist destinations	no	Evidence suggests this was an al-Qaeda plot

TABLE 4.1 Al-Qaeda's Use of the Maritime Domain, 1998 Onward *(Cont.)*

Where	When	Event	Success?	Outcome
Strait of Gibraltar[h]	2002	Attacks planned on shipping in the strait; Afghan-trained Saudis sent to Morocco to prepare for bomb-laden speedboat attacks on US and British warships as they passed through	no	Abd al-Rahim al-Nashiri, alleged mastermind of the *Cole* and *Limburg* attacks and linked to the 1998 East Africa attacks, captured in late 2002
Persian Gulf[i]	late 2002–3	Plan by al-Qaeda operatives to attack ships in the Gulf	no	Disrupted by US and a partner nation
Strait of Hormuz[j]	2002	Plan to attack vessels transiting the strait	no	Disrupted by US and partners
Strait of Hormuz	2001	Planned suicide attack in explosive-laden speedboats, backed up by an explosive-laden freighter, on US warships	no	Planned to coincide with 9/11; al-Nashiri called it off, fearing it was under surveillance
Philippines[k]	February 2004	Passenger ferry sunk by a bomb in Manila Bay	yes	116 killed—worst loss of life in maritime terrorist attack in recent years[l]; Abu Sayaff Group (al-Qaeda affiliate) responsible, according to Philippine officials
Philippines	August 2005	Bomb exploded on ferry, docked in harbor	yes	At least 30 people injured; Abu Sayaff blamed for attack
Singapore[m]	mid-1990s	Plan to attack US warships with explosive-laden small boats manned by foreign suicide bombers	well-developed but never carried out	Jemaah Islamiyah (al-Qaeda affiliate) blamed; plans revived in 2001 but no action taken
Malaysia[n]	2000, 2001	Planned attacks on US warships	no	Attacks foiled by Malaysian intelligence
Indonesia[o]	2002	Planned attack on US naval vessel in Indonesia's second-largest city	no	Planning disrupted by Omar al-Faruq's arrest; he was organizer and one of al-Qaeda's leading SE Asian liaison operatives

(continues)

TABLE 4.1 Al-Qaeda's Use of the Maritime Domain, 1998 Onward *(Cont.)*

Where	When	Event	Success?	Outcome
Japan[p]	2002–4	Attempt to organize an al-Qaeda cell in Japan; information gathered on US navy base on the outskirts of Tokyo	no	Lionel Dumont arrested in Germany in 2003; five foreigners arrested in Japan in 2004 who had been in contact with him

[a] John Mintz, "15 Freighters Believed to Be Linked to Al-Qaeda," *Washington Post*, December 31, 2002.

[b] "Two Sentenced to Death for Bombing of USS Cole," *New York Times*, September 29, 2004.

[c] "Limburg Attackers Had Inside Knowledge," *Lloyd's List*, May 15, 2003.

[d] Chip Cummins, "US Military Increases Oil-Facility Protection as Global Threats Rise," *Asian Wall Street Journal*, July 1, 2004.

[e] Hassan M. Fattah, "Search Continues for Clues and Suspects in Rocket Attack in Jordan," *New York Times*, August 21, 2005.

[f] On this and other attacks using waterborne improvised explosive devices, see "Small Vessel Security Strategy," Department of Homeland Security, April 2008, 11; available at www.dhs.gov/xlibrary/assets/small-vessel-security-strategy.pdf.

[g] Craig Whitlock, "In Morocco's 'Chemist', a Glimpse of Al-Qaeda," *Washington Post*, July 7, 2007.

[h] Office of the Director of US National Intelligence, September 6, 2006, press release, "Biographies of High Value Terrorist Detainees Transferred to the US Naval Base at Guantanamo Bay," section on Abd al-Rahim al-Nashiri. Available at www.odni.gov/.

[i] White House, "Fact Sheet: Plots, Casings and Infiltrations Referenced in President Bush's Remarks on the War on Terror," October 6, 2005.

[j] Rupert Herbert-Burns, "Terrorism in the Early 21st Century Maritime Domain," paper for the IDSS Maritime Security Conference, Singapore, May 20–21, 2004, page 10.

[k] James Hookway, "Philippines, a Dangerous New Alliance," *Far Eastern Economic Review*, May 6, 2004.

[l] Peter Chalk, "Christian Converts and Islamic Terrorism in the Philippines." Jamestown Foundation, *Terrorism Monitor* 4, no. 8 (April 20, 2006); www.jamestown.org/terrorism/news/article.php?articleid=2369967.

[m] "The Jemaah Islamiyah Arrests and the Threat of Terrorism," Singapore Government White Paper, January 7, 2003, pages 29–30.

[n] Office of the Director of US National Intelligence, September 6, 2006, Press release, "Biographies of High Value Terrorist Detainees Transferred to the US Naval Base at Guantanamo Bay," section on Walid Bin 'Attash. Available at www.odni.gov/.

[o] Maria Ressa, "Maritime Terror Attack Alert," CNN.com, October 23, 2002.

[p] "Deadly Muslim Convert: Trial of French Islamic Radical Sheds Light on the Role of Converts," *Washington Post*, January 2, 2006.

Table 4.1 summarizes examples of terrorist attacks on naval and commercial vessels or plans to attack them and the bases from which the terrorists operated. However, al-Qaeda has also shown interest in cargo containers on ships to ferry agents, weapons, and terrorist-related material around the world. Shortly before his capture in Pakistan in March 2003, al-Qaeda's head of global operations, Khalid Shaikh Mohammad, through two trusted lieutenants, offered to invest about $200,000 in an export firm in exchange for access to the containers used by the firm to ship garments to Port Newark in the New York–New Jersey harbor complex.[39] He wanted to use the containers to smuggle explosives into the US for various al-Qaeda attacks.[40] His interest in ships and their cargo containers, as well as the fact that he was prepared to invest an unusually large amount of al-Qaeda's money in a company that regularly moved textiles into the maritime heart of the US financial capital and sold them to leading retail outlets, is a chilling reminder of what armed groups may be considering.

Despite some agitated speculation, no convincing evidence has been produced to demonstrate links between piracy and al-Qaeda's operations in Southeast Asia. The motives of pirates are different from those of al-Qaeda terrorists, militia groups such as Hezbollah, and armed rebels such as the LTTE. However, the millions of containers that carry most of today's general cargo around the world are a security nightmare. These uniform steel boxes are potential Trojan horses in the twenty-first century when advanced technology, including weapons and the information needed to build and operate them, is increasingly accessible to terrorists and criminals. Just as goods and people are easily smuggled inside a container, so are weapons or bombs. Once a container is loaded and sealed, inspection is problematic. Contents can be misrepresented, and undeclared items can be hidden inside with relative ease. Even when sealed, contents can be removed or added without great difficulty by surreptitiously opening and reclosing containers. This is a made-to-order method of transport for terrorists—just as it is for drug and other contraband smugglers.[41]

More than 17 million containers are in circulation, crisscrossing the globe by sea and making more than 230 million journeys through the world's ports each year. Some 9 million containers arrive annually by sea in US ports alone. Physical checks of containers reaching American ports by sea increased to 5.2 percent of total arrivals by September 2003, up from 2 percent two years earlier. But worldwide, less than 1 percent of shipped cargo is screened using gamma-ray devices and radiation detectors to peer inside and check for explosives, radioactive substances, or other dangerous materials.

US Homeland Security officials have argued that the key to preventing a terrorist attack using cargo containers is not how much physical inspection takes place. It is the ability to marshal intelligence on the contents of the boxes so that only suspect ones are chosen for inspection while the genuine trade proceeds without delay. Critics of this approach, including the world's leading container terminal operator, say that the risk analysis method being used by the United States is flawed and that all containers moving through the global supply chain by sea should be monitored using nonintrusive inspection equipment to scan and clear containers quickly in terminals.[42]

The fear that terrorists could exploit the container transport system was confirmed barely a month after 9/11. In October 2001 authorities in the southern Italian port of Gioia Tauro discovered an unusually well-equipped and neatly dressed stowaway locked inside a shipping container loaded in Port Said, Egypt, which was furnished with a bed, water, and supplies for a long journey. Italian police identified the stowaway as Rizik Amid Farid and said he was born in Egypt but carried a Canadian passport.[43]

Unlike most stowaways, Farid was smartly dressed, clean-shaven, and rested as he emerged. He was found to be carrying two mobile phones, a satellite phone, a laptop computer, several cameras, batteries, and—ominously, given recent events in the US—airport security passes and an airline mechanic's certificate valid for four major American airports.[44] The port of Gioia Tauro is a leading transshipment hub for cargo in the Mediterranean. Had the occupant not been trying to widen ventilation holes when port workers were nearby, the box may well have passed unhindered to its final destination in Canada via Rotterdam. After he was discovered, Farid was investigated by Italian prosecutors, who suspected that he was an al-Qaeda operative. He was charged with illegal entry into Italy and detained. But a court released him on bail, and he disappeared before further information about him and his aims could be gathered.[45]

In summary, if one looks at the plans and operations of the first generation of al-Qaeda leaders such as Khalid Shaikh Mohammad, Abd al-Rahim al-Nashiri, and others, it is clear that by 2001 and 2002 they were conducting trial runs for opening a maritime-related front in global terrorism. An American think tank argued in 2006 that such attacks were particularly attractive to armed groups, given that the vast commercial shipping and cargo container business around the world is open to infiltration and abuse, that naval ships are iconic targets, and that busy ports provide tempting targets because they are key nodes through which so much of world trade is shipped.[46]

Given the assessment of al-Qaeda's maritime ambitions, why have terrorists not succeeded so far in causing greater damage to naval operations and to international shipping and the cargo container supply chain that carry the bulk of world trade? First, violent jihadists historically have lacked modern and lethal antishipping weapons. Their most effective weapons have been small boats packed with explosives and manned by suicide bombers. This mimics the use of suicide attack boats by the LTTE but on a much smaller scale. The LTTE had years to build its capability and, more importantly, sanctuary inside LTTE-controlled areas of Sri

Lanka to hide its swarming boats and practice operational maneuvers. Hezbollah's shocking attacks against the Israeli navy in 2006 raises the question of whether superior weapons might change this equation by putting increasingly lethal weapons into the hands of armed groups.

Second, the effect of the global counterterrorism effort against al-Qaeda should not be understated. The death of bin Laden in 2011 is just one example of many in which the transnational terrorist network's most capable and ruthless planners have been killed or captured. With key players such as Khalid Shaikh Mohammad, Abd al-Rahim al-Nashiri, and Khallad transferred to the Guantanamo Bay detention center in Cuba for trial before military tribunals, the expertise and organizational skills required to launch large-scale maritime attacks have been disrupted and dispersed. Moreover, constant pressure on midlevel leadership, particularly by US special operations forces, makes planning and coordination of maritime attacks more problematic.

Third has been a worldwide crackdown on the sources of terrorist financing, their communications, and their means of moving money around. Visa and border controls have been tightened, and counterterrorist cooperation and intelligence sharing between nations and among law enforcement agencies have been enhanced. This was one of the key factors that helped the Sri Lankan government tighten the noose around the LTTE. However, although the antiterrorism fight is enhanced by improved intelligence sharing among countries concerned, there is still room for improvement, especially given al-Qaeda's new geographic focus in the Arabian Peninsula and North Africa.[47]

Fourth, the shipping business, like the aviation industry, is now better protected by a range of measures to prevent terrorist attacks. So, too, are the US Navy and other naval forces around the world, which have learned protective lessons since the October 2000 attack on the USS *Cole*.[48] The international community, spurred by the United States, has tightened controls over the movement of containerized cargo at sea and on land through the Container Security Initiative and other measures. Indeed, a major focus of the Proliferation Security Initiative is on sea trade. Nearly ninety countries, about half the member states of the United Nations, now support this initiative, which aims to prevent illegal trade in weapons of mass destruction, related materials, and technology as well as their means of delivery.[49]

A fifth reason why terrorists have not succeeded, at least so far, in causing greater damage to shipping may lie in the breakdown of centralized control. In the past few years, following the loss of Afghanistan as a base and training area, al-Qaeda has franchised its ideology around the world. Holed up in the porous border zone between Afghanistan and Pakistan, al-Qaeda's leaders watched as affiliates and emulators, often in home-grown and largely autonomous cells, have taken root and launched their own terrorist activity in Asia, Europe, the Middle

East, North Africa, Australia, Canada, and the United States. However, as al-Qaeda senior leadership reorients itself to a post–bin Laden and post–Arab Spring world, and as organizations in and around the Horn of Africa start to mature, the same conditions that allow piracy to flourish open up opportunities for terrorist groups to use clandestine networks, move goods and people, and disrupt ports and shipping around the key Gulf of Yemen area.

CONCLUSION

This chapter has considered some of the recent uses of the maritime domain by armed groups—insurgents, terrorists, and militias—and some of their state sponsors. Although al-Qaeda's current capabilities have been disrupted and diminished by the global war on terror, both Hezbollah and the LTTE provide examples and inspiration for how armed groups can use the maritime domain to their advantage. However, two final trends should be considered in an assessment of terror groups and the sea: the threat of weapons of mass destruction (WMD) use by armed groups in the maritime context, as well as the conventional arms bazaar.

Officials and counterterrorism experts in Asia, Europe, and the United States have warned that the next step up in mass-casualty terrorism may be an attack with chemical, biological, radiological, or nuclear (CBRN) weapons. A ship or cargo container is a possible delivery device for a nuclear or radiological bomb.[50] Those who worry about such an attack believe that weapons of mass destruction and terrorism have become interlocking threats that could, if more effective safeguards are not put in place, fuse in an extremely dangerous challenge to international security, stability, and trade—and thus to the functioning of the globalized economy.

Achieving CBRN capability is a stated objective of al-Qaeda, which sees weapons of mass destruction as a strategic equalizer against better-armed enemies. Mustafa Setmariam Nasar (often referred to by the nom de guerre Abu Musab al-Suri), the Syrian-born strategist for decentralized global jihad who was arrested in Pakistan in October 2005 and then handed over to US intelligence agents, has urged clandestine terrorist cells to use weapons of mass destruction or radiological bombs if they can get them. Some analysts argue that the risk of terrorists being able to acquire or build a nuclear explosive device is overstated. Others say that the fissile material needed to build a bomb is available, or could become available, and that certain terrorists groups have already demonstrated the technical abilities and organizational reach to make an improvised nuclear device.[51] Officials in India and the West and at the International Atomic Energy Agency worry that some of Pakistan's nuclear weapons or fissile material may reach extremists, although Pakistan's leaders have given assurances that its stocks of both weapons and fissile material are under tight control and will not fall into the wrong hands.[52]

Many international officials and analysts argue that some form of CBRN attack is highly likely in the next decade. The nightmare scenario, in which terrorists would move from a position of relative technological weakness to approximate symmetry of power with their enemies in the United States and elsewhere, is certainly no longer unthinkable. A survey was commissioned in late 2004 and early 2005 by the US Senate Foreign Relations chairman Richard Lugar to canvas the views of more than eighty international arms control and national security experts. They put the likelihood of a CBRN attack occurring in the next ten years at 70 percent. There was strong, though not unanimous, agreement that any nuclear attack is more likely to be carried out by a terrorist organization than a government. A majority of those surveyed said a black market purchase was the most likely way for terrorists to get nuclear weapons or fissile material.[53]

Most experts believe that a radiological or "dirty" bomb (which uses conventional explosives to disperse radioactive material) is well within the technical capabilities of at least some terrorist groups and that they could acquire the components without much difficulty. Such a device would probably be designed as a weapon of mass disruption to cause panic, chaos, and prolonged economic dislocation in a metropolis or port city. US-led counterproliferation programs, such as the Container Security Initiative and the Megaports Initiative, are intended to prevent terrorists from shipping dangerous nuclear or radioactive material into US ports. But critics of existing measures say they fall far short of what is needed to detect the clandestine shipment of dirty bombs wrapped in lead shielding, bomb-grade highly enriched uranium, or even a nuclear weapon in cargo containers.[54]

Meanwhile, navies, coast guards, and government intelligence and law enforcement agencies must counter the illegal or clandestine spread of conventional weapons to nonstate actors including terrorist, military, and rebel organizations. Among the weapons that have been transferred through these channels are long-range antiship missiles, UAVs, and closer-range armor-piercing missiles and rocket-propelled grenades: all weapons capable of causing significant damage to ships, both big and small.

The trade in small arms and light infantry weapons is already extensive in conflict-prone parts of the IOR, and the demand for more advanced equipment is strong. This is a global problem; around one hundred countries make weapons and ammunition.[55] The Small Arms Survey estimates that China and Russia as well as Austria, Belgium, Brazil, Germany, Italy, and the United States each routinely export small arms, light weapons, and ammunition worth $100 million or more.[56] The *Small Arms Survey 2010* estimates that the annual trade in ammunition for both small arms and light weapons is worth $4.3 billion.[57] In October 2006 negotiations started in the UN General Assembly on a binding treaty to control the so-called light arms trade that kills at least three hundred thousand people each year, destabilizes nations, and ruins the lives of millions. Not surprisingly, the negotiations, which nearly collapsed in February 2012, have been contentious, slow, and fraught with disagreements over implementation.[58]

The US military intelligence community is concerned with these trends. In testimony to the US Senate Committee on Armed Services on February 27, 2008, Lieutenant General Maples, director of the DIA, said that highly accurate long-range guided weapons "help non-state actors inflict losses against technologically superior opponents at a relatively low cost and with little training. These weapons can produce operational and even strategic-level effects beyond the battlefield when used to their maximum effect at the tactical level and publicized through the media or Internet. This provides terrorist and insurgent groups with a magnified politico-military potential that exceeds their historical norm."[59]

In closing, it is worth considering the extent to which armed groups have challenged the perceptions of states in the maritime environment and successfully exploited seams in their coverage. In November 2008 terror attacks killed more than 170 people at Mumbai landmarks, including the Chhatrapati Shivaji Terminus, the Cama & Albless Hospital, the Chabad center, the Leopold Cafe, and two hotels, the Taj Mahal Palace and the Trident-Oberoi. The attacks were attributed to Lashkar-e-Taiba, a violent Islamic extremist group based in Pakistan. The attackers deliberately targeted US and British citizens in addition to attacking a Jewish community center. It is of note that the attackers sailed from Karachi on a Pakistani cargo ship and avoided detection by the Indian Coast Guard by hijacking an Indian fishing trawler. They killed the trawler's crew, beheaded the captain near Mumbai, and landed in two small inflatable boats to commence their attacks.[60]

Less than twelve months prior, in December 2007, M. K. Narayanan, national security adviser to the Indian prime minister, had argued in Bahrain that both the Gulf and South Asia must remain prepared for a new wave of terrorism and that Gulf nations, with major oil resources, were highly vulnerable to such threats. Quoting from Indian intelligence reports, he said that new schools specializing in training an international brigade of terrorists were being established on the Pakistan–Afghanistan border, with recruits from as many as fifteen countries. These schools' targets included high-profile political leaders; vital infrastructure and installations including large ocean liners, oil pipelines, oil storage depots, and electricity pylons; and military targets.

Narayanan's warnings were prophetic, considering that by April 2008 an al-Qaeda affiliated website was urging mujahedeen to establish naval terror cells, arguing that gaining control over the seas and sea passages, especially around the Arabian peninsula, was the next strategic step toward restoring the global Islamic caliphate.[61] As Narayanan argued and the Mumbai attacks tragically demonstrated, the sea is becoming a favored route for carrying out attacks.[62]

Taken with other developments set out in this chapter, the Mumbai attacks and al-Qaeda's interest in sea lines of communication and access should serve as a warning of what may be in store for both naval and merchant shipping in and around the Gulf and the wider IOR. It will be difficult, if not impossible, to block the arms and other support channels that empower nonstate actors unless states cooperate to exert both preemptive and disruptive pressure. This can be done if governments work more closely together to provide relevant and timely intelligence and then act on it using military, law enforcement, and diplomatic levers as required. Such a coordinated strategy was indispensable in helping the Sri Lankan government weaken the maritime and external support networks of the LTTE.

However, such a strategy will be harder to apply against both Hezbollah and al-Qaeda networks. Since Hezbollah has tried to shed its rebel reputation and is now part of a widely recognized government in Lebanon, its fighters often remain beyond the reach of the Lebanese military. In the case of al-Qaeda, since its leaders and fighters are spread over many countries, the principal challenges will continue to include identifying operatives, timely gathering of intelligence, disrupting networks, and, most importantly, preventing new attacks.

NOTES

1. Michael D. Maples, "Current and Projected National Security Threats to the United States, Statement for the Record, Senate Armed Services Committee," *Defense Intelligence Agency*, February 27, 2008; www.dia.mil/public-affairs/testimonies/2008-02-27.html, 33.
2. Catherine Philp, "Sri Lanka Tamil Tigers Say Struggle for Separate State Will Continue from Exile," *Times* (London), June 17, 2009; www.timesonline.co.uk/tol/news/world/asia/article6515025.ece (accessed July 6, 2009). According to this article, Selvarasa Pathmanathan, the LTTE head of international relations, stated that "the group was reorganizing to pursue its goal of a separate Tamil state from outside Sri Lanka. 'The struggle of the people of Tamil Eelam has reached a new stage,' he said. 'It is time now for us to move forward with our political vision towards our freedom.' Mr. Pathmanathan gave no indication that the group would renounce violence but announced the establishment of a 'provisional transnational government of Tamil Eelam,' which would decide on a course of action 'within democratic principles.'"
3. "World Oil Transit Chokepoints," country analysis brief, *US Energy Information Administration*, January 2008; www.eia.gov/countries/regions-topics.cfm?fips=WOTC.
4. Pranab Mukherjee, "India: A Rising Global Player," Second Plenary Session Address, Fifth IISS Asia Security Summit (Shangri-La Dialogue). Singapore, June 3, 2006, p. 6.

5. Sam Bateman, Catherine Zara Raymond, and Joshua Ho, "Safety and Security in the Malacca and Singapore Straits," RSIS Policy Paper (S. Rajaratnam School of International Studies, Singapore, May 2006), 8.
6. William C. Ramsay, "Asian Oil Outlook and Challenges," Presentation to the Roundtable Conference on Regional Cooperation: Key to Energy Security, New Delhi, January 6, 2005.
7. Peter Chalk, "Liberation Tigers of Tami Eelam's (LTTE) International Organisation and Operations: A Preliminary Analysis," Commentary no. 77 (Ottawa: Canadian Security Intelligence Service, March 17, 2000), 9.
8. Tim Fish, "Sri Lanka Learns to Counter Sea Tigers' Swarm Tactics," *Jane's Navy International*, March 2009, 20–25.
9. Vijay Sakhuja, "Terrorist Sea Strategy: The Kamikaze Approach," Peace Forum Essays (New Delhi: Jawaharlal Nehru University, April 2003).
10. Chalk, "Liberation Tigers," 5–6.
11. Organisation for Economic Co-operation and Development, Maritime Transport Committee, *Security in Maritime Transport: Risk Factors and Economic Impact*, July 2003; available at www.oecd.org/sti/transport/maritimetransport/18521672.pdf, 14–15.
12. Chalk, "Liberation Tigers," 8.
13. "Arms Ship Mystery Deepens, Possibility of LTTE Ploy: Zimbabwe Official Here for Probe," *Sunday Times* (UK), August 3, 1997.
14. "Dignity and Respect for Our People Is All We Ask—Pathmanathan," *TamilNet*, May 17, 2009, accessed July 2, 2009, www.tamilnet.com/art.html?catid=13&artid=29389.
15. See Brian White, "Six Indicted in Arms Brokering for Tamil Tigers and Indonesia," *Associated Press*, September 29, 2006; and "US Busts Asian Network Seeking Arms for Tamil Tigers," *AFP*, April 5, 2007. An Indonesian national was sentenced on July 10, 2008, in the United States to thirty months in prison for conspiracy to provide material support including firearms, machine guns and ammunition, surface-to-air missiles, and night vision goggles to the LTTE. See Department of Justice, "Major US Export Enforcement Prosecutions during the Past Two Years," Fact Sheet 08-959, October 28, 2008; www.usdoj.gov/opa/pr/2008/October/08-nsd-959.html.
16. Rafik Jalaldeen, "Navy's Pivotal Role in Battle against Terrorism," *Daily News* (Ceylon), December 10, 2007.
17. "British-Based Sri Lankan Jailed for Helping Tamil Tigers in Terror Attacks," *Telegraph* (UK), June 12, 2009; www.telegraph.co.uk/news/uknews/5517148/British-based-Sri-Lankan-jailed-for-helping-Tamil-Tigers-in-terror-attacks.html.
18. Ranil Wijayapala, "Navy Chief Assesses Navy's Role in the Forces' Successful Campaign to Eliminate LTTE Terrorism," *Daily News* (Ceylon), September 4, 2008.
19. Robert Karniol, "Tamil Tigers' Hangout: S-E Asia," *Straits Times* (Singapore), October 22, 2007; and Fish, "Sri Lanka Learns to Counter Sea Tigers."

20. Andrea Dew, interviews with Sri Lankan naval officers, February 2012.
21. Ibid. See also Fish, "Sri Lanka Learns to Counter Sea Tigers," 21.
22. Vice Admiral Karannagoda of the SLN argued in a recent interview that "[the LTTE] totally lost their supplies and that turned the war. . . . It was one of the major turning points of the war that has been going on for the last 30 years." Quoted in Fish, "Sri Lanka Learns to Counter Sea Tigers."
23. Matthew Rosenberg, "Sri Lanka's Tamil Tiger Rebels Run a Global Fund Raising and Weapons-Smuggling Network," *Associated Press*, November 5, 2007.
24. Nicholas Blanford, "Lebanon Resumes Defense Talks on Hezbollah's Military Wing," *Christian Science Monitor*, March 10, 2010.
25. US House of Representatives Committee on International Relations, *Hezbollah's Global Reach: Testimony of Frank C. Urbancic, Joint Hearing of the Subcommittee on International Terrorism and Nonproliferation and the Subcommittee on the Middle East and Central Asia*, September 28, 2006; http://democrats.foreignaffairs.house.gov/archives/109/30143.pdf, 7.
26. Amit Cohen, "The Hezbollah within Us," *Ma'ariv* (Tel Aviv), June 3, 2004.
27. Jewish Institute for National Security Affairs, "Israel's Navy Steps up to Security Challenge in Wake of Gaza Pullout," May 31, 2006.
28. Jewish Institute for National Security Affairs, "IDF Seizes Bomb Making Supply Ship Headed for Gaza," May 26, 2003. In July 2002 Israeli security officials in Ashdod seized a shipment of guns and other weapons intended for Palestinian militants. Two months earlier a container supposedly filled with a donation of toys sent to the Gaza Strip by an Islamic charity had been opened by officials in Ashdod and found to be packed with hundreds of pounds of guns, ammunition, telescopic lenses, and night-vision equipment.
29. Jim Garamone, "Iranian Government behind Shipping Weapons to Iraq," *American Forces Press Service*, September 28, 2006.
30. Melvin Singh, "Internal Security Department Opens Their Files," *New Paper* (Singapore), June 8, 2002.
31. "Minister for Home Affairs Comments on the Hezbollah Case," Press release, Ministry of Home Affairs, Singapore, June 8, 2002.
32. Steven Erlanger and Richard A. Oppel Jr., "A Disciplined Hezbollah Surprises Israel with Its Training, Tactics and Weapons," *New York Times*, August 7, 2006.
33. Joshua Brilliant, "Anti-Tank Rockets Menace Israelis," *UPI*, August 14, 2006.
34. "Hizbollah's Worrisome Weapon," *Newsweek*, September 11, 2006.
35. Richard Fisher Jr., "China Sows the Whirlwind: Implications of Hezbollah's Iranian-Chinese Weapons," *International Assessment and Strategy Centre*, July 26, 2006.
36. Mark Mazzetti and Thom Shanker, "Arming of Hezbollah Reveals US and Israeli Blind Spots," *New York Times*, July 19, 2006.
37. "C-802/YJ-2/Ying Ji-802/CSS-C-8/SACCADE," *GlobalSecurity.org*, http://globalsecurity.org/military/world/china/c-802.htm.
38. The phrase "maritime-related" encompasses activities that affect merchant and private shipping as well as the naval vessels that help protect the sea-lanes

carrying the bulk of global trade. It also covers activities that impinge on the cargo container supply chain that is an integral part of modern commerce and now stretches into most parts of the world. Sea trade does not begin and end in ports or at the dockside. For those who have to police international trade and keep it secure, responsibility starts in the factories and warehouses on land where containers are loaded. It ends where they are unloaded. In between, the containers may have been carried by road and rail, as well as by sea, on their journeys around the world.

39. FBI criminal complaint filed before Judge Andrew J. Peck, South District of New York, August 8, 2003. See Greg B. Smith, "Al Qaeda Sought Garment Center Tie," *New York Daily News*, August 22, 2003; http://articles.nydailynews.com/2003-08-22/news/18239931_1_al-qaeda-plot-sources.
40. "Biographies of High Value Terrorist Detainees Transferred to the US Naval Base at Guantanamo Bay; Jul–Sept," sections on "Majid Khan" and "'Ali 'Abd al-'Aziz 'Ali." Press release. Office of the Director of US National Intelligence, September 6, 2006.
41. Philippe Crist, "Report on Security in Maritime Transport: Risk Factors and Economic Impact" (Paris, France: OECD, July 2003).
42. US Senate Committee on Homeland Security and Governmental Affairs, Permanent Subcommittee on Investigations, *Neutralizing the Nuclear and Radiological Threat: Securing the Global Supply Chain (Part Two)*, testimony by Gary Gilbert, March 30, 2006; www.hsgac.senate.gov/subcommittees/investigations/hearings/neutralizing-the-nuclear-and-radiological-threat-securing-the-global-supply-chain-part-two.
43. Richard Owen and Daniel McGrory, "Terrorist in a Box," *Times* (UK), October 25, 2001.
44. Andrea Felsted and Mark Odell, "Agencies Fear Extent of Al-Qaeda's Sea Network," *Financial Times*, February 21, 2002.
45. "When Trade and Security Clash," *Economist*, April 4, 2002.
46. James Jay Carafano and Martin Andersen, "Trade Security at Sea: Setting National Priorities for Safeguarding America's Economic Lifeline," Backgrounder no. 1930, Heritage Foundation, April 27, 2006, 5.
47. Scott Shane and Lowell Bergman, "US Enters the Age of Foiled Plots," *International Herald Tribune*, September 9, 2006.
48. Department of Defense, USS *Cole* Commission, *USS Cole Commission Report*, Executive Summary (Washington, DC: US Department of Defense, 2001).
49. "Proliferation Security Initiative Participants," Department of State, Bureau of International Security and Nonproliferation, September 10, 2010, www.state.gov/t/isn/c27732.htm.
50. Thomas Lehrman, "Preventing Weapons of Mass Destruction Terrorism in the Maritime Supply Chain," Remarks made at the Maritime Security Expo, New York, September 20, 2006.
51. See Robin M. Frost, *Nuclear Terrorism after 9/11*, Adelphi Paper 378 (London: International Institute for Strategic Studies, December 2005); Anna M. Pluta

and Peter D. Zimmerman, "Nuclear Terrorism: A Disheartening Dissent," *Survival* 48, no. 2 (Summer 2006): 55–70; and Sammy Salama and Lydia Hansell, "Does Intent Equal Capability? Al-Qaeda and Weapons of Mass Destruction," *Nonproliferation Review* 12, no. 3 (November 2005): 615–53.

52. Ravi Velloor, "Worries over Pakistan's Nuclear Assets Unabated," *Straits Times* (Singapore), January 31, 2008.
53. Richard G. Lugar, *The Lugar Survey on Proliferation Threats and Responses*, Washington, DC, June 2005; http://lugar.senate.gov/nunnlugar/pdf/NPSurvey.pdf.
54. US Senate Committee on Homeland Security and Governmental Affairs, Permanent Subcommittee on Investigations, *Neutralizing the Nuclear and Radiological Threat: Securing the Global Supply Chain (Part One)*, testimony by Stephen E. Flynn, March 28, 2006; available at www.hsgac.senate.gov/subcommittees/investigations/hearings/neutralizing-the-nuclear-and-radiological-threat-securing-the-global-supply-chain-part-one.
55. Brian White, "Six Indicted in Arms Brokering for Tamil Tigers and Indonesia," *Associated Press*, September 29, 2006.
56. "Exporters," *Small Arms Survey*, www.smallarmssurvey.org/weapons-and-markets/transfers/exporters.html.
57. *Small Arms Survey 2010: Gangs, Groups, and Guns* (Geneva, Switzerland: Small Arms Survey, June 2010), www.smallarmssurvey.org/publications/by-type/yearbook/small-arms-survey-2010.html.
58. Louis Charbonneau, "Collapse of Arms Trade Treaty Talks Narrowly Averted," Reuters, February 17, 2012; www.reuters.com/article/2012/02/18/us-arms-treaty-idUSTRE81H03P20120218.
59. Maples, *Current and Projected National Security Threats*, 32–33.
60. Angel Rabasa, Robert D. Blackwill, Peter Chalk, Kim Cragin, C. Christine Fair, Brian A. Jackson, Brian Michael Jenkins, Seth G. Jones, Nathaniel Shestak, and Ashley J. Tellis, *The Lessons of Mumbai* (Santa Monica, CA: RAND Corporation, 2009), 3–9.
61. "Al-Qaeda Affiliated E-Journal: 'The Sea Is the Next Strategic Step towards Controlling the World and Restoring the Islamic Caliphate,'" *Middle East Media Research Institute*, May 1, 2008; www.memrijttm.org/content/en/blog_personal.htm?id=378.
62. International Institute for Strategic Studies, "Plenary Session No. 3, Energy and Regional Security," in *Manama Dialogue Report 2007* (London: International Institute for Strategic Studies, December 8, 2007), www.iiss.org/publications/conference-proceedings/manama-dialogue-report-2007/plenary-session-3.

PART II

Emerging Rivalries and Possible Triggers

CHAPTER 5

INDIA

Dominance, Balance, or Predominance in the Indian Ocean?

ANDREW C. WINNER

INTRODUCTION

After much anticipation, in 2007 the Indian Navy formally published a maritime strategy—officially, the Indian Maritime Military Strategy.[1] This document and supporting and supported documentation by the Indian government is a good place to start in examining how India sees the Indian Ocean, its place in it, and the place of the security of the Indian Ocean in its overall national security policy. Indeed, the contrast between the centrality of the Indian Ocean in Indian naval documents and its relative absence in other Indian official pronouncements on foreign policy and national security policy offers a useful window into India's traditional land-centric view of the world versus an emerging maritime consciousness that is being advocated by the Indian maritime services. Official government documentation, however, is insufficient and needs to be placed in a larger context to be analyzed with any degree of sophistication. This chapter focuses on policy statements and documents by officials and current strategic thinkers as well as India's capabilities to execute any sort of a strategy toward the Indian Ocean region (IOR), and examines how India may cooperate with other states in pursuing its aims in the region. The maritime military documents are also examined against India's other national objectives that relate to the Indian Ocean and that have a security component—such as transport of energy, trade generally, and use of ocean resources such as fisheries. This articulation of national objectives is drawn from official documents, public statements of senior officials, and a brief review of the writings of some of India's most prominent strategists.

After an examination of India's goals and strategies as they relate to the Indian Ocean, the next section of the chapter looks into India's current and future capabilities and capacity to achieve those goals and fulfill the strategies. All states have limitations and generally reach further than they can grasp, and India is no exception. Potential stumbling blocks to India achieving its objectives in the Indian Ocean include budgetary shortfalls, military limitations (both capability and capacity), policy and bureaucratic friction, and the potential actions of other actors in the IOR.

This last set of issues—the dynamic interactive effects—is the subject of the final section of the chapter. The views, objectives, and capabilities of key state and nonstate actors in the Indian Ocean region are examined with an eye to how those entities will likely interact with India in the IOR in the coming years. Ultimately, what the chapter demonstrates is that India wants to play a larger role in the Indian Ocean, but it will face a number of hurdles to realizing this goal—some technical and budgetary but some related to gaps in India's ability to articulate and operationalize a strategy at the whole-of-government level.

INDIA'S MARITIME MILITARY STRATEGY AND DOCTRINE

In 2004 the Indian Navy published the *Indian Maritime Doctrine*, a document whose purpose was to "provide every officer, irrespective of his rank, branch, or specialization, a common vocabulary and a uniform understanding of maritime concepts."[2] This document was updated and published again in August 2009.[3] Because it is primarily an education document for the officers of India's navy, it provides a very useful starting point for examining what the Indian Navy thinks about the Indian Ocean.

What is the Indian Navy telling its officers in its most basic of documents? In both the 2004 and 2009 versions of the doctrine, the Indian Ocean is detailed as the primary maritime environment in which India has to operate. Indeed, the 2009 version of the document breaks up India's maritime areas of interest in two parts—primary and secondary. The primary area encompasses the entirety of the Indian Ocean including all of "the choke points leading to, from and across the Indian Ocean" except the southern portion (reaching to Antarctica) and, interestingly, the Red Sea and its littoral states.[4] The discussion of India's maritime interests in the 2009 document, to the degree that they are couched in a geographic context at all, refer to the Indian Ocean or areas or territories contained within it.

The Indian Navy's second major publication, its October 2007 maritime strategy, provides a bit more information and insight into how India's major maritime military service views the Indian Ocean.[5] The strategy document devotes an entire chapter to the IOR and its geopolitics. While largely descriptive, the chapter does enumerate various facts and trends in the Indian Ocean that could affect India's security, including state failure, territorial and maritime disputes, population trends, and terrorism. In its "assessment" section, the document discusses the problematic trends along with the various efforts by regional navies to increase capabilities and capacities. The strategy document notes that the Indian Navy has been supportive of these efforts because they are aimed at improving good order at sea. The overall tenor of this assessment section is that India is at the forefront of cooperative initiatives in the region and that these types of efforts will increase in the future to the benefit of overall security in the IOR.

With regard to the volume's theme of the prospects for rivalry in the region, a section in the Indian maritime strategy's chapter on the Indian Ocean also discusses the increased presence of extraregional navies. In contrast to the views of Indian national security policymakers in the 1970s and 1980s, the discussion of these fleets is benign, going so far as to say that the "strategic objectives of a majority of extra-regional navies are broadly coincident with India's own strategic interests, there is no clash of overarching interests in the IOR."[6] This discussion of extraregional navies is written in a way that makes it clear that the maritime forces being described here are those from the United States, Europe, Japan, and Australia. A separate but fairly neutrally worded paragraph in the same section notes that the Chinese Navy is on the path to developing a blue water force and that its various building programs exist "along with . . . attempts to gain strategic toe-hold in the IOR." That intriguing but unfortunately curt statement ends the discussion of the IOR and its geopolitics.

It would be interesting, from the point of view of an outside analyst, to see more details of how the Indian Navy officially views these trends in capabilities and intentions in the Chinese Navy in particular. Unfortunately, due to both the nature of official Indian foreign and military documents and the tight political control of the military and over broad national security policy in India, we are not likely to see any time soon a detailed official and open discussion of how the Indian Navy views China. To obtain a more detailed understanding of how the Indian Navy, and indeed the rest of the Indian military, views China and China's role in the Indian Ocean, one must read the articles and speeches of retired flag and general officers from the Indian military services. This is true for much public discourse over national security issues (although this is changing; we later discuss India's evolving national security institutions). It is generally only after military officers retire that they enter the public discussion of national security interests and strategies and are allowed to publish and speak publicly. A speech in August 2009 by the then outgoing Indian Navy chief of staff Adm. Sureesh Mehta is a good example. While not quite retired at the time (his retirement was already set for a few weeks after the speech), Admiral Mehta gave a speech in which he candidly discussed the Indian–China competition in ways unlikely to be seen in any official Indian Navy document.[7] His speech is noteworthy because Admiral Mehta, in that window right before his retirement, had both an insider's detailed understanding of the United Progressive Alliance government's view of China as well as a solid sense of the government resources that India had, and was likely to have, at hand to engage in that competition.

Admiral Mehta's speech was an overview of India's national security challenges, but it received significant play in the Indian media because he addressed, in four paragraphs, how India should "cope" with China in the years ahead. He noted China's advantages over India in "GDP, defence spending or any other economic, social, or development parameter" and indicated that those gaps were growing and were, for India, too wide to bridge. He opined that this set of facts had to be taken into account when devising a strategy to deal with China, and posited that cooperation was the logical road to pursue. However, he noted that a "trust gap" existed between India and China, largely because of existing boundary disputes and because of China's predilection for "intervention in space" and "cyber warfare." Despite his prescription for cooperation, Admiral Mehta noted that there are areas where tension could arise between these two rising Asian powers. Specifically, he noted that "competition for strategic space in the Indian Ocean" needed to be watched diplomatically. In terms of military prescriptions, the outgoing service chief argued that India must reduce the military gap (despite his belief that on most measures of comparison China is ahead and pulling away) and "counter . . . the growing Chinese footprint in the Indian Ocean Region." Getting more specific, Admiral Mehta proposed that India not try to match China's military capabilities symmetrically but rather should adopt asymmetrical technical approaches, including "developing high situational awareness and creating a reliable stand-off deterrent."[8]

INDIA'S NATIONAL SECURITY AND FOREIGN POLICY

The views of military service chiefs, as noted in several newspapers immediately following Admiral Mehta's speech, are rarely articulated in public.[9] This is due to strong civilian control of the military and the accompanying fact that Indian military tradition defers public articulation of policy and strategy to the realm of the civilian politician or career civil servant. This delineation of public roles mirrors the very strong control over budgets and national security strategy that is also maintained by the Indian civilian national security elite. This means that simply examining the writings and speeches of navy officers, or indeed officers of any service, may be misleading in determining India's overall national view of the Indian Ocean and its importance in national security policy. Indeed, one only has to look at the Ministry of Defence's annual reports to see that the official views of the higher echelon have historically been decidedly land-centric. These documents represent the closest that India comes to a publicly articulated defense strategy or, indeed, a national security strategy. In the reports from 2003 to 2009, the Indian Ocean is hardly ever mentioned in the lead chapter, which is titled "The Security Environment."[10] In the 2008 version of the annual report the Indian Ocean is only mentioned twice. It is dubbed a "strategic region" once in a discussion of growing defense ties between India and the Maldives. The other mention is in the context of coastal security, which is embedded in a section discussing the aftermath of the November 26, 2008, terrorist attack on Mumbai, one in which the terrorists infiltrated the financial and entertainment capital of India from the sea.[11] These brief mentions contrast with the number of pages that cover land-based issues (Pakistan, Afghanistan, and China) and broader strategic relationships with Russia and the United States in the annual reports. This has changed somewhat in the 2009 and 2010 versions of the reports, which now discuss the Indian Ocean prominently in the opening section.[12] The discussion, however, remains largely descriptive vice analytical, but it represents a slowly changing viewpoint.

Earlier discussions of India's foreign policy and national security challenges by officials such as India's foreign secretary mirror this relative bias for looking either landward or toward relations with extraregional great powers. In a 2007 speech at a Delhi-based think tank, then foreign secretary Shivshankar Menon posited three sets of challenges for India, each of which potentially involved the Indian Ocean but were not discussed.[13] In his discussion of how to ensure that India's periphery remains peaceful, Menon mentions only India's landward neighbors. Regarding the challenge of managing relations with the world's major powers, the foreign secretary mentions the Indian Ocean in passing, noting the need for India to expand its "circles of engagement" including that area.[14] Even in his discussion of a basket of issues including energy, he did not refer to the maritime transport dimension in this 2007 speech.

This continental mindset, or "sea blindness," as it is sometimes referred to, may be slowly changing in India, perhaps due to efforts by the Indian Navy and others who more naturally think about the maritime realm. In September 2009 the Indian Navy's think tank, the National Maritime Foundation, invited the by now retired Foreign Secretary Menon to give a speech focused not broadly on India's foreign policy challenges but specifically on "the maritime imperatives of Indian foreign policy."[15] While the invitation and requested subject matter forced the matter of addressing the maritime realm, the content of the speech is revealing in terms of how thinking has evolved in India's foreign policy and national security establishment even in just two years' time. Indeed, Menon began this speech by echoing what has become a regular talking point among India's navy and maritime thinkers, that India indeed has long had a continental mindset. Menon attributes this, plus an accompanying resource constraint in the maritime realm, to its colonial legacy—where European powers exclusively dominated the seas around India. In the speech, the former foreign secretary outlines three areas where the maritime realm, and particularly the Indian Ocean, is central to India's foreign policy concerns. The first is trade, where he lists the standard statistics on the volume and value of seaborne trade that passes by India heading both east and west. On energy, he mentions that both India and China face a "Hormuz dilemma," an interesting recognition that India has proximate security issues as opposed to the more common discussion of China's "Malacca dilemma." Finally, he mentions classic security issues such as intrastate conflict but skips by these potential problems to focus the majority of his speech instead on a range of transnational security concerns including terrorism, smuggling, and piracy.

In response to these three maritime issues, Shivshankar Menon notes that India has been increasing its cooperation with friendly foreign governments in the Asia–Pacific region to enhance India's naval cooperation, but he notes that these cooperative efforts are still mostly in the declaratory stage with substantive progress far behind those in places such as the Atlantic or Mediterranean.[16] Such a statement acknowledges that India is relatively new to such cooperative ventures and seems to imply support by the official foreign policy apparatus for continuing and expanding such maritime cooperative efforts. However, his very next sentence in the speech points to caution and illustrates why maritime cooperative efforts with India are likely to be slow in developing. Menon notes that because the cooperative endeavors "occur in a regional and global context that is changing so rapidly, and when the relative balance of power in the area is shifting and evolving, we need to be careful of the effect of these formal and informal demonstrations of intent on others." Menon could be expressing the concern of the Ministry of External Affairs that too rapid a move toward cooperative endeavors by India could unnecessarily antagonize China, Pakistan, or both.

The Indian Navy has also made an attempt to engage in "maritime diplomacy," a strategy outlined in the Indian Navy's strategy document by which naval assets are used to support foreign policy by nonviolent methods. In the case of the Indian Navy, the naval assets were naval officers. In February 2008 the then chief of the Indian Navy, Admiral Mehta, convened an Indian Ocean Naval Symposium (IONS), inviting his counterparts from Indian Ocean littoral states to discuss maritime security, stability, safety, and consequent collective prosperity. The concept was to begin a sustainable dialogue among regional navies on topics of mutual interest with the goal of deciding upon courses of action on transnational issues that require bilateral or multilateral efforts. Despite requests, officials from outside powers who have interests in the Indian Ocean (including the United States, China, and the United Kingdom) were not invited. After the symposium, at least one article reported that the Indian Ministry of External Affairs had turned down a Chinese request to attend—showing at least some degree of interagency coordination and cooperation. The United Arab Emirates hosted the next IONS in May 2010.[17] South Africa hosted the most recent meeting in the spring of 2012. This initiative was in part an effort by the Indian Navy to demonstrate utility to the civilian national security and foreign policy establishment. Despite the follow-on meeting and plans for the next chiefs meeting, the exact impact of IONS in this regard remains to be seen.

CAPABILITY AND CAPACITY

Speeches, official documents, and one-off meetings are only part of any examination of India's view of and role in the Indian Ocean. Such documents and pronouncements may accurately reflect what a country is actually doing or they may be a substitute for capabilities or indeed reflect aspirations for which capabilities and capacity have yet to be developed. In India's case, the navy's vision, beginning gradually to be recognized and repeated by the broader national security and foreign policy establishment, is currently more ambitious than India's capabilities or capacity. The trends in the building of both India's specific technical capabilities and organizational capacity are positive, but many constraints remain. Moreover, real-world events and policy decisions could shift India away from a greater focus on the Indian Ocean back to concerns that are either land-centric or do not have a specific geographic focus at all, such as cyberspace or outer space.

The Indian Navy naturally focuses more heavily on the Indian Ocean than do other sections of India's national security establishment. The navy, however, has its limitations. The continental mindset predominates not only in the civilian hierarchy but in the other military services as well. Historically, the Indian Navy has been the smallest and least well-resourced of the three services; the 1-million-person-plus Indian Army dwarfs the 55,000-person Indian Navy. Historically, the Indian Navy has received the lowest budget allocation of the three Indian military services. In the 1980s and 1990s the Indian Navy averaged 12 percent of the overall military budget, despite the capital-intensive nature of the service.[18] This share has increased significantly since 2000, with the maritime service's percentage increasing to 15 percent in 2011–12.[19] The overall Indian defense budget has continued to grow within the past decade as well, and the capital portion of the defense budget has seen a significant increase. Percentage growth in either a single service or overall defense budget, however, only tells part of the story.

Both the absolute budget figures for India's military and the percentage of the national budget that the military receives provide another sense of how much the Indian government is able and willing to commit resources to security issues and particularly to security issues in the maritime realm. Indian expenditure on the military ranks ninth in the world in 2010, and it is unlikely to change in that relative ranking in the next two decades.[20] As a percent of gross domestic product,

India's military expenditure has not often breached the 3 percent mark since 1962, when New Delhi hiked its spending significantly after losing a border war to China. Some defense commentators have called for an increase to 3 percent or 4 percent of GDP in order to compete with China and generally to have the capability to influence the globe in a way that compares with India's size and goals.[21]

Even if India's defense budget were to increase and even if the Indian Navy were to receive a greater percent of the budget, there would remain significant constraints on what type of capability would result, at least over the next decade. One of those constraints is the current high average age of the Indian fleet, particularly major surface vessels. While, on the one hand, the Indian Navy chief has outlined plans for major purchases to make the fleet both larger and more modern, on the other, that same chief has lamented the ability of India's shipbuilding sector to deliver platforms in a timely manner.[22] In an ironic twist, higher operational tempos brought on by greater Indian Navy involvement in activities such as counterpiracy operations in the Gulf of Aden may actually accelerate a decline in the fleet's capabilities in the short to medium term. Finally, overall defense policy preferences (indeed requirements) for indigenous production of defense goods will only exacerbate this issue unless there are significant changes in the efficiency of Indian navy yards.[23]

Despite policy pronouncements that emphasize indigenization of the production of defense goods and services, India's defense establishment understands that a significantly higher degree of domestic defense production is a long-term goal at best.[24] Meanwhile, India must rely on a mix of indigenous design and production, licensed production, and direct purchases from foreign suppliers. The latter route, however, is not without its significant problems as highlighted by the drawn-out procurement drama involving the Russian aircraft carrier, the *Admiral Gorshkov*. Moscow and New Delhi's original deal, signed in 2004, was for delivery of the refitted and modernized Kiev-class aircraft carrier to India in 2008 at a cost of $1.5 billion dollars. Wrangling over cost and delivery dates began almost immediately, with a February 2008 Indian offer to add $600 million more to the price. Moscow countered with a request for another $1.2 billion, and in late 2009 the two sides had apparently reached an agreement on price and delivery, the latter being set for late 2012.[25] This was reaffirmed in December 2011 talks between India's prime minister and his Russian counterpart.[26] Delays due to disagreements on price as well as accidents during refit have slowed the delivery of a leased Russian Akula submarine to India.[27]

India's problems with reliable foreign defense supply have changed but they have not disappeared. In the 1970s and 1980s the Soviet Union was a reliable military supplier for India. This changed with the collapse of the Soviet Union in 1991. India was left with a large stock of Soviet equipment but with a fragmented supply chain for spare parts. New Delhi worked hard in the 1990s to rebuild this supply chain for its now former-Soviet equipment as well as to begin establishing better contacts with Western manufacturers. India became both more capable and more willing to purchase defense goods from the West and, over time, even from the United States. Its increased capability came from economic growth in the 1990s and first decade of the twenty-first century, enabling it to pay market prices rather than the largely barter arrangement it had worked out for politically discounted Soviet equipment in the Cold War days. Its increased willingness was derived from decreasing concerns in New Delhi that the West was attempting to keep India under a "technology denial regime"—a phrase used commonly in India to describe the panoply of technology and defense good sanctions that Washington and others had slowly put in place after India's 1974 nuclear test. In the wake of the US–Indian civilian nuclear accord in 2006, those restrictions—and India's perception of them—began to decline. However, even with increased willingness in both New Delhi and the West to engage in serious defense cooperation and sales, India's limited defense budget will continue to constrain India's options.

The issue for India is not only that it may not be able to afford some Western goods, but also that the Indian defense procurement system is slow and has restrictions on how money is spent that make large purchases difficult. Often, foreign purchase possibilities are slowed by advocates within India for indigenous development. Indigenous Indian weapons-development programs are notoriously slow in delivering useable military capabilities that are actually desired by the armed forces. Moreover, Indian procurement rules require any unspent funds to be returned to the treasury if they are not obligated by the end of each fiscal year—making large purchases, whether foreign or domestic, difficult. Such requirements also lead to some reports overstating the actual procurement purchasing power of the Indian armed services in recent years.

Despite the fiscal constraints on India's purchases of maritime capabilities and even in the light of obstacles in its procurement system, over ten to twenty years the age and composition of the Indian Navy will gradually shift to one of a younger average fleet with significantly greater capabilities. Projecting the exact capabilities of that fleet and what India will choose to use it for is difficult. The Indian Navy plans for a mixed fleet with blue water capabilities, with close to 140 major combatants. This includes plans for 24 modern conventional submarines by 2030, between 5 and 6 nuclear-powered submarines, 3 aircraft carriers, and a range of destroyers, cruisers, and frigates as well as modern land-based maritime patrol aircraft.[28] Whether these plans will be entirely fulfilled or fulfilled on time remains to be seen.

However, what can be analyzed with more certainty is what the Indian Navy has done over the past several years in the Indian Ocean. This provides at least some sense of how the Indian Navy is thinking about how its capabilities can support broader Indian national security and foreign policy goals.

The Indian Navy has been fairly active in the Indian Ocean in the first decade of the twenty-first century across a range of missions. In the 2001–2 crisis with Pakistan following terrorist attacks on the Indian parliament, the Indian Navy deployed elements of both its eastern and western fleets to guard Indian maritime assets and to deter Pakistan from horizontal escalation if the crisis had escalated to actual conflict. After the September 11 terrorist attacks on the United States, Indian Navy vessels escorted US resupply ships and warships through the Strait of Malacca. In addition to these traditional naval roles, the Indian Navy has more recently conducted a wider range of missions, reflecting the breadth of maritime mission areas outlined in its 2007 maritime military strategy. The Indian Navy has participated in tsunami relief operations in 2004–5 that ranged from affected Indian states to Sri Lanka, the Maldives, and Indonesia. In 2006 the Indian Navy undertook a noncombatant evacuation operation, helping more than two thousand Indian, Nepali, and Sri Lankan citizens from Lebanon during the Israeli conflict with Hezbollah. Finally, after what appeared to be some internal debates between the Indian Navy and civilian policy circles, the Indian Navy joined the efforts of numerous other navies in counterpiracy operations off the coast of Somalia and in the Gulf of Aden.[29] Most recently, the Indian Navy was put in charge of overseeing maritime security and the approaches to the Indian coast in the wake of the November 26, 2008, terrorist attacks on Mumbai.

This range of operations, in both type and geographic reach, show that the Indian Navy currently has the capability to influence many areas of the Indian Ocean in a variety of ways in support of Indian foreign policy. The question is whether the Indian Navy's capabilities are well integrated into that broader foreign and security policy or whether they are to some degree serendipitous. India's foreign and security policy formal and informal processes for generating ideas, integrating efforts, and implementation lag behind India's ambitions. The Indian government and broader analytic community recognize this, but it is taking time to make changes and develop a more modern set of processes, procedures, and institutions that reflects India's history, culture, and geopolitical position in the world. Three events since 1998 have pushed the Indian state to modernize how it thinks about, formulates, and implements foreign and national security policy, whether it is regarding the IOR or other geographic and functional issues. The first was India's testing of nuclear weapons in May 1998 and its declaration that it was a nuclear weapons state. The second was the Kargil War with Pakistan in 1999, and the third was the terrorist attack on Mumbai in November 2008.

The nuclear tests and declaration led to the establishment of a Nuclear Strategy Advisory Board that developed a draft nuclear strategic doctrine. The Kargil War resulted in the Indian government establishing a committee to examine how and why India was surprised by Pakistan and how it responded to the war in an environment where both antagonists now had declared nuclear arsenals.[30] That committee report cited numerous shortfalls in the way that the Indian security establishment went about its work. A Group of Ministers (GOM) was constituted in April 2000 to conduct a study and make recommendations on reforming the Indian national security system. The implementation of the GOM's recommendations began in 2001 and has yet to be completed as of this writing.

Many of these recommendations would impact the ability of India to develop and implement a wide-ranging and coherent security strategy for the Indian Ocean. At the recommendation of the GOM, the Integrated Defence Staff was established as was India's first triservice joint command for the Andaman and Nicobar islands in the Bay of Bengal. The establishment of a chief of defense staff is still pending. The personnel of the Integrated Defence Staff is provided by the three military services as well as representatives from the Ministry of External Affairs, the Defence Research and Development Organization, the Armed Forces headquarters civil services, and the Ministry of Defence. Such a staff is not only joint, it is interagency, a double step for a defense establishment that prior to this innovation had been very service oriented and that exhibited a wide gap between civilian and military entities involved in national security. Despite this new staff and other reforms concerning defense procurement, there remain significant concerns about whether sufficient coordination and consultation takes place between civilian authorities and the service staffs about issues as fundamental as military requirements for future weapons.

New institutions and working relationships are a necessary step, but often real integration among military services takes decades to achieve, as the United States acknowledged decades after passage of its seminal legislation in the mid-1980s to create a truly joint military. Laws and governmental institutions are not the only necessary step in establishing a robust foreign policy and national security community capable of generating ideas, evolving policies, and carrying out implementation. A broader set of foreign policy institutions that need reform and growth, dubbed "foreign policy software" by Daniel Markey, includes Indian think tanks, the Indian Foreign Service, Indian public universities, and India's media and private businesses.[31] Markey argues that these institutions need investment, reform, and expansion to allow India to achieve great power status. While developing and implementing a coherent and capable security strategy toward the IOR is something short of great power status, it requires the same type of depth of analysis, creativity, and cohesiveness of implementation that Markey argues is required for even broader Indian foreign policy aspirations.

INTERACTIVE EFFECTS: OTHERS IN THE INDIAN OCEAN

Regardless of whether India has a fully articulated and fully resourced maritime, joint, and interagency policy on the Indian Ocean, what it does say and do will have an impact on other states on the Indian Ocean littoral or with maritime interests there. This will in turn lead to reactions, some that may be suspicious or hostile and others that may see India's greater role in the Indian Ocean as a chance for improved cooperation. The result of these interactions could determine whether the Indian Ocean becomes a "zone of peace" or, alternatively, something more akin to Robert Kaplan's view that it will be a site of commercial and indeed military rivalries.[32]

Beginning with worst-case scenarios, Pakistan is almost certainly not going to see India's increased interest and capabilities in the Indian Ocean as benign. In fact, advances in India's naval capabilities, such as the launch of the long-rumored nuclear-powered and nuclear-armed submarine, the INS *Arihant*, were met with hostile reaction from both Pakistani official circles and national security analysts. A Pakistani navy spokesman declared that the launch was "a destabilizing step which would jeopardize the security paradigm of the entire Indian Ocean region."[33] Pakistan was one of two states not to send its chief of navy to the Indian-led and hosted IONS meeting in 2008 (the other was Iran). The long-standing animosity between India and Pakistan is likely only to be stoked as India acquires greater maritime capabilities and as it attempts to create and implement a strategic approach to the Indian Ocean, particularly if Pakistan is unable to keep up due to its relatively lower economic power and institutional capacity. In addition, Pakistan is, unfortunately, likely to see India's attempt at maritime diplomacy in the Indian Ocean as part of a zero-sum game. It may see India's greater activity levels as a diplomatic threat to its own historic close ties to the Gulf Arab states, particularly in the military field.

Pakistan is almost certainly likely to see India's increasing naval capabilities as a threat and will, within its resource limits, balance against them. Given the history of both wars and crises between India and Pakistan, each state will monitor military and political-military developments very closely. Islamabad is keenly aware that India was able to make very effective use of its navy in the 1971 war, isolating then–East Pakistan and bottling up the Pakistani fleet in the port of Karachi as well as launching missile strikes against Pakistani navy and port facilities.[34] Concern about India's ability to blockade Karachi and more generally isolate Pakistan's economy is evidenced by the fact that one of Pakistan's stated "red lines" for using nuclear weapons is if "India proceeds to the economic strangling of Pakistan."[35] Despite reports that India and Pakistan had been secretly negotiating a deal on Kashmir, it is unlikely that such a resolution of a core issue between the two states will occur any time soon.[36] Inevitable Indian actions in the area of increased capabilities and Pak reactions to them will therefore maintain or escalate a "security dilemma," that is, a situation in which actions that India takes to develop and implement a more complete or robust security policy in the Indian Ocean lead Pakistan to feel less secure.

In chapter 8 in this volume, James Holmes and Toshi Yoshihara analyze India redlines for Chinese behavior in and around the Indian Ocean that may cause Sino-Indian China rivalry to cross into hostilities. The authors note that China need not cross these redlines and indeed they predict competition over the medium term instead of open hostility. This leads to two questions. First is whether there is possibility for cooperation between India and China in the Indian Ocean, and if so, on which issues and under what circumstances. The second is whether and under what conditions might a competition escalate toward situations where redlines may become visible on the horizon or in which other redlines may arise. The areas where competition is most unpredictable and potentially destabilizing are those that involve third parties—states or substate actors over which New Delhi or Beijing are seeking to expand influence.

At the senior political level and even on the bilateral military level in both Delhi and Beijing, there is both talk and action on cooperation. At their fall 2009 summit, both leaders went to great lengths to demonstrate that they did not see the other country as a military threat.[37] The two states held the first joint military exercise—a land-based counterterrorism exercise—in December 2007 and have since engaged in low-level naval exercises in the Indian Ocean. Indian officials refer to this type of interaction with China in terms similar to how officials in Washington describe interactions with China—"constructive engagement."[38] While exercises are one thing, actual cooperative ventures in the field of maritime security in the Indian Ocean are another. Each country has sent forces to join in the multistate effort to counter piracy off the coast of Somalia, for example, yet each has also chosen to remain aloof from one another and from the more formal structures of the American-led combined task force. Mutual suspicion and minor diplomatic pinpricks, such as China's issuing stapled visas for Indian citizens from the Chinese-claimed Indian state of Arunachal Pradesh, keep both sides edgy and keep them from cooperating on other areas where they may have common interests.[39]

One area with a potential for crisis concerns the competition for access to and influence in the smaller countries in the region. Both states are providing economic and military assistance to a number of states. Whether true or not, this capacity building is often described in numerous press outlets as aimed at containing the other's growing influence.[40] Perception is as important as reality in some of these instances. To the degree to which maritime and diplomatic planners begin to see access to and influence over these small states as critical to countering the other, perceptions may morph into reality.[41] Even if China and India do not necessarily view themselves as rivals for influence in countries such as the Maldives, future political crises in these countries may push New Delhi and Beijing into situations where they are drawn into a situation not of their making, which may then escalate.

The degree to which both China and India are each seeking access (whether economic or military) and diplomatic influence in various states in the IOR correspondingly increases the chance that New Delhi and Beijing will find themselves more involved in the domestic politics of these sometimes unstable states. In India's case, in recent years it has significantly stepped up its interactions with African states on the Indian Ocean. In 2008 India sent a four-ship task force to the eastern coast of Africa for a two-month cruise to engage in port visits and bilateral exercises covering humanitarian assistance and disaster relief as well as search and rescues with African navies and coast guards.[42] Analysts note that this Indian engagement in Africa is about more than granting India access to energy resources. India has private enterprise eager to expand into other emerging markets along with a vast regional expatriate population for which New Delhi feels some political and security responsibility.[43]

India and China are also engaging in what has been called capacity building, helping small and relatively poor states on the Indian Ocean increase their military and law enforcement capabilities in the maritime domain. In the case of India and Mauritius, this has included gifts of a navy ship, a patrol boat, and a maritime surveillance plane. India is also not shying away from engaging states that are both close to Beijing and that carry with them some international stigma such as Iran and Myanmar.[44] Either of these states could clash with the United States or other Western states over nuclear weapons ambitions, democracy issues, or human rights. India and China could find themselves competing for influence in these states or caught in uncomfortable diplomatic situations vis-à-vis Washington or one another. It is more likely that India may find itself on the opposite sides of an African coup or other political clash with China rather than directly opposing Washington and the Europeans on issues such as Iran.

In sum, while India and China will continue to talk about cooperation and, indeed, possibly engage in some small-scale cooperative ventures in areas of peripheral interest to both, political-military competition in the Indian Ocean is more likely to be the norm. While that competition will, for the most part, almost certainly remain well below the level of overt hostilities, there exists the potential that actions by regional actors will put New Delhi and Beijing in situations where they may be forced to make choices or take actions that could raise hackles in the others' capital. It is situations that begin in third countries in the IOR, where Beijing and New Delhi have interests and where they have expended resources, that could draw the two into more fierce competition, potentially escalating to situations where the two Asian powers are faced with confrontation. What will be interesting, then, is how the two handle these situations where land borders are not in dispute but where less tangible political assets of influence and prestige are at stake.

At the other end of the spectrum, the interaction between India and the United States in the IOR is perhaps the most promising in terms of future cooperation that will address the myriad security issues in the region—including institution building and stability in many states on the Indian Ocean littoral. The security relationship between India and the United States has changed fundamentally over the course of the past two decades. The end of the Cold War coupled with India's economic reforms and the rise of the information technology age have opened the doors to greater economic, political, and finally military cooperation between the world's largest democracy and the world's oldest democracy. The rapprochement on the US side began with the Clinton administration, which recognized both the geopolitical opening that the end of the two-bloc system provided as well as the increased commercial interaction between the two countries in the areas of information technology. The improved relationship was set back by the Indian nuclear weapons tests in May 1998, but President Clinton was determined not to have this single issue impede the overall progress that had been made in the relationship. The president made a triumphant visit to India in 2000 while American officials continued discussions with the government of India about the two capitals' differences over India's vertical nuclear proliferation.[45]

The relationship continued to improve during the Bush administration and received a significant boost after the terrorist attacks of September 11, 2001. The prime minister of traditionally nonaligned India, which since independence had never allowed foreign military forces on its soil, made an extraordinary offer—to allow the basing of US military aircraft in India for use in the American offensive against the Taliban government of Afghanistan.[46] While the Bush administration had been working toward lifting military and high technology sanctions against India before September 11, the changed strategic circumstances helped push this change through Congress in short order. The Bush administration also made the decision that it was going to address the central political-military issue between the United States and India—the question of India's nuclear weapons program and the consequent restrictions on civilian nuclear technology sales from Western countries to New Delhi. After years of at times tense negotiations, Washington and New Delhi reached an agreement on October 2, 2008, regarding civilian nuclear cooperation. The deal meant that Washington and, through its offices, the other members of the Nuclear Suppliers Group tacitly recognized India's de facto nuclear weapons state status outside of the Nuclear Nonproliferation Regime and agreed to make sales in civilian nuclear technologies to New Delhi. India, for its part, agreed to divide its nuclear facilities into civilian and military lists and reached agreement with the International Atomic Energy Agency to a full-scope safeguards and inspection regime on its civilian facilities. The real importance of the deal was less in its details than in its symbolism, particularly for India. It represented acceptance of its great power status and the lifting of what Indian politicians and analysts termed a "technology denial regime" that dated from India's 1974 initial nuclear test.

Even prior to this landmark agreement, Indian and American cooperation in the military sphere was on the increase, particularly when compared to the Cold War era. This enhanced military interaction was led by the US and Indian navies and was centered largely on the Indian Ocean. In the 1990s the United States and India began a series of annual, increasingly complex naval exercises in the Indian Ocean. The Malabar exercises, named for the Indian coast near where they have often been held, were interrupted in the wake of the 1998 Indian nuclear tests, but they resumed after the September 11, 2001, terrorist attacks. In 2007 the exercise series expanded to include ships from Australia, Japan, and Singapore. In 2008 the exercises reverted to a bilateral endeavor, but the 2009 exercise included ships from the Japan Maritime Self Defense Force and took place in international waters off Japan. The 2010 and 2011 Malabar exercises remained bilateral, but the 2011 exercises included a new twist, with the exercise area being in the Pacific Ocean, near Okinawa. In 2006 President Bush and Prime Minister Manmohan Singh signed an Indo-US Framework for Maritime Security Cooperation, which committed the two sides to cooperate "in ensuring a secure maritime domain."[47] This short document set out the bureaucratic structures within which India and the United States would engage one another on maritime security issues, and it put forward the general view of senior political leadership that maritime security cooperation was an area ripe with promise. With the lifting of restrictions in the wake of September 11, the Indians began more seriously considering purchases of US military equipment, and the first major procurement was for the Indian Navy in the form of advanced maritime patrol aircraft—US-manufactured P-8s.

Annual exercises and the purchase of defense articles and goods are tangible demonstrations of improved cooperation in the maritime realm, but the maritime strategies of both the United States and India create the foundation for significantly greater cooperative activities and approaches to security in the Indian Ocean. The new US maritime strategy, issued by the US Navy, Marine Corps, and Coast Guard in October 2007, was at its time a forward-looking document. Its very title, *A Cooperative Strategy for 21st Century Seapower*, represented a departure from the emphasis on unilateral security efforts emphasized in earlier national security documents and statements by the administration of then president George W. Bush.[48] It appeared to anticipate the more cooperative, multilateral approach espoused by the administration of President Obama. One startling change in US maritime focus in the document was its statement that "credible combat power will be continuously postured in the Western Pacific and the Arabian Gulf/Indian Ocean to protect our vital interests, assure our friends and allies of our continuing commitment to regional security, and deter and dissuade potential adversaries and peer competitors." Since World War II, the US Navy has been a two-ocean navy—the Atlantic and the Pacific. This new strategy heralded a change in that focus. The US Navy was still a two-ocean navy, but the oceans had changed. The Atlantic Ocean has been supplanted by the Indian Ocean as the second area of strategic focus for the US Navy. The document was codifying what had been the reality of US Navy deployments since August 1990, when Saddam Hussein's Iraq had invaded Kuwait. Since that time, the United States had almost continuously kept at least one carrier battle group and often an expeditionary strike group deployed in the Northern Arabian Sea or the Persian Gulf, or both.

In addition to this focus on the Indian Ocean, the new US maritime strategy contains lists of mission areas for the US maritime services that almost exactly paralleled those in India's maritime strategy document. Each document emphasized the desirability of cooperative approaches to these maritime missions, and the US and Indian navies have already begun cooperative activities in some of the areas. In the area of humanitarian assistance and disaster relief, the US and Indian navies were both significant first responders after the 2004 tsunami in the eastern Indian Ocean. The two navies deconflicted their activities, but clearly there is significant scope for cooperative endeavors in this mission area, ranging from joint exercises and training to cross-decking and sharing lessons learned to joint contingency planning and operations.

In the mission areas of maritime security and protection of maritime commerce since November 2008, the United States and India have been cooperating as part of the broader international effort to combat piracy off the coast of Somalia and in the Gulf of Aden. The cooperation has been on a low level, with both attending UN-hosted contact group meetings and US Navy–hosted operational-level information sharing meetings at the US Navy facility in Bahrain. However, as of the end of 2011, India had not yet joined the US-led combined task force (CTF-151), which the United States set up as one central multilateral contribution to the counterpiracy effort.[49] Both the United States and India have undertaken other multilateral efforts at maritime security in the IOR—the United States as part of CTF-150, which patrols the North Arabian Sea on a broad maritime security mission that includes counternarcotics and counterterrorism, and India in joint counterpiracy patrols with countries bordering the Straits of Malacca. In several instances after September 11, Indian warships accompanied US high-value cargo ships through the Straits of Malacca to protect them against possible attack by terrorist groups or pirates.[50] There is clearly scope for greater cooperation in these areas, and it will likely come about over time.

Another maritime mission area of mutual interest is counterterrorism. As just noted, there has been some cooperation between the Indian and US navies. This cooperation, however, has been sporadic and is likely to continue to run up against political sensitivities. One such sensitivity is Indian participation in CTF-150, another US-led combined task force that evolved out of US efforts to stop potential exfiltration of al-Qaeda and Taliban terrorists from Pakistan in the wake of the 2001 US invasion of Afghanistan. This maritime mission broadened over time from one of checking for terrorists potentially fleeing Pakistan's Makran coast to the Horn of Africa to a more general set of missions that encompasses both counterterrorism and more general maritime security. Not only did the mission broaden but participation widened as well, with Pakistan joining the combined task force in 2004. Since that time, Pakistan has commanded the force (which rotates command every six months) three times. It is not clear why India is not part of this combined task force. There is little public information on the question. One possibility is that India has demurred from making such a request due to a desire to maintain some autonomy of operations (similar to it more recently not joining CTF-151 despite its dispatch of forces to conduct counterpiracy operations in the same area). Another is that the United States has not wanted to potentially annoy Pakistan by inviting or allowing Indian participation. Regardless of the reason, cooperation in maritime counterterrorism remains limited at least in these multilateral areas and could likely be increased if political conditions allowed on one or both sides.

The terrorist attack on Mumbai in November 2008 did open doors to increased cooperation between Washington and New Delhi on coastal security. India recognized its shortcomings both in monitoring coastal traffic and in coordinating efforts of its maritime security forces (local, coast guard, and navy). US law enforcement officials cooperated in the immediate investigation following the Mumbai attacks. In addition, the United States and India began other discussions about how each has integrated efforts of various levels of government in tackling issues such as coastal security. Indeed, Indian analysts have noted that the US experience after the September 11 attacks may provide useful lessons for India as it attempts to construct better institutions and policies designed to secure its own borders.[51] While the issues of US whole-of-government efforts on counterterrorism and Indian integration efforts on improving coastal security are not exactly analogous, and certainly India would have to tailor reforms it makes to meet its particular legal, bureaucratic, and geographic circumstances, the scope for further cooperation on internal integration efforts is certainly open.

As noted, India is using support for capacity building to increase its access and influence with a number of regional states as well as helping them to increase their capacities for monitoring and patrolling their areas of the Indian Ocean commons. The United States has engaged in such capacity-building programs in the IOR for decades, first as part of its Cold War containment policy and later as part of counterterrorism efforts. Both Washington and New Delhi will continue to contribute to the increased capabilities and capacities of smaller and relatively poorer states on the Indian Ocean rim. The question is whether and how the two states could increase their cooperation on capacity building to increase its overall efficiency and effectiveness. Current practice, in late 2011, is for New Delhi and Washington to go about their capacity-building programs in parallel with little to no information exchange or coordination. One possibility would be to exchange information on future capacity-building plans during one of the many bilateral defense meetings that now take place on a regular basis between India and the United States. An even more ambitious step would be to coordinate these programs, exchanging information in advance, building on one another's projects, and—when needed—dividing up labor among various Indian Ocean countries so that all important areas are addressed on a fairly regular basis. This would of course require some meeting of the minds between Washington and New Delhi on the goals and priorities for this capacity building. As noted, the similarities of the maritime strategies of the two nations, along with increasingly close relations, provide some hope that this alignment of interests in the Indian Ocean may not be that difficult to achieve.

In the area of counterproliferation, the United States and India have a difficult history. The potential for cooperation in this functional area, both writ large and in the maritime realm, has largely been limited by a range of international agreements and regimes set up under US leadership largely in the wake of India's nuclear test in 1974. In addition, the maritime component of counterproliferation is limited and falls under a broader, whole-of-government approach to the problem. Since the India–US civilian nuclear agreement, first agreed to in 2005 with implementation beginning in late 2008, the political space for more agreement on counterproliferation has widened. While India declined early US requests to become a participant in the US-founded Proliferation Security Initiative (PSI), it does appear that this position may change or at least may be under reconsideration.[52] Indeed, India has been undertaking counterproliferation actions in the maritime realm both before and after the establishment of PSI, including some at the behest of the United States, without formally associating itself with the initiative.[53] This slow and at times less-than-formal increase in cooperation in this area is likely to increase, particularly as the overarching legal framework for these activities expands through new UN Security Council resolutions and other new legal frameworks such as the 2005 protocol to the Convention for the Suppression of Unlawful Acts against the Safety of Maritime Navigation.

There are, however, potential barriers and challenges to Indo-US cooperation in the maritime realm in the Indian Ocean and beyond. None of these are insurmountable, but they may slow or stymie cooperative efforts between the two maritime powers. One challenge, as noted earlier in the discussion of interaction effects, is the potential reaction of other powers to increased US–Indian security cooperation. This includes potentially hostile reactions from a range of countries important to Indian Ocean security—China, Iran, and Pakistan. The United States and India could see these reactions differently and could differ about the way in which they would want to handle them diplomatically and potentially militarily. A second challenge is simply overcoming the long history of misunderstanding and real antagonism between India and the United States. While senior political leaders in both countries have made the commitment to improve relations and have taken many steps to make it so, progress may at times be hindered by long-held perceptions and misperceptions.[54] Building trust will take time, even between democracies that appear, on the surface, to share many common objectives.

Another challenge is institutional culture and structures. As noted, India is working hard to establish joint and interagency institutions. However, it is still quite limited in terms of capacity, particularly in terms of empowered decision makers in the Indian government. The United States often overwhelms partners and allies with its sheer size and its long-established mechanisms and procedures—often ones created for entirely different purposes and contexts, such as the Cold War. The United States has to examine its approach to improving cooperation with India with an eye toward seeing if its institutions, procedures, and policies make sense for a relationship with a regional power (aspiring to global or great power) who is neither a potential adversary nor a treaty ally. In terms of the Indian Ocean, the United States also has a significant bureaucratic challenge. Washington does not make military strategies for oceans. In fact, it divides the world in continental terms, and in the US military's unified command plan, responsibility for the Indian Ocean rests with four different regional commanders with dividing lines cutting across strategically critical locations. It is as though a line of invisible buoys in the waters of the Indian Ocean divide military responsibility among different US military commands. At times these invisible lines make policy coordination difficult, as is the case when the dividing line puts India in one command's area of responsibility and Pakistan in another's. Washington has to figure out how to overcome or otherwise blur these bureaucratic seams if it is going to effectively work with India on the range of questions involving maritime security in the Indian Ocean. New Delhi sees the Indian Ocean as a strategic whole. If Washington seeks to better coordinate its policies toward this maritime region with New Delhi, it has to be able, bureaucratically, to craft and implement a more seamless strategy.

Finally, there will be the more mundane technical issues of resources, capacity, and military interoperability. Again, here the issue is in part one of money and technology and in part one of diverging perceptions about what is most important in moving a relationship forward. For Washington, the most important sign that another nation is our security partner is their willingness and ability to conduct combined military operations. Conducting combined operations takes some technological commonality, but it largely takes political will and a familiarity with one another's tactics, techniques, and procedures. For New Delhi, the signal that another state is a true partner is its willingness to transfer military technology to it, even if that technology is not necessarily going to be used in combined operations. These different views have to be understood by both sides, and concrete policies and procedures to accommodate both have to be developed in both New Delhi and Washington. These challenges are not insignificant. They may slow or constrain the relationship in certain areas. However, the trajectory of the US–India relationship is clear and positive. Both nations have vital interests in the IOR and are going to develop and implement strategies designed to secure those interests. Many of those vital interests are either identical or congruent. It only makes sense that India and the United States will figure out ways to support one another in their pursuit.

CONCLUSION

For those in India who look toward the sea, the Indian Ocean is central to India's national security. The Indian Navy has begun to develop a doctrine and strategy that will support and defend India's maritime interests in the Indian Ocean and beyond. That strategy balances traditional military missions and tasks undertaken in time of war with the use of maritime forces in peacetime and crisis to support broader foreign policy goals. Therefore the strategy is both one of self-sufficiency when it comes to core defense missions, complete with a desire for more self-sufficiency in developing and producing the weapons systems that would be used for defense, and one of cooperation with other states of the IOR. The Indian Navy and the Indian government generally are taking a much more benign view of the presence of Western powers in the Indian Ocean. Gone are the days of proposals for an Indian Ocean zone of peace or, indeed, a nuclear-free Indian Ocean—both proposals designed to keep US and Soviet navies out of India's maritime backyard. The potential for cooperation with the United States in the Indian Ocean looms large. Yet there are challenges and potential obstacles to the pace and scope with which that cooperation can be expanded.

India is expanding its capabilities and capacity to affect events in the Indian Ocean—politically, economically, and particularly militarily. That expansion will continue to have fits and starts due to resource constraints, internal bureaucratic obstacles, and policies such as indigenization and offsets that are designed to meet other objectives. That expansion will produce reactions by other maritime powers either in or with interests in the Indian Ocean. In particular, Pakistan is likely to view India's growing maritime power and influence with suspicion and will seek to balance with both diplomatic and military initiatives of its own. China will watch Indian developments closely although perhaps not as closely as India will watch what China is doing in the Indian Ocean—from its sustaining counterpiracy operations in the Gulf of Aden to Beijing's support for construction of numerous commercial port facilities around the Indian Ocean. While New Delhi and Beijing talk of cooperation, the challenges and barriers to making that consistent and robust are very significant. While India and China are not likely to directly antagonize one another in the Indian Ocean, they will keep bumping into one another as both see access and influence with other states of the region. It is when a third state in the IOR becomes the object of both India and China's direct and serious attention that the prospects for crisis increase. In a case such as Pakistan, neither New Delhi nor Beijing is necessarily controlling events. Rather, they could be responding to situations well beyond their ability to control but within their need to attempt to influence the outcome. There are numerous candidates for such interaction in the Indian Ocean, and both New Delhi and Beijing are increasing their reach.

NOTES

The views expressed here are solely the author's and do not reflect the views of the Naval War College, the US Navy, or the US government.

1. *Freedom to Use the Seas: India's Maritime Military Strategy*, Indian Navy, Integrated Headquarters, Ministry of Defence (Navy), 2007.
2. *Indian Maritime Doctrine*, INBR 8, Indian Navy, Integrated Headquarters, Ministry of Defence, April 25, 2004.
3. *Indian Maritime Doctrine*, INBR 8, Indian Navy, Integrated Headquarters, Ministry of Defence, Sivakasi: Standard Press (India) Pvt., Ltd, August 2009.
4. *Indian Maritime Doctrine* (2009), 65–68.
5. *Freedom to Use the Seas.*
6. Ibid., 41.
7. Address by Admiral Sureesh Mehta, "India's National Security Challenges—An Armed Forces Overview," August 10, 2009; http://maritimeindia.org/sites/all/files/pdf/CNS_Lec_at_Habitat.pdf.
8. Ibid.
9. Rahul Singh, "India No Match for China, Says Navy Chief," *Hindustan Times*, August 11, 2009; available at www.hindustantimes.com.
10. Available at the Ministry of Defence website, http://mod.nic.in/reports/welcome.html.
11. Ministry of Defence, Government of India, *Annual Report 2008–2009*, 8.
12. Ministry of Defence, Government of India, *Annual Report, 2009–2010*, 2–3, 8; and Ministry of Defence, Government of India, *Annual Report, 2010–2011*, 2, 7.
13. Shivshankar Menon, "The Challenges Ahead for India's Foreign Policy," *Air Power Journal* 2, no. 2 (April–June 2007).
14. Ibid., 6.

15. Address by Ambassador S. Menon, "Maritime Imperatives of Indian Foreign Policy," September 11, 2009; http://maritimeindia.org/sites/all/files/pdf/SMenon.pdf.
16. Ibid., 4–5.
17. "Pak May Join IONS Summit in UAE Next May: Verma," *Zeenews.com*, December 2, 2009; http://zeenews.india.com/news/nation/pak-may-join-india-navy-summit-in-uae-verma_584052.html.
18. Rahul Roy-Chaudhury, *Sea Power and Indian Security* (London: Brassey's: 1985), 170.
19. Ministry of Defense, Government of India, *Annual Report, 2010–2011*, 16.
20. Stockholm International Peace Research Institute, *SIPRI Yearbook 2011: Armaments, Disarmament, and International Security*, Appendix 4A; www.sipri.org/yearbook/2011/04/04A.
21. Arun Kumar Singh, "The Weary State of the Indian Navy," *Secunderabad Deccan Chronicle*, December 4, 2009; http://theasiandefence.blogspot.com/2009/12/weary-state-of-indian-navy.html.
22. "Navy Fleet to Grow by 40 Warships Soon: Verma," *Outlook India.com*, December 2, 2009; http://news.outlookindia.com/item.aspx?670396; "Navy Chief Decries Warship Delivery Delays," *Pioneer* (India), December 3, 2009; available at http://epaper.dailypioneer.com.
23. Ministry of Defence, Government of India, *Defence Procurement Procedure, Capital Procurement*, 2008; http://mod.nic.in/dpm/welcome.html.
24. "New Policy to Boost R&D, Pvt Sector Role in Def Production," *Times of India*, December 25, 2010; http://timesofindia.indiatimes.com/india/New-policy-to-boost-RD-pvt-sector-role-in-def-production/articleshow/7160257.cms.
25. "Russia, India Finalize Deal on Warship Overhaul," *Riavovosti*, November 12, 2009; http://en.rian.ru/russia/20091207/157140513.html.
26. "Gorshkov Aircraft Carrier Should Arrive in Time: PM," *Hindustan Times*, December 18, 2011; www.hindustantimes.com/News-Feed/News/Gorshkov-aircraft-carrier-should-arrive-in-time-PM/Article1-783918.aspx.
27. "Leased Russian N-Submarine to Set Sail for India This Month," *India Today*, December 15, 2011; http://indiatoday.intoday.in/story/leased-russian-n-submarine-to-set-sail-for-india-this-month-end/1/164449.html.
28. Standing Committee on Defence (2010–11) (Fifteenth Lok Sabha), Ministry of Defense, "Action Taken by the Government on the Recommendations/Observations Contained in the Sixth Report (Fifteenth Lok Sabha) on Demands for Grants of the Ministry of Defence for the year 2010–2011," Ninth Report, New Delhi: Lok Sabha Secretariat, 2011.
29. Author's discussions with Indian Navy officials, September 2008.
30. *From Surprise to Reckoning: The Kargil Review Committee Report* (New Delhi: Sage Publications, 1999).
31. Daniel Markey, "Developing India's Foreign Policy 'Software,'" *Asia Policy* 8 (July 2009), 73–96.

32. Robert D. Kaplan, "Center Stage for the 21st Century: Power Plays in the Indian Ocean," *Foreign Affairs*, March/April 2009.
33. "INS Arihant Launch a Destabilizing Step: Pakistan," *Zeenews.com*, July 27, 2009; www.zeenews.com/news550677.html.
34. John H. Gill, *An Atlas of the 1971 India-Pakistan War: The Creation of Bangladesh* (Washington, DC: National Defense University Press, 2003).
35. Author's interview with then–major general Khalid Kidwai, director general, Strategic Plans Division, Pakistan, October 2000.
36. Steve Coll, "The Back Channel: India and Pakistan's Secret Kashmir Talks," *New Yorker*, March 2, 2009.
37. P. S. Suryanarayana, "Friendship First," *Frontline (India)*, November 7–20, 2009; www.frontlineonnet.com/fl2623/stories/20091120262304900.htm.
38. "India, China Aim to Hold Regular Joint Exercises," *Times of India*, November 4, 2008; http://timesofindia.indiatimes.com/India/India_China_aim_regular_exercises/articleshow/3670587.cms.
39. Emily Wax, "As Ties between India and China Grow, So Does Mistrust," *Washington Post*, December 13, 2009, A15.
40. Dean Nelson, "India Plans Naval Base on Maldives to Contain Chinese Influence," *Telegraph*, August 20, 2009.
41. Bhaskar Balakrishnan, "China Woos Mauritius and Eyes Indian Ocean," *Hindu Business Line*, July 1, 2009; www.thehindubusinessline.com/todays-paper/tp-opinion/china-woos-mauritius-and-eyes-the-indian-ocean/article1055443.ece?ref=archive.
42. "Indian Navy to Hold Military Exercises with France, African Navies," *Indiadefence.com*, August 17, 2008; www.india-defence.com/reports/3970.
43. Vibhuti Hate, "India in Africa: Moving beyond Oil," *South Asia Monitor*, Center for Strategic and International Studies, June 11, 2008.
44. Daniel Twining, "India's Relations with Iran and Myanmar: 'Rogue State' or Responsible Democratic Stakeholder?," *India Review* 7 (January–March 2008): 1–37.
45. Strobe Talbott, *Engaging India: Diplomacy, Democracy, and the Bomb* (Washington DC: Brookings Institution Press, 2004).
46. Rajiv Chandrasekaran, "India Offers Bases to US for Retaliatory Attacks," *Washington Post*, September 16, 2001.
47. US Department of Defense, "Indo-US Framework for Maritime Security Cooperation"; www.defense.gov/news/Mar2006/d200600302indo-usframeworkformaritimesecuritycooperation.pdf.
48. US Department of Defense, *A Cooperative Strategy for 21st Century Seapower*; www.navy.mil/maritime/MaritimeStrategy.pdf.
49. It is not clear whether the United States has not invited India (although the task force appears open to all comers) or whether India prefers to operate outside of such a command and control umbrella.
50. Pramit Mitra and John Ryan, "Gathering Steam: India and the United States

Extend Military Ties," *South Asia Monitor*, Center for Strategic and International Studies, October 2, 2006.

51. Arvind Gupta, "India Can Learn from the US Experience in Securing Its Borders," *IDSA Comment*, December 14, 2009; www.idsa.in/idsacomments/IndiacanlearnfromtheUSexperienceinsecuringitsborders_agupta_141209.
52. A. Vinod Kumar, "India's Participation in the Proliferation Security Initiative: Issues in Perspective," *Strategic Analysis* 33, no. 5 (2009): 686–700. Kumar notes on page 693 a March 2009 indication by a high-level Indian official that New Delhi may want to reexplore the issue with the Obama administration.
53. James R. Holmes and Andrew C. Winner, "A New Naval Diplomacy," *Proceedings* 133 (2007): 34–39; and Sreeram Chaulia, "Wary India Frisks North Korean Freighter," *Asia Times Online*, August 21, 2009; www.atimes.com/atimes/South_Asia/KH21Df03.html.
54. Juli A. McDonald, *Indo-US Military Relationship: Expectations and Perceptions* (Washington, DC: Booz Allen Hamilton, October 2002); and Bethany N. Danyluk and Juli A. McDonald, *The US–India Defense Relationship: Reassessing Perceptions and Expectations* (Washington DC: Booz Allen Hamilton, November 2008).

CHAPTER 6

PAKISTAN'S VIEW OF SECURITY IN THE INDIAN OCEAN

MOEED YUSUF

INTRODUCTION

Pakistan is one of the key states in the Indian Ocean littoral. It has always remained heavily dependent on sea access for its economic well-being. Currently, as much as 95 percent of the country's trade takes place through the sea.[1] Two-thirds of the country's oil imports approximating $10 billion originate in the Gulf region and thus flow through the Indian Ocean.[2] Moreover, until the Gwadar port in southwest Pakistan is fully operational, Pakistan has only one port city, which renders it highly vulnerable to any disruption in the Indian Ocean waters. While this amounts to a high premium on maritime security, Pakistan's strategic enclave has never accorded the maritime sector its due importance. The country has no maritime doctrine; arguably, there exists no long-term vision in the first place to reflect in such a document.

Not only have maritime concerns been ignored by the decision makers but even analysts studying Pakistan's security needs have shown lack of appreciation for this area. There have been few systematic studies of Pakistan's maritime sector that analyze why Pakistan neglects its maritime environment and the effects of this neglect on its security. Those who have written on the subject in an Indian Ocean context tend to gloss over Pakistan as a minor actor unable to make an impression upon the interests of larger powers in these critical sea-lanes. While true, Pakistan's maritime security concerns are likely to gain greater prominence over the coming years largely due to Pakistan's recent initiative to develop a new deep-sea port at Gwadar in the heart of the Indian Ocean littoral and its invitation to China to establish presence there.

The argument in this chapter is that since Pakistan's traditionally India-centric security policy has been narrowly defined within continental confines, this has limited the Pakistan Navy's role to coastal defense against an Indian naval attack; however, the development of the Gwadar port has led to a de facto expansion of the country's maritime interests. The Pakistani leadership considers Gwadar a masterstroke, one that has allowed their country to limit the Indian threat while opening up a lucrative economic avenue. It has managed this by providing Beijing sovereign guarantees and incentivizing heavy Chinese commercial presence at the port. That said, new balance-of-power politics have been spurred by this move. The Sino-Pakistan partnership has already raised eyebrows in India, the United States, and even Iran. In fact, India has moved to assist Iran in upgrading its Chabahar port at the mouth of the Strait of Hormuz to undermine Gwadar's economic potential. The United States has also made its discomfort about Chinese presence known. While it is too early to decipher the precise impact Gwadar will ultimately have on the Indian Ocean littoral's power struggle, whatever the implications, Pakistan is likely to be faced with a challenging task of balancing its foreign relationships deftly in order to reap economic dividends and enhance its maritime security at the same time.

The chapter begins by highlighting the country's traditional approach toward the maritime sector. Next, India's naval modernization is discussed in the context of Pakistan together with Pakistan's inability to maintain an acceptable level of asymmetry vis-à-vis its adversary as the key factor that pushed Pakistan to rethink its strategy to cope with the Indian threat. The subsequent section analyzes Pakistan's response and its impact on the state's maritime outlook. Finally, we consider the balance-of-power implications of the Gwadar port project.

PAKISTAN'S MARITIME SECTOR: A HISTORY OF NEGLECT

Pakistan has always neglected its maritime domain. The neglect applies not only to the security domain but also to the intrinsically linked commercial dimension of this sector. Despite being almost entirely dependent on the sea for its trade, Pakistan relies heavily on foreign carriers for both inward and outward shipping. The country's sole noticeable carrier, the publicly owned Pakistan National Shipping Corporation, carries only 5 percent of total trade.[3] This makes Pakistan inherently susceptible to enemy coercion as any stronger naval power can interfere with the sea lines of communication (SLOC) by positioning its naval vessels in threatening formations to dissuade commercial carriers from entering the area and thus reducing maritime traffic.[4] Indeed, for a country as heavily reliant on the sea as Pakistan, mortgaging its trade shipment to foreign carriers risks bringing it to an economic standstill in no time.

Countries that languish in their indigenous shipping capacity and are situated in hostile neighborhoods often attempt to compensate for the weakness by ensuring strong maritime security. However, in Pakistan's case, even this aspect has only fared marginally better than its commercial counterpart. Within the country's overall security strategy, the maritime dimension has received the least importance. Traditionally, the Pakistan Navy has been limited in its objectives to coastal defense. It has only been able to establish a token presence in the country's 240,000-km^2 exclusive economic zone. The service does have a three-dimensional capability (surface, subsurface, and air) consisting of thirty combat ships including seven frigates, five active-duty submarines, six missile patrol boats, three minesweepers, and air squadrons of the Atlantique, Fokker, and American P-3C Orion aircraft and aviation helicopters.[5] However, apart from the submarines, which provide a limited offensive punch, these platforms largely reflect defensive capabilities in the Pakistani context and will most likely be employed in protective or antisubmarine roles.[6] In essence, Pakistan's strategy lacks the offensive spirit that naval strategists consider an imperative for successful navies. Discussing the role of maritime warfare in a conflict among contiguous states, Adm. Raoul Castex argued that the burden would always be on the defender who ties itself to mere protection of limited geographical space.[7] This is precisely the goal that Pakistan's navy has been forced to limit itself to.

The Pakistan Navy's plight would be puzzling to a casual observer of Pakistani politics given that the country is renowned for maintaining a lopsided civil–military balance in favor of the latter. The military is widely believed to be the ultimate determinant of security and foreign policy in addition to having a strong voice in political matters. To be sure, the reality is that Pakistan has always been dominated by the army, not the navy; this is a key distinction that often tends to be ignored. Within this calculus, while the natural affinity between land and air services has still allowed the air force some clout, the navy has been kept at arm's length by the decision-making enclave. With only twenty-four thousand active personnel, the Pakistan Navy is by far the smallest service.[8] Moreover, despite the inherently capital-intensive nature of navies, the service receives one dollar for every forty dollars allocated to the army.[9] Traditionally, its share in the overall defense expenditure has remained less than 10 percent, only rising in a select few years when big-ticket items were procured.[10]

In a nutshell, this anomaly can be attributed to the inherently continental mindset of the army generals who have dictated defense strategizing from the very beginning. Apart from their obvious preference for ground combat, the continental outlook of the army top brass in Pakistan can also be attributed to the historical dimension of the recruitment pattern of the service. The ethnic Punjabis and Pukhtoons who make up the bulk of the Pakistan Army have always been reputed as formidable land warriors.[11] However, since both provinces lie inland, their natives have never had any noticeable affinity to the sea. Indeed, it is no coincidence that the British chose these ethnicities to form the backbone of the British Indian Army in the colonial era but never sought the same from them for the Royal Navy's presence in India.

The second major factor contributing to the continental view is the nature of the threat Pakistan has faced throughout its history. Islamabad takes pride in having a security policy that is India-centric; the country has never posed as having security ambitions beyond its eastern neighbor. Therefore, given that the two sides share approximately three thousand kilometers of land border, it is only natural that they expected conflict between them to be conducted over land.[12] Since India also neglected its navy for the same reason in its early years, the Pakistan Navy never had any real justification to ask for greater importance.[13] While India's propensity to turn the 1971 Indo-Pak war into a maritime affair on the country's eastern front and to blockade Karachi in the west did serve as a rude awakening, the generals saw the loss of East Pakistan as having simplified the navy's task to defending the lone remaining port in Karachi.[14] Therefore, while the 1971 debacle did allow the navy to procure new platforms, intermittent gains in this regard over the next two decades did not result in any coherent procurement vision.[15]

The 1990s seemed like a new beginning for the Pakistani navy's fortunes because it was the only service to conclude four major deals during the decade, these amounting to a procurement allocation of $1.6 billion.[16] The deals included three French Agosta 90-B submarines, six refurbished British Type-21 type frigates, three Eridian-class French mine hunters, and three American P-3C Orion maritime patrol aircraft.[17] Interestingly, however, even these procurements did not reflect a change in the continental mindset. Rather, as Ayehsa Siddiqa Agha pointed out, the navy managed these deals due to the presence of strong naval chiefs with clout among the decision makers. In fact, Agha argues that most of these procurements were objectionable on technical grounds but were still taken up by the navy to avoid deferring resources to the two larger services.[18] Moreover, a US embargo that had been in place against Pakistan since 1990 helped as the navy was the only service ready to procure from non-US sellers at the time.[19] That the 1990s were not representative of any fundamental shift in the country's overall security vision is evident from the fact that, post-2000, the navy has returned to its stepsister status, only receiving marginal attention from the army top brass. Since the turn of the century, it has only received one Chinese F-22 frigate (among major platforms) against a deal negotiated in the late-1990s in addition to having signed an agreement with the US for upgraded P-3C Orion aircraft.[20]

INDIA'S PROGRESS CAUSES A RETHINK

The Pakistani Army had always believed that naval defense was peripheral to any Indo-Pak conflict. The predominant view was that the ultimate fate of the war would be decided over land; essentially, a robust Pakistani land defense with sufficient aerial support was considered adequate to achieve a stalemate.[21] Moreover, since the army believed that Indo-Pak wars would always be halted within a matter of days—this was perhaps reflective of their confidence that the international community would pressurize both sides to pull back—the threat of an Indian coastal invasion or prolonged naval blockade at any stage of a conflict was not taken too seriously. Again, it is important to mention in this regard that the 1971 blockade of Karachi was explained away as an outcome of the navy's dispersed area of operations across the country's eastern and western wings, an issue it no longer had to deal with after the dismemberment of East Pakistan. In essence, then, the sea leg of security was considered to be largely irrelevant to the continental dimension. Notwithstanding, the navy's view on the threat from India was quite the opposite. Naval planners had constantly been pointing to Pakistan's high vulnerability given that all its naval assets were housed at Karachi (a small base was built at Ormara 120 nautical miles west of Karachi in 2000, which provided some relief).[22] The service contended that India could fight a protracted battle to choke Pakistan's maritime traffic, thus undermining the entire war effort.[23]

The continental mindset of the Pakistani defense planners never transformed. However, a number of external developments toward the 1990s—read: India's growing military advantage—reaffirmed the message that the continental and maritime aspects of national security were not isolated. The single most important external development was India's growing naval disparity vis-à-vis Pakistan. The Indian Navy, although the smallest of the services possessed by New Delhi, had been growing gradually in terms of capability just as Pakistan was constantly losing platforms to decommissioning and lease returns.[24] By the early-1990s, the Indian Navy enjoyed a 5:1 quantitative advantage over Pakistan's aging fleet; the qualitative edge was perceived to be wider. Of course, by itself, the disparity did not bother the land-centric outlook given the earlier-mentioned view that the naval arm would not need to undertake a drawn-out battle, and that land and air forces would hold off Indian advancement in a short war. While the argument was inherently shortsighted, it took a limited war at Kargil in Indian-administered Kashmir in 1999 to shake the army's belief.

The Kargil episode has largely been seen as a landmark event for being the first limited war Pakistan and India fought under the nuclear umbrella. However, relevant to our discussion is another largely ignored aspect of the crisis. Kargil also marked the first ever limited and geographically confined crisis since Indo-Pak independence, which saw New Delhi threaten a naval blockade of Karachi.[25] The only time India did so in the past was during the full-fledged conflict in 1971 (where it acted upon the threat successfully). For any student of maritime strategy, the implication should be obvious; India had realized that its navy had the strength to exploit the inability of its Pakistani counterpart to prevent a blockade of its sole port.[26]

This was precisely what the Pakistani Navy had been trying to warn the decision makers against. The navy was well aware of its weakness; in 1992–93 Pakistani naval planners had justified procurement of six British Type-1 frigates on the plea that they would have the capacity to repulse an Indian attack and prevent a blockade for a mere eight- to ten-day period.[27] Thus it would seem that the Kargil episode would have signaled to the Pakistani armed forces, army included, that if the advent of nuclear weapons had made the prospects of limited war more likely by allowing Pakistan to use the space below India's nuclear threshold with impunity, it also meant that India would counter Pakistan's advantage at the lowest rung of the escalation ladder by exploiting its naval superiority early on in any crisis. In essence, India was using the sea to neutralize Pakistan's low-end strategic space under the nuclear umbrella. The implication was that the maritime and the continental dimensions of war would be interdependent in every future conflict that saw India behave in a similar manner.[28] By simply blockading Pakistan's port, India would cause economic strangulation of the adversary, thereby altering the outcome of the continental war. Therefore, the Pakistan Navy's failure to deter its Indian counterpart would leave the army and air force compromised in their strategy.

Although the Kargil crisis has never been widely written about in terms of its naval implications, the author's conversations with Pakistani strategists and naval officers suggest that the maritime implications of Indian behavior during Kargil have not been lost on the armed forces. For the navy, with empirical evidence on their side, it was an opportunity to lobby even harder for a stronger role in the country's security. For the army, the episode would have brought about a grudging realization that sea and land could not be expected to remain delinked in Indo-Pak conflicts.

Moreover, in August 1999 India explicitly stated its intention to develop a triad of nuclear forces.[29] India's quest to achieve a sea-based deterrent was well known even earlier as its indigenous nuclear-capable submarine project, the advanced technology vehicle (ATV), had crawled along since the 1970s despite massive technical and bureaucratic glitches.[30] Its effort to develop the Sagarika, a submarine-launched ballistic missile, was also reportedly under way by the mid-1990s.[31] The Indian triad not only concerned the Pakistan Navy; it also served as a reminder of the continental-maritime link for the army. Indeed, there is a strong argument to be made that an Indian triad would require a matching response by

Pakistan to keep its own deterrent credible.[32] Again, for the Pakistan army, the dilemma was obvious: to ensure deterrence against Indian aggression, the navy had to be given the role of the ultimate guarantor of peace; land- and air-based launch capability would not be enough.

Add to this the fact that the Indian triad was only a small part of the Indian military's plans for upgrading its capabilities. As Andrew Winner discusses in chapter 5 in more detail, since the mid-1990s, India clearly stated its intention to undertake a concerted military modernization drive to correct its long-standing "vision-capability dilemma." The dilemma refers to the virtual consensus among the Indian elite that their country deserves a global status and thus should possess projectable military might, a vision that nonetheless has not been achieved owing partly to the Nehruvian mindset among Indians early on and partly to the Hindu economic growth rates till the 1990s. In essence, then, India's capability lagged its vision.

Beginning with the United Coalition government that took office in 1997, however, India decided to use its miraculous economic turnaround to fund military modernization.[33] Indeed, the beginnings of what the 2004 Indian Maritime Doctrine later described as a drive toward a blue water navy to be achieved by concentrating "at the arc from the Persian Gulf to the Straits of Malacca as a legitimate area of interest," essentially India's signal to its ambition of establishing outright primacy in the littoral, was in evidence by the late 1990s.[34]

India's modernization course presented itself as a major concern to Pakistan's defense planners. With an economy that had suffered throughout the 1990s and reached the verge of bankruptcy toward the end of the decade, Pakistan simply could not expect to match the Indian trend. Grim future prospects were adding on to a decade-long stagnation in Pakistan's military capabilities due to a US embargo that started in 1990 and multiple international sanctions after the country's nuclear tests in May 1998. Therefore, just when the military needed to compensate for a decade of stagnation for army and air force equipment, the country had reached its economic nadir. In hindsight, it is clear that Pakistan's defense establishment realized that they could not hope to keep up with India in all facets of military strategy. By the late 1990s they had shifted decisively to maintaining certain acceptable force ratios within an overall asymmetric relationship, thus representing a move away from their traditional tit-for-tat mentality. Moreover, the lack of funds due to the poor performance of the Pakistani economy forced the military to concentrate on updating its army and air force at the expense of the navy.

Post-2001, when Pakistan's international stature took a positive turn and it found willing sellers of military hardware, the navy's interests were put on the back burner. Admittedly, apart from the traditional mindset, this time an added justification was that unlike the navy, the two larger services had not managed to upgrade throughout the 1990s. Moreover, some of the requirements such as a sea-based nuclear capability were beyond Pakistan's technical expertise and financial capacity and thus were understandably not seriously contemplated.[35]

PAKISTAN'S MASTERSTROKE: THE GWADAR PORT

If our thesis is correct, Pakistan's propensity to put upgrading its maritime force on the back burner even after an economic revival post-2001 is puzzling. It would imply that the army, despite realizing that a decisive Indian advantage at sea would impact the continental battle and knowing that it may lose its second-strike capability over the long run, had decided not to seek an antidote. Indeed, the defense planners sought an alternate route to satisfy their concern in this regard: they aimed at checking India's hegemonic ambitions in the Indian Ocean through a mortgaging arrangement with China. This was done by initiating the development of a new deep-sea port at Gwadar on the Makran coast in southwestern Pakistan. The port is designated to be a military base as well as an industrial, investment, and transshipment hub, which makes it the single largest infrastructure project undertaken in Pakistan's history.

The idea to develop Gwadar was not new. In fact, the site had been identified as a potential naval base as early as 1964. At the time the rationale was solely to disperse Pakistan's naval assets to make it less vulnerable to an Indian attack.[36] However, Gwadar's importance increased tremendously after the fall of the Soviet Union. Pakistan now presented newly independent, energy-rich Central Asian Republics (CAR) with an attractive sea opening.[37] Keeping in mind that globalization of the world economy was sure to engulf these CARs, the potential of pumping Caspian Sea energy and other tradable goods through Afghanistan and into Pakistan became a lucrative proposition. While the security concerns remained important, the project was no longer seen solely through this lens.

It is interesting to note that while Gwadar's economic importance had become evident immediately after the fall of the Soviet Union, Pakistani governments in the 1990s did not explore the option seriously. That it took an army general who had taken over in a military coup to reach out to China—a strategic competitor to India—in 2000–2001 to jointly pursue the project is no coincidence. The importance accorded to Chinese involvement was evident from the very beginning. The Chinese premier Zhu Rongji underwrote the project during his visit to Pakistan in May 2001 and Vice Premier Wu Bangguo laid the foundation of the port in March 2002. Admittedly, it is impossible to distinguish whether economic or security interests took precedence in Gen. Pervez Musharraf's decision to initiate the process. The predominant view suggests that the move was principally aimed at satisfying economic interests. Indeed, as Musharraf's tenure proved, he had an inclination toward megadevelopment projects as a preferred development tool. Be that as it may, the choice of China as a partner and the timing of the move (Pakistan approached China when defense planners were already resigned to the fact that India would leap ahead in terms of naval capacity) suggest that the growing Indian disparity may have played a major role in Musharraf's decision.

For Musharraf and those who guided him through the Gwadar negotiation process, the initiative marked a milestone achievement. Gwadar presented one of the few examples where the commercial and the strategic pundits in Pakistan saw eye to eye. It satisfied a twin—inseparable—goal of reinforcing Pakistan's quest to deny India a decisive naval advantage as well as providing the country with a lucrative economic opportunity. Merely a naval base would not have been sufficient; while it would have allowed Pakistan to move away from the inherently dangerous limitation of banking on naval bases that are in close vicinity to each other, it would still not have resolved the problem of a naval blockade at Karachi. By engaging China directly, Pakistan sought to bring a ready antidote to Indian designs in the Indian Ocean, a fact that New Delhi has made explicit frequently in recent years. Moreover, Islamabad's accentuated interest in securing SLOC given the economic stakes in Gwadar would also be automatically addressed if China saw a strong enough incentive to maintain stability in the Indian Ocean. This is exactly what Pakistan has managed.

To ensure China's role as a guarantor of peace in the region—this implies foremost that India would be kept at bay—Pakistan sought to use the strategic importance and economic potential of the project as the bait. The Gwadar port is strategically located just 250 miles from the Strait of Hormuz, which sees 40 percent of the world's total oil supplies pass through it.[38] Pakistan has allowed China "sovereign guarantees," implying that it has the option of maintaining naval presence even in brown waters in addition to setting up a listening post. In fact, the Pentagon has already cast doubts over Chinese intentions and suggested that Beijing is operating eavesdropping posts from Gwadar to monitor ship traffic through the Strait of Hormuz and the Arabian Sea.[39] For China, Gwadar signifies an extension of its "String of Pearls" naval strategy; indeed, given Gwadar's strategic location, it would be no exaggeration to term this the jewel in the string.

That said, the potential for Chinese strategic gains should not be taken to imply that presence of offensive naval platforms in the Arabian Sea is a given. In fact, China has strenuously avoided any mention of Gwadar's military dimension in its statements. Indeed, a Chinese move to relocate its surface or subsurface crafts to Pakistan would quickly raise the diplomatic temperature in the area. In reality, even Pakistan realizes that physical presence of Beijing's navy is improbable. What Pakistan is banking upon, however, is not necessarily the actual relocation but the deterrence effect generated from the adversary's knowledge of such a possibility. Consequently, in contrast to Chinese silence on the security aspect, Pakistan has had no qualms about publicizing its willingness to allow Beijing to enter its waters. Pakistan's signaling has included the official designation of Gwadar as a "sensitive defense zone" where, according to President Musharraf, "as and when needed the Chinese Navy would be in Gwadar to give befitting reply to anyone."[40]

As for the economic aspect, Pakistan has created an arrangement with China that raises the latter's stakes such that it would not appreciate any effort by a third party to exert excessive influence in the Indian Ocean. Gwadar port's originally projected trade volume is presented in table 6.1. The actual gains will be realized much later than indicated, owing to the fact that the port only started servicing ships in 2008. It is not scheduled to be fully completed before 2015.[41]

China's economic expectations can be gauged from the fact that it has funded 80 percent of the $248 million first phase of the project and is assisting in raising funds for the $600 million second phase.[42] Moreover, it has provided 450 engineers on site to help finish the project. For China, Gwadar fulfills its long-standing quest to find alternate routes for its energy imports.[43] Having become the energy consumption hub of the world, China is desperate to diversify its modes of oil import. Currently, imports into China make their way through the Strait of Malacca, a route fraught with piracy.[44] Furthermore, the route has always remained susceptible to a US blockade that could be exercised in case of an eventuality in the Taiwan Straits. By establishing presence in the Arabian Sea, not only will China be able to secure SLOC leading to the Malacca straits, it will also find an alternate route to transport oil originating from Iran and Africa.[45] China has already signaled its intention to use Gwadar as a crude oil transport hub. Its leading petroleum company, the Great United Petroleum Holding, is also setting up a refinery and petrochemical complex at Gwadar.[46] In April 2006 a proposal for Pakistan to supply China with oil and gas originating in the central and western Asian region through pipelines from Gwadar was also considered.[47]

In addition to its concern regarding energy, China will have a large industrial stake in Gwadar. Chinese companies are tipped to get preferential treatment

TABLE 6.1 Gwadar's Trade Forecast

	Year		
Category	**2005**	**2010**	**2015**
Dry cargo (million tons)	3.96	4.74	5.77
Liquid cargo (million tons)	16.62	17.54	18.77
Container (1,000 TEUs)	200	241	295
Transshipment (1,000 TEUs)	200	250	300

Source: Data from "Pakistan Country Brief" World Bank; available at http://siteresources.worldbank.org/PAKISTANEXTN/Resources/293051-1114424648263/Session-VII-Fazal-Ur-Rehman.pdf.

within the Gwadar Special Economic Zone (GSEZ); this will be on top of the seven-year tax holiday planned for all investors operating in the GSEZ.[48] The idea is for Beijing to use the zone as its factory floor for labor-intensive export products that would incur a higher per-unit cost in China. Moreover, to realize the full potential of the arrangement, the Gwadar agreement envisions a network of road and rail connections between the two countries and beyond. China is helping develop a highway inland from Gwadar through Balochistan. It has also agreed to connect the Karakoram Highway to the CARs.[49] Further, Pakistan is upgrading road links to Afghanistan and Iran. There is also talk of developing a rail link between China's western Xinjiang province and Peshawar in Pakistan. Once completed, the road and rail networks would present Pakistan's Gwadar port as the shortest route for Xinjiang's global trade.[50]

While the economic interest is crucial in its own right, it also ties in directly with the security dimension. Earlier we had mentioned the adequacy of the mere possibility of Chinese naval presence at Gwadar for Pakistan's purposes. However, Chinese economic stakes make Pakistan's task of ensuring its security even simpler. There is a strong case to be made that India would not contemplate aggression against a port that constantly hosts a significant number of Chinese merchant ships. New Delhi would realize that precisely such an act may cause China to exercise the option of relocating naval forces, a development that the former would want to avoid at all costs. In short, Chinese strategic and economic stakes in Gwadar seem to be high enough for it to act as a dependable Pakistani ally in terms of ensuring stability in the Indian Ocean littoral.

THE POWER BALANCE AND THE STRATEGIC IMPLICATIONS

Pakistan's anticipation that Gwadar would solve its security dilemma while providing an extremely lucrative economic opportunity should not imply that the process is likely to be straightforward.[51] By bringing China directly into the Indian Ocean, Pakistan has set into motion balance-of-power politics that is likely to prompt interested states to pursue contradictory policies at multiple levels.

A number of existing competitive relationships will be further accentuated due to Gwadar. Foremost among them is the Sino-Indian equation. Notwithstanding their improved ties on the economic front, the manner in which India is pursuing a blue water agenda in the Indian Ocean clashes directly with Beijing's objective of denying anyone hegemony in the littoral. Therefore, to see India express its discomfort with Chinese presence and acknowledge that the port presents strategic challenges to its naval ambitions is no surprise.[52] While India may well have lost its ability to readily threaten interference or interdiction of Pakistan-bound ships or wage a coastal war on Pakistan, both due to the presence of a new

Pakistani naval base cum port at Gwadar and due to Chinese presence, it seems determined to check the Sino-Pakistani alliance. Its principal strategy is to undermine the economic prospects of the Gwadar port by assisting Iran in upgrading its Chabahar port at the mouth of the Strait of Hormuz. Chabahar presents the shortest route for the CAR to the sea; should American isolationist policies toward Tehran subside, it could well out-shadow Gwadar to some extent.[53] As reflected by a Pakistani official, "Pakistan is pinning huge hopes on the Gwadar project as the transit point for goods from Russia and the CARs bound for the Gulf and the East, but Chabahar port would inflict a huge financial setback for Pakistan."[54] India has simultaneously increased its presence in Afghanistan and has become a major player in the country's infrastructure development. The idea, as New Delhi has hinted previously, is to bypass Pakistan in forging alliances with western and central Asian states—from Pakistan's perspective, this amounts to its de facto encirclement—in addition to finding alternate routes of access to western and central Asia for itself.[55] An additional limb to this strategy, of course, is to encourage other states to use Iranian port facilities over Gwadar and thus dampen Chinese interest in the project. Pakistan and China may have some room for optimism about the project with the potential to offer Iran a high incentive not to side with India overtly. Pakistan has moved in that direction by recently inking a twenty-five-year gas import deal with Iran. The project was initially framed as the Iran-Pakistan-India (IPI) pipeline; New Delhi, however, has chosen to stay away, citing pricing concerns.[56] Moreover, there is already a Pakistani offer for China to join the IPI project.[57] In addition, China has separately signed a twenty-five-year oil and gas import deal with Iran worth $70 billion, which should keep the latter from explicitly undermining Chinese interests to favor India.[58]

Resentment about the Sino-Pakistani relationship in the littoral is exacerbated due to the American discomfort with Chinese presence. The Indo-US relationship has experienced a quantum leap in recent years; the United States is set to be India's long-term strategic partner, one seen as a counterweight to China. Moreover, the United States has received China's presence in the Indian Ocean cautiously because it has always been interested in these waters and has long sought to establish its own primacy in the area. The United States is also pursuing an aggressive foreign policy with the CARs in a bid to capture oil resources.[59] China, for its part, is wary of a US role, as was evident from its displeasure at a Pakistani move to provide America with air bases within miles of Gwadar just when the project's deal was being inked.

The Sino-US equation puts Pakistan in a quandary. Islamabad, while preferring Beijing, cannot afford to isolate Washington completely. After all, Pakistan has been receiving substantial aid from the United States, the latter is Pakistan's largest export market, and Islamabad is desperate to avoid any break in the relationship that may cause Washington to contemplate a move to neutralize

Pakistan's nuclear capability. But if Pakistan is attempting to signal its preference toward China while maintaining amenable ties with the United States, how would it react if America requested permission to establish a naval base or listening post at Gwadar?[60] On the one hand, Pakistan's need to keep China squarely in its camp could prompt it to deny the United States. On the other hand, however, it might find China annoyed if it obliged the United States. Consider that, although allowing China to develop large stakes in Gwadar implies that China's presence and interest in undermining what it believes to be India's Mahanian naval vision is guaranteed, it does not follow that Pakistan can conduct a parallel policy that runs counter to China's interest without considering the possibility, however remote, that Beijing may resort to coercive tactics of its own against Islamabad. Therefore, deft diplomacy will be required to balance the Sino-US interests at Gwadar.[61]

The alliance maze gets even more complex by including Afghanistan into the calculus. Here Pakistan's interests are clearly paradoxical. The US campaign in Afghanistan has been unable to bring peace to the country. Nonetheless, Pakistan's support for the United States has caused a tremendous backlash within its heartland. Moreover, while the current Pakistani authorities seemed willing in 2009–10 to initiate military action on their own terms, satisfying the United States' persistent calls to "do more" remains a remote possibility at best.[62]

Much more fundamental, however, is a lingering disconnect in the very objectives of the two sides. Despite American pressure, Islamabad has not lost sight of its interest in installing an amenable regime in Kabul once Western troops pull out. From Pakistan's perspective, this is important even to ensure that Afghanistan is willing to allow transit of CAR exports to Gwadar rather than preferring Chabahar in Iran. Again, this implies that Pakistan may accept a prolonged tussle in Afghanistan as long as it does not end up with a government that sides overtly with India or Iran. Inherently contradictory, however, is the fact that the bulk of Gwadar's economic promise is contingent on Afghanistan's stability since the latter provides the only route for CARs to reach Pakistan. This should prompt Islamabad to find the quickest means to stabilize Kabul. How Pakistan resolves this dilemma remains to be seen. However, Pakistan would be conscious of the fact that if Afghanistan remains unavailable as a dependable transit route for too long, the very premise that has guaranteed the Chinese role as a "front state" to cater to Pakistan's strategic and economic interests—that is, Beijing's high economic stakes—would be undermined.

LOOKING AHEAD

Pakistan has lacked any coherent vision regarding its maritime interests in the Indian Ocean. Concern about maritime security was only considered seriously after the growing disparity between Pakistani and Indian capabilities made it obvious that the sea leg of security could not be divorced from its continental dimension. Notwithstanding, in terms of Pakistan's view of security in the Indian Ocean, the Gwadar port does not alter the India-centric outlook of the Pakistan Navy. In fact, Chinese presence in the port reflects a realization of the navy's inability to perform its traditional function effectively; the answer was to partly mortgage its responsibilities. By doing so, the navy has simultaneously made itself less susceptible to a naval blockade and to an Indian coastal attack. Gwadar has also expanded Pakistan's overall maritime interests in the Indian Ocean littoral by giving it a role as a major transshipment hub. The pressure to ensure secure SLOCs is automatically satisfied by raising Chinese stakes in the project and, consequently, its interest in preventing any disruption in waters south of Pakistan.

While the Gwadar port does present a way out of Pakistan's otherwise irresolvable lacunae, it also opens up a Pandora's box in terms of alliance politics. Pakistan is now caught in seemingly contradictory foreign policy objectives that will not be easy to reconcile. Ideally, Pakistan would want to maintain excessive Chinese interest in keeping India's hegemonic designs at bay while retaining an amenable relationship with the United States. Equally important is Pakistan's concern about not being encircled; this would entail thwarting an Indo-Iranian-Afghan alliance that is pitted against the Sino-Pakistani relationship. It follows, then, that Pakistan would prefer the absence of any development that forces China to actually situate naval forces in its waters. This would make it easier for Islamabad to deny the United States permission to establish naval presence at Gwadar, should it request to do so. Moreover, Pakistan would want to remain engaged in the IPI project with Iran while hoping that American isolationist tactics keep the Chabahar port underutilized. It would also be looking for an amenable government in Afghanistan that is able to stabilize Kabul to the point that the territory could be used as a transit route on a regular basis.

In terms of concrete policy prescriptions, then, the situation calls for extremely deft maneuvering. Pakistan's aim should be to ensure that Chinese commercial interests in the port continue to grow. This necessitates swift completion of the port and of the road infrastructure that is to allow shipments to be transported to and from western China. At the same time, however, Pakistan must not see the port as a license to provoke India militarily. Ultimately, success would be gauged by Pakistan's ability to continue gaining economically from Gwadar while discrediting any future Indian threats to blockade Pakistan's sea-lanes. Shrewdness on Pakistan's part calls for periodic signaling to reinforce the deterrent effect of Chinese presence without actually forcing a situation that necessitates testing the deterrent's robustness.

Balancing the relationships with China and the United States is likely to prove even trickier for Pakistani leaders in the coming years. As indicated earlier, Pakistan cannot afford to alienate either of the two parties. The most realistic course is to keep the United States away from direct presence at Gwadar (apart from any private, nonstrategic investment originating from the United States). Prospects of any US demands for listening posts or naval presence can be prevented if political tensions in the littoral are kept in check.

Finally, Pakistan ought to continue pursuing its own interests vis-à-vis its western neighbors without allowing excessive US (or, for that matter, Chinese) interference. Its decision to proceed with the IPI deal despite staunch US opposition may serve as a model in this regard. Islamabad should treat the Chabahar port strictly as an economic competitor and should attempt to outmaneuver the Indo-Iranian initiative by classic cost-cutting and efficiency-enhancing measures. Moreover, a quick return to relative stability in an Afghanistan controlled by a government amenable to Islamabad stands out as the most desirable outcome. Admittedly, however, short of Pakistan playing a dangerous game—this approach is certainly not recommended—to actively support anti-US forces in Afghanistan in the hope of hastening the United States' withdrawal, the policy levers to bring about a stable, pro-Pakistan Afghanistan are under US control for the most part.

Indeed, all this is a tall order. Nonetheless, it is plausible to envision Pakistan achieving an amenable balance of power reasonably close to the optimal. By 2020 Gwadar could well have provided Pakistan with an answer to the otherwise outright Indian naval advantage, it could have further cemented Sino-Pak ties while allowing Pakistan to retain its partnership with the US, and the interest of all concerned parties to keep tensions in the littoral low may even have vindicated the liberal interdependence theory, thereby allowing the economic interests to buffer against conflict. To the contrary, however, having brought global attention on its southern borders, Pakistan may well fall prey to power politics whereby active efforts to undermine Gwadar's success are undertaken. External interference in the restive Balochistan province or an effort to maintain a setup in Afghanistan that is antagonistic to Pakistan cannot be ruled out.[63] Indeed, should the global power play pit the United States and India irreconcilably against China, and should Pakistan's domestic troubles at the time result in its inability to thwart external challenges, Gwadar could well hasten Pakistan's further decline. Be that as it may, one thing is certain: the Indian Ocean will remain the center of global maritime power politics for the foreseeable future, and Gwadar will continue to be an important pawn in the game.

NOTES

1. Ammad Hassan, "Pakistan's Gwadar Port: Prospects of Economic Revival," Master's thesis, Naval Postgraduate School, June 2005, 27; available at www.nps.edu/Academics/Centers/CCC/Research/index.html.

2. This figure reflects Pakistan's total oil import bill as projected for the fiscal year 2008–9.
3. UNESCAP, "Country Report of Pakistan," www.unescap.org/ttdw/Publications/TFS_pubs/Pub_2217/pub_2217_Pakistan.pdf. The minimum recommended contribution of local shipping to a country's total trade under the World Trade Organization's general agreement on trade in services regime is 40 percent. To encourage domestic private investment in the sector, Pakistan instituted a merchant marine policy in 2000–2001. However, the policy has not had the requisite effect and has suffered from a glaring disconnect between its vision and implementation.
4. Raja Rab Nawaz, "Maritime Strategy in Pakistan," Master's thesis, Naval Postgraduate School, December 2004, 69, www.nps.edu/Academics/Centers/CCC/Research/index.html.
5. For details of the platforms that the Pakistan Navy is equipped with, visit the service's official website at www.paknavy.gov.pk/.
6. Malik Ayaz Hussain Tiwana, "Pakistan's Security Concerns and the Navy," *Defense Journal*, April 2002; www.defencejournal.com/2002/april/navy.htm.
7. Castex was vice admiral in the French Navy in 1934. See Raoul Castex, *Strategic Theories*, trans. by Eugenia C. Kiesling (Annapolis, MD: Naval Institute Press, 1993). For a succinct summary of his key ideas, see Raja Menon, *Maritime Strategy and Continental Wars* (London: Frank Cass, 1998), 41–46.
8. The Pakistan Army is by far the largest service, with 550,000 active personnel, whereas the air force has 45,000 servicemen.
9. Raja Menon, "Admiral Gorschkov and the Navy," *Daily Times*, January 30, 2003.
10. Vijay Sakhuja, "Pakistan's Naval Expenditure," *Institute of Peace and Conflict Studies*, January 21, 2003, www.ipcs.org/article/military/pakistan-naval-expenditure-956.html. The naval expenditure rose to 16–17 percent as a percentage of total defense spending in the late 1990s. However, as we discuss shortly, this was not reflective of any change in the overall strategy.
11. Three-quarters of the servicemen in the Pakistan Army come from just three districts of the Punjab (Rawal Pindi, Jhelum, and Campbellpur) and two districts of NWFP (Mardan and Kohat). Ian Talbot, *Pakistan: A Modern History* (Lahore: Vanguard Books, 1999), 15.
12. Even before the dismemberment of East Pakistan in 1971, when arguably the need for naval defense was stronger given the eastern wing's vulnerability to the sea, the Pakistani high command's belief that the "defense of the East lies in the West" forced it to neglect maritime security.
13. The army was so oblivious to naval requirements that it never allocated a requisite budget for Pakistan Navy to meet its requirements. In 1959 this even led HMS Chaudri, one of Pakistan's most respected naval chiefs, to resign on the account that Gen. Ayub Khan, the then president cum army chief, was neglecting the navy.

14. The Pakistan Navy was so far outside the decision-making loop that it was not even informed of hostilities in 1971 and only came to know through a public radio message.
15. Between 1971 and the early 1980s, the navy did receive a boost as it acquired the Atlantique maritime patrol aircraft, Sea King and Alouette III helicopters, Daphne- and Agosta-class submarines, a guided missile destroyer, US harpoon missiles, and US Navy Gearing-class destroyers.
16. Sakhuja, "Pakistan's Naval Expenditure." The total procurement expenditure during the decade was $2.7 billion.
17. Ayehsa Siddiqa Agha, *Pakistan's Arms Procurement and Military Buildup* (New York: Palgrave, 2001), 160–65.
18. For Agha's argument on the lack of institutionalization in naval decision making, see ibid., 64–66. For specific discussion of naval arms procurement during the 1990s, see ibid., 160–68.
19. The Pakistan Air Force was the most affected service because it depended heavily on the United States for spares of its aircraft. Moreover, at the time it had concluded and paid for a deal to acquire F-16 fighter jets from the United States, which the latter refused to deliver owing to the embargo.
20. In total, China and Pakistan have signed an agreement for four F-22P frigates. As for the Orion, the first upgraded system was delivered to the Pakistan Navy in 2007.
21. Rather interestingly, in the 1965 war, Pakistan's sole submarine, the *Ghazi*, did play a significant role by limiting India's use of its offensive capability, thereby allowing Pakistan to successfully attack India's key Dwarka naval station. Yet the eventual halt of the Indian offensive across the international border was largely credited to the army. Indeed, as already discussed, the Pakistan Navy was paid no attention till after the 1971 debacle.
22. "Jinnah Naval Base at Ormara Completed at a Cost of 4.5 Billion Rupees Was Inaugurated Today," *Federation of American Scientists*, June 22, 2000, www.fas.org/news/pakistan/2000/000622-pak-ptv1.htm.
23. Agha, *Pakistan's Arms Procurement*, 161.
24. The number of Pakistan's combat ships declined from a high of sixty in 1980 to thirty by the end of the 1990s. See Rodney W. Jones, "Force Modernization Trends—India and Pakistan," Presentation at the APCSS Conference on Conventional Arms Rivalry in Asia-Pacific Region, October 23–25, 2001, www.policyarchitects.org/pdf/ForceModern_IndiaPakistan2.pdf.
25. "India Says It Threatened Naval Blockade," *Dawn*, July 27, 1999.
26. At Kargil, Pakistan's naval inventory consisted of 30 combat vessels, as compared to India's 110-strong fleet.
27. Agha, *Pakistan's Arms Procurement*, 164.
28. A clear indication that Indian threat of a blockade at Kargil was representative of a future trend is that India emphasized the naval dimension of war in the next bilateral crisis in 2001–2 as well. During the ten-month-long crisis that had two

distinct spikes, India moved its eastern naval fleet including its aircraft carrier from the Bay of Bengal to the Arabian Sea immediately after the trigger events that caused the two spikes. The move was widely publicized, perhaps as an intentional signal to Pakistan. See Wallace J. Thies and Dorle Hellmuth, "Critical Risk and the 2002 Kashmir Crisis," *Nonproliferation Review* 11, no. 3 (2004): 1–24.

29. This was stated in India's Draft Nuclear Doctrine that was leaked and later rescinded in August 1999.
30. India has recently launched the ATV, named INS *Arihant*, thus formally completing the triad. A deployable sea-based capability, however, is still some way away. "India Launches 1st Nuclear Submarine," *IBN*, March 19, 2007; "India's Nuclear Submarine to Trigger Arms Race: Pak Navy," *Dawn*, July 27, 2009.
31. M. Shamsur Rabb Khan, "Sagarika: A Feather in India's Defense Hat," March 8, 2008, *Institute of Peace and Conflict Studies*, www.ipcs.org/article_details.php?articleNo=2512.
32. Pakistan was certain to feel vulnerable if it remained completely dependent on a land-based capability in the face of an Indian triad. The Pakistani military continues to entertain the possibility of a "bolt out of the blue" attempt at preemption by India. Coupled with India's growing capabilities, particularly its plans to acquire sophisticated early-warning and ballistic missile defense systems, a triad would undermine Pakistan's self-belief. There are also technical requisites that may force Pakistan toward a triad. For one, Pakistan faces an acute always/never dilemma in that its entire chain of command is based within one hundred kilometers in Islamabad and Rawalpindi and thus is under real threat of debilitation during a conflict. This then raises the attractiveness for Islamabad to predelegate nuclear weapons to field commanders early on in a crisis. Not only is this dangerous, since it leaves the decision to the whims of the commander, but for Pakistan such a move carries a heavy diplomatic cost given that it is largely perceived to have a program dominated by a military that has been known for its belligerence. In essence, any Pakistani move that may be seen as destabilizing is sure to carry greater sanction due to its perceived recklessness and thus would prompt Islamabad to compensate by signaling extreme prudence in crises. Therefore, while operational requirements should push Islamabad toward predelegation, diplomatic concerns may not allow such a choice. For military planners then, land- and air-based nuclear forces would be vulnerable. Finally, Pakistan has always remained wary of the US outlook toward Pakistan's nuclear weapons. Throughout the 1990s, and especially after the 1998 nuclear tests, Pakistan was under tremendous pressure to rethink its nuclear future. More recently, a proliferation scandal and domestic instability in Pakistan have led to persistent murmurs from Washington that hint at the need to neutralize the Pakistani program. This increases the attractiveness of a capability that cannot be constantly monitored by outside powers, that is, a triad.
33. The navy was allocated $7.5 billion from 1997 to 2001. David Scott, "India's Drive for a 'Blue Water' Navy," *Journal of Military and Strategic Studies* 10, no. 2 (Winter 2007–8): 13; www.jmss.org/jmss/index.php/jmss/article/download/90/100.

34. See *The Indian Maritime Doctrine* (New Delhi: Ministry of Defense, 2004), 56. The doctrine has since evolved into a maritime strategy. Since the turn of the century, India has further accelerated its naval modernization and is well on its way to attaining its blue water vision. Its budget allocation reached $18.3 billion from 2002 to 2007. Currently it has 156 combat vessels, and another 27 are on order. India's sea-based deterrent has also been launched and it has already conducted a successful full subwater test of its ballistic missile, dubbed K-15. For an overview of India's naval ambition and its modernization in recent years, see Scott, "India's Drive," 13–38.
35. In light of the exorbitant costs involved in developing a triad, it is hardly surprising that there are no signs of any aggressive Pakistani effort to achieve a sea-based capability. Even the few statements made by some naval officers signaling the country's seriousness about acquiring a sea-based capability in the early years of nuclearization have subsequently been rescinded. While this is not to say that the ultimate vision for a triad has disappeared, there are few who believe that Pakistan's present efforts have gone much beyond the drawing board.
36. In another example of the navy's continued neglect, the proposal was continuously put off by decision makers citing lack of resources as the reason.
37. The Central Asian region is an oil- and gas-rich area with proven reserves of 6,609 million barrels of oil and 232.6 trillion cubic feet of natural gas. In addition, CARs' current trade potential is $20 billion, a major share of which could be captured by Gwadar. Hassan, "Pakistan's Gwadar Port," 30.
38. Urvashi Aneja, "Pakistan–China Relations: Recent Developments (January–May 2006)," *Institute of Peace and Conflict Studies*, Special Report 26, June 2006, 8.
39. Ibid.
40. Rajeev Rajan Chaturvedy, "Interpreting China's Grand Strategy at Gwadar," *Institute for Peace and Conflict Studies*, February 14, 2006.
41. "Gwadar Port to Be Fully Completed by 2015: Chairman," *ARY News*, January 18, 2009; www.thearynews.com/english/newsdetail.asp?nid=20411.
42. Ziad Haider, "Baluchis, Beijing, and Pakistan's Gwadar Port," *Politics and Diplomacy* (Winter–Spring 2005): 97.
43. For a discussion of Chinese energy interests in the Indian Ocean, see James Holmes, "China's Energy Consumption and Opportunities for US–China Cooperation to Address the Effects of China's Energy Use," Testimony before the US–China Economic and Security Review Commission (Washington DC: US–China Economic Security Review Commission, June 14, 2007), 1–4.
44. Haider, "Baluchis, Beijing," 98.
45. Holmes, "China's Energy Consumption," 6.
46. Syed Fazl-e-Haider, "Pakistan Port Opens New Possibilities," *Asia Times Online*, March 22, 2007; www.atimes.com/atimes/South_Asia/IC22Df02.html.
47. Aneja, "Pakistan–China Relations," 7.
48. Syed Fazl-e-Haider, "Singapore Takes Over Pakistani Port," *Asia Times Online*, February 8, 2007; www.atimes.com/atimes/South_Asia/IB08Df03.html. The seven-year concession has recently been enhanced by declaring Gwadar a "tax

free" zone for ten years. "Gwadar Port Declared Tax Free Zone for Ten Years," *News*, May 21, 2009.

49. Chaturvedy, "Interpreting China's Grand Strategy."
50. Xinjiang is 2,500 km away from Gwadar, whereas China's eastern ports are 4,000 km away from the country's western province.
51. Pakistan's total expected revenue from Gwadar over a forty-year period is between $17 billion and $31 billion. Haider, "Singapore Takes Over."
52. "Gwadar Port Has Strategic Implications for India: Indian Naval Chief," *Daily Times*, January 23, 2008; www.dailytimes.com.pk/default.asp?page=2008%5C01%5C23%5Cstory_23-1-2008_pg7_53.
53. Tarique Niazi, "Gwadar: China's Naval Outpost on the Indian Ocean," *Jamestown Foundation*, February 28, 2005; and Haider, "Baluchis, Beijing," 96, 99.
54. "New Iranian Port to Hurt Gwadar Port's Prospects," *Daily Times*, September 15, 2003.
55. See, for example, "Strategic Shift in South Asia," *Jane's Defense Weekly*, January 29, 2003; http://india.indymedia.org/content/2003/02/3192.shtml.
56. Syed Fazl-e-Haider, "Pakistan, Iran Sign Gas Pipeline Deal," *Asia Times Online*, May 27, 2009; www.atimes.com/atimes/South_Asia/KE27Df03.html.
57. "Pakistan Asks China to Join IPI Gas Line," *United Press International*, April 17, 2008; www.upi.com/Business_News/Energy-Resources/2008/04/17/Pakistan-asks-China-to-join-IPI-gas-line/UPI-47951208444864/.
58. Christopher J. Pehrson, "String of Pearls: Meeting the Challenge of China's Rising Power across the Asian Littoral," *Strategic Studies Institute*, US Army, 6; available at www.strategicstudiesinstitute.army.mil/pubs/display.cfm?pubid=721.
59. Hassan, "Pakistan's Gwadar Port," 48.
60. Hassan highlights this possibility in a discussion of US interests in the Gwadar project. See ibid., 46–50.
61. For a similar view on the complex alliance structure developing in South Asia, see Ejaz Haider, "Pakistan and the 'Alliance Maze,'" *Himal*, September 2006; www.himalmag.com/component/content/article/1541-Pakistan-and-the-%E2%80%98alliance-maze%E2%80%99.html.
62. For a detailed discussion on the incentives for Pakistan to avoid "doing more," see Moeed Yusuf, "Rational Institutional Design, Perverse Incentives, and the US–Pakistan Partnership Post-9/11," *Defense against Terrorism Review* 2, no. 1 (Spring 2009): 15–30; www.tmmm.tsk.tr/publications/datr3/02_Moeed%20Yusuf.pdf.
63. Pakistan has already been alleging for some time that Indian intelligence is funneling unrest in Balochistan by assisting the secessionist Balochistan Liberation Army. It has also reportedly passed on a dossier containing evidence of the same to the Indian authorities. "RAW Camps in Balochistan," *Dawn*, August 31, 2004; "The RAW Dossier," *Dawn*, July 23, 2009.

CHAPTER 7

CHINA AND THE INDIAN OCEAN

New Departures in Regional Balancing

JINGDONG YUAN

INTRODUCTION

China's perspectives on security developments and its growing interest in the Indian Ocean have been informed and influenced by three sets of key considerations. First, China's perceived maritime interests have expanded and constitute an increasingly crucial component of the country's overall economic development due to the rising international trade portion of its gross domestic product (GDP) and its growing energy and raw materials imports. Second, Beijing sees a "Malacca Dilemma" in the form of a potential bottleneck or, at a minimum, a node of extreme vulnerability should one or more hostile states seek to block transits of energy and other resources headed to China. And finally, as its dependence on and stakes in access to maritime traffic continue to rise, China is witnessing an expanding internal debate about whether it is a continental or maritime power and, to the extent that it is the latter, how a balance can be struck between developing the necessary naval capabilities in order to assert China's maritime rights and interests and not causing unnecessary alarm in the Indian Ocean region (IOR).

This chapter seeks to provide some preliminary analysis of Chinese perspectives on the growing importance of the Indian Ocean and how Beijing develops strategies to promote its diplomatic and commercial interests in and with the region, particularly its energy security. The following section briefly summarizes China's growing demands for oil and its increasing dependence on its imports. This is followed by a discussion of the rising importance of the IOR for China and Beijing's strategies to maintain and expand ties to a number of countries critical to safeguarding transports of its energy supplies. The chapter then reviews and assesses an emerging debate in China on the desirability and feasibility of pursuing the status of a sea power to protect its growing maritime rights and interests. It concludes by arguing that, despite the uncertainty and challenges of ensuring undisrupted energy and trade flows, Beijing has so far determined that diplomacy and stable relationships with key powers such as India and the United States may better serve its interests than other alternatives, including an open pursuit of blue water naval capabilities.

CHINA'S GROWING DEMANDS FOR RESOURCES

China's economy has registered an average of 9–10 percent annual growth rate over the past three decades. Its GDP surpassed Japan's in 2010 and reached $4.7 trillion in 2011, making the country the second-largest economy in the world.[1] Despite the global economic downturn in 2008, China continued to attract significant inflows of foreign direct investment, which reached $105.7 billion in 2010.[2] Likewise, its foreign exchange reserves reached $3.181 trillion by the end of 2011, up from $2.39 trillion in 2009.[3] One recent study predicts that China will overtake the United States as the world's number one economy by 2025.[4]

China's phenomenal economic growth over the past three decades has been marked by an export-oriented industrial policy and facilitated by its ever-growing economic interdependence and integration at both the global and regional levels. As a result, a significant portion—close to 60 percent of the total—of China's GDP is represented by its international trade ($2.62 trillion of $4.42 trillion in 2008), with approximately 85 percent of Chinese international trade being seaborne.[5] By 2006 China's maritime economy accounted for 10 percent of Chinese GDP (about $270 billion), and by 2011 the Chinese government had announced three new maritime economic development zones as part of its twelfth Five-Year Plan.[6]

As discussed in chapter 1, fueling this growth has been China's growing and insatiable appetite for raw materials and resources—in particular, energy.[7] As of 2010 China was the world's second-largest oil consumer after the United States, with an estimated total consumption of more than 8 million barrels per day (b/d). China became a net oil importer in 1993, and in 2010 imported 4.8 million b/d.[8] At the current rate of growth (around 8–10 percent annually), China is projected to import 7.1 million b/d by 2015 and 13.1 million b/d by 2030, representing 80 percent of its projected oil consumption.[9]

This growing dependence on energy imports raises serious security issues for policymakers in Beijing. Oil price hikes could drive up total costs of production and fuel inflation. Potential and real disruption of transportation of oil supplies could seriously affect economic growth, leading to loss of employment. China's pursuit for oil also drives up international prices.[10] With its own oil fields already matured and overdrilled, its dependence on global oil supplies would likely continue to rise. In response to these growing demands, China's national oil companies have been busy securing oil supplies, developing oil fields in foreign countries, and diversifying sources of supplies by moving into the Central Asian markets.[11] Overconcentration of supply sources and dependence on potential choke points for oil transportation are but two imminent concerns for Beijing.

THE IMPORTANCE OF THE INDIAN OCEAN

With 74.9 million square kilometers, the Indian Ocean is the third-largest ocean in the world. It is strategically situated, connected with some of the world's most important oil (and trade) transport lines: the Strait of Hormuz, the Malacca Strait, the Suez Canal, Bab el-Mandeb (Djibouti-Yemen), and the Horn of Hope. The Malacca Strait alone accounts for sixty-five thousand ships annually. Of the globe's seaborne trade, 50 percent travels through the Indian Ocean, of which about 20 percent are energy resources. Two-thirds of the global oil reserves and an estimated 40 percent of the world's offshore oil production are located in and come from the IOR. Because of its growing importance in both maritime security and global energy transports, the Indian Ocean has attracted increasing attention from major powers.[12] In recent years it has also become a hotbed for international piracy, threatening maritime commerce in one of the world's busiest arteries.[13]

The Indian Ocean's strategic importance is by no means a recent discovery. For more than three hundred years, the Indian Ocean has been an arena of great power competition. According to Chinese analysts, Napoleon's ambition was to control the Indian Ocean as the first step toward global hegemony. Britain and Russia collided in Afghanistan over their attempts to control the Indian Ocean. Japan and Nazi Germany had planned to achieve victories in the Pacific and European theaters, respectively, and link up in the Indian Ocean. And the late twentieth century witnessed superpower rivalry in Afghanistan.[14]

As the largest country in the region, India has always regarded the Indian Ocean as its backyard and has extensive security interests that stretch from the Strait of Malacca to the Strait of Hormuz and from the coast of Africa to the sea-lanes of western Australia. Renowned Indian strategic thinker and historian K. M. Panikkar emphasized the crucial importance of India's need to control the Indian Ocean in the early days of independence. However, it was not until the end of the Cold War that India began to devote more resources and debate to its naval strategy and capabilities.[15] The 2004 Indian Maritime Doctrine and the 2007 Maritime Military Strategy make it clear that India's maritime interests are in no small measure influenced by recognition of its unique geographical location and the important role it is entitled to and should play. This impacts its strategy; thus it is no surprise that the official Indian document is unequivocal in asserting that "by virtue of our geography, we are . . . in a position to greatly influence the movement/security of shipping along the [sea lines of communication] SLOCs in the [IOR] provided we have the maritime power to do so. Control of the choke points could be used as a bargaining chip in the international power game, where the currency of military power remains a stark reality."[16]

Given its unique geographic location and the growing recognition of the critical importance of the Indian Ocean to its strategic and commercial interests, India naturally is concerned with the activities of external powers—most prominently, the United States and China.[17] Indeed, from New Delhi's perspectives, China's interests in the Indian Ocean are not a recent phenomenon but have deep roots and have long reflected Beijing's strategic intentions.[18] In that context, New Delhi has always been wary of Beijing's efforts, in particular its defense ties with countries in the region, which range from visits by ranking People's Liberation Army (PLA) officers to Chinese arms sales, and the People's Liberation Army Navy (PLAN) activities such as naval port calls and joint exercises.[19] And reports in 2008 about China's construction of a new naval base on the Hainan Island that could house more than twenty submarines have caused significant concerns in India.[20]

According to Chinese analysts, India has been implementing the so-called Indian Ocean dominance strategy since the early 1990s by establishing absolute military supremacy over countries in the region and deterrence against attempts by major maritime powers to extend influence or establish outposts in the region.[21] They note that New Delhi's ambitious maritime strategy is driven by its traditional and newfound interests in the Indian Ocean, including regional dominance and protection of energy supplies. The extent to which it can control or aspire to control the Indian Ocean will be countered by US interests in the region, which range from freedom of navigation and control of the Persian Gulf to the need to guarantee logistic support of its antiterrorism military operations in Afghanistan. In recent years New Delhi and Washington have forged close ties and expanded cooperation in a number of areas; however, differences and even potential conflicts remain between the two countries. For one thing, the United States seeks balance of power and opposes dominance by any power in the Indian Ocean.[22]

Nonetheless, Beijing is attentive to what it sees as New Delhi's ambitions for building a blue water navy by 2015: a fleet of 145 oceangoing surface ships capable of operating beyond the Indian Ocean. The Indian Navy has shifted from its past doctrine of active defense to a new one of offensive defense to move beyond the Indian Ocean. Chinese media suggest that India has the ambitious plan to control the Strait of Malacca with its eastern naval command and Project Seabird, which includes the consolidation and expansion of the Kadamba naval base to control the Indian Ocean. India maintains two important overseas territories, the Andaman Islands and the Nicobar Islands, that can be used to block the Malacca Strait and control the entire Bay of Bengal. Once India controls the area, it will control some of the key arteries of the global economy. This could have serious implications for China's energy security.[23] In recent years India has begun to extend its maritime reach to the eastern African coastline with development of the Mauritian islands and a planned intelligence-gathering facility to be opened on a leased island in northern Madagascar.[24]

For this purpose, India has significantly increased its defense budget and lent urgency to its naval buildup. India's defense budget is around $20 billion and is growing. India currently has one aircraft carrier, the INS *Viraat*, and is retrofitting another, the 44,570-tonne Russian *Admiral Gorshkov*. A third and indigenously built carrier was scheduled for commission by 2012, although this date has been moved to 2015.[25] India's naval strategy has also shifted from area control to deep-sea operations. From 1986 to 1991 alone, India purchased eight Silo-class submarines from the former Soviet Union. In January 2004 New Delhi and Moscow entered into a $1.5 billion contract whereby Russia would give the *Gorshkov* to India as a gift while the latter would pay $650 million in retrofitting expenses and would purchase twelve MiG-29 shipborne fighter aircraft and four MiG-29 coach aircraft. India also received a leased nuclear-powered Russian submarine (INS *Chakra*), which is among the most advanced submarines, in early 2012.[26]

Against this background, it is not surprising that China's own interests in the Indian Ocean have been growing in recent years, not the least of which is driven by the need to secure SLOCs for its commerce and farther waterways for uninterrupted energy supplies. Beijing's Indian Ocean strategy therefore aims at forging friendly relationships with countries along these critical transportation routes and developing the ability to neutralize any potential hostile action to choke its energy shipments. Within this context, strategic alliances with Pakistan, Myanmar, Bangladesh (which has immense natural gas reserves), and Sri Lanka have become a critical component of Beijing's new maritime strategy and inform Chinese decisions to expand influence westward toward the Indian Ocean.[27] And Beijing is increasingly concerned with its excessive reliance on oil transport in the Malacca Strait, through which approximately 80 percent of China's 3.19 million b/d in crude oil imports passed in 2007. For this level of dependence, the PLAN does not possess the ability either to protect its tanker fleet or to secure access to critical ports along the routes in the Indian Ocean. Energy security requires free passage from China's coastline to the Indian Ocean, with the Strait of Malacca playing a particularly central role.[28]

CHINA EYES THE INDIAN OCEAN

Chinese activities in the IOR have drawn growing attention to and speculation about Beijing's intentions, in particular by Indian analysts.[29] Some analysts argue that China's strategy toward the Indian Ocean forms part of its grand strategy and long-term objectives of undermining US influence in the region and establishing and consolidating its own.[30] They point to Chinese initiatives over the past decades, in particular Beijing's efforts to establish what has now been described as a "string of pearls" with ongoing and proposed construction of sea ports and pipelines—a nexus of Chinese geopolitical influence or military presence in Indian Ocean littorals: Hainan Island; Woody Island in the South China Sea; Chittagong in Bangladesh; the 1,200-km pipeline from the port of Sittwe in Myanmar to China's Kunming in Yunnan Province; the Gwadar Port in Pakistan; a $1 billion port in Hambantota of Sri Lanka; and the reported (and likely aborted) $20 billion Kra Isthmus in Thailand.[31] In recent years China has provided significant aid to Indian Ocean countries in an effort to secure safe passage of its tanker fleet, which provides more than 80 percent of China's oil as well as 65 percent of India's. New Delhi, not to be outdone, has been active in countering China's moves, successfully beating out the latter to develop a port in Myanmar.[32]

Others view the "string of pearls" as simply motivated by economic necessities, that is, China's growing demands for oil and the need for securing reliable SLOCs. Typically, this could be accomplished through one or both of two ways: to have naval escorts or to develop alternative routes along the Indian Ocean passageway so any disruption would have minimum impact. Until the December 2008 PLAN deployment of naval ships to the Gulf of Aden, Chinese officials tended to disavow any plan to use the military to protect commercial vessels.[33] On the other hand, the latter consideration probably explains why China has been rather active in the past decade in developing and potentially linking various "pearls" in the IOR.[34] Some analysts have suggested that the "string of pearls" is accidental rather than deliberate and far from strategically conceived by Beijing as part of its overall scheme for control and dominance of the region. This being the case, the reactions to the so-called string of pearls and, indeed, some carefully thought-out countermeasures may be based more on myth than on realities.[35]

Clearly, China's growing interest and emerging maritime strategy in the Indian Ocean should be seen as driven by its preoccupation with the SLOCs that affect the security of its energy supplies from the Middle East, from the Gulf region, and increasingly from Africa as well. While the 1980s and 1990s witnessed Beijing's efforts to expand and promote bilateral ties with a number of IOR countries, including economic assistance and conventional arms sales, China recently has become increasingly involved in projects in Myanmar, Pakistan, and

Sri Lanka, among other countries, that appear to be aimed at developing alternative land routes for oil transports should maritime passages be disrupted.[36]

China began to develop close ties with Myanmar in the early 1990s. Beijing provided up to US$1.4 billion in conventional weapons to the military junta in Rangoon. China also reportedly helped Myanmar build a naval base on Hainggyi Island as well as set up intelligence-gathering posts on the Coco Islands in the east Indian Ocean. Presumably, China may be expected to have access to these naval facilities and thus will have projected power capabilities into the Indian Ocean.[37] China's intentions might be to revitalize the wartime Burma Road and hence facilitate its southwestern region's ("Develop the West") economic interactions with South Asian countries and, where nontraditional security is concerned, combat pirates and terrorists that threaten maritime safety and security. However, New Delhi could regard this as potentially threatening to its maritime interests in the eastern Indian Ocean and the Bay of Bengal.[38] It has been suggested that the reason India cozied up with Vietnam and the Association of Southeast Asian Nations (ASEAN), and even with Myanmar, was to counter Beijing's growing influence in the region.[39]

While Beijing maintains an amicable relationship with Rangoon, Myanmar's junta has also been seeking to broaden its external relationship so as not to rely solely on China.[40] India has been making great efforts in courting Myanmar in recent years, after years of policies of isolating the military regime. Some analysts suggest that China and India are now competing for influence over Myanmar, even though Beijing may retain the lead in a wide range of areas, such as access to gas supplies and contracts to build pipelines.[41] In October 2004 the pro-Beijing prime minister Khin Nyunt was sacked, followed by Myanmar's top leader Gen. Than Shwe's visit to India. There was much media speculation that Beijing was losing ground. However, analysts point out that may not be the case because China's influence remains deeply entrenched, as are its strategic interests in the region.[42] During a 2004 visit to Myanmar Chinese vice premier Wu Yi pledged to expand bilateral trade from the current level of $1 billion to $1.5 billion in 2005. And after five years of discussion, construction began in 2010 on oil and gas pipelines running from Myanmar's port city of Kyaukphyu to Kunming, thereby providing China's southwestern region more direct access to Middle Eastern oil.[43] Additionally, the Irrawaddy River waterways have been proposed to link China's Yunnan Province with Myanmar ports on the Bay of Bengal.[44]

The Gwadar port is another strategic point. During his visit to Pakistan in May 2001, then Chinese premier Zhu Rongji announced that China had agreed in principle to help Pakistan to build a new deepwater port at Gwadar in Pakistani Baluchistan. The port construction would entail three phases with twenty three deep-sea ship berths along with new wharves, warehouses, and other facilities.

The first phase, which began in early 2002, was completed by the end of 2004. In March 2007 the port was formally opened. The total cost of the project was estimated at $1.16 billion. Chinese investment in the first phase (2002 to 2005, with three berths completed) amounted to $198 million, with another $200 million committed to building a highway connecting Gwadar and Karachi. The second phase is estimated to cost $526 million with the construction of nine more berths. The port will offer landlocked Central Asia and Xinjiang with access to the Arabian Sea. It could therefore serve as a hedge against US blockade. With its location some 240 miles away from the Strait of Hormuz, where a huge percentage of the world's oil and gas exports flow, Gwadar could be used to monitor maritime activities through this critical choke point. A Pakistani navy chief also describes Gwadar as the country's third naval base after Karachi and Ormara with strategic importance: it is 450 kilometers further from the Indian border than Karachi, which currently handles about 60 percent of Pakistan's seaborne trade and could be vulnerable to potential Indian blockade, as it was during the 1971 Indo-Pakistani War.[45]

China's diplomatic offensives in the IOR have rapidly reached the African continent—with annual trade reaching $107 billion in 2008, more than eight hundred companies operating on the continent, and $12 billion in accumulated investment. Beijing hosted the China–Africa summit in 2006, writing off $10 billion in bilateral debts.[46] Africa provided 32 percent of China's oil imports in 2008.[47] Energy security and access to Africa's rich resources are clearly part of Beijing's renewed interest in and strategy toward the continent.

As will be addressed later, if there is a deliberate Chinese Indian Ocean strategy, it is less about establishing Chinese naval presence and dominance in the IOR and more about how China can use a combination of diplomatic and economic means to influence the littoral states and, to the extent possible and feasible, the development over time of naval power projection capabilities to protect its own maritime interests, should all else fail and should it have to confront hostile security environments with its critical supply lines at stake.[48] Concerns over potential blockades against choke points in the IOR by hostile powers aside, China's Indian Ocean strategy has always been and likely will continue to be informed by its relationships with India, Pakistan, and the smaller South Asian countries. China sees as its right to develop and maintain cordial relationships through trade, investment, and military assistance with states in what New Delhi may regard as its sphere of influence. Indeed, both Beijing's efforts to make inroads in South Asia and New Delhi's Look East Policy reflect the two Asian powers' perceptions of each other's intents and their pursuit of opportunities and relative power.[49] In that context, Sino-Pakistani naval cooperation in recent years has attracted attention, especially from India. Since 2003 the two navies have conducted a series of joint exercises and Beijing has supplied Islamabad with naval ships. China's close ties with Sri Lanka, including its political and military support of Colombo's fight against and eventual victory over the Liberation Tigers of Tamil Eelam and the joint Hambantota Development Zone project, provide Beijing with a growing footprint in the Indian Ocean.[50]

At the moment, China does not have a powerful oceangoing navy. The PLAN's limitation remains telling: it lacks access to ports for refueling, repairing, and replenishing; it has inadequate numbers of at-sea-replenishment vessels; and it has little experience in long-distance operations. Perceived Chinese encroachment into the IOR will incur strong Indian reaction as well as raise suspicion from the United States. At the same time, its unfinished business of unification with Taiwan and the reemergence of a military Japan may continue to keep Beijing's eyes on the bigger prize in East Asia.[51] Even in the IOR, littoral states may not welcome Chinese military presence, including Myanmar.[52] Beijing would rather avoid stoking fear of a "China threat" in the region, and not without good reasons. In the early 1990s Beijing's assertiveness in its claims to sovereignty over the Spratly Islands in the South China Sea, its ongoing military buildup, and the occasional uses of force in asserting its territorial claims (South Vietnam in 1974, Vietnam in 1988) cast a shadow over the Southeast Asian states at a time of uncertain US commitment and military drawdown in the region (e.g., the closing of the Subic and Clark military bases in the Philippines in 1991). It was no accident that the China threat thesis found a receptive audience in Southeast Asia. China has no interest in repeating that mistake and has so far been very careful in crafting a benign image to soften the perceived edges of its emerging maritime strategy in the IOR.[53]

That said, late 2008 witnessed a major development in Chinese naval deployment beyond its traditional near-sea environs. In response to heightened piracy threats to Chinese-flagged cargoes, the PLAN dispatched two destroyers and one supply ship carrying a total crew of about eight hundred off the Somali coast to the Gulf of Aden to participate in international antipiracy patrols. About 20,000 ships pass through the Gulf of Aden annually, including more than 1,265 Chinese commercial vessels, 7 of which were attacked in 2008.[54] The PLAN's Aden expedition drew close attention. Analysts suggested that protection of Chinese seaborne commerce and energy supplies aside, the deployment would provide unique training opportunities for the Chinese navy; at the same time, it also demonstrated its growing confidence and interest in maritime affairs.[55]

BEYOND THE INDIAN OCEAN: CHINA'S PURSUIT OF SEA POWER

The past ten-plus years have witnessed an emerging Chinese debate between two competing interpretations and visions of the defining nature and direction of the country's future power status: whether China is and should remain a continental power or pursue becoming a great sea power. Without a doubt, China's growing integration into the global economy has raised its awareness of its maritime rights and interests, as have its maritime activities. The Chinese economy is heavily dependent on international trade, and continued growth relies on the safe and secure supply of raw materials and energy, especially oil. While Beijing has been paying increasing attention to the IOR, a so-called sea consciousness has been introduced into the pages of Chinese media and academic journals in recent years. "Blue territories" and "invisible boundaries" have become hot topics as China's interest in and dependence on the oceans increase.

Based on the United Nations Convention on the Law of the Sea (UNCLOS), China has more than three million square kilometers in maritime territories under its management, including continental shelves and the three-hundred-mile exclusive economic zones (EEZs) in the East China Sea and South China Sea. Taken together, these vast maritime territories provide potentially enormous resources for China's large population. Oceans provide economic lifelines, serve as platforms for military command of the commons, and could be the high frontier of science and technology, and are therefore fertile grounds for competition and control.[56]

Chinese analysts differentiate between three distinct types of maritime rights for the country: coastal maritime interests and rights; offshore maritime interests and rights; and maritime interests and rights in the high seas. The first covers 18,000 km of coastal lines and an area that contains 40 percent of China's total population and 60 percent of its annual GDP, with major cities and ports. The second refers to areas stretching from Taiwan all the way to the entire South China Sea, the Diaoyu/Senkaku Islands, the Spratlys, and some 6,900 other small islands and atolls. These constitute both strategic shields for China and passageways into the Pacific and Indian Oceans. The third touches regions of increasing and vital importance to China's continued economic growth, regions that provide critical resources, raw materials, and energy supplies, from the Middle East to the Gulf, from the Arabian Sea to the Horn of Africa, and from the Indian Ocean to Latin America.[57]

China has suffered humiliating defeats in the past, and historians argue that one reason was its failure to recognize and develop its sea power. China's defeat in the Sino-Japanese war of 1894–95 was largely attributed to its backwardness in naval power; in contrast, the US emergence as a global power was based to a great extent on its own sea power. Its decisive defeats of the Japanese fleets and its effective control of the western Pacific helped it prevail over Japan in World War II. During the Cold War, the two superpowers engaged in fierce maritime competition, and the current US global strategy of dominance depends significantly on its ability to control the so-called global commons both in space and on the high seas. The conclusion: historically great powers competed for supremacy and focused on the ocean; China's ability to protect its maritime interests and project its power thus requires that it develop and strengthen its naval capabilities.[58] As keen students of Alfred Thayer Mahan, advocates of Chinese sea power argue that there has never been a greater need to raise the nation's awareness of the importance of sea control or the command of the commons to protect one's own rights and to unify maritime rights and sea power.[59]

The past decade has witnessed a growing body of Chinese literature on the following issues: (1) the concept, characteristics, and functions of China's maritime rights and the differentiation of three separate terminologies: *haiyang shili* (maritime capabilities), *haiyang quanyi* (maritime rights and interests), and *haiyang quanli* (sea power, both hard and soft power); (2) whether China should develop a strong sea power represented by a strong navy, and how to protect China's blue national territory; (3) how China should solve its maritime disputes with other countries; and (4) the path to developing China's sea power, its principles and difficulties.[60] Ni Lexiong, a professor in Shanghai's Eastern China Science and Engineering University and perhaps one of the most ardent advocates for China's sea power, provides the following rationales: (1) international trade is an important component of the nation's economy; (2) national economy depends on SLOC, which is a maritime lifeline; (3) overseas investment and free trade areas are essential; (4) the protection of maritime rights and interests rely on military power; (5) threats to China's economy security interests are not confined to the continent but extend to maritime interests.[61]

However, Ye Zicheng, a professor of international relations at Beijing University, maintains that China's fundamental interests have always been and will remain anchored on land; sea, space, and cyber power in the end serve the interests of land power. Continental power is more permanent, while sea power is temporal and less sustainable over time. In the final analysis, command of commons—land or sea—will ultimately depend on changing geopolitics and the ability to adapt. For China, Ye argues, focusing on land is critical to its strategy of peace and development. Like Mearsheimer, Ye emphasizes the importance of land power as the basis and foundation of all other power and capabilities, from cyberspace to maritime. China's external environment for peaceful development depends on the stability of the Eurasian heartland, which is the departure point of China's policy.[62]

Other analysts argue that China should develop limited maritime power, which should focus on regions of immediate concern and should not constitute a challenge to US maritime dominance; pursuing maritime power has the potential to stoke "China threat" fear in the region and trigger a strong US response.[63] With the end of the Cold War and the relief of pressure of threats from land, it becomes increasingly important to focus on China's maritime interests and the development of necessary resources and capabilities to protect such interests. China's growing economy depends on securing its maritime rights; territorial disputes with some neighboring countries pose serious challenges. Nontraditional security challenges are also on the rise, such as maritime terrorism, drug trafficking, transnational crimes, and piracy. This does not mean that China should compete with other powers for maritime hegemony, but only for its legitimate rights.[64]

While most would submit that the country has never been more secure regarding land invasions, China's unique geographical position makes it at once easily accessible to maritime resources and vulnerable to being blocked by foreign powers. The two island chains in particular cut off that natural connection to the outside world, which can easily be threatened under uncertain circumstances. However, there is lack of consensus among Chinese analysts on the significance of the so-called Malacca Dilemma to China's safe transports of oil and energy security. To some, the potential risk of the Malacca Strait being disrupted or even blocked exposes China's vulnerability. For others, more likely threats are disruptions caused by piracy, terrorism, illicit armed attacks and hijacking, and transport accidents during peacetime. The responses to such risks could include better strategic dialogue and cooperation on securing the safe passages of trade and development of alternative routes of transportation.

Short of open hostility or direct military conflicts or war, China is unlikely to face deliberate blockade by a major power.[65] Resorting to military resolution by strengthening naval capabilities could trigger regional reactions and unnecessary suspicion of China's military intentions. Even if a major power were to attempt such blockade or strangulation of Chinese oil imports, such attempts could hardly be easy. Only 10 percent of China's oil imports are carried on Chinese tankers, with the remaining 90 percent on foreign-flagged tankers.[66] With 90 percent of such imports by sea, Chinese-owned tankers deliver less than 20 percent, and the Japanese-registered tanker fleet carries up to 90 percent of its crude. China is expanding its fleet of supertankers from the current twenty-five to ninety by 2015 to transport oil imports critical to the country's continued economic growth.[67]

Chinese leaders from Mao Zedong to Hu Jintao have emphasized the importance of protecting and advancing China's maritime rights and interests. Mao called for building a strong navy (*yizhi qiangda de haijun*). Deng Xiaoping promoted exploration of maritime resources as a critical component of China's economic development strategy. Jiang Zemin pointed out that oceans are critically related to China's economic and security interests and are an important element for the country's sustainable economic development. Hu Jintao calls on the PLAN to shoulder more responsibility not only in protecting China's sovereignty but also in terms of securing and protecting the country's growing maritime rights and interests beyond its coastline and near sea.[68] During a speech in 2003, he specifically referred to the Malacca Dilemma, stating that "certain powers have all along encroached on and tried to control navigation through the strait."[69] In December 2006, attending the PLAN Communist Party congress, Hu stated that China needs a powerful blue navy to uphold its national interests: "We should strive to build a powerful navy [*qiangda de renmin haijun*] that adapts to the needs of our military's historical mission in this new century and at this new stage." In the same speech he also referred to China as a sea power (*haiyang daguo*).[70]

Chinese military leaders echo such sentiments and the historical mission under the new economic and security environments. In a 2007 article in the Chinese Communist Party's flagship magazine *Qiushi*, PLAN commander Adm. Wu Shengli called for a "powerful navy" that should "protect fishing, oceanic resource development, and oceanic investigation and tests; maintain the safety of oceanic transportation and the strategic passageway for energy and resources; ensure the jurisdiction of our nation."[71] Gen. Mi Zhenyu and Gen. Li Jijun, both former vice presidents of the PLA Academy of Military Science, call for greater recognition of the importance of oceans to China's national interests and advocate the strengthening of the navy.[72]

The Chinese government in recent years has issued various laws and documents as a reflection of its growing recognition of maritime rights. For instance, the eleventh Five-Year Plan states that the country needs "to strengthen the protection of islands ... improve the demarcation of maritime areas, regulate the orderly use of the sea," and "develop in a focused way the resources in the exclusive economic zone, continental shelf, and international seabed." The 2006 Defense White Paper states that the PLAN is charged with developing a "gradual extension of strategic depth for offshore defensive operations." Chinese maritime laws and regulations include the following: National Regulation on Uninhabited Islands (June 2003; jointly issued by the State Oceanic Administration, the Ministry of Civil Affairs, and the PLA); Exclusive Economic Zone and Continental Shelf (January 1998); and Law of the Territorial Sea and the Contiguous Zone (February 1992).[73]

Chinese media and commentators argue that the West, and in particular the United States, often exaggerates Chinese military capabilities, intending to stoke fears of a growing Chinese threat.[74] They note recent reports by the US government and intelligence community that deliberately and publicly highlighted China's ambition to build a blue water navy to operate in the open ocean beyond the Taiwan Strait. They also argue that, contrary to the allegation that China's growing submarine capability is posing a threat to US maritime interests, it is the United States that is posing a new threat in the region by strengthening its naval presence in the western Pacific with the redeployment of three nuclear-powered *Los Angeles*–class subs to Guam and the transfer of four *Ohio*-class SSBNs from the Atlantic Fleet to the Pacific Fleet.[75]

Chinese analysts note that with globalization and growing maritime interests, many powers are now paying more attention to building up their naval capabilities, especially those that enable power projection for deep-sea operations. The

Indian Navy's plan to develop aircraft carrier-centered blue water capabilities, stretching all the way from the Strait of Hormuz to the South China Sea, is but one example.[76] Chinese analysts call for a naval development plan and strategy befitting China's objectives in asserting its maritime rights and exploring maritime resources while at the same time developing and maintaining harmonious relationships with other maritime powers. This would include the exercise of sovereignty over one's maritime national territory; having jurisdiction over and developing one's contiguous zones, EEZs, and continental shelf; carrying out (and escorting) sea-lane transportation; and developing and using resources, all of which require the development of a strong and oceangoing navy.[77]

Nonetheless, some Chinese analysts point out the growing importance of sea and maritime interests in the development of China's overall military capabilities. They argue that China should transition from its status as a traditional land power to one capable of pursuing and defending its maritime geo-strategic interests.[78] Some Chinese analysts have argued for a blue water navy and power projection capabilities commensurate with China's growing international role and reflecting the country's increasing dependence on overseas oil and its need to secure crucial SLOCs.[79] Indeed, in recent years, China has built up its naval capabilities through the acquisition of Russian destroyers and Russian *Kilo*-class diesel attack submarines—of which it purchased twelve at a cost of more than $1.6 billion—as well as through domestic production of the new SSBN and attack submarines. The latter have included the new nuclear-powered *Shang*-class (Type 093) SSN attack submarine and new *Yuan*-class nuclear-powered (Type 041) and *Song*-class diesel-powered (Type 039/039G) attack submarines. Between 1995 and the end of 2007, at least thirty-one of the above five classes of submarines were planned to have been built or procured and commissioned. These will supplement, rather than replace, China's aging *Ming*- and *Romeo*-class diesel-powered attack subs.[80]

If the place of maritime rights and interests in the country's economic and national security policymaking has been elevated, how is one to accomplish the goals and objectives set by policymakers, and where should the navy's role be? In China's specific case, how and to what extent can the PLAN be deployed as the primary component of its emerging maritime security strategy? To date, the PLAN remains a coastal and—at best—an offshore to near-sea navy. This in turn is related to and affects the evolution of different scenarios. The first is what type of navy China is going to build, and whether this will be based on the Mahanian vision of sea control or a limited version with Chinese characteristics. Second is the issue of what messages, concerns, and threats such developments will send and how they will be perceived, and whether maritime confrontation then becomes inevitable between China and the United States or between China and other regional powers such as India and Japan, and how such rivalry can be managed if not avoided. Third is how China, with a strong navy, will manage its relationship with its neighboring countries and, in particular, for the purpose of this chapter, handle its ties with the Indian Ocean nations. These remain unanswered.[81]

To date, the choices between a blue water navy that focuses on aircraft carrier groups and submarines thus far remain biased toward the latter due to a combination of political-diplomatic and technical-financial considerations. For some Chinese analysts, whether a country will pursue and own aircraft carriers has less to do with its financial capabilities than where and how its national interests inform that decision. However, they do note that India's aircraft carrier development reflects its maritime strategy of securing its interests in the Indian Ocean, offshore control, and expansion beyond the Indian Ocean.[82]

At the same time, most Chinese analysts continue to urge that China's maritime strategy should remain one of "near-sea offense and deep-sea defense."[83] The latter strategy is based on China's near-term objective of preventing Taiwanese independence and blocking US intervention to support such a development, as well as on recognition of the practical limits of China's current and projected naval capabilities. Recognizing that China has unresolved territorial disputes with a number of Southeast Asian countries and that the contested areas may contain oil and gas resources, such a strategy would also enable China to defend its sovereignty and maritime economic interests in this arena.

Disputes over the Spratly Islands in the South China Sea began to emerge in the 1980s, especially after the signing of UNCLOS in 1982. The reported rich deposits of maritime resources, including oil and natural gas, led to scrambling for atolls and islets in the South China Sea and disputes among six claimants—Brunei, China, Malaysia, the Philippines, Taiwan, and Vietnam.[84] While Beijing sought to improve relations with ASEAN, its assertiveness in sovereignty claims almost derailed such efforts. The construction of shelters on the disputed Mischief Reef was seen by some contenders as an act of aggressiveness. In addition to strengthening its claims to the disputed territories, China's South China Sea policy also reflected its growing interest and ambitions in extending its influence and, as a result, its greater efforts in developing a navy that could go beyond coastal defense.[85]

Chinese assertiveness in its claims over the Spratly Islands was informed both by its strong sense of sovereignty and territorial integrity and by more pragmatic economic security considerations such as securing a peaceful external environment for economic development and protecting the country's economic interests, including protecting its land, air space, and territorial waters. The growing attention to maritime interests and the cultivation of a "conception of sea as territory" (*Haiyang guotuguan*) reflect both a recognition of the potential of maritime resources for national economic development and a realization that China must enhance its ability to protect its perceived maritime territories. One Chinese analyst suggested: "To make sure that such [maritime] resources are fully tapped and utilized, China needs to ensure the security of its maritime economic activities. A strong naval defense is essential to reducing the threat posed by seaborne smuggling and piracy to China's tariff incomes, ocean fishery and marine transportation."[86]

Chinese analysts argue that the reason that China cannot resolve the South China Sea issue is due to its weak navy, especially its open-ocean (*yuanyang*) operating and control capabilities. The ratio of major surface battle ships is low compared to those of other navies. Some essential components either remain underdeveloped or are nonexistent. Most notable among those are aircraft carriers, naval maritime satellites, early-warning systems, and long-distance precision strike capabilities. This also affects China's interest in the area, where 80 percent of its oil imports come through; 60 percent of the cargoes going through the Strait of Malacca are Chinese vessels.[87]

The PLAN's mission, therefore, is not just coastal areas but also toward blue navy posture and expansion of scope of maritime strategic defense; however, for the time being, the goals seem to be rather modest and focus on control of China's adjacent waters and a sea-denial capability within the first island chain by 2010–20. A regional navy will be down the road that in theory could meet China's growing maritime interests. Others suggest that China may have a much more ambitious plan, with PLAN officers talking about three oceangoing fleets that cover the East China Sea, the western Pacific, and the Indian Ocean and the Strait of Malacca. Should the PLAN adopt a "far sea" strategy, it would have major implications for the future development of its naval capabilities and far-reaching impacts on the Indian Ocean.[88]

While analysts may be debating these points of strategy, it appears that China's current naval order of battle will leave the PLAN little choice but to focus on the near-sea option, rather than deploy a powerful blue water surface fleet.[89] Chinese naval development priorities have strongly favored submarines over aircraft carriers, given the latter's high cost and technological complexity as well as the political issues carriers would raise because of the major threat they would pose to regional states.[90] Along this line, Chinese maritime focus will remain on the offshore or near-sea areas that extend to include the Taiwan Strait, the latest Department of Defense report on Chinese military power to the contrary. The PLAN's likely midterm ambition (ten to fifteen years) could lead it to pursue capabilities that go up to and even beyond the so-called second island chains and possibly the Malacca Strait. Any ventures toward deep seas, including the Indian Ocean, will largely be a function of how the Taiwan Strait and the South China Sea issues are managed and resolved. In sum, while current Chinese discussions and debates on maritime strategy recognize the critical link between interests, rights, and naval capabilities, these remain by and large aspirations for the time being.[91]

However, while the PLAN's general orientation has remained unchanged, there is growing recognition of the multiple roles that the PLAN's submarine force must play; thus, China is developing and procuring different types of submarines for maritime blockade, near-sea offensive operations, and survivable nuclear second-strike operations. Indeed, the last mission has received strong support for a number of years, with Adm. Liu Huaqing, former vice chairman of China's powerful Central Military Commission (1989–97) and the PLAN commander (1982–87), one of its key proponents.[92] China's no-first-use policy, which requires that it maintain an ability to survive a nuclear first strike, also elevates the importance of developing a reliable SSBN deterrent force.[93]

Although the United States is obviously concerned with these growing Chinese capabilities—the attack submarines, for example, could significantly complicate US offensive naval operations in a future Taiwan Strait crisis—the new *Jin*-class SSBN could have a more positive effect by potentially increasing bilateral nuclear stability in such a confrontation. Chinese analysts have expressed concern that at present China's land-based retaliatory systems may be vulnerable to US preemptive attack with conventional weapons, a situation that could lead China to use these missiles early in a crisis, before they might be lost.[94] A sea-based deterrent would be less vulnerable to preemption and could reinforce China's no-first-use policy, reducing the risk of sudden escalation to the nuclear level. However, beyond nuclear deterrence, and with regard to developing China's power projection capabilities in anticipating its ever-growing maritime interests and the need to protect its rights, the Chinese navy will have to address the issue of platforms. The aircraft carrier issue not surprisingly has surfaced and become the focus of discussions in the aftermath of the PLAN Gulf of Aden dispatch and the marking of the navy's sixtieth anniversary. It is back on the agenda, and the debate is increasingly passing the point of "whether" to focus on "how" and "when."[95]

CONCLUSION

There is no doubt that the Indian Ocean is increasingly on Chinese policymakers' radar screen. The country's growing dependence on SLOCs for secure and reliable supplies of critical raw materials and energy is key to China's continued economic growth and prosperity. The fact that energy security and economic security became important considerations in Beijing's overall foreign policy strategies means that such interest will only grow.

The IOR holds a particular place in China's emerging maritime strategy, given its unique position in the global arteries of commercial transports and, more critically for China, the large volumes of its trade and energy imports through the Indian Ocean and the Straits of Hormuz and Malacca. The "Malacca Dilemma" and its responses inform Beijing's adoption of hedging strategies by trying to win friends and neutralize potentially hostile forces that could choke its supply lines. In this context, building a string of pearls is more for defensive reasons than driven by deliberate and offensive schemes, still less naval ambitions.

Despite these challenges, Beijing has decided that the optimal strategy for protecting its lifeline remains diplomacy. This includes maintaining stable relationships with India and the United States, which could involve cooperation in SLOC security from antipiracy or joint antiterrorism operations to cooperative energy security.

Over the longer term, and beyond the Indian Ocean prism, are emerging Chinese debates on how the country should redefine itself in the era of globalization and economic interdependence. China's economic future will largely depend on whether and to what extent its newfound maritime interests and rights can be asserted and protected, given the vulnerability it can be exposed to and the gap between what it needs to do and its existing ability. Although strong arguments have been made that China must seek to become a sea power, the jury is out whether the most efficient path to that status is through naval buildup and how that can be accomplished without raising unnecessary attention and un-called-for alarms by countries in the region. Such negative attention could do significant harm to the growing maritime interests China seeks to protect. This balance remains a serious challenge for Beijing's civilian and military leadership.

China is rising in the political, economic, and military spheres, and its policies are increasingly having important impacts on regional and global developments. Managing China's rise and facilitating its integration into the existing international system without the typical repercussions and instability that were associated with past eras of power transition poses a serious challenge for the United States and other major powers in and interested in the Indian Ocean. A policy that seeks cooperation in energy security, safe and secure SLOCs against international piracy and potential shipping accidents, and the development of multilateral maritime security institutions would go a long way toward mitigating misunderstanding and misperceptions on the one hand and avoiding major conflicts on the other. Clearly, Washington holds great stakes in regaining its leadership role in promoting multilateral efforts to address the multiple challenges that the international system faces and managing peace and stability in the IOR in cooperation with all the important stakeholders—China included.

NOTES

1. David Barboza, "China Passes Japan as Second-Largest Economy," *New York Times*, August 15, 2010; www.nytimes.com/2010/08/16/business/global/16yuan.html?pagewanted=all.

2. Xinhua, "China's R&D Spending Surges," February 22, 2012; www.china.org.cn/china/2012-02/22/content_24704247.htm; Central Intelligence Agency, *The World Fact Book: China*, accessed February 24, 2012; https://www.cia.gov/library/publications/the-world-factbook/geos/ch.html; and "Foreign Direct Investment in China in 2010 Rises to Record $105.7 Billion," *Bloomberg News*, January 17, 2011; www.bloomberg.com/news/2011-01-18/foreign-direct-investment-in-china-in-2010-rises-to-record-105-7-billion.html.
3. Andrew Batson and Jason Dean, "Quarterly Foreign-Exchange Reserves Surge," *Wall Street Journal*, July 16, 2009; http://online.wsj.com/article/SB124762045424342595.html; and Lingling Wei, "China's Forex Reserves Decline," *Wall Street Journal*, January 14, 2012, http://online.wsj.com/article/SB10001424052970204542404577157852552391774.html.
4. Albert Keidel, *China's Economic Rise—Fact and Fiction*, Policy Brief No. 61 (Washington, DC: Carnegie Endowment for International Peace, July 2008); www.carnegieendowment.org/files/pb61_keidel_final.pdf.
5. Dipanjan Roy Chaudhury, "China: Boosting Maritime Capabilities in the Indian Ocean," Worldpress.org, August 23, 2007, www.worldpress.org/Asia/2908.cfm; and CIA, *World Fact Book: China*.
6. Sun Xiaohua, "Report: 10% of GDP Comes from Sea," *China Daily*, April 10, 2007; www.chinadaily.com.cn/china/2007-04/10/content_846707.htm; and Liu Shuguang, "China's Marine Economy: Opportunities for International Cooperation?" *RSIS Commentaries*, October 25, 2011; www.rsis.edu.sg/publications/Perspective/RSIS1542011.pdf.
7. International Crisis Group, *China's Thirst for Oil*, Asia Report No. 153, June 9, 2008.
8. "Country Analysis Briefs," Energy Information Administration (EIA), US Department of Energy, May 2011; www.eia.gov/countries/cab.cfm?fips=CH.
9. International Energy Agency, *World Energy Outlook 2007: China and India Insights* (Paris: OECD/IEA, 2007), 168.
10. Zha Daojiong, "China's Energy Security: Domestic and International Issues," *Survival* 48, no. 1 (Spring 2006): 179–90.
11. Peter Cornelius and Jonathan Story, "China and Global Energy Markets," *Orbis* (Winter 2007): 5–20; Heinrich Kreft, "China's Quest for Energy," *Policy Review* 139 (October–November 2006): 61–70; and David Zweig and Bi Jianhai, "China's Global Hunt for Energy," *Foreign Affairs* 84, no. 5 (September–October 2005): 25–38.
12. Martin Walker, "Indian Ocean Nexus," *Wilson Quarterly* (Spring 2008): 21–28; and Donald L. Berlin, "Neglected No Longer: Strategic Rivalry in the Indian Ocean," *Harvard International Review* 24:2 (Summer 2002): 26–31.
13. "The Indian Ocean: The Most Dangerous Seas in the World," *Economist*, July 19, 2008, 57–58.
14. Zhang Wenmu, "Shijie baquan yu yinduyang [World Hegemony and the Indian Ocean]," *Zhanlue Yu Guanli* [*Strategy and Management*], no. 4 (2001): 13–23; Yu Fengliu, "Shijie baquan weihe zongxiang kongzhi yinduyang [Why Have Global

Hegemons Always Wanted to Control the Indian Ocean]?" *Dangdai Haijun* [*Modern Navy*], no. 4 (2008): 15–19; and Emrys Chew, "Crouching Tiger, Hidden Dragon: The Indian Ocean and the Maritime Balance of Power in Historical Perspective," Working Paper No. 144 (Singapore: S. Rajaratnam School of International Studies, October 2007).

15. Harsh V. Pant, "India in the Indian Ocean: Growing Mismatch between Ambitions and Capabilities," *Pacific Affairs* 82, no. 2 (Summer 2009): 279–97; and James R. Holmes and Toshi Yoshihara, "India's 'Monroe Doctrine' and Asia's Maritime Future," *Strategic Analysis* 32, no. 6 (November 2008): 997–1011.
16. Government of India, *Indian Maritime Doctrine*, INBR 8 (New Delhi: Integrated Headquarters, Ministry of Defence [Navy], April 25, 2004), 64, cited in James R. Holmes and Toshi Yoshihara, "China and the United States in the Indian Ocean," *Naval War College Review* 61, no. 3 (Summer 2008): 44.
17. Eric S. Margolis, "India Rules the Waves," US Naval Institute *Proceedings* (March 2005): 66–70; Gurnam Singh, "China and the Indian Ocean Region," *China Report* (May–June 1984): 15–23; and Geoffrey Kemp, "The East Moves West," *National Interest* (Summer 2006): 71–77.
18. Donald L. Berlin, "India in the Indian Ocean," *Naval War College Review* 59, no. 2 (Spring 2006): 58–89; Holmes and Yoshihara, "China and the United States"; and Pant, "India in the Indian Ocean."
19. Gurpreet S. Khurana provides extensive lists of these activities in "China's 'String of Pearl' in the Indian Ocean and Its Security Implications," *Strategic Analysis* 32, no. 1 (January 2008): 1–39. See also Rahul Bedi, "India Expresses Concern at China's Visit to Coco Islands," *Jane's Defence Weekly*, August 13, 2008.
20. Richard D. Fisher Jr., "China's Naval Secrets," *Asian Wall Street Journal*, May 5, 2008, 13; and Siddharth Srivastava, "China's Submarine Progress Alarms India," *Asia Times*, May 9, 2008; www.atimes.com/atimes/South_Asia/JE09Df02.html.
21. Yin Fang, "Cong diyuan zhengzhi lilun kan xinshiji de yindu haiyang zhanlue [India's Maritime Strategy in the New Century from the Perspective of Geo-Politics]," *Jiefangjun Waiguoyu Xueyuan Xuebao* [*Journal of PLA University of Foreign Languages*] 24, no. 5 (September 2001): 102–5; and Xu Hua, "Yindu zhongshi haiyang junshi weishe [India Emphasizes Maritime Deterrence]," *Xiandai Junshi* [*Conmilit*], April 2000, 54–56.
22. Zhen Li, "Yindu de haiyang zhanlue ji yinmei zai yinduyang de hezuo yu maodun [India's Maritime Strategy and Indo-US Cooperation and Conflict in the Indian Ocean]," *Nanya Yanjiu Jikan* [*South Asian Studies Quarterly*], no. 1 (2005): 113–20; and Song Zhihui, "Meiyin zai yinduyang shangde boyi dui shuangbian guanxi de Zhiyue yu tuidong [US-India Maneuverings in the Indian Ocean and the Impacts on Bilateral Ties]," *Nanya Yanjiu Jikan* [*South Asian Studies Quarterly*], no. 3 (2008): 22–26, 77.
23. Hu Qingliang, "Yindu haiyang zhanlue jiqidui zhongguo nengyuan anquan de yingxiang [India's Maritime Strategy and Its Impacts on China's Energy Security]," *Nanya Yanjiu Jikan* [*South Asian Studies Quarterly*], no. 1 (2008): 21–25, 83; Chen Jihui, "Yindu haijun yaoguan maliujia [INS Wants to Control Malacca

Strait]," *Huanqiu Shibao* [*Global Times*], March 1, 2006, http://world.people.com.cn/GB/14549/4152188.html; and Lai Yang, "Yindu quanmian tisheng junshi shili [India Enhances Overall Military Capabilities]," *Shijie Xinwenbao* [*World News Journal*], March 4, 2008, http://gb.cri.cn/12764/2008/03/04/2945@1964796.htm. See also "India's Project Seabird and the Indian Ocean's Balance of Power," *IntelliBriefs*, July 20, 2005, http://intellibriefs.blogspot.com/2005/07/indias-project-seabird-and-indian.html.

24. Steven J. Forsberg, "India Stretches Its Sea Legs," *US Naval Institute Proceedings* (March 2007): 38–42.
25. "India's Naval Posture: An Assessment," *Military Technology* 30, no. 2 (February 2006): 28–33; and "India Will Have Two Aircraft Carrier Strike Forces by around 2015," *Times of India*, January 20, 2011.
26. Luo Xiaobing and Ou'yang Zhao, "Yindu shuze induyang haibu anfen [A Restless India Even with the Indian Ocean at Its Doorstep], *Dangdai Haijun* [*Modern Navy*], no. 3 (2007): 50–53; Bai Yanlin, "Yindu li 'dahaijun' meng haiyou duoyuan [How Far Away Is India from Its Dream of 'Great Navy']?" *Dangdai Haijun* [*Modern Navy*], no. 2 (2008): 6–11; and Wen Jiafeng, "Yindu jiangzai mingnian jieshou shousou erzhi alakula ji gongji heqiantin [India to Receive First Russian-Made Akula-Class Nuclear Submarine in Coming Year]," Zhongguo Guofang Keji Xinxiwang, July 5, 2008; http://mil.eastday.com/m/20080705/ula3695774.html.
27. Tarique Niazi, "The Ecology of Strategic Interests: China's Quest for Energy Security from the Indian Ocean and the South China Sea to the Caspian Sea Basin," *China and Eurasia Forum Quarterly* 4, no. 4 (2006): 97–116; and Lee Jae-hyung, "China's Expanding Maritime Ambitions in the Western Pacific and the Indian Ocean," *Contemporary Southeast Asia* 24, no. 3 (December 2002): 549–68.
28. Marc Lanteigne, "China's Maritime Security and the 'Malacca Dilemma,'" *Asian Security* 4, no. 2 (May 2007): 143–61; Zhao Hongtu, "'Maliujia kunju' yu zhongguo nengyuan anquan zaisikao [The 'Malacca Dilemma' and Second Thoughts on China's Energy Security]," *Xiandai Guoji Guanxi* [*Contemporary International Relations*], no. 6 (2007): 36–42; and James Holmes, "China's Energy Consumption and Opportunities for US–China Cooperation to Address the Effects of China's Energy Use," Testimony before the US-China Economic and Security Review Commission (Washington DC: US–China Economic Security Review Commission, June 14, 2007).
29. "Into the Wide Blue Yonder," *Economist*, June 7, 2008, 53–54; and Khurana, "China's 'String of Pearls.'"
30. David Walgreen, "China in the Indian Ocean Region: Lessons in PRC Grand Strategy," *Comparative Strategy* 25 (2006): 55–73.
31. Christopher J. Pehrson, *String of Pearls: Meeting the Challenge of China's Rising Power across the Asian Littoral* (Carlisle, PA: Strategic Studies Institute, US Army War College, July 2006); Sudha Ramachandran, "India Chases the Dragon in Sri Lanka," *Asia Times Online*, July 10, 2008; www.atimes.com/atimes/South_Asia/

JG10Df03.html; and Vijay Sakhuja, "China-Bangladesh Relations and Potential for Regional Tensions," *China Brief* 9, no. 15 (July 23, 2009): 10–12.

32. Gavin Rabinowitz, "India, China Jostle for Influence in Indian Ocean," *USA Today*, June 7, 2008; www.usatoday.com/news/world/2008-06-07-2762331882_x.htm; Graham Lee, "China Seeks Burmese Route around the 'Malacca Dilemma,'" *World Politics Review*, February 20, 2007; www.worldpoliticsreview.com/article |.aspx?id=562; and Chaudhury, "China."
33. He Huifeng, "Port Projects in Indian Ocean 'Not Strategic,'" *South China Morning Post*, June 19, 2008, 6.
34. Pehrson, *String of Pearls*.
35. James R. Holmes and Toshi Yoshihara, "China's Naval Ambitions in the Indian Ocean," *Journal of Strategic Studies* 31, no. 3 (June 2008): 377–78; and Lawrence Spinetta, "Cutting China's 'String of Pearls,'" *US Naval Institute Proceedings* 132, no. 10 (October 2006): 40–42.
36. John W. Garver, "Development of China's Overland Transportation Links with Central, Southwest and South Asia," *China Quarterly* 185 (2006): 1–22.
37. Michael Richardson, "China-Burma Ties Upset Neighbors," *International Herald Tribune*, April 7, 1995, 4. See also Andrew Selth, "Burma, China and the Myth of Military Bases," *Asian Security* 3, no. 3 (September 2007): 279–307; and William Ashton, "Chinese Naval Base: Many Rumors, Few Facts," *Asia-Pacific Defence Reporter* (June–July 1993): 25.
38. "Asia's Navies: Into the Wide Blue Yonder," *Economist*, June 7, 2008: 53–54; and Sameer Suryakant Patil, "New Sun on the Horizon: The Rise of the PLA Navy," *China Report* 43, no. 4 (December 2007): 521–29.
39. J. Mohan Malik, "Sino-Indian Rivalry in Myanmar: Implications for Regional Security," *Contemporary Southeast Asia* 16, no. 2 (September 1994): 137–56.
40. Andrew Selth, "Burma and Superpower Rivalries in the Asia-Pacific," *Naval War College Review* LV, no. 2 (Spring 2002): 43–60.
41. Ashild Kolas, "Burma in the Balance: The Geopolitics of Gas," *Strategic Analysis* 31, no. 4 (July 2007): 625–43; and Jürgen Haacke, *Myanmar's Foreign Policy towards China and India*, Adelphi Papers 381 (London: Routledge, June 2006).
42. Robert Sutter, "China-Southeast Asia Relations: Progress with Limitation," *Comparative Connections*, January–March 2006; Mohan Malik, "Regional Reverberations from Regime Shake-up in Rangoon," *Asia-Pacific Security Studies* 4, no. 1 (January 2005): 1–4; and Sudha Ramachandran, "Yangon Still under Beijing's Thumb," *Asia Times*, February 11, 2005; www.atimes.com/atimes/South east_Asia/GB11Ae01.html.
43. C. S. Kuppuswamy, "Sino-Myanmar Relations and Its Impact in the Region," Paper 4357 (Noida, India: South Asia Analysis Group, March 2, 2011); Bruce Vaughn and Wayne M. Morrison, *China-Southeast Asia Relations: Trends, Issues, and Implications for the United States*, CRS Report for Congress, Updated April 4, 2006: 23–24; Zha Daojiong, "Oil Pipeline from Myanmar to China: Competing Perspectives," *RSIS Commentaries*, July 24, 2009; and "China to Myanmar Pipelines," *Straits Times*, November 20, 2008.

44. Garver, "Development of China's Overland Transportation," 11–14.
45. David Montero, "China, Pakistan Team Up on Energy," *Christian Science Monitor*, April 13, 2007; www.csmonitor.com/2007/0413/p06s01-wosc.htm; Ziad Haider, "Baluchis, Beijing, and Pakistan's Gwadar Port," *Georgetown Journal of International Affairs* 6, no. 1 (Winter 2005): 95–103; Garver, "Development of China's Overland Transportation"; Tarique Niazi, "Gwadar: China's Naval Outpost on the Indian Ocean," *China Brief* 5, no. 4 (February 15, 2005); www.jamestown.org/single/?no_cache=1&tx_ttnews[tt_news]=3718; and Steve Inskeep, "Karachi Calling!" *NPR Morning Edition*, June 1, 2008; www.npr.org/templates/story/story.php?storyId=91007621.
46. Xinhua, "China-Africa Trade Up 45% to $107 Billion," *China Daily*, February 11, 2009; www.chinadaily.com.cn/china/2009-02/11/content_7467460.htm; and Walker, "Indian Ocean Nexus." For a more sanguine view of China's relationship with Africa, see Serge Michel, "When China Met Africa," *Foreign Policy* 166 (May–June 2008): 38–46.
47. ICG, *China's Thirst for Oil*, 40.
48. James R. Holmes and Toshi Yoshihara, "Soft Power at Sea: Zheng He and Chinese Maritime Strategy," *US Naval Institute Proceedings* 132, no. 10 (October 2006): 34–38.
49. On Sino-Indian rivalry in the Indian Ocean from a historical perspective, see John W. Garver, *Protracted Contest: Sino-Indian Rivalry in the Twentieth Century* (Seattle: University of Washington Press, 2001), ch. 10. On Chinese views of India's Look East Policy, see Zhao Gancheng, "Yindu 'dongxiang' zhengce de fazhan ji yiyi [The Evolution and Implications of India's Look East Policy]," *Dangdai Yatai* [*Contemporary Asia-Pacific Studies*], no. 8 (2007): 10–16, 64.
50. Itamar Y. Lee, "Deepening Naval Cooperation between Islamabad and Beijing," *China Brief* 9, no. 13 (June 24, 2009): 11–13; and Vijay Sakhuja, "Sri Lanka: Beijing's Growing Foothold in the Indian Ocean," *China Brief* 9, no. 12 (June 12, 2009): 7–10.
51. Andrew S. Erickson, "The Growth of China's Navy: Implications for Indian Ocean Security," *Strategic Analysis* 32, no. 4 (July 2008): 655–76; and Holmes and Yoshihara, "China's Naval Ambitions in the Indian Ocean."
52. Selth, "Burma, China and the Myth of Military Bases."
53. Holmes and Yoshihara, "Soft Power at Sea."
54. Mark McDonald, "China's Navy to Join Pirate Patrols," *New York Times*, December 26, 2008; www.nytimes.com/2008/12/26/world/asia/26china.html.
55. Mingjiang Li, "China's Gulf of Aden Expedition and Maritime Cooperation in East Asia," *China Brief* 9, no. 1 (January 12, 2009): 5–8.
56. Liu Zhongmin, "Zhongguo guoji wenti yanjiu shiyuzhong de guoji haiyang zhengzhi yanjiu shuping [An Analytical Review of Scholarship on International Maritime Politics in China's International Studies Researches]," *Taipingyang Xuebao* [*Journal of Pacific Studies*], no. 6 (2009): 78–89; "Zhuanti baodao: jinglue 'lanse guotu' [Special Report: Managing 'Blue Territories']," *Liaowang Xinwen Zhoukan* [*Outlook News Weekly*], September 4, 2006: 20–29; "Fengmian huati:

haiyang: lanse de jiaozhuo [Cover Story: Ocean: the Blue Competition]," *Shijie Zhishi* [*World Affairs*], no. 22 (2007): 16–23; and Zhang Wei, "Guojia haishang anquan lilun tanyao [Discussion on National Maritime Security Theories]," *Zhongguo Junshi Kexue* [*China Military Sciences*] 20, no. 1 (2007): 84–91.

57. Wang Shumei, Shi Jiazhu, and Xu Mingshan, "Lvxing jundui lishi shiming, shuli kexue haiquanguan [Carry out the Historical Mission of the Armed Forces and Establish the Scientific Concept of Sea Right]," *Zhongguo Junshi Kexue* [*China Military Science*] 20, no. 2 (2007): 139–46.
58. Xu Qi, "Maritime Geostrategy and the Development of the Chinese Navy in the Early Twenty-First Century," translated by Andrew S. Erickson and Lyle J. Goldstein, *Naval War College Review* 59, no. 4 (Autumn 2006): 46–67; Zhang Wenmu, "Sea Power and China's Strategic Choices," *China Security* 2, no. 2 (Summer 2006): 17–31; and Zhang Wenmu, "Xiandai zhongguo xuyao xinde haiqunguan [Contemporary China Needs New Thinking on Maritime Power]," *Huanqiu shibao* [*Global Times*], January 12, 2007, 11.
59. Shi Jiazhu, *Haiquan yu Zhongguo* [*Seapower and China*] (Shanghai: Shanghai sanlian shushe, 2008); Shi Chunlin, "Jin shinianlai guanyu zhongguo haiquan wenti yanjiu shuping [A Review of Research on China's Sea Power in the Past Decade]," *Xiandai Guoji Guanxi* [*Contemporary International Relations*], no. 4 (2008): 53–60; and Li Yihu, "Cong hailu erfen dao hailu tongchou—dui zhongguo hailu guanxi de zaishenshi [Sea Power and Land Power: From Dichotomy to Overall Plans—A Review of the Ties between Chinese Sea Power and Land Power]," *Xiandai Guoju Guanxi* [*Contemporary International Relations*], no. 8 (2007): 1–7.
60. Shi, "Review of Research on China's Sea Power"; and Zhang Wenmu, "Lun zhongguo haiquan [On China's Sea Rights]," *Shijie Jingji yu Zhengzhi* [*World Economics and Politics*], no. 10 (2003): 8–14.
61. Ni Lexiong, "Cong luquan dao haiquan de lishi biran [The Historic Destiny from Land Power to Sea Power], *Shijie Jingji Yu Zhengzhi* [*World Economics and Politics*], no. 11 (2007): 22–32.
62. Ye Zicheng, "Cong Dalishiguan kan diyuan zhengzhi [Viewing Geopolitics from Broader Historical Perspectives]," *Xiandai Guoji Guanxi* [*Contemporary International Relations*], no. 6 (2007): 1–6; Ye Zicheng, "Zhongguo de heping fazhan: luquan de huigui yu fazhan [China's Peaceful Development: The Return to Continental Power and Its Development]," *Shijie Jingji yu Zhengzhi* [*World Economics and Politics*], no. 2 (2007); and John J. Mearsheimer, *The Tragedy of Great Power Politics* (New York: W. W. Norton, 2001).
63. Liu Zhongmin, "Guanyu haiquan yu daguo jueqi wenti de ruogan sikao [Some Thoughts on Sea Power and the Rise of Great Powers]," *Shijie Jingji Yu Zhengzhi* [*World Economics and Politics*], no. 12 (2007): 6–14; Tang Shiping, "Zailun zhongguo de dazhanlue [On China's Grand Strategy: A Second Take]," *Zhanlue Yu Guanli* (*Strategy and Management*), no. 4 (2001): 29–37; and Zhang Wenmu, "Zhongguo guojia anquan zhexue [Chinese National Security Philosophy], *Zhanlue Yu Guanli (Strategy and Management)*, no. 1 (2000): 24–32.

64. Lu Binyan, "Cong dalu dao haiyang—zhongguo diyuan zhengzhi de zhanglue quxiang [From Continent to Ocean: The Strategic Orientation of China's Geopolitics]," *Taipingyang Xuebao* [*Journal of Pacific Studies*], no. 5 (2009): 62–67; Feng Liang and Duan Tingzhi, "Zhongguo haiyang diyuan anquan tezheng yu xinshiji haishang anquan zhanlue [Characteristics of China's Maritime Geostrategic Security and Its Maritime Security Strategy in the New Century]," *Zhongguo Junshi Kexue* [*China Military Sciences*] 20, no. 1 (2007): 22–29; and Mi Zhenyu, "Luelun woguo de haifang, haiquan he haiyang anquan [On Our Country's Maritime Defense, Maritime Rights and Maritime Security]," *Zhongguo Shehui Kexue Neikan* [*Chinese Social Sciences*], no. 1 (2008): 62–69.
65. Andrew Erickson and Lyle Goldstein, "Gunboats for China's New 'Grand Canals'? Probing the Intersection of Beijing's Naval and Oil Security Policies," *Naval War College Review* 62, no. 2 (Spring 2009): 43–76; and Zhao, "'Malacca Dilemma.'"
66. Gabriel B. Collins and William S. Murray, "No Oil for the Lamps of China?" *Naval War College Review* 61, no. 2 (Spring 2008): 79–95.
67. Andrew Erickson and Gabe Collins, "Beijing's Energy Security Strategy: The Significance of a Chinese State-Owned Tanker Fleet," *Orbis* (Fall 2007): 665–84; and David Lague, "China Begins Expanding Its Supertanker Fleet," *International Herald Tribune*, May 16, 2007.
68. Mi, "On Our Country's Maritime Defense," 67–68.
69. Ian Storey, "China's Malacca Dilemma," *China Brief* 6, no. 8 (April 12, 2006): 4–6, www.jamestown.org/programs/chinabrief/single/?tx_ttnews[tt_news]=31575&tx_ttnews[backPid]=196&no_cache=1.
70. "China: Hu Calls for Powerful, Combat-Ready Navy," *Washington Post*, December 27, 2006; www.washingtonpost.com/wp-dyn/content/article/2006/12/27/AR2006122701888.html.
71. "OSC Analysis: China: Debate Suggests Leadership Differences over 'Sea Power' Concept," Open Source Center, August 9, 2007; available at https://www.opensource.gov.
72. Li Jijun, "Qiangbian gufang, jinglue haiyang [Strengthen Border Defense, Manage and Use Oceans]," *Zhongguo Shehui Kexue Neikan* [*Chinese Social Sciences*], no. 1 (2008): 58–61; and Mi, "On Our Country's Maritime Defense."
73. "OSC Analysis: China: Measures Aim to Bolster Control of Maritime Interests," Open Source Center, May 31, 2007; available at https://www.opensource.gov.
74. "Meijun cheng zhongguo zhengzai jianzao zhiyao wusou xinxing heqiantin" [US Military Claims China Is Building at Least Five New-Type Nuclear Submarines], *Dongfang junshi* [Eastday Military Section], March 5, 2007, http://mil.eastday.com/eastday/mil1/m/20070305/ula2660279.html; and Yong Bo, "Zhongguo haijun wenbu shixiang 'shenlan'" [Steady Advance of China's Navy Toward the 'Deep Blue'], *Jinbao yuekan* [*Ching Pao*], April 2007, 31–33.
75. Li Yutong, "Meiguo haijun heqiantin jinchang zai zhongguo donghai nanhai huotong" [US Nuclear Subs Regularly Move around East China Sea and South

China Sea], *Xinlang junshi* [*Sina Military News*], January 16, 2007; http://jczs.news.sina.com.cn/2007-01-16/1213426920.html; and Hu Gang and Lu Ping, "Meijun xiang weidu zhongguo heqiantin [US Military Seeks to Encircle Chinese Nuclear Subs]," *Guoji zaixian* [*China Radio International*], March 9, 2007, http://gb.cri.cn/12764/2007/03/09/2225@1488396.htm.

76. Liu Yijian, "Zhihaiquan lilun ji fazhan qushi [Theory of the Command of the Sea and Its Trends of Development]," *Zhongguo Junshi Kexue* [*Chinese Military Science*] 18, no. 1 (2005): 42–46.
77. Shi, *Seapower and China*; and Shi, "A Review of Research."
78. Xu, "Maritime Geostrategy"; and Zhang Wenmu, "Sea Power and China's Strategic Choices," *China Security*, Summer 2006, 17–31.
79. See, for example, Zhang Wenmu, "Jingji quanqiuhua yu zhongguo haiquan [Economic Globalization and China's Maritime Rights]," *Zhanlue yu Guanli* [*Strategy and Management*], no. 1 (2003): 86–94.
80. Lyle Goldstein and William Murray, "Undersea Dragons: China's Maturing Submarine Force," *International Security* 28, no. 4 (Spring 2004): 161–96; Eric A. McVadon, "China's Mature Navy," *Naval War College Review* 59, no. 2 (Spring 2006): 90–107; and Andrew S. Erickson and Andrew R. Wilson, "China's Aircraft Carrier Dilemma," *Naval War College Review* 59, no. 4 (Autumn 2006): 13–45.
81. James R. Holmes and Toshi Yoshihara, *Chinese Naval Strategy in the 21st Century* (London: Routledge, 2007); and David Lei, "China's New Multi-Faceted Maritime Strategy," *Orbis* (Winter 2008): 139–57.
82. Erickson and Wilson, "China's Aircraft Carrier Dilemma"; Ian Storey and You Ji, "China's Aircraft Carrier Ambitions," *Naval War College Review*, 57, no. 1 (Winter 2004): 76–93; and Dong Ruifeng and Liu Demao, "Hangmu zheshe guojia zhanlue liyi [Aircraft Carriers Reflection of National Strategic Interests]," *Liaowang Xinwen Zhoukan* [*Outlook News Weekly*], no. 15 (April 9, 2007): 54–56.
83. Jin Heng, "Zhongguo haijun ying jianchi jingong yuanfang zhanlue" [PLAN Should Maintain a Near-Sea Offensive and Deep-Sea Defensive Strategy], *Jianchuan zhishi* [Naval & Merchant Ships], May 2007; http://mil.eastday.com/m/20070528/ula2864541.html.
84. Mark J. Valencia, *China and the South China Sea Disputes*, Adelphi Papers No. 298 (London: IISS, 1995); and Mark J. Valencia, "Building Confidence and Security in the South China Sea: The Way Forward," in *Non-Traditional Security Issues in Southeast Asia*, edited by Andrew T. H. Tan and J. D. Kenneth Boutin, 528–69 (Singapore: Select Publishing for the Institute of Defence and Strategic Studies, 2001).
85. Lee, "China's Expanding Maritime Ambitions"; and Shee Poon Kim, "The South China Sea in China's Strategic Thinking," *Contemporary Southeast Asia* 19, no. 4 (March 1998): 369–87.
86. Yan Xuetong, "Economic Security, Good-Neighbor Policy Emphasized in Post-Cold War Security Strategy," *Xiandai guoji guanxi* [*Contemporary International Relations*], no. 8 (August 1995): 23–28.

87. Du Wenlong and Shi Zhikun, "Wohaijun yuanyang zuozhanli youxian shi nanhai wenti nanjiejue shouyao yuanying [Limited Naval Long-Distance Combat Capabilities a Prime Reason Why Spratly Issue Difficult to Resolve]," *Bingqi Zhishi* [*Ordinance Knowledge*], no. 1 (2008); http://mil.news.sina.com.cn/p/2008-01-21/0840482058.html.
88. Nan Li, "The Evolution of China's Naval Strategy and Capabilities: From 'Near Coast' and Near Seas' to 'Far Seas,'" *Asian Security* 5, no. 2 (May 2009): 144–69; You Ji, "Dealing with the Malacca Dilemma: China's Efforts to Protect Its Energy Supply," *Strategic Analysis* 31, no. 3 (May 2007): 467–89; and Gordon Fairclough, "As China Grows, So Does Its Long Neglected Navy," *Wall Street Journal*, July 16, 2007, A1.
89. Jin, "PLAN Should Maintain a Near-Sea Offensive."
90. Wang Xiangsui, "Zhongguo zhuanjia: hangmu yibu shiying dangjing haijun zhanlue xuqu" [Chinese Expert: Aircraft Carrier No Longer Meeting the Strategic Needs of Today's Navy], *Zhongguo guofangbao* [*China's National Defense*], May 31, 2007; http://mil.eastday.com/m/20070531/u1a2873959.html.
91. James R. Holmes and Toshi Yoshihara, "A Chinese Turn to Mahan?" *China Brief* 9, no. 13 (June 24, 2009): 8–11.
92. See Liu Huaqing, *Liu Huaqing huiyilu* [*The Memoir of Liu Huaqing*] (Beijing, People's Liberation Army Press, 2004).
93. Zhang Wenmu, "Zhongguo qianghua haiquan yingyuxian fazhan heqiantin" [China Should Put Nuclear Sub Development as a Priority to Strengthen Its Sea Power], *Guangmingwang*, June 5, 2007; and "Zhongguo yingyongyou gengxianjin de heqiantin" [China Should Possess More Advanced Nuclear Subs], *Jianchuan zhishi* [*Naval & Merchant Ships*], February 23, 2005.
94. Jing-dong Yuan, "Beyond No-First-Use: Recent Chinese Discussions of Nuclear Strategy," *WMD Insights*, September 2006; www.wmdinsights.org/I8/I8_EA3_BeyondNoFirstUse.htm.
95. Andrei Chang, "Analysis: China to Build Aircraft Carrier," *UPI*, June 4, 2009; www.spacewar.com/reports/Analysis_China_to_build_aircraft_carrier_999.html (accessed on July 27, 2009); "China Confirms It Will Build Aircraft Carrier: State Press," *Taipei Times*, March 24, 2009; and Holmes and Yoshihara, "Chinese Turn to Mahan?"

CHAPTER 8

Redlines for Sino-Indian Naval Rivalry

JAMES R. HOLMES AND
TOSHI YOSHIHARA

INTRODUCTION

It is commonplace for states to sketch "redlines" to signal competitors that they take certain actions only at high and unacceptable cost. Redlines are a kind of threat. As political scientist Thomas Schelling observes, a threat is most effective when the actor issuing it convinces the target of the threat that unacceptable repercussions will flow automatically from the target's own actions.[1] In a sense, then, the actor issuing the threat removes itself from the chain connecting action to reaction. Deterrence is almost self-enforcing, provided that the state drawing the redlines artfully persuades prospective adversaries that it is irrevocably committed to enforcing its will and possesses sufficient wherewithal to do so. Redlines are nothing new to South Asia, where a senior Pakistani officer famously announced a set of redlines that would trigger a nuclear response if breached by India.[2] New Delhi has inscribed its own redlines vis-à-vis Chinese activities in the Indian Ocean, with the goal of deterring Beijing from actions that infringe unacceptably on Indian interests as India interprets them. The result could be an action–reaction dynamic between India and China. Helping manage Sino-Indian interactions is a pressing interest for the United States, which sees the Indian Ocean as the western half of the grand "Indo-Pacific" theater and one of two oceans that engage vital American interests.[3]

It has recently become fashionable to declare that the Indian Ocean is emerging as a new geopolitical locus of great-power rivalry. Writing in *Foreign Affairs*, Robert Kaplan attests to the growing interest in a body of water that has generally suffered neglect over the years, especially when compared to the attention lavished on the Pacific and the Atlantic. Kaplan declares that "the Indian Ocean—the world's third-largest body of water—already forms center stage for the challenges of the twenty-first century."[4] The maritime services of the United States appear to concur with this assessment in the latest US maritime strategy. For the first time in postwar maritime history, Washington reoriented its two-ocean strategy from the Atlantic and Pacific to the Pacific and Indian Oceans. Emerging geopolitical and geo-economic realities documented throughout this volume largely explain this heightened strategic awareness. Yet, while the logic and the rationales underpinning competition in the Indian Ocean have been well treated in academic and policy circles, the processes and mechanisms by which such dynamics might unfold remain largely unexplored. Those inclined to pessimistic forecasts of the South Asian nautical environment tend to assume away the specific sequence of events that could trigger enmity among the maritime powers, particularly between India and China. As such, there is an urgent analytical need to assess the potential escalatory thresholds that, when crossed, could invite a more intense struggle in the Indian Ocean.

Our purpose in this chapter is threefold. First, we consider whether and when the Chinese navy will cross three redlines set by New Delhi, and we will project how India may respond to such an infraction. While some analysts are resigned to Indian Ocean rivalry, we render more granular judgments about the likelihood of such an outcome. In the process we shatter some myths and preconceptions surrounding future Sino-Indian interactions in the maritime domain. Second, we consider the possibility of a self-fulfilling prophecy. The tenor of Indian commentary on China's "string of pearls," Chinese navy counterpiracy operations in the Gulf of Aden, and other Chinese endeavors suggests that New Delhi might perceive a Chinese bid for naval supremacy in the Indian Ocean even if Beijing makes no such bid. In effect, Indians could lower the threshold for competition so low that China cannot help but cross it—even if its force posture and strategy in the region remain static. And third, while our focus is not on US strategy in South Asia, we hint at how the United States can manage any Sino-Indian competition in the interests of preserving the system of seagoing trade and commerce.

OUT LEAPT A MAHANITE!

Commentary on Sino-Indian relations in the Indian Ocean is taking on decidedly ominous overtones. The Asia columnist for *The Economist* magazine attended the May 2009 meeting of the Shangri-La Dialogue, which convened in Singapore under the auspices of the International Institute of Strategic Studies. As "Banyan" tells it, whenever he "prodded a military man from India or China, out leapt a Mahanite."[5] These days the name of Alfred Thayer Mahan—the fin de siècle American sea captain who urged seagoing nations to found "sea power" on the "pillars" of international commerce, merchant and naval fleets, and forward bases—is shorthand for a fatalistic resignation to zero-sum international competition and war on the high seas.[6] Robert Kaplan maintains that "whereas the US Navy pays homage to Mahan by naming buildings after him, the Chinese avidly read him; the Chinese are the Mahanians now."[7] Declares Kaplan, it is not just the Chinese; "his books are now all the rage among Chinese and Indian strategists."[8] Indian scholar Harsh Pant testifies to the "centrality" of Mahan in Indian maritime strategic thought.[9]

There is something to this. Yale University professor Paul Kennedy points to a historical curiosity.[10] Six centuries ago China's Ming Dynasty disbanded the world's most advanced navy, Adm. Zheng He's "treasure fleet," evidently to appease Confucian factions at court that opposed maritime profit making. As it happened, Portuguese explorer Vasco da Gama dropped anchor at the Indian seaport of Calicut scant decades later, an eyeblink by historical standards. Da Gama's voyage ushered in an epoch in which Europeans—Portuguese, Dutch, French, and ultimately British—commanded the Indian Ocean.[11] With command of the sea came control of the national lives of India and other coastal nations, ultimately including China.[12] Asians let control of their maritime periphery pass to outsiders by default, with fateful results.[13]

Today, says Kennedy, the reverse is happening. Europeans are letting their fleets atrophy, in effect relinquishing their claim to sea power. Britain's Royal Navy, which bestrode the world's sea-lanes a century ago, is in danger of dropping to second-class status following the radical cuts recommended in the British government's 2010 Strategic Defense and Security Review. Having decommissioned large numbers of warships to free up funds for two big-deck carriers, the navy now finds the carrier program under scrutiny from the Treasury, as well as from the air force and army, whose service chiefs urge canceling the flattops. Vice Adm. Sir Jonathon Band, the recently retired first sea lord, publicly inveighed against the British government's "sea blindness."[14] The Royal Navy is now smaller than the French navy for the first time since the 1805 Battle of Trafalgar—and even the French navy finds its force structure under severe downward pressure amid the global financial crisis. Barring a very improbable turn of events—say, a dramatic reversal of economic trends or an effort to pool resources, creating a combined European Union navy—the outlook will only worsen. Seldom has Mahan seemed more remote.

Where Kennedy dwells on the material dimension of naval strategy, King's College London professor Geoffrey Till takes a more abstract, almost Hegelian perspective on the different trajectories along which Asian and European navies are tracking. Naval development, that is, takes place in the realm of consciousness as well as in the material world. Till maintains that the West has transcended Mahan, entering a "postmodern," "post-Mahanian" age in which high-seas combat appears almost unthinkable. Upholding the system of globalized trade and commerce, not sending rival battle fleets to the bottom, is the main function of sea power in this view. Battle in the open ocean has given way to force protection, control of littoral seas, projecting power ashore, and preserving "good order at sea." Knitting together "a global maritime community of major stakeholders in the system" takes precedence over traditional rivalry for postmodern navies.[15] Asians, by contrast, inhabit a "modern," "neo-Mahanian" world in which naval war remains a real, deadly possibility. Having endured colonial rule until relatively recent times, Asians guard their sovereignty jealously. "Modern navies," observes Till, "often regard the sea as a frontier needing to be defended individually and exclusively."[16]

For neo-Mahanians, then, fleet-on-fleet battle remains a possibility that must be prepared for in intellectual and material terms. A vocal school of thought in China looks to Mahan for strategic inspiration, viewing sea combat as the arbiter of political and economic disputes. Long stigmatized in China for advocating imperialism and colonialism, Mahan has inspired a flurry of interest in Chinese scholarly and policy circles. Studies parsing terms such as "command of the sea" (*zhihaiquan*) and "command of communications" (*zhijiaotongquan*) have proliferated, while some neo-Mahanians appear spellbound by the American theorist's portrayal of command of the sea as "that overbearing power on the sea which drives the enemy's flag from it, or allows it to appear only as a fugitive."[17] Indeed, this bellicose-sounding phrase is by far the most common Mahan quotation in Chinese commentary. Maj. Gen. Jiang Shiliang sees the contest for "absolute command" of the Asian commons as an elemental fact of life in the region.[18] Beijing's 2004 Defense White Paper is couched in Mahanian-sounding terms, ordering the armed forces to "strengthen the capabilities for winning both command of the sea and command of the air."[19]

If many Chinese scholars and officials regard Mahanian command of the sea as the sine qua non of naval strategy, Indians seize on an evidently apocryphal Mahan quotation on the surpassing importance of the Indian Ocean.[20] Proclaimed an official Indian press release in 2002, "Mahan, the renowned naval strategist and scholar had said over a century ago 'whosoever controls the Indian Ocean, dominates Asia. In the twenty-first century, the destiny of the world will be decided upon its waters.'"[21] Rear Adm. Rakesh Chopra, the one-time head of sea training for the Indian Navy, offered a somewhat less bellicose-sounding but equally evocative version of the quotation at a seminar on maritime history: "Whoever controls the Indian Ocean controls Asia. This ocean is the key to the Seven Seas."[22] Aside from invoking Mahan to stress the importance of the region, however, Indians seldom mention his name. Their misuse of Mahan's words casts doubt on whether they draw useful guidance from his works, but there is no questioning Indian navalists' sincerity about naval preparation.

Till is right to use Mahan as a proxy for traditional naval strategy predicated on combat at sea. Both Indians and Chinese accept the need to compete for favorable geographic positions and diplomatic and economic advantage. Indeed, improving the nation's political and economic standing represents the core of peacetime maritime strategy. And they accept the likelihood of naval war. Determining what constitutes a neo-Mahanian grand strategy for China and India, then, is a matter of some consequence. New Delhi and Beijing interpret Mahan quite differently, to the extent that there *is* a unified interpretation within each nation's strategic community. Nor will they apply Mahanian precepts by rote. They will factor in other sources of strategic thought, their national interests, and the shifting external environment. Importing ideas from abroad, or even from one's forebears, always involves such analysis, interpretation, and synthesis. Certain precepts endure, but no static body of ideas animates strategy.

Combined with other strands of Indian strategic thought, Mahan will prime Indians to look with alarm on the entry of outside navies into the Indian Ocean region (IOR), India's maritime domain, and to enact strategies that will keep India at the forefront of regional power politics. At the same time, Mahan may spur the Chinese to establish a robust naval presence in the region to uphold Chinese commercial interests and, ultimately, Chinese economic prosperity. Now as in his own day, then, Mahan's works lend themselves to zero-sum competition among great seafaring nations. While New Delhi has not sought to bar Chinese entry into the Indian Ocean, it has sketched several "redlines" that, if crossed, will prompt India to step up its fairly leisurely naval buildup. A far different Indian naval strategy and fleet could emerge. We examine three of the most commonly cited triggers for Sino-Indian naval competition:

- A forward deployment of People's Liberation Army Navy (PLAN) nuclear submarines to the Indian Ocean
- A militarized Chinese "string of pearls," or network of Chinese naval stations, spanning the IOR
- A Chinese effort to shut New Delhi out of the South China Sea, complicating India's broader "Look East" policy in Southeast Asia

Our analysis projects likely interactions among the great Asian powers in a strategic environment in flux. As the US Navy's margin of physical superiority diminishes in the IOR, despite the importance placed on the region in the 2007 Maritime Strategy (which vows to stage "credible combat power" there for the foreseeable future[23]), Indians and Chinese may well play out a neo-Mahanian rivalry of their own in regional waters. It behooves American strategists and decision makers to understand the asymmetries these disparate visions are likely to produce and whether and how the United States can manage them.

An Indian Monroe Doctrine

Indian sea-power specialists strike a prickly attitude toward real or perceived encroachment in the IOR. As noted earlier, Indians seemingly draw little substantive guidance from Alfred Thayer Mahan, who merely seems to ratify their preconceived policy preferences. But they do look to nineteenth-century America as one model for how a nonaligned great power can manage its geographic surroundings to ward off outside threats. In particular, they look to the Monroe Doctrine, the 1823 US foreign policy statement that proclaimed the Western Hemisphere off-limits to European territorial expansion or a restoration of European political control over American republics that had newly won independence from the imperial powers. The practical application of this "Monroe Doctrine with Indian characteristics," to borrow the Chinese formula, would likely demand the kinds of policies and maritime strategies that Mahan himself—a "disciple of Monroeism"—would have advocated and applauded.[24] In other words, even if New Delhi does not explicitly invoke or credit the naval theorist, India's rendition of the doctrine will likely rhyme with his writings.

Americans saw the doctrine as a joint defense of North and South America against great-power predations. The threat of European inroads grew over the course of the nineteenth century, as the imperial powers built modern armies and navies, sought out foreign markets and resources, and partitioned much of Africa and Asia among themselves. As US power grew, Americans were prone to interpret the doctrine more forcefully, taking an expansive view of their rights and responsibilities as self-appointed guardian of the New World's independence. In the 1880s the United States set out to build its first modern steam navy. By 1895 the US Navy was strong enough that the Grover Cleveland administration could interpose itself in a border dispute between Venezuela and British Guiana. Secretary of State Richard Olney interpreted the Monroe Doctrine in extravagant terms. He informed Britain that Washington was "practically sovereign" in the Americas, and that its "fiat" was "law" on any matter in which the US leadership saw fit to involve itself. Olney maintained that its combination of moral standing, geographic separation from the great powers, and sheer physical might entitled Washington to such a lofty status.[25]

Clearly, then, each generation of Americans reinterpreted the doctrine as US interests, the strategic environment, and the nation's capacity to project power varied. Several things are worth pointing out about the doctrine. In its earliest form, the doctrine was a statement of principle, an effort to shape the diplomatic environment. The United States was woefully short on the physical means to enforce it. Its navy in particular was too small and too outdated to fend off European navies. But overlapping national interests helped. Great Britain had reasons of its own for keeping rival empires out of the Americas. In effect its Royal Navy acted as co-guarantor of James Monroe's principles. The United States free-rode on British naval mastery for much of the century, concentrating its resources and energies on subduing a continent and building the infrastructure for an industrial economy. And finally the US leadership was open to working with outsiders—even a former enemy like Britain—absent a geopolitical threat. Indeed, in the same message to Congress in which he enunciated his famous doctrine, President Monroe noted that the US Navy and the Royal Navy were jointly patrolling the Caribbean to suppress the slave trade.

The Monroe Doctrine evolved through several phases before Theodore Roosevelt affixed a "corollary" to Monroe's precepts in 1904, asserting a US right to exercise "an international police power" in vital parts of the Western Hemisphere. In practice this meant the Gulf of Mexico and the Caribbean Sea, where the sea-lanes to the isthmian canal would run. Keeping European navies from establishing bases along these shipping routes was vital. In essence, Roosevelt foresaw US administrations' mediating between European creditors and weak Caribbean states that had defaulted on their debts to these creditors. An aggrieved lender typically appealed to its government for redress, whereupon the government sent warships to seize customhouses in the debtor nation, exacting the tariff revenue needed to repay the debt. American observers such as Roosevelt and Mahan feared they might parley temporary possession of Caribbean territory into permanent naval bases along crucial sea communications.

This was no idle worry. In 1897, for instance, Imperial Germany had used the murder of two German missionaries as an excuse to wrest the seaport of Kiaochow from China's Qing Dynasty. Having matured into a strong power, the United States was finally in position to enforce a venerable foreign policy principle. It did so unilaterally and preventively, and it did so with considerable restraint. No shots were fired in the Caribbean basin under the Roosevelt presidency. Roosevelt's America took a relaxed attitude toward fellow great powers, provided they posed no threat to vital US interests. Ultimately the United States took advantage of burgeoning Anglo-German naval competition, ushering even a relatively benign sea power, Britain, out of the Americas. This left the US Navy to police hemispheric seas. Indians regard this as a model for foreign policy and strategy. Consider Prime Minister Jawaharlal Nehru's 1961 speech justifying the use of force to evict Portugal from its longstanding coastal enclave of Goa, along the subcontinent's western coast. Nehru first invoked the Monroe Doctrine saying: "even some time after the United States had established itself as a strong power, there was the fear of interference by European powers in the American continents, and this led to the famous declaration by President Monroe of the United States

[that] any interference by a European country would be an interference with the American political system."[26] Nehru then argued that

> the Portuguese retention of Goa is a continuing interference with the political system established in India today. I shall go a step further and say that any interference by any other power would also be an interference with the political system of India today. . . . It may be that we are weak and we cannot prevent that interference. But the fact is that *any attempt by a foreign power to interfere in any way with India is a thing which India cannot tolerate, and which, subject to her strength, she will oppose. That is the broad doctrine I lay down.*[27] (emphasis original)

Nehru's statement is extraordinarily rich. Several themes are worth stressing. First, while a European presence on the Indian landmass was the prime mover for his doctrine, Nehru took the opportunity to warn *any* external power against taking *any* action anywhere in the region that New Delhi might construe as a threat to the Indian political system. His injunction against outside interference laid the intellectual groundwork for a policy aimed at regional primacy. Indeed, his "broad doctrine" represented a more sweeping injunction against external meddling than the doctrine framed by James Monroe and John Quincy Adams, who left existing European holdings in the hemisphere intact and did not proscribe European interference unless it reinstituted European political control.

Second, notwithstanding the wide scope of his principles, Nehru acknowledged realities of power and geography. Like Monroe's United States, Nehru's India remained weak by most measures. Even so, the prime minister wanted New Delhi to enjoy the discretion to implement his doctrine with greater vigor as Indian national power grew—opening up new political vistas and supplying Indian leaders with new instruments of statecraft.

Third, while removing the Portuguese presence from the subcontinent was his immediate concern, Nehru implied that India could enforce his precepts beyond the subcontinent. It was up to future prime ministers to decide how far beyond. Prime ministers Indira Gandhi and Rajiv Gandhi did just that, invoking his doctrine to justify diplomatic or military intervention in such places as Sri Lanka, Nepal, and the Maldives. One leading commentator, C. Raja Mohan, matter-of-factly states that the Monroe Doctrine is part of Indian grand strategy.[28] Declares Mohan, the "Indian variation of the Monroe Doctrine, involving spheres of influence, has not been entirely successful in the past, but it has been an article of faith for many in the Indian strategic community."[29]

And fourth, Nehru asked no one's permission to articulate a hands-off doctrine. While his doctrine—like the Monroe Doctrine before it—was not international law, which derives its force from the consent of states, it was a unilateral statement of purpose to which New Delhi would give effect as national interests demanded and as national power permitted. India did expel the Portuguese from Goa, applying an exclamation point to Nehru's words.

Over time, if the American case is any indication, fellow Indian Ocean powers may silently acquiesce in India's Monroe Doctrine, lending it a kind of quasi-legal standing, or at least an air of permanence. But their acquiescence will depend on whether New Delhi can replicate the American example, fortifying its comprehensive national power and thus its capacity to uphold its claim to regional leadership. A weak India would stand little chance of fulfilling Nehru's vision of a beneficent great power. Should the Indians eventually align their maritime capability with strategic aspirations, however, then their interactions with other sea powers could very well assume an assertive if not bellicose character. A competitive nautical environment is especially likely if extraregional powers refuse to acquiesce in Indian ambitions, or if New Delhi's presumptions about its dominant place in the Indian Ocean predispose Indians to cast the intentions of other interested actors in the dimmest possible light. Worse, both factors could come into play at the same time—prodding Indian Ocean powers toward an escalatory cycle of competition. It is in this context that the future of Sino-Indian naval dynamics deserves scrutiny.

UNDERSEA DRAGONS IN THE INDIAN OCEAN

Indian officials and scholars are frank about the thresholds that, if crossed by the PLAN, will prompt an Indian naval buildup far more vigorous and more offensive in outlook than the unhurried, fairly complacent efforts at naval development New Delhi has undertaken to date. A former Indian Navy chief, Adm. Arun Prakash, implores New Delhi to acknowledge the Chinese naval threat and take it seriously. "It is time for India to shed her blinkers," declares Prakash, "and prepare to counter PLA Navy's impending power-play in the Indian Ocean."[30] New Delhi's Mahan-, Monroe-, and Nehru-inspired conviction that India should preside over a benign regional order helps explain the redlines inscribed by Indian officials. Thomas Mathew, the deputy director-general of the Institute for Defense Studies & Analyses, a leading Indian think-tank, doubts that China will "countenance a competitor in India." Mathew is apprehensive that "it may already be getting too late" for the Indian Navy to catch up with the PLAN.

Nuclear submarines in particular obsess Indian sea-power thinkers. In 2008, for instance, one officer bluntly told a gathering of Indian and American naval experts in Newport, Rhode Island, that a forward deployment of Chinese nuclear submarines would breach the threshold set by New Delhi. In the spring of 2009, fanning such fears, a Chinese officer reportedly joked that the United States and China should partition maritime Asia. Adm. Timothy Keating, head of the US

Pacific Command, recounted the exchange in a meeting with Indian Navy chief Adm. Sureesh Mehta: "You, the US, take Hawaii East and we, China, will take Hawaii West and the Indian Ocean. Then you will not need to come to the western Pacific and the Indian Ocean and we will not need to go to the eastern Pacific. If anything happens there, you can let us know and if something happens here, we will let you know."[31] Despite such breezy Chinese statements, Indians take them seriously. A high-ranking Indian diplomat frets that "China now displays its military might openly and calls on the commander of the US Pacific Fleet to recognize the Indian Ocean as a Chinese sphere of influence to be managed by Chinese nuclear submarines and aircraft carriers."[32]

Since PLAN carriers remain some way off (reports project that the refitted Soviet flattop *Varyag* will join the fleet in 2012, presumably as a training platform), such worries arise mainly from the disparity between the two navies' submarine construction rates and foreign acquisitions.[33] PLAN submarine construction has outpaced Indian Navy construction by a 3:1 margin since 1995, observes Mathew, while the comptroller and auditor general of India has documented the rapid aging of the Indian Navy submarine force.[34] China, moreover, has devoted substantial resources to the buildup of its conventional and nuclear submarine force since the earliest days of the Cold War. Undersea warfare has long been a strategic forte for Beijing, whereas New Delhi is a relative newcomer to the field. The potential asymmetries are clearly cause for concern.

Curiously, though, Indian navalists rarely specify which kind of Chinese submarine they consider most menacing. Presumably they mean nuclear attack submarines (SSN). At first glance, fleet ballistic-missile submarines (SSBN) would appear most likely to alarm New Delhi, if only because they pack enormous punch with their battery of submarine-launched ballistic missiles (SLBM). But China can already range all of India with its current arsenal of nuclear weapons, consonant with Beijing's deterrent strategy. China's second-generation, road-mobile intercontinental ballistic missiles can fulfill almost all of Beijing's nuclear strike missions against India while maintaining a high level of survivability.

SSBN deployments, consequently, would hold less military value for Beijing than it might seem. SSBN cruises in the Indian Ocean would have important strategic and symbolic import despite their limited military utility, creating the impression that China was bullying India in its own backyard. This could well prompt a political backlash on India's part. New Delhi's propensity to overreact would be particularly acute if India could not respond in kind with its own undersea deterrent patrols in the Indian Ocean or the South China Sea. The immature state of India's SSBN program suggests that such a strategic embarrassment is entirely conceivable. (Only in 2009 did the first Indian SSBN, christened *Arihant*, take to the sea for trials. It did so without working SLBM for armament.[35]) Thus, those in New Delhi predisposed to draw the worst conclusions about China would see the presence of SSBNs as evidence of Beijing's intent to contend for dominance in the region.

On the other hand, nuclear attack submarines can interdict merchant or naval shipping through torpedo or antiship missile attack, conduct antisubmarine warfare (ASW)—it is a commonplace among US submariners that one submarine is the best ASW platform against another—and even project power ashore using conventional or nuclear-tipped cruise missiles. Chinese SSNs could loiter on station for extended intervals, threatening the Indian Navy's control of the sea lines of communication on which India's claim to preponderance in maritime South Asia—its Monroe Doctrine—rests. The aircraft-carrier task forces around which the Indian Navy will be built would be especially vulnerable to undersea warfare. Fitted with land-attack cruise missiles, Chinese SSNs could even strike at Indian Navy bases on the subcontinent.

Chinese attack boats, then, could hold at risk all three elements of Mahanian sea power, namely Indian overseas commerce, commercial and military shipping, and naval stations. SSNs represent a working weapon system, not simply a token of Chinese power cruising off the subcontinent. While scenarios involving a Sino-Indian nuclear exchange can be easily dismissed as the product of an overactive imagination, the prospects of commerce warfare and precision strikes at sea and ashore led by nuclear-powered wolfpacks are far more likely to resonate with Indian strategists.

Or perhaps Indian strategists mingle the SSBN and SSN threats, seeing them as indivisible. Both represent challenges to Indian primacy. The mere fact of forward PLAN submarine deployments would signal, to recall Jawaharlal Nehru's words, a foreign power's attempt to interfere with India—"a thing which India cannot tolerate," that is, and which, "subject to her strength, she will oppose." A more permanent Chinese undersea presence in the Indian Ocean, a maritime arena to which Beijing has paid little attention until recently, would signify an unprecedented strategic turn of events for India. Public perceptions that India had failed to deter Beijing's projection of maritime power into its backyard, or that New Delhi lacked a credible countermove, would very likely magnify the intolerable nature of China's position in the Indian Ocean.

If so, several strategic shifts are probable in New Delhi. First, it will pay new attention to the material dimension of naval strategy. Indian governments will orient naval development efforts increasingly toward ASW capabilities, investing in indigenous and foreign-bought diesel and nuclear attack boats, ASW-capable surface vessels, and fixed- and rotary-wing ASW aircraft. With only six modern diesel boats under construction—of the *Scorpene* class being built at Indian yards under contract with France—bolstering the Indian Navy's ASW force clearly represents an arduous, expensive, time-consuming task. (A contract for an additional six diesel boats is reportedly in the works.[36])

Second, New Delhi will redouble its effort to upgrade Indian industrial capacity, reducing the military's dependence on foreign suppliers like Russia, France, and the United States. This will also cut back on the inefficiencies that invariably arise when using (as the Indian Navy does) an assortment of equipment manufactured by different firms in different countries. Self-sufficiency in defense matters has long been a priority for the Indian military. The urgency military chiefs attach to industrial independence will only grow should the threat environment deteriorate. Since foreign policy success rests in part on a foundation of national power, the fate of India's Monroe Doctrine will be decided at Indian shipyards, aircraft manufacturers, and arms facilities. Whether a defense-industrial sector known for erratic performance can put substance into India's security doctrine, fielding ships, aircraft, and armaments of sufficient quality and in sufficient numbers to hold PLAN submarines at bay, remains an open question.

Third, New Delhi could essay some diplomatic and military maneuvers of its own. India instituted a "Look East" policy in 1992, turning its attention to the South China Sea basin. It did so primarily for economic reasons, in conjunction with its economic liberalization program. But New Delhi could also find political and military value in its eastward turn. Should the PLAN deploy SSBNs in the Indian Ocean, New Delhi's maritime preserve and then the Indian Navy may repay the favor, inaugurating SSBN cruises in China's domain. Turnabout is fair play.

Exploiting historic, cultural, and political affinities there only makes sense from an economic standpoint, but it could also pay dividends should naval rivalry ensue with China. There are military-technical reasons for forward-deploying Indian missile boats. Indian engineers have found it difficult to resolve technical issues relating to nuclear propulsion plants, the range of sea-launched cruise and ballistic missiles, and the payloads these missiles would deliver against Chinese targets. As a practical matter, Indian Navy commanders may find themselves compelled to dispatch missile-firing submarines to the South China Sea—or through the South China Sea into patrol grounds off East Asia—to reach Chinese targets. The geometry of nuclear deterrence will shift accordingly. Not only political imperatives but also military-technological constraints, then, could compel the Indian Navy to operate beyond Malacca. Whether India can effectively meet its strategic needs while managing its relations with Association of Southeast Asian Nations (ASEAN) states, committed as they are to a regionwide nuclear-free zone, remains to be seen.

Again, Indian foreign policy success depends in large measure on industrial capacity, just as it depends on the skill and daring of Indian mariners. Whether the Indian Navy, like the fin de siècle US Navy, can assert local sea control around its periphery preoccupies Indian officials. Misquoted or not, Mahanian theory and Indian threat perceptions promise to raise the political and strategic stakes for New Delhi in the struggle for maritime preeminence.

MILITARIZING THE "STRING OF PEARLS"

Securing beachheads in the Indian Ocean basin represents a precursor to a more vigorous future Chinese strategy in the region, as Indians well know. Forward bases constitute one of three pillars of Mahanian sea power, without which a nation's vessels are like "land birds," unable to fly far from home.[37] Many Indians believe the PLAN is acting on this logic. China has cultivated close ties with South Asian coastal states likely to approve of—or, at a minimum, refrain from objecting to—a Chinese naval presence in their vicinity. Chinese efforts to negotiate basing rights have earned the moniker "string of pearls" in the United States.[38] This term refers to bases and seaports scattered along the sea routes linking the Middle East and Africa with coastal China, augmented by diplomatic relations with states inhabiting these regions. The notion of a string of pearls almost instantly took on an aura of legitimacy, with analysts and officials incorporating it into everyday discourse in the United States and abroad.[39] It has become common parlance if not an article of faith among Indian sea-power analysts, many of whom view it as a Chinese attempt at geographic encirclement.[40]

It is worth pointing out, consequently, that the term is not a Chinese one. US and Indian observers have inferred it not from a coherent national strategy codified in Chinese doctrine, strategic commentary, or official statements but from a pattern of Chinese activities in the region. Beijing can use informal strategic alliances with Myanmar and Pakistan, to name two countries that have granted basing rights, to counterbalance US power, check India's rise, and monitor maritime activities carried on by these maritime competitors.[41] Some Southeast and South Asian states also provide alternative routes bypassing the narrow sea at Malacca. Chinese strategists urge Beijing to build oil pipelines through Myanmar and Pakistan. The more ambitious among them advocate digging a canal across Thailand's Kra Isthmus. While the political merits, technical feasibility, and cost-effectiveness of many such proposals remain doubtful, the interest paid to them suggests an acute sensitivity on Beijing's part to the nation's energy security dilemma.

China, in short, is gradually laying the foundations of a strategic maritime infrastructure that will enhance both its economic prospects in and its military access to the Indian Ocean. Observes Thomas Mathew, "China has quietly obtained a string of naval facilities around India, called the 'string of pearls,'" to facilitate Chinese naval power projection into the IOR.[42] For many Indians, this is simple fact—not a proposition to be put to the test. If it is axiomatic that Beijing is proceeding according to a coordinated national strategy, then it is reasonable for New Delhi to foretell incremental gains in Chinese leverage and presence in the IOR.

And so many Indians do. Says Gurpreet Khurana, "in the longer term, it is not inconceivable for some littorals to even permit China to build dedicated naval infrastructure, like depots for ammunition stores and equipment spares, for use of these facilities as forward operating bases."[43] Such straight-line projections help explain the disproportionate, overwhelmingly negative Indian commentary on the modest PLAN deployment of surface vessels off Somalia for counterpiracy duty. "The People's Liberation Army's decision to deploy its warships to fight piracy in the Gulf of Aden marks the beginning of a major shift in the Indian Ocean balance of power," grouses the respected *Indian Express* newspaper in a typical commentary.[44]

It is notable that the nature and character of military access a host nation grants to an outside power can vary widely, ranging from lightly attended military sites underwritten by informal agreements to massive basing infrastructure codified by treaty. US bases have ranged from comprehensive installations such as Yokosuka to a single submarine tender anchored at Holy Loch, Scotland. To date, Beijing has made little effort to convert the string of pearls into a true network of naval bases, and Chinese officials strenuously disavow any such intention. Speaking on behalf of PLA naval headquarters, for example, Senior Col. Xie Dongpei insists that Sri Lanka merely makes a convenient port of call for Chinese vessels passing through the region. No naval station is in the making, according to Colonel Xie.[45] (It is worth recalling that the Indian military waged a counterinsurgency on Sri Lanka in the late 1980s, in part to deny the United States a base at the port of Trincomalee. Chinese port calls on the island strike a chord with Indians for similar reasons, while the Chinese port project at Hambantota has elicited tart commentary.[46]) Such denials represent Beijing's standard line not only on Sri Lanka but on high-visibility port projects such as Gwadar, a major Chinese-financed facility in western Pakistan.

How can outsiders gauge Beijing's sincerity? Creating a PLAN Indian Ocean squadron with a standing headquarters, shipyards and other facilities for depot-level maintenance, and stockpiles of spares and weapons would telegraph Chinese plans for a bigger, more persistent, and more offensively minded presence than it has ventured to date. As a frame of reference, the Yokosuka naval base in Japan, the homeport of the US Navy's only permanently forward-deployed aircraft carrier, is the most potent symbol of American military presence in Asia. The relatively modest Chinese arrangements in the Indian Ocean pale in comparison. For now, then, it seems safe to say that Chinese strategy in the Indian Ocean reflects aspirations more than near-term realities. Having built the substructure for a base network, Beijing can defer a decision to add the superstructure.

Opening up new diplomatic and military options in a region of vital interest represents simple prudence for China. It bears repeating that, notwithstanding Indian fears, Beijing will lack the capacity for overt naval competition in South Asia for some time to come, while priorities far closer to home will hamper the pace and scope of its activities in the Indian Ocean. The Taiwan question lingers, while China is determined to exert more control of the waters around its maritime periphery, sorting out resource and territorial disputes with neighboring states such as Japan, the Philippines, and Vietnam. Barring the emergence of far more serious threats to seagoing traffic in the Indian Ocean, Beijing must tend to matters in the China seas before mounting a serious push in South Asia, if indeed it decides such a push is necessary. As an interim measure, Chinese diplomats have sought to burnish China's reputation as a benign great power through soft-power diplomacy. They hope this will win legitimacy for a Chinese naval presence in the Indian Ocean.

Any Chinese attempt to transform its web of basing rights in the Indian Ocean into a network of naval bases, akin to the US base network in the western Pacific, will profoundly aggravate Indian perceptions of an external threat—engaging New Delhi's Monroe Doctrine. First, military power will rise in importance for Indian decision makers as conditions degenerate. A Chinese military and naval threat will militate for an Indian response in kind. Second, the imperative to maintain preponderant naval power will spur New Delhi to intensify its naval buildup. At present, the Indian Navy fleet is centered on one small aircraft carrier of 1950s vintage. The navy is pursuing indigenous aircraft carriers with uncertain success. This may suffice while the US Navy rules the waves, and while a PLAN threat remains years distant. It will not suffice once Chinese warships and aircraft establish a sizable presence in India's environs. A carrier fleet of some six to nine flattops organized into three fleets (one on the western coast of the subcontinent, another on the eastern coast, and a third for expeditionary operations outside the Indian Ocean) may ultimately be necessary to assure Indian supremacy should US Navy numbers continue their downward drift.[47] (This assumes that the Indian Navy, like the US Navy, needs three vessels to keep one fully ready for combat service.)

Third, New Delhi will continue and step up its drive for defense-industrial self-sufficiency, freeing itself of the prospect of seeing shipments of weapons and spares halted in wartime (as indeed occurred during the Cold War, souring relations between Washington and New Delhi). Russia and China have remained on good terms since the Cold War—meaning that Indian officials would have cause to fear such a cutoff in a future Sino-Indian naval clash. Fourth, a real Chinese string of pearls would warrant feverish efforts in naval nuclear propulsion. The Indian Navy has never managed to build naval nuclear reactors to power its surface combatants or submarines, extending their range and at-sea endurance. Keeping pace with the PLAN will demand keeping pace in engineering.

And finally, Indian military strategy would have to assume a far more regionally and offensively oriented posture. Under crisis or wartime conditions, New Delhi would presumably have to be prepared to neutralize third-party bases across the Indian Ocean basin from which Chinese naval forces could sortie, thereby cutting off or disrupting critical supplies and logistical support to the PLAN. Operationally, India would need the capacity to conduct sea-based precision strikes ashore with all the sophisticated command-and-control assets that such missions entail. At the same time, the Indian military would likely rely on shore-based, long-range air power and possibly conventionally armed ballistic missiles to bolster the striking power of its naval forces.

The Chinese themselves have set a precedent for the latter option by targeting US bases across the Pacific with nuclear-tipped and conventional ballistic missiles. In any event, a regional conflagration would require unprecedented joint action on the part of the Indians. Politically and diplomatically, such a regional posture would likely prove nettlesome, especially given the dangers of horizontal and vertical escalation. Would India risk a wider regional war against a nuclear-armed Pakistan should Chinese naval forces launch operations from, say, Gwadar? Would New Delhi be willing to countenance the hostile international reaction likely to follow if it attacked or threatened to attack Chinese bases in energy-rich Burma, or in nearby Sri Lanka? The emergence of a more menacing Chinese string of pearls and India's corresponding countermoves would likely add a new and complex set of politico-military dilemmas for New Delhi.

This second scenario in essence represents a broader-based, more intense version of the first, and thus India's strategic response to PLAN submarine deployments would be a subset of its strategy to counter a string of pearls. Sending nuclear submarines into the Indian Ocean on independent cruises is bad enough from New Delhi's vantage point, warranting intensive ASW efforts. But erecting the infrastructure for a PLAN Indian Ocean fleet, presumably made up not only of submarines but of surface combatants, aircraft, and support facilities, would signal that China is in South Asia to stay. In all likelihood, India would reply to a militarized string of pearls with a crash naval construction program of its own, complemented by a far more comprehensive and aggressive contingency plan against Chinese use of Indian Ocean base infrastructure.

SHUTTING INDIA OUT OF THE SOUTH CHINA SEA

Indian officials have not explicitly defined Chinese dominance of the South China Sea as a redline, but it is worth speculating about the strategic effects that might ensue should Beijing try to thwart Indian policy goals east of Malacca. In

1992, consonant with its economic interests and its long-term threat assessments, the Indian government instituted its Look East policy, shifting its largely westward strategic gaze.[48] The policy is predicated on the belief that binding together South and Southeast Asian economies will foster prosperity, stability, and peace. Observes India's *Maritime Military Strategy*, New Delhi's most authoritative statement of how it sees the nautical milieu and the proper responses to it, the Look East policy "is now an essential element of India's foreign policy," and "part of an irreversible process of integration of India's economy with that of South East Asia."[49]

But economic integration has strategic implications, as Indian thinkers well know. Under the policy, which in part constitutes a riposte to Chinese endeavors in the Indian Ocean, New Delhi has begun to court governments in Southeast Asia. Beijing could attempt to block Indian diplomatic outreach, using its own growing diplomatic, economic, and military influence as a lever to dislodge India from the region. This would presumably foreclose a forward Indian Navy strategy in the region, dissuading Southeast Asian coastal states from offering basing rights. The South China Sea, then, is shaping up as a theater for Sino-Indian competition. The extent to which each side uses naval diplomacy to undermine the other's regional clout will indicate the direction Sino-Indian naval rivalry may take.

In Clausewitzian parlance, New Delhi attaches major value to the object of accumulating influence east of Malacca, not only because of historic and cultural affinities but because of a range of pragmatic national interests. Secure sea-lanes, economic integration, and counteracting Chinese influence are some of the interests Indians see at stake to the east. Coping with such challenges merits diplomatic, economic, and military effort commensurate with the value of the political object.[50] With regard to India's Monroe Doctrine, the Strait of Malacca is a rough counterpart to the Panama Canal, the maritime "gateway" to Asia for American commerce and military might that obsessed Alfred Thayer Mahan and Theodore Roosevelt. Malacca is India's gateway to Southeast Asia and to the engines of the global economy residing in Northeast Asia. India's security doctrine predisposes New Delhi to view the South China Sea as a theater of nautical enterprise.

India enjoys certain advantages in the current low-key competition among outside powers for regional influence. New Delhi has regained credibility lost during the economic malaise of the late Cold War. India's reputation suffered among "Asian tigers" such as Thailand, Singapore, and Malaysia during the 1980s, when Southeast Asians saw it as an economically backward power pretending to regional grandeur. Having liberalized its own economy and generated robust annual economic growth, India has restored its standing in the region. It has matched its claims to preeminence with real, quantifiable performance.[51]

China lies closer by than India. It has surpassed India's economic performance since its own economic opening. It enjoys marked geographic advantages, namely a South China Sea coast, common frontiers with the likes of Vietnam, and a forward naval base on Hainan Island. And the PLA is further along with its modernization program. But India has performed well enough by these standards that Southeast Asian governments believe they can rely on it to help maintain the regional equilibrium. They see in New Delhi a counterpoise to China that helps them preserve their liberty of action. Notes Stephen Cohen, "India is welcome in the region as another (and nonthreatening) state, part of a mix of insiders and outsiders that Southeast Asian strategists hope will prevent any one power from dominating the region."[52] Through engagement in the region—including maritime engagement—New Delhi puts Beijing on notice that it can reply asymmetrically to any Chinese meddling in South Asia. For India, soft power—a mode of diplomacy at which India excels—can pay off in hard-power terms.

While Sino-Indian competition has remained harmless to date, with Beijing and New Delhi jockeying for influence and goodwill in the region, events could intervene. A souring of Sino-Indian relations could see the Indian Navy step up its naval deployments in the South China Sea. At the same time, India may seek to raise the profile of its naval diplomacy by stepping up the rate of port visits to and the rigor of its military exercises with Southeast Asian states that are traditionally wary of Chinese influence. Vietnam and Indonesia number prominently among these. More provocatively, New Delhi could outflank Beijing from a new direction by developing even closer naval ties with Japan and South Korea. Diplomatic or military considerations could prompt such moves. As discussed before, China's evident pursuit of basing rights in the Indian Ocean basin would spur Indian countermeasures.[53] India could repay the favor by increasing its visibility in China's own self-declared preserve. Tensions would rise should the Indian Navy commence naval (let alone submarine) patrols in the South China Sea. Having claimed virtually all of the South China Sea as territorial waters—codifying its maritime claims in domestic law in 1992—Beijing would doubtless view Indian warships cruising offshore with alarm.

Should events skew the Sino-Indian relationship toward competition in Southeast Asia, what kinds of capabilities will the Indian Navy need? First, if indeed New Delhi opts for sea-based nuclear deterrence (a likely prospect whose timetable remains unsure), it will need to perfect its nuclear-propelled boats and their armament. Should Indian SSBNs start patrolling the South China Sea, Sino-Indian relations would clearly suffer, as would Indian relations with coastal states. For diplomatic reasons, accordingly, Indian engineers will need to develop missiles of sufficient range to deter Chinese aggression from the relatively safe, politically inoffensive confines of the Indian Ocean. Second, the Indian Navy would need numbers—that is, an expeditionary fleet capable of sustained forward operations, comparable to the US Seventh Fleet. Third, to sustain operations in Southeast Asia or beyond, the navy would need some combination of basing rights in the

South China Sea and underway logistics, embodied in oilers, ammunition vessels, and refrigerated-stores ships. For now, these sustainment capabilities remain out of reach.

If indeed China attempts to lock the Indians out of Southeast Asia, then, New Delhi will have to undertake an effort of unprecedented magnitude and duration to frustrate Beijing's efforts. Its capacity to prevail in such a competition is dubious in light of China's manifold advantages in the region. Even a United States in decline might again find itself the guarantor of last resort for regional security, with New Delhi seeking US help to offset Chinese naval power and Southeast Asians looking for an honest broker.

ASSESSING THE THREE REDLINES

We apply feasibility and risk as the two standard measures to assess the likelihood of China's crossing the three redlines over the next decade. First, China already possesses the wherewithal to deploy its SSBNs and SSNs in the Indian Ocean. Open-source satellite imagery reveals that China has commissioned at least three second-generation *Jin*-class SSBNs that could sortie from the Sanya naval base on Hainan Island. A first-generation *Han*-class SSN reportedly circumnavigated Guam in 2004 before triggering a crisis with Japan by entering Tokyo's territorial waters. China's basing options and improved at-sea training suggest that the PLAN may possess the technical capacity and operational skills to assert its undersea presence west of the Malacca Strait.

The tactical feasibility of widening PLAN patrol grounds, however, must be weighed against the potential strategic risks. Beijing's leadership is surely aware of the provocative nature of such an unprecedented submarine deployment. Indeed, it would likely conjure up memories of the Soviet Union's attempts to demonstrate its global naval prowess in the 1970s, and of the international alarm that Moscow's muscle-flexing triggered. Undersea patrols in the Indian Ocean would not only put India on notice but would certainly compel an American response, in the form of more aggressive patrols, tracking of Chinese submarine activity, and efforts to rebuild US ASW capacity after years of post–Cold War inattention. At the moment, it appears doubtful that the PLAN is prepared or willing to engage in dangerous cat-and-mouse games like those endured by Soviet and American submariners throughout the Cold War, especially in underwater terrain more familiar to Indians.

Second, in contrast to the first scenario, which involves exclusively military options, China's capacity to maintain a robust forward presence in the Indian Ocean remains confined largely to the realm of aspirations. The term "string of pearls" connotes far more coherence than is warranted by the assortment of relationships Beijing has crafted with other South Asian capitals in recent years.

China appears unwilling or unable to exert the leverage necessary to secure guaranteed naval access rights and a more permanent, sizable presence in the Indian Ocean basin. Forward basing almost always involves compromises to the sovereignty of host nations. For postcolonial states of the South Asian littoral, such concessions could prove politically unpalatable. Establishing a network of naval facilities usable in crisis or wartime, moreover, would require Beijing to disavow its longstanding pledge never to leave Chinese troops on foreign soil—a central pillar of its foreign policy.

Diplomatic sensitivities, then, could foreclose basing options similar to those enjoyed by the United States in Asia and Europe. From an operational perspective, forward presence entails major risks. In a major trial of arms, India could either cut off Chinese forward-deployed detachments from follow-on forces based on the mainland, or New Delhi could exercise its own version of antiaccess/area-denial tactics against PLAN units that rely on the pearls for resupply and maintenance. Many of the pearls are within easy reach of Indian forces based on the subcontinent; New Delhi could administer punishing strikes from land and sea while China would have to make do with the limited number of units available in the theater of operations. In short, it is no easy feat for the Chinese to operate in someone else's backyard.

Third, China's ability to shut India out of Southeast Asia is highly questionable. The small and medium-sized states of the region would not be inanimate objects in any hypothetical Sino-Indian tug-of-war. Southeast Asian capitals recognize that they cannot afford to play power politics. Consequently, ASEAN states have pursued a disciplined, prudent strategy of equidistance among the great powers. They have adroitly avoided choosing sides, thereby precluding competitive balancing behavior. Unless New Delhi pursues expansionist ambitions in the South China Sea or other hegemonic objectives, which seems highly unlikely, Beijing would find it difficult to forge an anti-Indian maritime coalition.

Furthermore, as an extraregional power carrying the least historical and strategic baggage of the great powers with Southeast Asian states, India seldom spurs zero-sum thinking. In contrast, China suffers from a severe image deficit. Given the lingering memories of imperial Chinese dominion over parts of Southeast Asia, China's export of highly unsettling radical ideology to the region during the Maoist era, and Beijing's expansive territorial claims over the South China Sea, Chinese influence remains a source of discord rather than unity. China thus risks resistance to or an overt backlash against attempts to counterbalance a nonthreatening, stabilizing Indian presence in the region. Any Sino-Indian competition for influence in the region, moreover, would not be confined exclusively to these two powers. Other interested parties, including the United States, Japan, and Australia, would likely enter the fray—perhaps in concert—should an imbalance result from exclusionary policies by either China or India.

These three analytical caveats on the redlines suggest that the apparent imminence of rivalry in the Indian Ocean predicted by some writings is somewhat off the mark. The strategic risks of escalating or counterbalancing will likely deter China from crossing certain thresholds, even if Beijing possesses the technical capacity and the material means to do so. At the same time, China lacks sufficient reserves comprehensive national power to emplace sizable military resources in forward positions in the Indian Ocean or to reorder regional politics along its southern flank. Nevertheless, the three scenarios outlined above provide a useful benchmark by which to measure the trajectory of Indian Ocean politics. As we noted, the existing literature presumes competition without providing adequate evidence of specific steps that key players would have to take to trigger rivalry. We hope this analytical exercise offers some baseline for more concrete extrapolations of Sino-Indian interactions, neither exaggerating the potential for enmity nor discounting the possibility of competition.

A FLEETING OPPORTUNITY

As we have tried to show, neither rivalry nor naval war is fated between India and China. As long as the strategic environment remains reasonably benign in the Indian Ocean and other matters consume its energies, China has neither the need to cross Indian redlines nor adequate resources to spare for naval competition. Chinese strategists strike a scornful attitude toward the Indian Navy. Beijing simply does not consider New Delhi a serious rival at sea, nor does it see India's reversing its relative inferiority any time soon. For their part, Indians may talk about a Chinese maritime threat, but their defense budgets and strategy suggest complacency. An India that really saw itself under threat would not content itself with a single, antiquated carrier to anchor its battle fleet. Why the disparity between rhetoric and concrete action? First, the stridency of Indian commentary on China may be a function of Indian's vibrant, at times unruly democracy. Those who prophesy a Chinese bid for dominion represent one faction among a cacophony of voices clamoring for New Delhi's attention and resources. Second, absent the physical capacity to keep the PLAN out of the region, India's Monroe Doctrine may lead New Delhi to threaten to abandon its restraint, erecting a deterrent to Chinese adventurism in South Asia. While these factors may not represent a policy consensus, they may still impel the Indian leadership to overreact in times of crisis.

The presence of Chinese submarines and bases in the Indian Ocean, accordingly, would channel Indian strategy toward competition, inducing New Delhi to plow new resources into naval construction. Though more speculative, a Chinese effort to bar India from the South China Sea could have the same effect, especially if combined with a growing Chinese naval presence in India's marine environs. Again, Indian commentary on Chinese naval affairs tends toward alarmism at times. This raises the possibility that New Delhi may lower the threshold for Chinese naval activity in South Asia so low that Beijing cannot help but cross it. If Indians interpret, say, Chinese participation in counterpiracy operations as evidence of malice toward India, the prospects for friction and conflict will increase. Adroit maritime diplomacy on the part of the United States, which has embarked on a maritime strategy premised on multinational partnerships designed to defend the system of global commerce, could help ease such tensions. There is at least some chance to forge a kind of maritime condominium in the Indian Ocean, bringing together the Indian, Chinese, and US navies to work together on matters of mutual concern. But this opportunity could evaporate unless the three seafaring powers manage their relations wisely.

NOTES

1. Thomas C. Schelling, "An Essay on Bargaining," in *The Strategy of Conflict* (Cambridge: Harvard University Press, 1960), 21–80.
2. In January 2002, Gen. Khalid Kidwai, head of the Pakistani Army's Strategic Plans Division, which oversees nuclear-weapons development and deployment, listed the redlines in an interview with Paolo Cotta-Ramusino and Maurizio Martellini of the Landau Network, an Italian arms-control organization. Quoted in Kaushik Kapisthalam, "Pakistan Leaves Arms Calling Card," *Asia Times*, February 10, 2005; www.atimes.com/atimes/South_Asia/GB10Df06.html.
3. Australian commentator Rory Medcalf has helped popularize the concept of the Indo-Pacific, along with American Enterprise Institute scholar Michael Auslin and a handful of others. For a sampling of the literature, see Rory Medcalf, "An Alliance for the Indo-Pacific Region," *Lowy Interpreter*, March 7, 2011; www.lowyinterpreter.org/post/2011/03/07/An-alliance-for-the-Indo-Pacific.aspx; Michael Auslin, "Tipping Point in the Indo-Pacific," *American Interest* 6, no. 4 (March/April 2011); www.the-american-interest.com/article-bd.cfm?piece=924; and Robert D. Kaplan, "Robert Kaplan on the 9/11 Decade," *Center for a New American Security*, September 6, 2011; www.cnas.org/node/6926.
4. Robert D. Kaplan, "Center Stage for the 21st Century," *Foreign Affairs*, March/April 2009; www.foreignaffairs.com/articles/64832/robert-d-kaplan/center-stage-for-the-21st-century. See also Robert D. Kaplan, *Monsoon: The Indian Ocean and the Future of American Power* (New York: Random House, 2010).
5. "Chasing Ghosts: The Notion That Geography Is Power Is Making an Unwelcome Comeback in Asia," *Economist*, June 11, 2009, 48; www.economist.com/displayStory.cfm?story_id=13825154.
6. Alfred Thayer Mahan, *The Influence of Sea Power upon History, 1660–1783* (1890; reprint, New York: Dover, 1987), 71.
7. Robert D. Kaplan, "America's Elegant Decline," *Atlantic*, November 2007; www.theatlantic.com/doc/200711/america-decline.

8. Robert D. Kaplan, "The Revenge of Geography," *Foreign Policy*, May/June 2009; www.foreignpolicy.com/story/cms.php?story_id=4862&print=1.
9. Author correspondence with Harsh Pant, November 15, 2010.
10. Paul Kennedy, "The Rise and Fall of Navies," *New York Times*, April 5, 2007; www.nytimes.com/2007/04/05/opinion/05iht-edkennedy.1.5158064.html.
11. K. M. Panikkar, *Asia and Western Dominance: The Vasco da Gama Epoch of Asian History, 1498–1945* (London: George Allen & Unwin, 1953).
12. Sir Julian Corbett equates control of communications, whether on land or at sea, to control of an enemy's national life. K. M. Panikkar applies this logic to explain India's loss of its independence to Great Britain, an external power that ruled the waves. Julian S. Corbett, *Some Principles of Maritime Strategy*, with an introduction by Eric J. Grove (1911; repr., Annapolis, MD: Naval Institute Press, 1988), 94.
13. See, for instance, Louise Levathes, *When China Ruled the Seas: The Treasure Fleet of the Dragon Throne, 1405–1433* (Oxford: Oxford University Press, 1994).
14. Neil Tweedie, "The Navy Strikes Back," *Telegraph*, June 18, 2009; www.telegraph.co.uk/news/newstopics/politics/defence/5560746/The-Navy-strikes-back.html.
15. Geoffrey Till, "Maritime Strategy in a Globalizing World," *Orbis* 51, no. 4 (fall 2007): 573; see also Geoffrey Till, *Seapower: A Guide for the Twenty-first Century* (London: Frank Cass, 2004), 310–50.
16. Till, "Maritime Strategy in a Globalizing World," 574.
17. Mahan, *Influence of Sea Power upon History*, 138.
18. Jiang Shiliang, "The Command of Communications," *Zhongguo Junshi Kexue*, October 2, 2002, 106–14, FBIS-CPP20030107000189.
19. State Council, *China's National Defense in 2004*, December 2004; www.fas.org/nuke/guide/china/doctrine/natdef2004.html.
20. Rahul Roy-Chaudhury traces this statement on the Indian Ocean to a 1970 article by an Italian journalist—but not to any source in Mahan's voluminous writings or lectures. Roy-Chaudhury, *Sea Power and Indian Security* (London: Brassey's, 1995), 199.
21. Government of India Press Information Bureau, "Guarding the Coastline of the Country," August 28, 2002; http://pib.nic.in/feature/feyr2002/faug2002/f280820021.html.
22. R. Chopra, "A Seminar on Maritime History," *Sainik Samachar* 49, no. 4 (February 16–28, 2002); http://mod.nic.in/samachar/html/ch15.htm.
23. US Navy, Marine Corps, and Coast Guard, *A Cooperative Strategy for 21st Century Seapower* (Washington, DC: Department of the Navy, 2007), 9.
24. Dexter Perkins, *A History of the Monroe Doctrine*, rev. ed. (Boston: Little, Brown, 1963), 186; and Mahan, *Influence of Sea Power upon History*, 346.
25. Richard Olney to Thomas F. Bayard, July 20, 1895, in Ruhl J. Bartlett, ed., *The Record of American Diplomacy: Documents and Readings in the History of American Foreign Relations*, 4th ed. (New York: Knopf, 1964), 341–45.
26. Jawaharlal Nehru, *India's Foreign Policy: Selected Speeches, September 1946–April 1961* (Delhi: Government of India, 1961), 113–15.

27. Ibid.
28. C. Raja Mohan, "Beyond India's Monroe Doctrine," *Hindu*, January 2, 2003; http://hindu.com/2003/01/02/stories/2003010200981000.htm. See also C. Raja Mohan, "SAARC Reality Check: China Just Tore up India's Monroe Doctrine," *Indian Express*, November 13, 2005, LexisNexis Database.
29. C. Raja Mohan, "What If Pakistan Fails? India Isn't Worried . . . Yet," *Washington Quarterly* 28, no. 1 (winter 2004–5): 127.
30. Thomas Mathew, "Mighty Dragon in the Sea," *Hindustan Times*, June 24, 2009; www.hindustantimes.com/News-Feed/ColumnsOthers/Mighty-dragon-in-the-sea/Article1-424622.aspx.
31. Manu Pubby, "China Proposed Division of Pacific, Indian Ocean Regions, We Declined: US Admiral," *Indian Express*, May 15, 2009; www.indianexpress.com/news/china-proposed-division-of-pacific-indian-o/459851/.
32. G. Parthasarathy, "Games Neighbors Play," *Times of India*, June 29, 2009; http://timesofindia.indiatimes.com/articleshow/msid-4712987,prtpage-1.cms.
33. Andrei Chang, "Varyag Aircraft Carrier Fully Restored at Dalian," *Kanwa Intelligence Review*, November 30, 2010; Open Source Center-CPP20101130715054.
34. Mathew, "Mighty Dragon in the Sea"; and "Gaps in Defense Preparedness of Submarines: CAG," *Hindu*, October 26, 2009; www.hindu.com/2008/10/26/stories/2008102655070900.htm.
35. Raja Menon, "Just One Shark in the Deep Blue Ocean," *Outlook India*, August 10, 2009; http://outlookindia.com/article.aspx?261048; and Adm. Nirmal Verma, quoted in "Indian N-Sub to Be Operational in Two Years," *Domain-b.com*, February 8, 2010, http://domain-b.com/defence/sea/indian_navy/20100208_n_sub_operational.html.
36. "Navy Gears Up for Biggest-Ever Deals," *Pioneer News Service*, November 29, 2010; www.dailypioneer.com/299836/Navy-gears-up-for-biggest-ever-deals.html.
37. Mahan, *Influence of Sea Power upon History*, 83.
38. The term first appeared in a *Washington Times* article after originating in a Booz Allen study commissioned by the Pentagon's Office of Net Assessment. See Bill Gertz, "China Builds Up Strategic Sea Lanes," *Washington Times*, January 18, 2005; www.washtimes.com/national/20050117-115550-1929r.htm.
39. See, for example, Christopher J. Pehrson, *String of Pearls: Meeting the Challenge of China's Rising Power across the Asian Littoral* (Carlisle: Strategic Studies Institute, US Army War College, July 2006); Lawrence Spinetta, "Cutting China's 'String of Pearls,'" US Naval Institute *Proceedings* 132, no. 10 (October 2006): 40–42; Sudha Ramachandra, "China's Pearl in Pakistan's Waters," *Asia Times*, March 4, 2005; www.atimes.com/atimes/South_Asia/GC04Df06.html; and Hideaki Kaneda, "The Rise of Chinese "Sea Power,"" *Philippine Daily Inquirer*, September 22, 2005, 11.
40. Author's discussions with Indian analysts, Institute for Defense Studies & Analyses, New Delhi, November 6–16, 2006. See also Rajat Pandit, "China's Deep

Sea Plans Alarm India," *Times of India*, May 3, 2008; http://timesofindia.indiatimes.com/articleshow/3005889.cms.

41. Lee Jae-Hyung, "China's Expanding Maritime Ambitions in the Western Pacific and the Indian Ocean," *Contemporary Southeast Asia* 24, no. 3 (December 2002): 553–54.
42. Mathew, "Mighty Dragon in the Sea."
43. Gurpreet Khurana, "China's 'String of Pearls' in the Indian Ocean and Its Security Implications," *Strategic Analysis* 32, no. 1 (January 2008): 22.
44. "Blue Water Marks," *Indian Express*, December 22, 2008; www.indianexpress.com/news/blue-water-marks/401259.
45. Goh Sui Noi, "China Not Planning Sri Lanka Naval Base," *Straits Times*, June 24, 2009.
46. Dilip Bobb, "Cautious Optimism," *India Today*, August 31, 1987, 69. See also Devin T. Hagerty, "India's Regional Security Doctrine," *Asian Survey* 31, no. 4 (1991): 351–63.
47. We derive these numbers from a US Navy rule of thumb that three ships are necessary to keep one readily deployable. That is, one ship is fully combat-ready, another is undergoing training and workups, and a third is in extended overhaul. The Indian Navy might make do with a 2:1 ratio, however, since it will not face the world-spanning operational requirements assigned to the US Navy.
48. C. Raja Mohan, "India and the Balance of Power," *Foreign Affairs* 85, no. 4 (July/August 2006): 17–32.
49. Indian Navy, Integrated Headquarters, Ministry of Defense, *Freedom to Use the Seas: India's Maritime Military Strategy*, May 2007, 29.
50. Vijay Bakhuja, "India's Growing Profile in Southeast Asia," in *Regional Outlook: Southeast Asia, 2008–2009*, edited by Deepak Nair and Lee Poh Onn, 15–18 (Singapore: Institute of Southeast Asian Studies, 1993–).
51. Stephen P. Cohen, *India: Emerging Power* (Washington, DC: Brookings Institution Press, 2001), 255.
52. Ibid., 252.
53. Pehrson, *String of Pearls*.

PART III

Third Powers and the Way Forward

CHAPTER 9

INTERNATIONAL LAW AND THE FUTURE OF INDIAN OCEAN SECURITY

JAMES KRASKA

INTRODUCTION

Hans J. Morgenthau argued that the struggle for power takes two forms: preservation of the status quo or the pursuit of imperialism, which has as its goal the replacement of the balance of power with hegemony.[1] Both of these tendencies can be observed in the Indian Ocean region (IOR), and although the significance of international law as an instrument for suppressing the politics of the IOR should not be oversold, it remains a vital aspect of the geopolitical and geostrategic picture.

As most legal experts will note, in most respects, international law is a lagging rather than a leading indicator of international politics, meaning that the law springs from political developments, rather than causing them. Yet the importance of international law to international politics and its significance is increasing, especially in the maritime domain. In particular, the framework and associated rules and treaties that have emerged from development of the international law of the sea are facilitating maritime security cooperation as well as defining the parameters of interstate competition in areas such as the South China Sea and the Indian Ocean.[2] Thus, the claims and counterclaims made within the law of the sea provide more than just a backdrop to Indian Ocean politics; they provide a set of boundaries that affect how the struggle for power plays out.

This chapter unfolds as follows: this introduction lays out the broad canvas of Indian Ocean geopolitics and some of the features of applicable international law. The second section presents the essential rules on the law of the sea, which mostly derive from a collection of legal regimes that balance the interests of coastal states in restricting freedom of navigation with the interests of the international community in unhampered access to the seas. Coastal states are entitled to draw baselines, assert sovereignty over a territorial sea, and maintain sovereign rights and jurisdiction over an exclusive economic zone (EEZ), and the width of these zones can be a source of national pride and legal and political wrangling. Therefore, the second part also analyzes how the states of the region have applied the rules of the law of the sea and the resulting frictions and sensitivities. For example, many of the states in the region have made formal declarations outlining their understanding of the law of the sea. The declarations, which are formal instruments of treaty interpretation, highlight some of the more intransigent diplomatic positions held by the states.

The third section takes a tour of the strategic geography of the Indian Ocean from a legal perspective, moving generally from west to east, from the Arabian Sea to the Central Indian Ocean and on to the Bay of Bengal. The states enjoy cooperative relationships as well as disagreements over maritime boundaries and access to marine resources. Although nominally a land-based competition, the clash between India and Pakistan particularly resonates at sea, with both nations seizing fishing vessels and crew belonging to the other. This section focuses most closely on the maritime law dimension of an emerging bipolar security complex, with India supported by a new pseudo-alliance with the United States to resist an energized and dynamic alliance between Pakistan and China. Concern in Washington over what the rise of Chinese power means in the Indian Ocean has produced a turnaround in bilateral relations with Delhi. As India has abandoned its reliance on the Soviet Union after the Cold War, the United States has had an increasingly frosty relationship with Pakistan. Meanwhile, Indian leaders fear encroachment by China in Delhi at sea as China for the first time develops a forward and permanent naval presence throughout the Indian Ocean.

In the fourth section, the chapter concludes that the maritime competition in the Indian Ocean between the world's two most populous states is gathering. International law is important to this struggle because it may help to restrain the powers by providing a measure of predictability and confidence building. Just as likely, however, is that the law of the sea provides a basis for increased friction between India and China. The liberal order of the world's oceans is designed to facilitate freedom of the seas, and China's new forays into the Indian Ocean—albeit lawful—aggravate India.

For more than sixty years, India and Pakistan have been the center of regional security. Including the mass violence arising from the breakup of the British Raj in 1947–48, the two nations have fought three wars. Although their last major war was fought in the 1970s, there is an uneasy peace between the two states. While Russia and China have large nuclear arsenals, both are members of the Nuclear Nonproliferation Treaty. India and Pakistan, however, have successfully detonated nuclear devices, and both possess nuclear weapons and the means to deliver them, but neither country is a party to the Nuclear Nonproliferation Treaty. Terrorist attacks inside both countries are destabilizing and risk outbreak of interstate conflict. The highest altitude conflict in the world—Kashmir—continues to drive a wedge between the two nuclear-armed neighbors, and the stage is set for dangerous confrontation on the subcontinent.

The stark example of nonparticipation in a cornerstone multilateral regime by the two most powerful states in the region is a reminder that international law and international politics on the Indian subcontinent are intertwined. At sea, the situation is even more complex—in terms of both maritime geopolitics and international law. The reason: unlike the contiguous land territory, the Indian Ocean is a domain of movement and a shared commons, with functional regulatory and enforcement authority divided between the coastal state and the international community. Shipping traffic from throughout the world passes through the region, and the Indian Ocean encompasses the busiest shipping lanes in the world. Each day 15 million barrels of oil transits from the India Ocean through the Strait of Malacca—almost as much as the 17 million barrels per day that flows through the Strait of Hormuz.[3]

Naval forces of distant water states are operating in the Indian Ocean for the first time, potentially affecting the strategic balance. International law provides a framework within which these activities take place. Thus, whereas most chapters of this volume are dedicated to the strategic and political aspects of Indian Ocean security, the legal context in this chapter—including rules for resolving resource and maritime boundary disputes, navigational rights and freedoms, and flag state and coastal state authorities—is another important dimension of Indian Ocean security. Moreover, the international law of the sea is particularly important for South Asian security. Just as Plato remarked in the fourth century BC that the Greeks sat around the Mediterranean likes frogs around a pond,[4] the coastal populations of the Indian Ocean states occupy a littoral shoreline inundated by seasonal monsoons that blow from Indonesia toward East Africa, northward through the Somali Basin and the Arabian Sea, and then eastward to the Bay of Bengal.

LAW OF THE SEA

Against the political-military backdrop, this chapter next turns toward sketching out a legal roadmap of the most pressing issues affecting Indian Ocean security, beginning with the international law of the sea, as codified by the United Nations Convention on the Law of the Sea (UNCLOS).[5] The provisions of UNCLOS, including navigational regimes through international straits, territorial seas, and EEZs, reflect a common rule set that is designed to facilitate peacetime global shipping and naval activities. The effect of UNCLOS on naval forces is tactical and operational as well as strategic. The rules governing recognition of archipelagic nations, such as the Maldives and Indonesia, for example, also affect tactical aviation and doctrine and operations for surface and subsurface navigation. At the same time, UNCLOS shapes the strategic seascape, affecting force structure and foreign policy.[6]

The law of the sea also reflects principles for nations to use in demarcating disputed maritime boundaries. By providing a template for resolving nationalist and resource conflicts, the law of the sea can promote conflict avoidance and war prevention. On the other hand, although the terms of the treaty are rather clear with respect to rights and duties of coastal states and distant water, foreign-flagged ships and aircraft, clashing interests, creative lawyering, and diplomatic brinksmanship could combine with ethnic and nationalist sentiment to trigger a crisis at sea. Whether disputes in the Indian Ocean are resolved peacefully or will erupt into conflict, the international law of the sea will be the point of departure for legal analysis and may even be dispositive in diplomacy, just as UNCLOS was at the center of the controversies over the collision of the US EP-3 and Chinese F-8 fighter jet in 2001 and the USNS *Impeccable* dispute between the United States and China in 2009.[7]

The rules and regimes in the Indian Ocean are a product of UNCLOS, to which nearly all states in the region are a party. The Convention also reflects the rules and state practice embodied in customary international law. The starting point for all analysis of the rights and duties of states in the Indian Ocean is determination of coastal state baselines. The international law of the sea recognizes that coastal states may assert sovereignty or other lesser forms of national jurisdiction over certain areas within designated offshore zones. Normally the outer perimeters of these zones, including the territorial sea, are measured from baselines running along the low-water mark of the coast, as displayed on large-scale charts officially recognized by the coastal state.[8]

Coastal states may, however, depart from normal baselines and under some circumstances draw straight baselines in accordance with articles 5–11 and 13–14 of UNCLOS. Article 7(1) of UNCLOS contains geographical conditions that must be used by nations establishing straight baselines. First, states may draw straight baselines "in localities where the coastline is deeply indented and cut into," or "if there is a fringe of islands along the coast in its immediate vicinity." Second, in either case, the straight baselines must meet additional criteria set forth in article 7(2), in that they may not "depart to any appreciable extent from the general direction of the coast, and the seas areas lying within the lines must be sufficiently linked to the land domain."[9]

Straight baselines allow the coastal state to enclose waters that have, as a result of their close interrelationship with the land, the character of internal waters. Internal waters are akin to national territory and, unlike territorial seas, do not include a right of innocent passage by foreign ships. A state also may use straight baselines to account for and smooth out particularly complex or irregular local shoreline patterns and small enclaves in its territorial sea that would otherwise result from the use of normal baselines. Article 14 of UNCLOS permits states to alternate between normal and straight baselines, as conditions suggest. Simply put, straight baselines permit the coastal state to exercise sovereignty or jurisdiction over a greater amount of ocean space. Because the writ of additional authority granted to the coastal state using straight baselines is so broad, they are supposed to be applied with great caution. The spirit as well as the letter of the law should be respected in determining straight baselines.[10] Unfortunately, in actual practice the rules pertaining to straight baselines are routinely discarded, and the Indo-Pacific region contains the most egregious serial violators.

There are no specific distance limits for the span of a straight baseline, but generally segment lengths are expected to extend no more than twenty-four to forty-eight nautical miles.[11] The US position on the issue is quite conservative—straight baseline segments should not exceed twenty-four miles.[12] The twenty-four-mile maximum segment length is implied from a close reading of the relevant articles of UNCLOS because that is the maximum distance at which territorial seas could overlap. Article 7(1) requires straight baselines to be set in the "immediate vicinity" of the coast. Article 7(3) states that "the sea areas lying within the line must be sufficiently closely linked to the land domain to be subject to the regime of internal waters." In both of these descriptions, the implication is strong that the waters to be internalized would otherwise be part of the territorial sea.

It is difficult to envision a situation where international waters (those waters lying beyond twelve miles from the beach) could be somehow "sufficiently closely linked" as to be converted by the coastal state into internal waters over which it exercises exclusive and complete sovereignty. This implication is reinforced by article 8(2), which guarantees the right of innocent passage in areas converted to internal waters by straight baselines. Thus, even in cases in which the coastal state is permitted by UNCLOS to draw straight baselines and convert international water to internal water, there is a special regime of nonsuspendable innocent passage that applies to the newly enclosed area. Yet nations that draw straight baselines typically fail to recognize article 8(2), denying the international community the right to use a portion of the global commons.

Coastal states are entitled to exercise national sovereignty over the territorial sea—a zone that may extend no more than twelve nautical miles from the baseline. The regime of innocent passage is applicable to the territorial sea. Although the territorial sea is under the complete sovereignty of the coastal state, the international community enjoys the right to travel through the zone under the innocent passage regime. Preservation of the regime of innocent passage prevails over preexisting rights in waters that were territorial in nature before the application of straight baselines. Creation of new straight baselines, then, may not close off waters that previously were open. Given the concept of close linkage to territorial waters and the foregoing rules, it follows that logically no straight baseline segment should exceed twenty-four nautical miles in length.

A number of nations in the IOR have adopted straight baselines, most of which appear excessive in light of the rules in UNCLOS. These excessive baselines generally are a local affair and are addressed in the sections that follow. Some straight baseline claims, however, stand out as particularly abusive of the treaty. Burma, for example, has the embarrassing distinction of having the longest nonconforming straight baseline in the world. The closing line across the Gulf of Martaban in the northern reaches of the Andaman Sea extends 222.3 nautical miles from the mouth of the Irrawaddy River to the coastal town of Ye, near the southern tip of the Mon State. Rather than adhering to the coastline, at one point along the stretched straight baseline, the nearest land is 75 nautical miles away, and the broad mouth of the Sittaung at the northernmost tip of the Gulf of Martaban is more than 120 nautical miles distant.[13]

Territorial Seas and International Straits

Immediately seaward of the baseline lies the territorial sea. The territorial sea is a belt of ocean that may extend a maximum of twelve nautical miles from the baseline of the coastal nation, and the area is subject to the sovereignty of the coastal state. Ships of all nations, however, enjoy the right of innocent passage in the territorial sea, although aircraft are not entitled to assert a similar right to overfly the territorial sea. The right of innocent passage means ships but not aircraft may exercise continuous and expeditious traversing of the territorial sea. Innocent passage may even include stopping and anchoring but only insofar as incidental to ordinary navigation or as rendered necessary by force majeure or by distress. All civilian vessels and warships enjoy the right of innocent passage, which cannot be conditioned on consent or notification by the coastal state. Generally passage is innocent so long as it is not prejudicial to the peace, good order, or security of the coastal nation. An exhaustive list of such prejudicial activities deemed inconsistent with innocent passage is contained in article 19 of UNCLOS, and these include any threat or use of force against the sovereignty, territorial integrity, or political independence of the coastal state.

A coastal nation may enact certain reasonable and necessary restrictions upon the right of innocent passage for purposes of resource conservation, environmental protection, and navigational safety. Such restrictions, however, may not have the practical effect of denying or impairing the right of innocent passage, and they may not discriminate in form or in fact against the ships of any nation, nor can they prohibit the transit rights of nuclear-powered sovereign warships. A number of countries in the IOR have laws pertaining to their territorial sea that are inconsistent with UNCLOS, typically by purporting to deny the right of innocent passage to foreign-flagged ships. Oman, for example, requires prior permission for innocent passage for warships and nuclear-powered vessels and vessels carrying dangerous substances. Such rules can lead to conflict because the coastal state may try to enforce rules that are not recognized by other nations—setting up a confrontation in which neither state presumes to back down as a crisis escalates.

International straits constitute a special permutation of the territorial seas. International straits are those areas of overlapping twelve-nautical-mile territorial seas that connect one area of the high seas or EEZ to another area of the high seas or EEZ, and that are used for international navigation. The US position is that the requirement that the strait be "used" for international navigation means that it is merely capable of being used.

There are more than 125 international straits throughout the world. These waters are simultaneously territorial seas and constitute an international strait; because of the dual nature of the waterway, the regime of transit passage, rather than the rules of innocent passage, applies to foreign-flagged vessels and aircraft. Transit passage, which permits continuous and expeditious transit by surface ships, submarines, and aircraft, exists throughout the entire strait (shoreline-to-shoreline) and not just the area overlapped by the territorial sea of the coastal nations. Unlike innocent passage, transit passage may not be suspended. Vessels and aircraft may transit in the "normal mode," meaning that submarines may travel under the water and aircraft may overfly the strait. While conducting transit passage, ships may conduct formation steaming and launch and recover aircraft and other military devices, such as unmanned underwater vehicles.

Several of the major international straits feed traffic into the Indian Ocean. The Strait of Hormuz separating Iran and Oman, for example, has particular strategic importance. The passage is only twenty-one miles wide at its narrowest point.[14] Forty percent of the world's oil passes through the Strait of Hormuz—each day 16 to 17 million barrels of oil are on southbound tankers going through the narrow passageway. Periodically Iranian patrol craft will threaten to close the strait to international shipping, and Iranian Revolutionary Guard Corps small boats overtly practiced such a closure by swarming US naval vessels in January 2008.

Similarly, approximately twenty thousand ships, or about 20 percent of global commercial shipping, passes through the Gulf of Aden and Strait of Bab el-Mandeb each year, with most traffic either going to or coming from the Suez Canal.[15] The Straits of Malacca and Singapore are even busier, although Singapore, Malaysia, and Indonesia do a commendable job of maintaining security, traffic management, and vessel services throughout the strait. The two-way shipping channel is less than three kilometers wide at its narrowest point off Singapore.

The rules concerning rights and duties of transit passage through international straits may give rise to a clash between the right of the coastal state to manage and use its territorial sea and the right of the international community to enjoy unimpeded freedom of navigation and overflight through an international waterway. Iran, for example, has asserted that nations that are not party to UNCLOS, such as the United States, do not enjoy the right of transit passage through the Strait of Hormuz. While the regime of transit passage was created specifically in UNCLOS, the United States responds that customary international law applies to all nations regardless of their acceptance of UNCLOS, and customary law recognizes a historic right of free transit.

Even friendly nations can disagree on the limits of transit passage and attendant coastal state rights, and these disputes can have strategic and military implications. In October 2007, for example, Indonesia approved a plan to construct a sixteen-mile road and railway bridge connecting the islands of Sumatra and Java.[16] Construction began in 2012 and the bridge could open by 2020. The Sunda Strait Bridge will be the world's longest suspension bridge, consisting of a series of bridges carrying a six-lane highway and double-track railway traversing the three islands of Prajurit, Sangiang, and Ular.[17] The bridge is also in one of the world's most active earthquake zones.

In December 2004 a 9.0-magnitude quake in Sumatra set off a tsunami that killed more than 230,000 people in the area. Krakatoa volcano is only forty kilometers away; when it erupted in August 1883, tens of thousands of people were killed.[18] But besides the fascinating geophysical features of the area, the construction of a bridge across a strait used for international navigation raises the issue of whether the landmark affects the right of all nations to exercise transit passage through the strait. A bridge across the strait likely will impede some types of shipping—tall vessels, such as aircraft carriers will no longer have access to the strait, much as the construction of the Øresund Bridge across the Danish strait connecting Sweden and Denmark forever foreclosed US aircraft carrier operations in the Baltic Sea. Although the US protested construction of the bridge at the time, the Danish built it anyway. Thus, coastal states can take seemingly innocuous steps that may end up limiting the movement of commercial shipping and reducing the mobility of naval forces.

Exclusive Economic Zones

Beyond the territorial sea, coastal states may claim an EEZ, a resource-related zone adjacent to the territorial sea in which a coastal state may exercise certain sovereign rights and jurisdiction, but not sovereignty, out to a distance of two hundred nautical miles from the baseline.[19] Ships and aircraft of all nations, including warships and military aircraft, enjoy complete freedom of movement and operation on, over, and under the waters of the zone. Unlike sovereignty over the territorial sea, however, the scope of sovereign rights in the EEZ applies only to living and nonliving resources of the water column, seabed, and subsoil, and to jurisdiction over artificial installations related to such purposes as well as jurisdiction over marine scientific research and a more limited authority to prescribe internationally accepted rules for marine environmental protection.[20]

The UNCLOS recognizes the sovereign rights of a coastal nation to prescribe and enforce its laws in the EEZ for the purposes of exploration, exploitation, management, and conservation of the natural resources of the waters, seabed, and subsoil of the zone as well as for the production of energy from the water, currents, and winds. Coastal nations also may exercise jurisdiction over the establishment and use of artificial islands, installations, and structures, but only those having economic purposes. In the EEZ, all nations enjoy the right to exercise the traditional high-seas freedoms of navigation and overflight, of the laying of submarine cables and pipelines, and of all other traditional high-seas uses by ships and aircraft that are not resource related.

Codification of the EEZ in UNCLOS has brought nearly 38 percent of the high seas under some form of national administration.[21] Unlike the territorial sea, however, the balance of rights and interests in the EEZ inures to the international community, and the rights and freedoms enjoyed by ships and aircraft of all nations are akin to those associated with the high seas. Naval forces may conduct task-force maneuvering, flight operations, military exercises, surveillance, intelligence-gathering activities, and ordnance testing and live firing in the EEZ. Despite the fact that coastal nations lack the legal authority or competence to restrict or impede the exercise of high-seas freedoms in the EEZ, a number of nations in the IOR place restrictions on foreign-flagged warships and aircraft. The efforts to assume greater coastal state authority over the EEZ often are reflected in declarations made by states upon signing UNCLOS.

Archipelagic States

The Indian Ocean contains four nations composed exclusively of islands—Comoros, Seychelles, Maldives, and Mauritius. The first three meet the legal requirements in UNCLOS for claiming archipelagic status and therefore may draw straight baselines to enclose the islands and oceans separating them to form a coherent area of national territory and internal waters. The former French colony of Comoros is located on the eastern shore of Africa. Comoros claims the French-administered Mayotte Island, and also challenges France's and Madagascar's claims to Banc du Geyser, a drying reef in the Mozambique Channel. Comoros has not delineated straight baselines but qualifies as an archipelagic state. Archipelagic status is determined according to objective criteria in article

47(7) of UNCLOS concerning the ratio of the water area to the land area located within the baseline system, and it must fall within the range of 1:1 and 9:1 of water to land. In contrast to Comoros, for example, Mauritius does not meet the test and may not claim archipelagic status.[22] Any nation that has too much land, such as Greece or Canada, or a nation with too much water, such as Mauritius, is ineligible to be recognized as an archipelago.

MAURITIUS. Mauritius consists of the principal island of Mauritius and its adjacent islets, Rodrigues Island, a coralline near-atoll located 300 nm eastward of Mauritius; the Cargados Carajos Shoals, 220 nm north-northeast of Mauritius; and the Agalega Islands, located nearly 650 nm north of Mauritius. Thus, the country of Mauritius has too little land territory and too much water in between its island groups to form a legally recognized archipelagic state.

Mauritius has drawn straight baselines in an apparent effort to gain recognition as an archipelagic state. The Mauritius Territorial Sea Act of 1970 extended the Mauritian territorial sea to 12 nm. But the law also established a system of straight baselines, and the system is not in accord with UNCLOS. Sections 5(a) and 5(b) of the act provide language for the drawing of a straight-baseline system, but the text is not specific enough to draw single sets of baselines.

MALDIVES. The Maldives, on the other hand, is an archipelagic nation located south-southwest of India.[23] Consisting of numerous atolls that range in size from 3 to 3,200 km^2, the state meets the test for archipelagic status.

The Maldives archipelagic straight baseline system meets the water-to-land-area ratio standard, with the following area measurements:

- Total area = 21,350 nm^2 (73,100 km^2)
- Water area = 15,500 nm^2 (53,000 km^2)
- Land area = 5,900 nm^2 (20,130 km^2)

Thus, the water-to-land ratio is 2.63:1. The length of any individual baseline may not exceed 100 miles in length, except that up to 3 percent of the total number of baselines may extend to a maximum of 125 miles. The atolls that make up the Maldives run in a north-south direction in two approximately parallel columns.

There are major benefits to archipelagic states. First, the nation may claim the oceans separating the islands as internal waters. Although the international community of states still enjoy the right to transit the area with ships and aircraft, the navigational regime is more limited than on the high seas. In particular, foreign-flagged ships and aircraft enjoy the regime of archipelagic sea-lanes passage, which has many similarities with the regime of transit passage through international straits.

Article 53 of UNCLOS permits archipelagic states to "designate sea lanes ... suitable for the continuous and expeditious passage of foreign ships ... through ... its archipelagic waters and the adjacent territorial sea." But if an archipelagic state does not designate such sea-lanes, then foreign-flagged ships and aircraft may exercise the right of archipelagic sea-lanes passage through all of the routes normally used for international navigation." Since the Maldives government has not formally designated any archipelagic sea-lanes, the international community may use all routes normally used for such purposes. Outside of archipelagic sea-lanes, foreign-flagged ships and aircraft are restricted to the regime of nonsuspendable innocent passage, which means, among other things, that submarines must travel on the surface and show their flag.

Although the Maldives is entitled to archipelagic status, not all of its maritime laws are consistent with the provisions of UNCLOS. Article 13(b) of the Maritime Zones of Maldives, for example, provides that foreign warships or foreign nuclear-powered ships (or ships carrying nuclear or other inherently dangerous or noxious substances) must receive authorization from the government of the Maldives prior to entering the territorial sea.[24] This provision is not in accordance with Part II of UNCLOS, and the United States has protested the claim.[25]

Archipelagic states may claim a normal EEZ, measured to a distance of two hundred nautical miles from the straight baselines. Here again, Maldives has rules inconsistent with UNCOS. Article 14 of the Maldives Act violates the provisions pertaining to the EEZ. Maldives claims that foreign vessels entering its EEZ must first obtain prior authorization, an assertion of authority that likewise is inconsistent with UNCLOS articles 59 and 87. Article 58(1) of UNCLOS states that in the EEZ, all states enjoy "the freedoms referred to in article 87 of navigation and overflight and of laying of submarine cables and pipelines, and other internationally lawful uses of the sea related to those freedoms, such as those associated with the operation of ships, aircraft and submarine cables and pipelines, and compatible with the other provisions of this Convention."

SEYCHELLES. Seychelles is an archipelagic state situated off the southwest coast of Africa. The tiny nation implemented straight baseline legislation in March 1999.[26] Two years later the country reached an EEZ and continental shelf boundary agreement with France between Ile de la Grande Glorieuse and Ile du Lys, and Assumption and Astove Islands. In January 2002 Seychelles signed a similar agreement with Tanzania, resolving its maritime boundary disputes.

The island nation signed UNCLOS in 1982 and ratified the Convention in 1991. Although the geographic maritime claims appear to be consistent with the rules set forth in UNCLOS, Seychelles has claimed coastal state competence to regulate foreign-flagged vessels in the territorial sea and EEZ that is inconsistent with the provisions of UNCLOS. Thus, in addition to compliance with the geographic or physical tests for establishing maritime zones, coastal states also may be tempted to prescribe and enforce laws in the zones that are greater than the authority permitted in UNCLOS.[27]

The 1999 law considers any act of pollution as qualifying as a violation of innocent passage by claiming that it is a priori prejudicial to peace, good order, and security in the territorial sea. This provision is not consistent with UNCLOS, and the United States protested the pollution claim in 2000. Finally, the most excessive maritime claim made by the Seychelles is the requirement of notice and permission for warships and nuclear-powered ships or ships carrying nuclear cargo to transit the territorial sea in innocent passage. The United States also protested these requirements by conducting operational freedom of navigation assertions in 1998 and 1999, and by filing a diplomatic demarche in protest in 2000.[28]

Southern Indian Ocean

The Southern Indian Ocean features numerous islands. Madagascar dominates the east coast of Africa, and it is virtually surrounded by a ring of islands belonging to Comoros in the northwest, Seychelles in the north, and Mauritius in the east as well as scattered French possessions on all three sides.[29] South Africa owns Prince Edward Islands, which are in excess of one thousand nautical miles due south of the Mozambique Channel.

Farther south, Antarctica, along the southern reaches of the Indian Ocean, is a demilitarized continent governed under the terms of the Antarctic Treaty of 1959.[30] Although seven nations assert sovereignty over portions of the continent, the claims are not recognized in international law. Yet the claimants have persisted in adopting laws governing the waters off the coast of Antarctica, particularly for marine environmental protection. While the legal competence of states to prescribe and enforce coastal state zones and associated navigational regimes is doubtful but legally untested, there is widespread agreement on the status of Antarctica. For all practical purposes, the Antarctic Treaty demilitarized the continent and surrounding waters, dedicating the region to peaceful purposes. Nuclear detonations and disposal of radioactive material are specifically proscribed, and freedom of scientific research for all nations is protected.[31]

Declarations

During the negotiations for UNCLOS from 1973 to 1982, the creation of a comprehensive oceans law always was considered a "package deal" in which nations would craft an interlocking set of rules and regimes. The provisions interrelate, so nations were barred from accepting some and rejecting others. The concept of an integrated treaty underpins all of UNCLOS and is the agreement's most durable and significant quality. The issues involved in assigning the maritime balance of authority and power have a close interrelationship, so nations made numerous compromises to conclude the treaty.[32] Consequently, article 309 of UNCLOS forbids states parties from making reservations or exceptions to sections of the Convention—states must accept the treaty as a whole, or not at all.

Article 310 of UNCLOS allows, however, that states and entities may make declarations or statements regarding their application at the time of signing, ratifying, or acceding to the Convention. Declarations may not purport to exclude or modify the legal effect of the provisions of UNCLOS but instead they may be used to harmonize local regulations with the terms of the treaty. Article 310 reads:

> *Declarations and statements*
> Article 309 does not preclude a State, when signing, ratifying or acceding to this Convention, from making declarations or statements, however phrased or named, with a view, inter alia, to the harmonization of its laws and regulations with the provisions of this Convention, provided that such declarations or statements do not purport to exclude or to modify the legal effect of the provisions of this Convention in their application to that State.

Reservations permit states to derogate from specific treaty articles or provisions, excepting some and accepting others. Declarations are different from treaty reservations. Many nations have used declarations as a way of making what one author calls "disguised reservations" or what I have termed elsewhere "stealth reservations."[33] A treaty reservation "modifies for the reserving State in its relations with that other party the provisions of the treaty to which the reservation relates to the extent of the reservation."[34] This means that if a treaty permits reservations (UNCLOS does not), states are free to modify or terminate sections or articles of the treaty by indicating an intention to do so at the time of accession. Since the nature of UNCLOS as a "package deal" does not allow nations to make reservations that preserve positions or modify the terms of the treaty, nations that are not satisfied with certain provisions of the text have sought to change them—or at least the way that they are applied—through the force of declarations.

The issue of "stealth reservations" and what they may mean for freedom of navigation has particular saliency in the Indian Ocean. The most powerful states in the region, India and Pakistan, announced declarations to UNCLOS that on their face constitute impermissible reservations purporting to limit freedom of navigation of foreign-flagged warships and civil shipping. Since both nations are acting outside the boundaries of the law, however, there is increased room for misunderstanding and miscalculation. Without a common understanding of the rule set, the two nations are primed for naval encounters to both feed existing maritime disputes and create new ones.

STRATEGIC GEOGRAPHY OF THE INDIAN OCEAN

The international law of the sea applies throughout the Indian Ocean within a milieu of geography, politics, and rivalry. The politics in the region are dominated by India and Pakistan, rivals that have had virtually no official bilateral naval collaboration. China, a new entrant to the region, is bolstering Pakistan and worrying India. Mutual hostility and suspicion between India, on the one hand, and Pakistan and China, on the other, reduces their ability to peacefully manage a crisis.

Fishing in the disputed maritime zone seaward of the Sir Creek that divides India's Kutch from Pakistan's Sind has become a serious bilateral issue, with coastal fishermen on both sides caught in the middle. In 2001 a group of retired admirals from the two nations met to begin a "Track II" dialogue to press for prompt release of detained fishermen.[35] The participation of the retired senior officers was influential in the release of detained fishermen, with India releasing 160 Pakistanis and Pakistan reciprocating with the release of 84 Indian fishermen. The retired admirals have pressed their governments to arrest fishing vessels alleged to have been caught fishing illegally but not to detain the crews. Article 73 of UNCLOS mandates that detained civilian crew members are entitled to "prompt release"—an expeditious repatriation to the flag state. There are, however, another 156 Pakistani and 28 Indian fishermen still waiting to be freed. The Indian Coast Guard and the Pakistan Maritime Security Agency could improve compliance and cooperation in this regard.

Even on land, there is little direct cooperation between India and Pakistan. The Indus River watershed agreement, for example, remains the most functional relationship between the two countries.[36] There are glimmers of hope for greater cooperation, however. Retired officers from both countries have proposed other avenues of maritime cooperation between the two rivals, including the feasibility of an "Incidents at Sea" arrangement as a confidence-building measure within a multilateral framework. Several maritime confidence-building measures have been negotiated between India and Pakistan, but they have seldom been sustained during time of crisis.

Further steps include a memorandum of understanding as part of the Lahore Declaration, signed in February, 1999. The Lahore Declaration obliged both nations to conclude an agreement on prevention of incidents at sea in order to safeguard navigation by their naval vessels and aircraft and prescribed a joint review of bilateral communication links. In early December 2011 the Indian Navy chief Adm. Nirmal Verma suggested that creation of a hotline between the two navies—akin to an incident at sea arrangement—makes sense to prevent maritime skirmishes. The maritime agreement could mirror the new Sino-Indian land border mechanism to prevent crises along the 4,057-km Line of Actual Control. That agreement would have been finalized in November 2011, but for an interruption in relations because of India's support for the Dali Lama, which derailed talks between Indian national security adviser Shiv Shankar and his Chinese counterpart Dai Bingguo.[37]

The India-Pakistan axis is now much more complicated due to the presence of China and the United States. China and the United States are becoming more significant factors in Indian Ocean security. Although Pakistan is nominally a US ally, differences over the US-led "war on terror" and increasing Indian-American coziness have pushed Pakistan toward China.[38] Meanwhile, China is spreading its influence throughout the Indian Ocean, with Pakistan as the bulwark in the west. Analysis of the interplay between international security and law of the sea emerges from a clockwise "walk" around the Indian Ocean, beginning with Pakistan and the Arabian Sea—the entranceway to the Persian Gulf in the west. The review begins with a quick look at Oman.

Western Indian Ocean

The country of Oman consists of two noncontiguous regions separated by the United Arab Emirates. The country extends to the northern extremity of the Ru'us al Jibal, comprising the Musandam Peninsula and offshore islands. In the south and west, the nation occupies an area below the 25th parallel of north latitude, along the shores of the Gulf of Oman and the Arabian Sea.[39]

Oman has a variety of excessive maritime claims. First, the country maintains excessive straight baselines based upon assertion of historic waters. In general, the coastline of the country is quite smooth and therefore inappropriate for the use of straight baselines. The United States has protested Oman's straight baselines using diplomatic demarches and operational freedom of navigation patrols by warships.[40]

Under Royal Decree, Oman also recognizes only the right of innocent passage rather than transit passage through Omani territorial seas that overlap the Strait of Hormuz.[41] The limitation on transit through the strait is not recognized by the United States and other nations, which conduct routine ship, aircraft, and submarine operations on their way into or out of the Gulf. Oman also purports to require prior permission for the conduct of innocent passage by warships, nuclear-powered ships, submarines, and ships carrying dangerous substances in the territorial sea. Oman signed UNCLOS on July 1, 1983. Upon ratification on August 17, 1989, Oman delivered the following declaration:

> Declaration No. 2, on the passage of warships through Omani territorial waters
>
> Innocent passage is guaranteed to warships through Omani territorial waters, subject to prior permission. This also applies to submarines, on

condition that they navigate on the surface and fly the flag of their home State.

> Declaration No. 3, on the passage of nuclear-powered ships and the like through Omani territorial waters
>
> With regard to foreign nuclear-powered ships and ships carrying nuclear or other substances that are inherently dangerous or harmful to health or the environment, the right of innocent passage, subject to prior permission, is guaranteed to the types of vessel [*sic*], whether or not warships, to which the descriptions apply. This right is also guaranteed to submarines . . . on condition that they navigate on the surface and fly the flag of their home State.[42]

In sum, Omani law requires foreign nuclear-powered ships and "ships carrying nuclear or other substances that are inherently dangerous or harmful to health or the environment" to seek prior permission in order to exercise the right of innocent passage. The provision purports to apply to both civilian vessels and warships.[43] Finally, Oman has signed boundary agreements with Yemen and Pakistan, so the maritime borders are stable among these states.[44]

Like Oman, Pakistan is a party to UNCLOS. Islamabad signed the treaty in 1982 and ratified the agreement in 1997.[45] Pakistan was a leader in objecting to US opposition to the 1982 treaty, when Washington sought renegotiation of the seabed mining provisions.[46] The government of Pakistan has published geographic coordinates defining straight baselines, from which Islamabad measures the breadth of its territorial sea and other maritime zones.[47] Pakistan claims the waters inside the baselines constitute internal waters.[48] The baselines are asserted under authority of Pakistan's domestic laws and include nine baseline segments that extend 396 miles along the coast.[49] The baseline segments range in length from 10 miles to 85 miles in length.[50] Pakistan's baselines were created under authority of the Territorial Waters and Maritime Zones Act of December 22, 1976. Paragraphs 2(3) and 2(4) of the act state:

> (3) The baseline from which such limit (territorial waters) shall be measured and the waters on the landward side of which shall form part of the internal waters of Pakistan shall be specified by the Federal Government by notification in the official Gazette.
>
> (4) Where a single island, rock or a composite group thereof constituting a part of the territory of Pakistan is situated off the main coast, the baseline referred to in such-section (3) shall be drawn along the outer seaward limits of such island, rock, or composite group.

In 1996 the Pakistani government issued specific latitude and longitude coordinates demarcating its maritime claims, which immediately drew an official protest from India.[51] The 1996 law is the first straight baseline claim made by the country.[52] A 1996 analysis by the Office of the Geographer at the US Department of State found that the normal low-water mark running along the coast would be the appropriate baseline along the vast majority of Pakistani coastline. Closing lines across bays and small rivers could be employed, but only in a few local stretches of coast was the use of straight baselines justified.[53] Pakistan's coastline generally does not meet either of the two geographic tests appropriate for straight baselines; furthermore, "for the most part, the waters enclosed by the new straight baseline system do not have the close relationship with the land, but rather reflect the characteristics of the territorial sea or high seas."[54]

Pakistan purports to require foreign warships to obtain permission prior to transiting territorial sea, and foreign supertankers, nuclear-powered ships, and ships carrying nuclear or other noxious materials are required to give Pakistan prior notification of transit.[55] The United States protested these claims of coastal state authority in 1982 and 1997, and the US Navy conducted operational freedom of navigation assertions to challenge them in 1986, 1991, 1996, 1998, and 1999.[56]

Pakistan also does not recognize the right of foreign-flagged warships to exercise high-seas freedoms in the EEZ. Pakistan claims authority to regulate passage of foreign ships through "designated areas" of the economic zone.[57] In a declaration made on February 26, 1997, at the time of ratification of UNCLOS, Pakistan stated: "It is the understanding of the Government of the Islamic Republic of Pakistan that the provisions of the Convention on the Law of the Sea do not in any way authorize the carrying out in the exclusive economic zone and in the continental shelf of any coastal State military exercises or maneuvers by other States, in particular where the use of weapons or explosives is involved, without the consent of the coastal State concerned."[58] Pakistan's law requires foreign state aircraft to file flight plans with the civil aviation authority before conducting overflight of the EEZ. This requirement is not in accord with article 3 of the International Convention on Civil Aviation, which exempts state aircraft from foreign state jurisdiction.[59]

Central Indian Ocean

India is situated at the geographic and political center of this enormous sweep of territory, with Pakistan and an Islamic influence gravitating from the west and Chinese power encroaching from the east. The Seychelles and Maldives also lie in the central Indian Ocean, and both are being heavily courted by China. The

Republic of the Maldives, along with Sri Lanka, is situated along the Laccadive Sea, which is between the southern tip of India and the equator. The Maldives shares religious and cultural connections with Pakistan, and there are reports that some Maldivian nationals have been drawn to Pakistan to join the Lashkar-e-Taiba and other Islamic terrorist groups.[60]

South of the Maldives, the islands of the Chagos Archipelago, British Indian Ocean Territory, is the location of Diego Garcia. Diego Garcia is the most important western strategic outpost in the Indian Ocean. France discovered the Chagos Archipelago in the sixteenth century, and at that time there were no indigenous inhabitants. In 1814 at the Treaty of Paris, Britain assumed control of the islands, which were governed from Mauritius until 1965.

The United Kingdom purchased the islands from Mauritius in 1965 and enacted the British Indian Ocean Territory (BIOT) Order that same year.[61] The United Kingdom and the United States executed an exchange of notes in 1966 to depopulate the island and permit the United States to construct military facilities on Diego Garcia. The agreement permits the United States to lease the BIOT for fifty years. An extension clause would permit US basing on Diego Garcia for an additional twenty-year period—to 2036—if the parties agree to do so by December 2014.

In 2006 the DC Circuit Court dismissed an appeal of a lawsuit based on alleged US complicity in the illegal depopulation of the Chagos Archipelago on grounds that the issue was a nonjusticiable "political question."[62] In doing so, the court affirmed the limitation of individual rights in foreign policy–related cases, and preserved the right of US forces to operate unimpeded under the long-term lease.[63]

The atoll of Diego Garcia has been the primary staging area for American power in the Indian Ocean. The airfield has two twelve-thousand-foot runways and extensive fuel farms, and has been used by US B-52, B-1 and B-2 strategic bomber aircraft to conduct missions into South Asia. The US Navy has located Maritime Prepositioning Squadron (MPS) Two in the lagoon of Diego Garcia, the crystal clear aqua-green center of the horseshoe-shaped atoll. Although the composition of MPS Two varies, generally the military sealift command ships in the squadron carry armored vehicles, heavy equipment, and supplies to equip a marine air-ground task force for up to one month. The ships have provided support for Operations Desert Storm, Restore Hope in Somalia, Support Hope in Kenya and Rwanda, and Iraqi Freedom.

INDIA. The Indian subcontinent projects into the Indian Ocean, providing a commanding geographic position. India has a continental coastline of 6,100 km in length. Including the coastlines of the Andaman and Nicobar Islands in the Bay of Bengal and Lakshadweep Islands in the Arabian Sea, India's shore stretches

7,517 km. The remote archipelagos located about 750 miles off India's southeastern coast (but only 175 miles south of Burma, an ally of China) are areas of high Indian Navy activity.[64] The Lakshadweep Islands in the Arabian Sea and the Andaman Islands in the Bay of Bengal form two geographic (but not legal) archipelagos. India also owns Minicoy Island, in the Southern Hemisphere.

Military support facilities on the outlying Andaman, Nicobar, Lakshadweep, and Minicoy Islands are being bolstered to enhance the country's forward operating capability.[65] A series of naval air "enclaves" are being developed along the outer perimeter of Indian territories in order to be able to enable military aircraft to refuel, rearm, and redeploy without having to return to main bases on the subcontinent.[66] The move has major implications for India's ability to interdict Chinese energy supplies transiting from the Persian Gulf through the Indian Ocean and Strait of Malacca. Nicobar Island, for example, sits astride the western entrance to the Strait of Malacca, just north of the island of Sumatra. Already 60 percent of China's oil imports from the Gulf transit the area, and that figure will increase to 75 percent by 2015. Like China, India purports to restrict military activities in the EEZ. Thus, India's interpretation of coastal state rights and freedom of navigation in its EEZ is important for China, placing Beijing in an ironic position. Whereas China has pushed for restrictive views of navigation in its own EEZ, it now must contend with the possibility that in the event of a crisis between the two countries, India could impede with Chinese oil shipments. Delhi might do so through the exercise of belligerent right of visit and search, or through the enforcement of peacetime restrictions on "military activities" or "dangerous or noxious cargoes" in the EEZ.

India was one of the original signatories to UNCLOS in 1982, and it also signed the Part XI implementing agreement on seabed mining in 1994. In June 1995 India ratified the 1982 Convention and the 1994 Implementing Agreement. The union cabinet stated at the time that ratification would "enhance India's navigational interests and protect the economic security under the legal regime."[67] In 1999 Judge P. Chandrasekhara Rao of India was elected president of the International Tribunal on the Law of the Sea in the German port of Hamburg, replacing Thomas Mensah of Ghana.[68]

India maintains a handful of excessive maritime claims in the Indian Ocean. First, the waters of Palk Bay between the mainland coast and maritime boundary with Sri Lanka are claimed as internal waters, and the Gulf of Mannar is claimed as historic waters.[69] India and Sri Lanka reached agreement during a meeting on June 26 to 28, 1974, to delimit a "historic waters" boundary through Palk Bay.[70] Several years after the 1974 agreement on the Palk Bay, India and Sri Lanka extended their maritime boundary eastward into the Bay of Bengal and southward through the Gulf of Mannar, claiming additional area as "historic waters."[71] The Palk Bay delimitation used a selective or modified equidistance formula. Traditional fishing rights of both parties were preserved. The two nations also settled a dispute over the ownership of Kachchativu Island, which is a historic Tamil Nadu fishing ground.[72] But the war against the Liberation Tigers of Tamil Eelam restricted access to the waters by Indian fishermen, causing the local Indian regional government in Tamil Nadu to contest Sri Lankan ownership in 2010.[73]

Second, India's laws concerning innocent passage in the territorial sea are not in accord with UNCLOS. Indian law provides that foreign warships must provide notice before entering territorial sea, a rule that is inconsistent with part II of UNCLOS.[74] But in a unique court case in 2006 following the grounding of a Taiwanese fishing vessel, *Isabel III*, in the Lakshadweep Islands off the country's west coast, India upheld the long-standing principle of the right to innocent passage.[75] In the first judgment of its kind, the court upheld the right of foreign vessels to enjoy innocent passage through the territorial sea as set forth in UNCLOS and reflected in the country's Merchant Shipping Act. Furthermore, in the case of a wreck or other accident, seafarers in distress can seek the help of a nearby state and refuge in that state at the expense of the vessel's owner until repatriated to their own country. The Kerala High Court in Cochin quashed the case against thirty-three crew members, including four Taiwanese, twelve Filipinos, twelve Chinese, three Vietnamese, and two Indonesians, after finding them not guilty of illegal entry into India.

Third, India claims authority over areas of the contiguous zone for security purposes. The contiguous zone extends from a distance of twelve nautical miles from the shoreline out to a maximum of twenty-four nautical miles from the shoreline. Since article 33 of UNCLOS specifies that the contiguous zone is for the purpose of preventing infringement of customs, fiscal, immigration, or sanitary (health) laws of the coastal state, the assertion of security jurisdiction is unlawful.[76]

Fourth, India has a fairly long pedigree of asserting that the coastal state may exercise a high degree of offshore jurisdiction over foreign-flagged ships. During the UNCLOS negotiations during the 1970s, India insisted that the treaty create a pollution regulation zone extending between fifty miles and two hundred miles from shore of coastal states.[77] The United States and other nations rejected the proposal, and instead the two-hundred-mile EEZ was created and formed part V of the Convention. Even today, however, Indian law requires prior consent for military exercises or maneuvers in the EEZ or on the seabed of the continental shelf.[78] India also purports to require twenty-four-hour prior notification from vessels entering its EEZ with cargoes "including dangerous goods and chemicals, oil, noxious liquid and harmful substances and radioactive material."[79] India's excessive EEZ claims place it within a small group of states, led by China and joined by Pakistan, that purport to regulate foreign military activities out to two hundred nautical miles from the shoreline.[80]

In 2001 India lodged diplomatic protests against the United States and the United Kingdom for the presence of US Navy and Royal Navy military survey ships operating in the Indian EEZ without permission. The USNS *Bowditch* was detected in the Indian EEZ on November 28, 2000, and the HMS *Scott* was detected by India twice in December 2000 and once in January 2001.[81] India claimed that these warships were conducting "marine scientific research" in the Indian EEZ without permission of the coastal state. The United States and the United Kingdom, however, have long held the position that military surveys constitute naval operations that are beyond the jurisdiction of the coastal state, as permitted under articles 58 and 87 of UNCLOS.[82]

India and Pakistan have struggled to resolve a five-decade-old maritime boundary dispute involving three segments—a horizontal sector, a maritime zone, and Sir Creek itself. During the 2007 round of talks on Sir Creek in Rawalpindi, Pakistani president Pervez Musharraf told the Indian delegation that the maritime boundary segment of the dispute "could be settled in 10 minutes."[83] The two nations are at loggerheads, however, over the methodology for resolving the dispute. While India has insisted on excluding the maritime zone from the negotiations, Pakistan has demanded a composite dialogue involving all the three sectors.[84] The issue involves fisheries and oil and gas rights but is complicated because the terrorists that struck the business district of Mumbai in 2008 staged from Sir Creek, along the border with Pakistan.[85] India has been more successful in resolving maritime boundary disputes with its other neighbors. The most important agreements are included in table 9.1.

Recently, India joined Burma in a dispute against Bangladesh in the International Tribunal for the Law of the Sea over maritime boundary demarcation in the Bay of Bengal.[86] Situated between India and Burma, Bangladesh estimates that the disputed areas of the Bay of Bengal hold promise for significant offshore oil development. Bangladesh has objected to the Indian and Burmese baseline claims, the division of territorial waters in the bay, and contending continental shelf claims. Dhaka is digging in for a protracted legal battle against its larger neighbors, and the ministry of foreign affairs has requested funding for the lawsuit.[87] In June 2010 Bangladesh and India appointed legal consultants in the case to serve on the arbitration panel.[88]

Aside from the maritime boundary negotiations with its neighbors, India is also becoming more active in cooperative maritime security. Despite initial resistance from communists inside the Indian government, for example, India has been a leader in counterpiracy operations in the Somali basin. As India's navy grows, there may be additional opportunities for it to play a larger role in regional security. The US and Indian navies are working more closely together to ensure regional stability. In 2006, during President George Bush's state visit to India, the two maritime powers signed a maritime security cooperation agreement as one

TABLE 9.1 Indian Maritime Boundary Agreements

Nation(s)	Location	Date of Agreement
Sri Lanka	Palk Strait maritime boundary[a]	July 1974
Sri Lanka	Gulf of Mannar and Bay of Bengal	May 1976
Indonesia	Continental shelf boundary	December 1974 and August 1977
Sri Lanka and the Maldives	Trijunction point in Gulf of Mannar	July 1976 and November 1976
Maldives	Arabian Sea maritime boundary	June 1978
Thailand and Indonesia	Fix the "Common Trijunction Point" in Andaman Sea between Thailand, India, and Indonesia, which is equidistant from India and Indonesia but not from Thailand; it is approximately 31.5 miles farther from Thailand.[b]	June 1978
Thailand	Continental shelf in the Andaman Sea	December 1978
Indonesia and Malaysia	Maritime boundaries	March 1979
Burma	Maritime boundary of the Andaman Sea in the Coco Channel and in the Bay of Bengal	December 1986
Burma and Thailand	Trijunction point in Andaman Sea between Burma, India, and Thailand	October 1993

[a] US Department of State, "Limits in the Seas No. 66, Historic Water Boundary: India-Sri Lanka" (Washington, DC: Bureau of Intelligence and Research, December 12, 1975); www.state.gov/documents/organization/61460.pdf.

[b] US Department of State, "Limits in the Seas No. 93, Continental Shelf Boundaries: India-Indonesia-Thailand" (Washington, DC: Bureau of Intelligence and Research, August 17, 1981); www.state.gov/documents/organization/58818.pdf.

of the many side agreements to the deal on nuclear collaboration. In conjunction with the visit, the two governments also penned a number of tertiary agreements to strengthen the bilateral relationship in other areas of cooperation.

One agreement in particular presages greater naval collaboration between Delhi and Washington—the 2006 Indo-US Framework for Maritime Security Cooperation. The agreement recognizes the "global strategic partnership" the two nations are fashioning, and forges a commitment to develop "comprehensive cooperation in ensuring a secure maritime domain." In addition to pledging to support existing multilateral efforts to strengthen maritime security, including initiatives at the International Maritime Organization, India and the United States also agreed to collaborate against maritime threats, including piracy and armed robbery at sea, threats to ship and crew safety, transnational organized crime, and suppression of illicit trafficking in weapons of mass destruction. The framework contains provisions for regular maritime security policy discussions in the bilateral Defense Policy Group, the Naval Executive Steering Group, and the Military Cooperation Group. So far the agreement has been underutilized, but it remains as a ready framework for ramping up bilateral cooperation.

But the United States and India are still recovering from decades of distance, a result of India's warm relationship with the Soviet Union during the Cold War, US support for Pakistan, and the memory of Delhi's nonaligned leadership. Despite big electoral defeats on May 13, 2011, including the loss of power in the large state of West Bengal, the Indian communist party is still a potent political force in the government of India.[89] Many Indians remain wary of a closer relationship with the United States.

Recently, India opted against purchasing 126 US fighter aircraft manufactured by Boeing (F/A-18E/F) and Lockheed Martin (F-16IN) in favor of either the Eurofighter Typhoon or the Dassault Rafale.[90] The $12 billion purchase illustrates India's reluctance to mesh too closely to Washington, and to bargain shop for the best deal. India recoiled at what it viewed as untoward pressure to sign a communication interoperability and security memorandum of agreement, which manages spectrum management and interoperability between the two nations. There were even suggestions in the Indian media that the US platforms may include surreptitious "kill switches" that could be flipped by the United States to shutdown systems sold to India.

India already has purchased eight P8i antisubmarine aircraft, and it may buy ten C-17 military transport aircraft, worth $4 billion.[91] The Indian Army is also interested in obtaining Apache attack helicopters and the Chinook heavy-lift helicopters.[92] India has a diversity of suppliers, however. Moscow sold the aircraft carrier *Gorshkov* to Delhi in 2010 for $2.3 billion. The ship will carry Russian aircraft once it is refitted as the INS *Vikramaditya* and inducted into the Indian fleet in 2013.[93]

Eastern Indian Ocean

On the eastern edge of the Indian Ocean lie Bangladesh, Burma, Thailand, the Indonesian Islands of Sumatra and Java, and the west coast of Australia. Australia owns Christmas Island and the Cocos (Keeling) Islands, which are located between Australia and Indonesia, as well as Heard Island and McDonald Island on the approach to Antarctica.[94]

Although nominally a Southeast Asian nation, Indonesia also fronts the eastern edge of the Indian Ocean. The Straits of Malacca and Singapore, the Sunda Strait, and transit through the Timor Sea provide access into the South China Sea and Pacific Ocean from the Indian Ocean. The Strait of Malacca, like the

Strait of Hormuz on the western edge of the Indian Ocean, constitutes one of the most important geographic infrastructures in the world. Just beyond the Straits of Malacca and Singapore is the South China Sea—an area Beijing hopes to place under its suzerainty. China is also expanding its presence beyond the South China Sea into the Indian Ocean.

The United States and India appear to be natural allies in the Indian Ocean, with the interests of both nations aligned against an ever-powerful and expansive China. There is a global shift in the balance of power under way. Traditional military powers such as Russia and the United Kingdom are waning. Russia, for example, has seen its defense budget increase 566 percent in the past decade—the country's greatest military spree since the end of the Cold War.[95] But with a military-age population in free fall, endemic corruption, low morale, and plaguing problems of quality, Russia's military might is uneven.[96] With Britain, the problem is cash. As the power of the Royal Navy ebbs under the crush of London's debt burden, the perennial sea power will be reduced to a single aircraft carrier. Washington, also facing defense reductions in the coming years, will be in need of allies with the will and capability to stand up to China in the Indian Ocean.[97]

China has launched a charm offensive to attract support for access to naval and aviation facilities in other countries—described as the "string of pearls" strategy. The strategy links Hong Kong and southern China to the port of Sudan and the Persian Gulf through a series of way stations and port-use agreements and facilities in the Indian Ocean. Beijing established basing access and facilities at Gwadar, a small Pakistani fishing village only 240 miles from the Strait of Hormuz.[98] China also uses facilities in Bangladesh, strengthening Beijing's sea lines of communication to the Persian Gulf but also encircling India.[99] Broad-spectrum diplomacy and outreach, combined with bags of money, is helping China entice Sri Lanka, Mauritius, Seychelles, Maldives, Burma, and, of course, Bangladesh and Pakistan to open their facilities to Chinese naval visits.

Fan Hongming, a Burma expert at Xiamen University, explained in 2010 that 80 percent of China's oil imports come through the Strait of Malacca, "and the United States has control over it."[100] In an effort to reduce dependence on a long and vulnerable maritime supply chain from the Gulf, Chinese state-owned companies are building a 1,100-km oil pipeline through Burma. The line connects southwest China to energy producers in the Middle East and Africa. By bypassing the Indian Ocean and the chokepoint of the Straits of Malacca and Singapore, Beijing hopes to make its supply of energy less vulnerable to disruption by the Indian Navy or US Navy.[101] China's goal is to reduce the percentage of its oil that travels by sea from Africa and the Middle East from more than 77 percent today to 54 percent by 2014, when the pipeline is expected to flow 440,000 b/d into China.[102] It is unlikely, however, that China can significantly lessen its reliance on the sea-lanes.

Even an optimistic evaluation by the International Energy Agency points out that it is only the share of Chinese oil imports through the Indian Ocean and Straits of Malacca and Singapore that actually could fall—not the total volume. By any measure, the total volume of oil flowing into China each year from the Middle East and Africa is expected to increase. By 2015, 3.5 million b/d will be shipped, up from about 3.1 million b/d presently.[103]

In Southeast Asia, Beijing is working with Cambodia to build a rail line from southern China to the Gulf of Thailand and with Burma to build a massive dam to supply power to China. China also has proposed construction of a $20 billion canal across Thailand's Kra Peninsula, which would enable Chinese ships to bypass the choke point at the Strait of Malacca.[104] Whether China solidifies its string of pearls strategy or develops the Kra Canal, it will have greater naval forces in the Indian Ocean to facilitate maritime trade. With the deployment of warships from the People's Liberation Army Navy (PLAN) to the Gulf of Aden and western Indian Ocean, China has for the first time demonstrated an ability to operate in distant waters.

Delhi hopes to leverage American power to offset what it views as accelerating Chinese encroachment into the region. China remains India's foremost conventional threat, whereas unstable Pakistan poses a potential nuclear danger as well as a vector for extremist groups and terrorists. An armed forces brief to Prime Minister Manmohan Singh, Defense Minister A. K. Antony, National Security Adviser Shivshankar Menon, Principal Secretary T. K. A. Nair, and Defense Secretary Pradeep Kumar in April 2011 reportedly advised that China was now capable of deploying and sustaining five hundred thousand troops along the Line of Actual Control on the border with India, giving China an advantage of thirty-four divisions to India's nine.[105]

China also has inserted itself into the volatile Kashmir dispute. Indian intelligence agencies suggest that several hundred People's Liberation Army (PLA) engineers are assisting in the construction of bunker fortifications in Pakistani-occupied Kashmir, affirming previous US intelligence reports of a Chinese military presence in the region.[106] In March 2011 the commander of Northern Command, Lt. Gen. K. T. Parnaik, stated that China's increasing proximity to Pakistan through Kashmir was driving India's security fears.[107]

Against this geopolitical backdrop, India's approach to the international law of the sea has important implications for China. Should India adhere to its EEZ claims that require notice in advance of foreign military activities, the stage could be set for a dispute over maritime international law. Likewise, China's well-publicized and more vocal efforts to eject foreign-flagged warships from operating in its own EEZ could be put to the test by Indian Navy warships. Delhi has been less insistent than China at enforcing its excessive maritime claims. Speaking informally, Indian Navy officials have stated that the only reason India purports to regulate foreign military activities in the EEZ is because Pakistan has the same rule. (For its part, Pakistan makes the same claim, so neither nation appears to be invested in enforcing its excessive EEZ claim).

CONCLUSION

The Indian Ocean features an emerging clash between the world's most populous states—India and China—as well as the confluence of three great religions, Islam, Hinduism, and Buddhism. Demographic and economic growth in the region portends increasing interaction among nations from within and outside the Indian Ocean. The possibility of further conflict does not appear remote, although it is uncertain whether India's wars with Pakistan and China in the past necessarily foreshadow naval warfare in the future. The center stage in the drama of Indian-Pakistani-Chinese-American politics is the Indian Ocean.

The international law of the sea serves to help alleviate as well as in some ways contribute to potential conflict in the Indian Ocean. First, UNCLOS has provided a framework that offers stability and predictability, balancing the rights and duties of coastal states with those of the international community. The treaty also created several mechanisms whereby neighboring states can negotiate to resolve competing maritime claims. The certainty created by UNCLOS and the availability of binding dispute resolution has aided states in reaching bilateral solutions to maritime disputes. Thus, while India has worked methodically with its neighbors to reach agreement on maritime boundaries in the Indian Ocean, Delhi has been less successful in finalizing borders with Pakistan in the Kashmir or China in the Himalaya.

Contending interpretations of UNCLOS, however, risk contributing to tension and increase the risk of conflict. Specifically, disagreements exist concerning the right of foreign-flagged warships and commercial vessels to enjoy innocent passage in the territorial sea, transit passage through international straits, and high-seas freedoms of navigation and other internationally lawful uses of the sea in the EEZ and on the high seas. For the nations that hold an expansive view of coastal state authority, such as India and China, it appears that their interpretations of the rules are very much ad hoc and case-specific—with the country asserting broad rights to freedom of navigation and overflight for its ships and aircraft while purporting to limit the exercise of those rights by other nations in areas under its national jurisdiction.

While India and Pakistan have settled into a rather routinized maritime relationship that is quite stable, India's relationship with China in the Indian Ocean is in a state of flux. Just as US naval power is in relative decline in East Asia, perhaps giving promise to a greater Chinese presence in the oceans, or even emboldening the PLAN, India's powerful and growing fleet in the Indian Ocean may frustrate Chinese ambitions in developing a "string of pearls."

NOTES

1. Hans J. Morgenthau, *Politics among Nations: The Struggle for Power and Peace*, 6th ed., edited by Kenneth Thompson (New York: Knopf, 1985) 52–53.
2. James Kraska, "Grasping 'The Influence of Law on Seapower,'" *Naval War College Review* 62, no. 3 (Summer 2009): 113–35. For analysis of how international institutions can facilitate cooperation in the Indian Ocean region specifically, see Lee Cordner, "Progressing Maritime Security Cooperation in the Indian Ocean," *Naval War College Review* 64, no. 4 (Autumn 2011): 69–88.
3. US Joint Forces Command, "The JOE 2010: Joint Operating Environment"; www.jfcom.mil/newslink/storyarchive/2010/JOE_2010_o.pdf, 28.
4. Plato, *Platonis Phaedo: The Phaedo of Plato*, edited by W. D. Geddes (London: Williams & Norgate, 1863), 145.
5. United Nations Convention on the Law of the Sea, completed December 10, 1982, UN Doc. A/CONF.62/122 (entered into force November 16, 1994), reprinted in 21 I.L.M. 1261, 1348; www.un.org/Depts/los/convention_agreements/convention_overview_convention.htm [hereinafter UNCLOS].
6. James Kraska, *Maritime Power and Law of the Sea: Expeditionary Operations in World Politics* (New York: Oxford University Press, 2011), 157–220.
7. See Raul Pedrozo, "Close Encounters at Sea: The USNS *Impeccable* Incident," *Naval War College Review* 62, no. 3 (Summer 2009): 101–11; Shirley A. Kan, Richard Best, Christopher Bolkcom, Robert Chapman, Richard Cronin, Kerry Dumbaum, Stuart Goldman, Mark Manyin, Wayne Morrison, Ronald O'Rourke, et al., *China-US Aircraft Collision Incident of April 2001: Assessments and Policy Implications*, Report RL30946 (Washington, DC: Congressional Research Service, October 10, 2001); and Margaret K. Lewis, "An Analysis of State Responsibility for the Chinese-American Airplane Collision Incident," *New York University Law Review* 77 (2002): 1404–41, at 1406–7.
8. Article 5, UNCLOS states: "The normal baseline for measuring the breadth of the territorial sea is the low-water line along the coast."
9. Article 7(2), UNCLOS.
10. United Nations, *The Law of the Sea: Baselines: An Examination of the Relevant Provisions of the United Nations Convention on the Law of the Sea* (New York: United Nations, 1989); www.un.org/Depts/los/doalos_publications/publications texts/The%20Law%20of%20the%20Sea_Baselines.pdf, 17.
11. See J. Ashley Roach and Robert Smith, *United States Responses to Excessive Maritime Claims*, 2nd ed. (The Hague: M. Nijhoff Publishers, 1996), 64 (24 miles); Robert D. Hodgson and Lewis M. Alexander, "Towards an Objective Analysis of Special Circumstances: Bays, Rivers, Coastal and Oceanic Archipelagoes and Atolls," *Law of the Sea Institute* Occasional Paper No. 13 (1971), 8 (45 miles);

Peter B. Beazley, "Maritime Limits and Baselines: A Guide to Their Delineation," *Hydrographic Society Special Publication No. 2*, 2nd rev. ed. (August 1978), 9 (45 miles); and US Department of State, "Limits in the Seas No. 106, Developing Standard Guidelines for Evaluating Straight Baselines" (Washington, DC: Office of the Geographer, Bureau of Intelligence and Research, August 31, 1987); www.state.gov/documents/organization/59584.pdf, (48 miles).

12. US Department of State Dispatch Supplement, "Law of the Sea Convention, Letters of Transmittal and Submittal and Commentary," vol. 6 (February 1995), 8.
13. US Department of State, "International Boundary Study, Series A: Limits in the Seas No. 14, Burma Straight Baselines" (Washington, DC: Office of the Geographer, Bureau of Intelligence and Research, March 14, 1970); www.state.gov/documents/organization/61607.pdf. One nautical mile equals 1,852 meters.
14. "World Oil Transit Chokepoints, Strait of Hormuz," *US Energy Information Administration*; www.eia.gov/countries/regions-topics.cfm?fips=WOTC&trk=p3.
15. "Piracy: No Stopping Them," *Economist*, February 3, 2011; www.economist.com/node/18061574.
16. John Aglionby, "Indonesia Plans World's Longest Bridge," *Financial Times*, October 3, 2007; www.ft.com/cms/s/0/b971a73c-71c4-11dc-8960-0000779fd2ac.html#axzz1Lx41VK6M.
17. The longest span of the Sunda Strait Bridge will be about 3 km, or more than 50 percent longer than the longest existing structure, the Akashi-Kaikyo Bridge in Japan.
18. The story of Krakatoa is set forth in Simon Winchester, *Krakatoa: The Day the World Exploded: August 27, 1883* (New York: Harper, 2005).
19. Articles 5–16 and 57, UNCLOS.
20. Article 56(1), UNCLOS.
21. Ken Booth, *Law, Force & Diplomacy at Sea* (Sydney, Australia: Allen & Unwin Pty., 1985), 38.
22. US Department of State, "International Boundary Study, Series A: Limits in the Seas No. 41, Straight Baselines, Mauritius" (Washington, DC: Office of the Geographer, Bureau of Intelligence and Research, March 7, 1972); www.state.gov/documents/organization/61537.pdf, 5–6.
23. Maldives ratified UNCLOS on September 7, 2000.
24. "Maritime Zones of Maldives Act No. 6/96"; www.un.org/Depts/los/LEGISLATIONANDTREATIES/PDFFILES/MDV_1996_Act.pdf. See also "United Nations Law of the Sea Bulletin No. 41" (New York: United Nations, 1999); www.un.org/Depts/los/doalos_publications/LOSBulletins/bulletinpdf/bulletinE41.pdf, 16–20.
25. Sally J. Cummins and David P. Stewart, eds., *Digest of United States Practice in International Law 2001* (Washington, DC: International Law Institute, 2002); www.state.gov/documents/organization/139600.pdf, 711–14.
26. "Maritime Zones Act, 1999" (Act No. 2 of 1999); http://faolex.fao.org/docs/pdf/sey34741.pdf.

27. The tendency is described in Bernard H. Oxman, "Centennial Essay: The Territorial Temptation: A Siren Song at Sea," *American Journal of International Law* 100 (October 2006): 831–51, at 851. Oxman recounts that excessive maritime claims reflect "a unilateralist impulse often born of narrow agendas, impatience, frustration, or political and bureaucratic ambition. It tends to confuse substance with inspiring rhetoric and useful tactics."
28. Under Secretary of Defense for Policy, *Maritime Claims Reference Manual*, DOD 2005.1-M (Washington, DC: US Department of Defense, June 23, 2005); www.jag.navy.mil/organization/documents/mcrm/MCRM.pdf.
29. Bassas da India, Europe Island, and Juan de Nova Island are in the Mozambique Channel separating Mozambique from Madagascar. France also owns Glorioso Island, Tromelin Island, and Reunion Island, which are near Madagascar, and numerous French Southern and Antarctic lands located in southern Indian Ocean.
30. *The Antarctic Treaty*, December 1, 1959, 12 U.S.T. 794, T.I.A.S. No. 4780, 402 U.N.T.S. 71. The fifteen consultative parties are the twelve states named in the preamble: Argentina, Australia, Belgium, Chile, France, Japan, New Zealand, Norway, South Africa, the Soviet Union, the United Kingdom, and the United States, and three acceding states that since have become qualified—Brazil, Poland, and Germany. See also, Robert D. Hayton, "The Antarctic Settlement of 1959," *American Journal of International Law* 54 (1960), 349–71, at 349, 355.
31. Karen N. Scott, "Managing Sovereignty and Disputes in the Antarctic: The Next Fifty Years," *Yearbook of International Environmental Law* 20, no. 1 (2009): 3–40; doi:10.1093/yiel/20.1.3.
32. "Introduction," UNCLOS, Agreement relating to the Implementation of Part XI of the United Nations Convention on the Law of the Sea with Index and Excerpts from the Final Act of the Third United Nations Conference on the Law of the Sea 1-2 (2001).
33. L. D. M. Nelson, "Declarations, Statements and 'Disguised Reservations' with Respect to the Convention on the Law of the Sea," *International and Comparative Law Quarterly* 50, no. 4 (October 2001): 767–86, at 767.
34. Article 21, Vienna Convention on the Law of Treaties, completed at Vienna on May 23, 1969 (entered into force on January 27, 1980), 1155 UNTS 331.
35. Sarosh Bana, "Law of the Sea," *Business India*, March 5, 2001.
36. Indus Waters Treaty, September 19, 1960, India-Pak., 419 U.N.T.S. 125. See also, James Kraska, "Sustainable Development Is Security: The Role of Transboundary River Agreements as a Confidence Building Measure (CBM) in South Asia," *Yale Journal of International Law* 28 (Summer 2003): 483–87, at 485.
37. Rajat Pandit, "India Seeks to Prevent Skirmishes with China on the High Seas," *Times of India*, December 3, 2011; http://articles.timesofindia.indiatimes.com/2011-12-03/india/30471461_1_ins-arihant-sea-trials-jin-class.
38. Christopher Bodeen, "Pakistan, China Premiers Meet amid Tension with US," *Associated Press*, May 18, 2011.

39. US Department of State, "Limits in the Seas No. 113, Straight Baseline Claims: Djibouti and Oman" (Washington, DC: Bureau of Oceans and International Environmental and Scientific Affairs, April 22, 1992); www.state.gov/documents/organization/58382.pdf.
40. Government of Oman, Royal Decree 38/82, July 1982, reproduced in "Law of the Sea Bulletin No. 1," 33–37 (Office of the Special Representative of the Secretary-General for the Law of the Sea, September 1983). The United States protested the excessive straight baseline claims in 1997 and 1999. *Maritime Claims Reference Manual*, DOD 2005.1-M.
41. Government of Oman, Royal Decree 15/81, February 1981.
42. Government of Oman, Declaration made upon ratification of UNCLOS, August 17, 1989, reproduced in, "Law of the Sea Bulletin No. 14" (Office for Ocean Affairs and Law of the Sea, United Nations, December 1989), 8.
43. Government of Oman, Declaration made upon ratification of UNCLOS, August 17, 1989.
44. Oman signed a land and maritime agreement with Yemen in October 1992, and a maritime boundary agreement with Pakistan in June 2000.
45. "Law of Sea Convention Ratified, Extending Resource Zone," *BBC Summary of World Broadcasts*, May 28, 1997.
46. "Third World Nations Assail US Position in Law of the Sea Talks," *New York Times*, August 11, 1981; www.nytimes.com/1981/08/11/world/third-world-nations-assail-us-position-in-law-of-sea-talks.html.
47. Ministry of Foreign Affairs, *Gazette of Pakistan*, August 29, 1996; reproduced in United Nations Division of Ocean Affairs and the Law of the Sea, "Law of the Sea Bulletin No. 34" (1997), 45.
48. Annex, "Pakistan Notifies Establishment of Baselines" (Islamabad, Pakistan, September 9, 1996), reproduced in US Department of State, "Limits in the Seas No. 118, Straight Baseline Claim: Pakistan" (Washington, DC: Bureau of Oceans and International Environmental and Scientific Affairs, December 20, 1996), 8.
49. "Limits in the Seas No. 118," 5.
50. Ibid.
51. United Nations, "Law of the Sea Bulletin No. 34" (United Nations Division for Ocean Affairs and Law of the Sea, 1997); www.un.org/Depts/los/doalos_publications/LOSBulletins/bulletinpdf/bulletinE34.pdf, 45.
52. "Limits in the Seas No. 118," 2.
53. Ibid., 6.
54. Ibid., 4.
55. "Territorial Waters & Maritime Zones Act" (1976); www.un.org/Depts/los/LEGISLATIONANDTREATIES/PDFFILES/PAK_1976_Act.pdf.
56. Under Secretary of Defense for Policy, *Maritime Claims Reference Manual*, DOD 2005.1-M.
57. "Territorial Waters & Maritime Zones Act" (1976).

58. Government of Pakistan, "Declaration Made upon Ratification," February 26, 1997; www.un.org/Depts/los/convention_agreements/convention_declarations .htm#Pakistan%20Upon%20ratification.
59. The United States protested Pakistan's overflight claims in 1982 and 1997, and it conducted operational assertions in 1986, 1991, and 1998. *Maritime Claims Reference Manual*, DOD 2005.1-M.
60. Praveen Swami, "Nine Maldives Jihadists Held in Pakistan," *Hindu*, April 4, 2009; www.hindu.com/2009/04/04/stories/2009040452281100.htm.
61. The British Indian Ocean territory Order 1965 provides for the constitution of a separate colony consisting of Diego Garcia, Egmont or Six Islands, Peros, Banhos, Salomon Islands, Trois Feres, including Danger Island and Eagle Island (previously included in the British Dependency of Mauritus), and West Island Middle Island, South Island, Cocoanut Island and Euphratis Island (formerly forming part of the Colony of the Seychelles). British Indian Ocean Territory Order 1965, S.I. 1965 No. 1920 (November 8, 1965), reproduced in *International and Comparative Law Quarterly* 15 (April 1966): 582.
62. *Bancoult v. McNamara*, 445 F.3d 427 (DC Cir. 2006). See also, "DC Circuit Holds Claims of Harms to Native Inhabitants of the British Indian Ocean Territory Caused by the Construction of a US Military Base Nonjusticiable," *Harvard Law Review* 120 (2007): 860–67.
63. *Carr v. Baker*, 369 US 186 (1962). See also *Tel-Oren v. Libyan Arab Republic*, 726 F. 2d 774, 803 n.8 (DC Cir. 1984) (Bork, J., concurring, stating that the "murky and unsettled" nature of the political question doctrine is demonstrated by the "lack of consensus about its meaning").
64. Amol Sharma, Jeremy Page, James Hookway, and Rachel Pannett, "Asia's New Arms Race," *Wall Street Journal*, February 12, 2011.
65. Sandeep Unnithan, "China Threat, Indian Navy Unveils Forward Policy in Indian Ocean," *India Today*, December 2, 2011.
66. Ibid.
67. "Cabinet Approves Ratification of Convention on Law of the Sea," *BBC Summary of World Broadcasts*, June 12, 1995.
68. "Law of the Sea Court in Germany Gets Indian President," *Deutsche Presse-Agentur*, October 5, 1999.
69. Ibid. This claim is not recognized by the United States, which conducted operational assertions in the Palk Strait in 1993 and 1994, and in the Gulf of Mannar in 1999. *Maritime Claims Reference Manual*, DOD 2005.1-M.
70. The agreement, which entered into force on July 8, 1974, is printed in the government of India's "Notice to Mariners," no. 9, 133–156, April 15, 1975, reproduced in US Department of State, "Limits in the Seas No. 66, Historic Water Boundary: India-Sri Lanka" (Washington, DC: Bureau of Intelligence and Research, December 12, 1975); www.state.gov/documents/organization/61460 .pdf, 3–4. The status of Palk Bay as historic waters has at least some legal authority, having been the subject of a judicial decision in the case of *Annakumaru*

Pillai v. Muthupayal, heard in the Appellate Criminal Division of the Indian High Court in Madras in 1903–4. During that time, both Sri Lanka (Ceylon) and India were under administration of the United Kingdom. The lawsuit involved rights to chank (Indian conch) beds and pearl grounds in Palk Bay and the adjacent Gulf of Mannar (Manaar). The Court ruled that the Bay was "landlocked by His Majesty's dominions for eight-ninths of its circumference ... [and] effectively occupied for centuries by the inhabitants of the adjacent districts of India and Ceylon respectively." "Limits in the Seas No. 66," 4. The court continued that, "we do not think that Palk's Bay can be regarded as being in any sense the open sea and therefore outside the territorial jurisdiction of His Majesty." Finally, the British occupation had attracted the "acquiescence of other nations."

71. US Department of State, "Limits in the Seas No. 77, Maritime Boundaries: India-Sri Lanka" (Washington, DC: Bureau of Intelligence and Research, February 16, 1978); www.state.gov/documents/organization/58833.pdf, 3–5.
72. "Notice to Mariners," no. 9, 133–156, in "Limits in the Seas No. 66."
73. The disagreement involves a rather complex mixture of conservation, fisheries, and ethnic pride. See, Charitha Ratwatte, "Fishy Happenings in Palk Bay," *Daily FT*, April 26, 2011; www.ft.lk/2011/04/26/fishy-happenings-in-palk-bay/.
74. Act No. 80 (Territorial Waters, Continental Shelf, Exclusive Economic Zone & Other Maritime Zones Act), August 1976.
75. Donald Urquhart, "Indian Court Acquits Crew of Grounded Taiwanese Ship; in First Such Case, India Gives Right to Innocent Passage to Ships in Distress," *Business Times Singapore*, October 6, 2006.
76. Act No. 80 (Territorial Waters, Continental Shelf, Exclusive Economic Zone & Other Maritime Zones Act), August 1976. This claim is not recognized by the United States, and the US Navy conducted operational assertions in protest in 2001. *Maritime Claims Reference Manual*, DOD 2005.1-M.
77. Information Bank Abstracts, *New York Times*, November 11, 1972, at 3 (bloc of thirty nations led by India and Canada propose an offshore pollution zone that is opposed by the United States as conferring validity on a claim of jurisdiction beyond territorial sea).
78. The government of India declaration made upon ratification (June 29, 1995) states: "The Government of the Republic of India understands that the provisions of the Convention do not authorize other States to carry out in the exclusive economic zone and on the continental shelf military exercises or maneuvers, in particular those involving the use of weapons or explosives without the consent of the coastal State." The United States does not recognize this claim, and the United States conducted operational assertions in Indian EEZ in 1999 and 2001. *Maritime Claims Reference Manual*, DOD 2005.1-M.
79. This requirement is not recognized by the United States and was protested in 1998, and the United States conducted operational assertion in 1999. *Maritime Claims Reference Manual*, DOD 2005.1-M.
80. Kraska, *Maritime Power and the Law of the Sea*, 310–11.

81. "Defence Minister Says US, UK Naval Ships Violating Territorial Waters," *BBC Monitoring South Asia*, April 19, 2001.
82. See Kraska, *Maritime Power and the Law of the Sea*, 270–77.
83. "Disputed Area Unlikely to Be Solved in July India–Pakistan Talks; Navy Chief," *BBC Monitoring South Asia*, March 1, 2011.
84. Ibid.
85. Krishna Pokharel, "Attacks Stir Another India-Pakistan Border Dispute," *Wall Street Journal Abstracts*, January 13, 2009, 10.
86. "Bangladesh Prepares for Legal Battle against India, Burma over Maritime Disputes," *BBC Monitoring South Asia*, March 14, 2010.
87. Ibid.
88. Bangladesh secured Alan Vaughan Lowe, a former professor of international law at the University of Oxford, to be a member of the five-member arbitration tribunal. India has selected Judge P. Sreenivasa Rao, a former legal adviser to India's external affairs ministry. The ITLOS nominated Rudiger Wolfrum of Germany, Tullio Treves of Italy, and Ivan A. Shearer of Australia to serve as the other three arbitrators, with Wolfrum presiding.
89. Amol Sharma, "Big Loss for India Communists," *Wall Street Journal*, May 14–15, 2011, A9.
90. Rahul Bedi, "India Shortlists Typhoon, Rafale for Medium Multi-Role Combat Aircraft (MMRCA) Race," *Jane's Defense Weekly*, May 4, 2011, 6.
91. "Boeing Eyes Asia for Its Defence Sales; It Says India Is the 'Jewel in the Crown' as the Country Opens Up Its Defence Sector," *Business Times Singapore*, June 7, 2010.
92. Ibid.
93. Ravi Velloor, "Putin's India Visit to Focus on Arms Deals; Delhi, a Long-time Ally, Also Aims to Tap Russian Leader's Views on Afghan Situation," *Straits Times* (Singapore), March 12, 2010.
94. Chas W. Andrews, "A Description of Christmas Island (Indian Ocean)" *Geographical Journal* 13 (January 1899): 17–35.
95. Richard Boudreaux, "Russia's Fading Army Fights Losing Battle to Reform Itself," *Wall Street Journal*, April 20, 2011, A1, A12. Russia, like India, faces potential foes in both the east and west. Moscow is worried about the enormous Chinese military buildup but cannot shake its historic preoccupation with NATO and the West.
96. Ibid.
97. Alistair MacDonald, "Sun Setting on British Power," *Wall Street Journal*, May 14–15, 2011, A1, 12.
98. Sudha Ramachandran, "China's Pearl in Pakistan's Water," *Asia Times Online*, March 17, 2005.
99. See, generally, Christopher J. Pehrson, "String of Pearls: Meeting the Challenge of China's Rising Power across the Asian Littoral," *Strategic Studies Institute*, US Army; available at www.strategicstudiesinstitute.army.mil/pubs/display.cfm?pubid=721.

100. Ho Ai Li, "Myanmar Becoming More Crucial to China; Reclusive Nation Key to Reducing Its Reliance on Strait of Malacca," *Straits Times*, September 10, 2010.
101. "China Sets Sail on Strategic Voyage for Oil Security," *Canberra Times* (Australia), March 14, 2011, A9.
102. Ibid.
103. Ibid.
104. "String of Pearls: Military Plan to Protect China's Oil," *Agence France Presse*, January 18, 2005.
105. Shishir Gupta, "Army Warns PM: China Can Deploy 500,000 Troops on LAC," *Indian Express.com*, May 11, 2011.
106. Josy Joseph, "Indian Confirms Chinese Military in PoK [Pakistan occupied Kashmir]," *Times of India*, May 12, 2011.
107. "China-Pak Nexus Cause of Concern: Parnaik," *Daily Excelsior*, March 27, 2011, www.dailyexcelsior.com/web1/11mar28/news1.htm#4.

CHAPTER 10

A MERLION AT THE EDGE OF AN AFRASIAN SEA

Singapore's Strategic Involvement in the Indian Ocean

EMRYS CHEW

INTRODUCTION

Seas and oceans are wide-ranging zones of interaction. They provide critical planes of analysis that allow for careful evaluation of large-scale historical processes and strategic currents. The Indian Ocean, however, presents a more highly textured and complex framework of analysis.[1] This analysis is challenging from a historical perspective because of an extensive oceanic history of contacts and exchanges between a kaleidoscopic array of human societies, which involve myriad forms of political and economic organization and which render this maritime domain more culturally variegated and historically layered than any other sea or ocean basin. The analysis is difficult in terms of grand strategy because of the strategic realities of an interregional geographic entity with widely divergent national interests and political economies, where civilizational fault lines in oceanic history have the potential to generate a clash of indigenous and outsider discourses. Certainly, the interpenetration of military-strategic and economic interactions with political and social fluctuations across this ocean, from the local to the global dimension, continues to demonstrate a higher degree of interdependence and intensity—as revealed by shockwaves from a twenty-first-century tsunami triggered by an earthquake epicenter some 450 km southwest of Singapore but felt some 6,900 km away in Kenya.

Strategic analysis may be skewed by an excessive emphasis on current events insofar as it repeatedly characterizes the Indian Ocean as an "emerging" geostrategic region while reacting to some recent turn of events or headline news racing across the immediate horizon.[2] But the interplay of forces in nature along with interactions of trade, politics, ideas, and strategy throughout Indian Ocean history—whether pursued by free agents or official representatives of large empires, small states, and private companies that impact or influence the region from outside or within—underscore the fact that a geostrategic arena of the first order was long emergent and well established over "a hundred horizons."[3] While the ocean's contours and characteristics have indeed altered with shifting relationships between its invaders and inhabitants, as with its maritime zones and landmasses, many of its strategic concerns still emanate from underlying structures and forces operating in the long run.

History never repeats in exactly the same way, but strategic analysis can ill afford to ignore underlying elements that would drive historical change or sustain historical continuity, not least in the Indian Ocean. Strategists must therefore engage with the layers of the intermediate historical space, as American journalist Robert Kaplan echoed recently for the benefit of policy elites and popular audiences.[4] What was held as strategically significant at any particular time would always depend on a critical convergence (or divergence) of the political ambitions, economic interests, ideological convictions, religious beliefs, and cultural preferences of the ocean's invaders and inhabitants. Of prime strategic importance would be the imperative to secure scarce commodities deemed either valuable or vital, including raw materials, luxury products, and energy resources.

The Indian Ocean region (IOR) was animated from the earliest antiquity by waves of cross-cultural interaction between Eastern and Western Hemispheres. Asians, Africans, and Caucasians became collective participants in a sophisticated structure of commerce and politics shaped by the annual cycle of monsoon winds and a lively subculture of bargaining with "value added" services. Applying key metaphors associated with British geographer and strategist Sir Halford Mackinder, this multidimensional transoceanic milieu extending as far as the South China Sea became the strategic "heartland" and geographical "pivot" of world history well before the rise of the Mediterranean-Atlantic and the Pacific. It encompassed as a core region the earliest processes of "archaic" as well as "modern" globalization, in which varied indigenous patterns of commercialization and consumption were only gradually subordinated to the market-driven, profit-maximizing forces of Euro-American capitalism and thereby subsumed within an evolving industrial world economy.[5] Yet the ocean never became a "lake" controlled or owned by any single power, regardless of exclusive claims made by proponents of Pax Indica, Pax Sinica, Pax Islamica, Pax Britannica, or Pax Americana. Bounded by the continental landmasses of Africa and Asia, there is a sense in which it was less of an "Indian" ocean than a cosmopolitan and increasingly globalized "Afrasian Sea."[6] The Indian Ocean's strategic significance would be recalibrated over the second half of the twentieth century, with the end of the Western colonial empires, the emergence of independent nation-states throughout Africa and Asia, and the extension of the US–Soviet Cold War not unlike the Anglo-Russian "Great Game" of the previous century. Strategic perspectives would again shift with the conclusion of the Cold War, the concurrent rise of India and China, the growing concerns over energy supplies, and the continuation of post-9/11 asymmetric conflicts.[7]

But what would it all mean for Singapore, a "global" maritime city-state located at the eastern periphery of that globalizing arena? To what extent are its fortunes bound up with the security and destiny of that wider Indian Ocean? From a geo-economic viewpoint, the stability of the IOR remains vital to Singapore, situated astride a key choke point and sea-lanes between two oceans, and thus reliant on seaborne commerce for its long-term viability. From a geostrategic viewpoint, Singapore continues to espouse a multiplicity of policies and partnerships that it perceives would better guarantee its survival and success in the region.

This chapter explores the evolutionary dynamics of Singapore's strategic involvement in the Indian Ocean: from Singapore's genesis amid the cycles of Indian Ocean history, as a "Merlion" at the edge of an "Afrasian Sea,"[8] to Singapore's growing ability to "value add" to Indian Ocean security, springing from its unique role in Southeast Asia as a leader in multinational approaches. The chapter addresses the multifaceted influences shaping Singapore's strategic outlook toward the IOR before analyzing its realistic, pragmatic approach to the region's ills. Singapore uses a combination of "internal balancing" or capability building alongside arms procurement and defense partnerships with external powers. While simultaneously engaging and balancing with the major powers, it continues to develop serious naval, air, and counterterror capacities. Finally, this chapter discusses Singaporean perspectives on recent multilateral security proposals, explaining why Singapore's highly responsive, adaptable strategic approach is likely to remain at the forefront of small states' solutions to Indian Ocean regional problems.

SINGAPORE'S LONG-TERM INTEREST IN THE INDIAN OCEAN

Singapore's significance in Indian Ocean history has derived mainly from its strategic location on the India-China maritime trade route, at the crossroads between the Indian and Pacific Oceans. Such strategic geography had been crucial to ensuring the commercial and political viability of the ancient island-emporium called Temasek-Singapura. That the increasingly "globalized," modern port city of Singapore could arise on the same site after a significant period of discontinuity and then make progress from colony to republic simply proves the dictum that geography is destiny.[9]

Early Greek references to the eastern periphery of the IOR had hinted dimly at the commercial significance of various places in maritime Southeast Asia. Based on those topographical sketches, thirteenth-century European cartographers drew a map of the Indian Ocean depicting the southern end of the Malay Peninsula as an *emporion*, a node in a network of international commerce.[10] But the earliest surviving eyewitness account has a distinctly oriental perspective; the fourteenth-century Chinese traveler Wang Dayuan composed a fairly detailed narrative about two oceans—a western ocean and an eastern ocean—with their division at the Malacca-Singapore Straits.[11]

Even more compelling is fourteenth-century archaeological evidence confirming the existence of an ancient emporium on Singapore Island, which likely prospered from seaborne trade until the twilight of the famous maritime "silk route" that ended around 1400. In the analysis of archaeologist-historian John Miksic, this Indo-Islamic *negara* had served "as a major node of the long-distance maritime communication network on the routes between the Indian Ocean and the South China Sea."[12] Indeed, the two names accorded to the archaic island-polity reflect its maritime orientation as much as the cultural influence of Indianization, rippling over much of the eastern Indian Ocean in previous centuries: Temasek ("Sea Town" in Javanese) and Singapura ("Lion City" in Sanskrit). But while Temasek-Singapura flourished for a time as an outpost of local Malay empires, it declined once the Malay imperium began to disintegrate and then crumbled into obscurity after the Portuguese, entrenched at Malacca since 1511, burnt down the Malay trading post at the mouth of the Temasek (Singapore) River in 1613.[13]

Given the apparent finality of that disruptive episode, underscoring the transitory nature of so many of the Indian Ocean's maritime emporia, what underlying factors then led to the emergence of a colonial port city over the ruins of the ancient *negara*? And how would Singapore's reinvention as a modern "global city" enable it to either endure or engage more contemporary cycles of international crisis and transformation around the IOR? The development of a British colony and then an independent republic on Singapore Island, following centuries after the rise and demise of Temasek-Singapura, emphasizes the importance of applying to strategic analysis no less than historical narrative what the great oceanic historian Fernand Braudel termed the *longue durée*: historical events or movements in politics, economics, and society yield particular consequences in the short to medium term, but these are regulated by underlying structures or forces of geography, climate, and culture that shape the destinies of particular communities over the long term, predisposing them to certain strategic choices or behavioral patterns.[14]

Colonial Singapore combined geo-economic factors that had defined its precolonial past with globalizing features that would shape its postcolonial future. The British official widely credited with the founding of the new trading settlement, Sir Stamford Raffles, was cognizant of the prior existence of "the ruins of the ancient capital of Singapura" that contemporaries in the Mediterranean-Atlantic region and IOR had both become "ignorant of."[15] Yet the factors of strategic geography that had once ensured the success of a local polity were unashamedly adapted to new global imperatives, which saw Singapore established from 1819 onward as a bastion of British free-trade imperialism: its raison d'être was to counter Dutch expansion from Batavia as well as secure British maritime trade routes running further eastward to China. Nonetheless, the British colonial regime in Singapore did not simply reconstruct the traditional Indian Ocean maritime emporium with its typically cosmopolitan bazaar culture; nor did they simply reproduce the Regency-period fabric or Victorian architecture of a British coastal municipality transformed by the engines of industry. Colonial Singapore was a hybrid port city that incorporated indigenous, imperial, and industrial features; a "free port" that presented a more attractive alternative to the monopolistic Dutch colonial ports; a regional transshipment center that served maritime Southeast Asia in addition to the oceans on either side; and, increasingly, an international entrepôt that operated to maximize profits within the larger industrial world economy. Singapore's migrant communities, drawn from diasporic movements and demographic shifts across the Indian Ocean and South China Sea, formed a "plural society" not merely cosmopolitan in character but internationalist in outlook—in the long term better able to appreciate and adapt to the socioeconomic and cultural requirements of modern globalization.[16]

The opening of the Suez Canal in 1869 would significantly enhance Singapore's prospects as a global port city. The canal not only accelerated the passage of steamships from Europe to the Far East but also augmented the volume of seaborne commerce transiting the Malacca and Singapore Straits. Wong Lin Ken, formerly Raffles Professor of History at the National University of Singapore, has observed: "Singapore's trade showed a greater rate of growth between 1869 and 1914 than in the first fifty years of its modern existence, for it became an essential link between the industrial world of the West and the developing export economies of colonial Southeast Asia."[17] Even when the Panama Canal was opened in 1914, shortly before the outbreak of World War I, it was still cheaper to convey goods from East Asia to the Atlantic seaboard ports of the United States via Singapore, the Indian Ocean, and the Suez Canal.[18] The poet Rudyard Kipling would pay tribute to Singapore's pivotal role in the expansion of cross-cultural commerce on a global scale. In Kipling's "The Song of the Cities," we hear the voice of Singapore personified:

> *. . . East and West must seek my aid*
> *Ere the spent hull may dare the ports afar.*
> *The second doorway of the wide world's trade*
> *Is mine to loose or bar.*[19]

Poetic license aside, Singapore was undoubtedly the greatest port of the eastern IOR before World War II.

But just how significant during the colonial period were Singapore's commercial interests within the IOR? Annual trade returns from between 1824 and 1937 indicate that the proportion of Singapore's trade with countries along the Indian Ocean littoral—including India, mainland and maritime Southeast Asia, Australasia, Arabia, the Persian Gulf, and East Africa—experienced a fairly consistent downward trend. It was at its highest around 1825, when trade with India and Southeast Asia alone amounted to 68 percent of Singapore's total trade, and at its lowest in 1937, when trade with India, Southeast Asia, and Australasia amounted to 44 percent of Singapore's total trade.[20] Such "decline" was, of course, only proportional: it reflected Singapore's progressive integration into the emerging global economy; and it was relative to the expansion of a worldwide trade that also encompassed East Asia (mainly China) and, increasingly, the West (Britain, Europe, and the United States).

These evolving patterns of regional integration and global interdependence could, on the other hand, lead to more pronounced vulnerabilities. The Great Depression of the 1930s had a decidedly dampening effect. Another hiatus occurred during the Japanese invasion and occupation of Singapore (1942–45) as attempts were made to forcibly integrate Singapore—renamed Syonan ("Light of the South")—into an exclusive "Greater East Asia Co-Prosperity Sphere" focused on the Pacific. Fortunately, modern Singapore did not go the way of ancient Temasek-Singapura. The decades of peaceful growth under the aegis of Pax Britannica had instead generated sufficient economic infrastructure and global trade connections to enable Singapore to survive both the trauma of wartime occupation and the long winter of the Cold War (1945–89) when it descended upon the Indian Ocean.

Nevertheless, changes in the political climate after 1945 would bring about shifts in both the balance of Singapore's interests between two oceans and the direction of Singapore's economic development. The geopolitics of bipolar superpower rivalry, regional nonalignment, and British decolonization "east of Suez" would draw Singapore increasingly into the orbit of a new Asia-Pacific system under the wings of the United States.[21] Protracted nationalist struggles and protectionist economic nationalism across the IOR further raised doubts over Singapore's long-term reliance on entrepôt trade to generate increased employment and economic growth.

Under the astute supervision of its first finance minister (later defense minister and deputy prime minister), Goh Keng Swee, self-governing Singapore would embark on a new phase of economic restructuring from the 1960s, oriented toward the Asia-Pacific. Having secretly negotiated Singapore's separation from Malaysia in August 1965, Goh proceeded to formulate economic and fiscal policies geared toward ensuring Singapore's survival as a fledgling nation-state. Coming from a thinking patriot who had obtained a doctorate in economics from the London School of Economics and was a voracious reader of Sun Tzu's *Art of War* and other military-strategic texts, it demonstrated, above all, a broader understanding of strategy empowered by the engines of economic development, with rapid industrialization, defense modernization, and education reform all tempered by fiscal discipline. The Jurong Industrial Estate (which the skeptics dubbed "Goh's Folly") would supply vital infrastructure, while institutional support was forthcoming through agencies and organizations such as the Economic Development Board, the Chartered Industries of Singapore, and the Development Bank of Singapore. It was an ambitious program for a time of transition, radical and rigorous in promoting the development as well as diversification of manufacturing, along with service and strategic industries, based on the free-enterprise capitalist model.[22]

This transition would lead ultimately to Singapore's reinvention as a global city, linked to other cities and continents not simply by the waves of a historic ocean but also the waves of modern technology. In the words of S. Rajaratnam, Singapore's first foreign minister, speaking in 1972:

> Singapore is transforming itself into a new kind of city—a Global City. . . . It is the city that electronic communications, supersonic planes, giant tankers and modern economic and industrial organization have made inevitable.
>
> If we view Singapore's future not as a regional city but as a Global City, then the smallness of Singapore, the absence of a hinterland, or raw materials and a large domestic market are not fatal or insurmountable handicaps. It would explain why, since independence, we have been successful economically and, consequently, have ensured political and social stability.
>
> Once you see Singapore as a Global City, the problem of hinterland becomes unimportant because for a Global City, the world is its hinterland.[23]

Rajaratnam's words in no way undermine Singapore's place within the earlier cycles of global interconnection that shaped Indian Ocean history as a whole. His speech at the time was prophetic, however, because it pierced through an uncertain horizon and pointed ahead to a type of globalization that had not fully dawned.

This would be a form of globalization that could simultaneously engage the arenas of the Indian Ocean, the Euro-Atlantic, and the Asia-Pacific, eventually linking all of them through networks in maritime space, air space, outer space, and cyberspace. Global cities such as Singapore would experience new levels of interdependence as nodes in multidimensional transoceanic networks. Already the demands of modern industry and technology were enlarging Singapore's dependence on oil from the western IOR: Saudi Arabia's share of Singapore's import trade rose from around 1 percent (in the early 1960s) to 13 percent (in 1975–77) owing to a massive increase in the volume and value of petroleum imports.[24] Yet the worldwide revolution in information technology and web-based Internet communication lay in the future, as did Singapore's post–Cold War regionalization strategy of investment in emerging economies.

In the aftermath of the Cold War, the radically altered global strategic environment of the early 1990s paved the way to a revival of Singapore's interest in the IOR. Faced with growing competition from a rising China "looking west," Singapore, as part of the Association of Southeast Asian Nations (ASEAN), soon pushed for greater economic integration in the eastern IOR.[25] From 1992 there would be increased flows of trade and investment involving Singapore and its neighbors within an ASEAN free-trade area. Further integration would be achieved through the e-ASEAN framework introduced in 2001, where information and communications technology has facilitated a paradigm shift in the way essential services are delivered, from e-health to e-education, e-commerce, and e-government. Regional economic integration would also be the theme of the ASEAN economic community, first proposed in 2003 by Singapore's then prime minister Goh Chok Tong and currently a blueprint with a schedule for implementation by 2015.[26]

Beyond Southeast Asia, Singapore has further engaged a rising India "looking east." Goh Chok Tong summed up the moment: "Just as India has looked east, Singapore has looked west towards India. Our ties are intertwined through history, language, and culture."[27] India's economic liberalization efforts have dovetailed nicely with Singapore's regionalization strategy of investing in emerging economies. Expansion in the volume and value of bilateral trade has proven phenomenal: whereas India would become Singapore's tenth-largest trading partner by 2004, Singapore would become India's ninth-largest trading partner by 2005–6, with the trade figures showing steady increase over the course of a decade, from $2.2 billion in 2001 to $9–10 billion in 2006 and $50 billion in 2010. Singapore would become the eighth-largest source of investment in India and the largest among ASEAN member states, with cumulative investment worth $3 billion in 2006, subsequently rising to S5 billion by 2010 and S10 billion by 2015.[28] Further growth would be achieved when Singapore and India signed a comprehensive economic cooperation agreement (CECA) in 2005, which included agreements on the trade in goods and services, investment, e-commerce, intellectual property, technology, educational exchanges, and dispute settlement.[29] The CECA has effectively linked India to ASEAN through its presence in Singapore, which

Singapore's current prime minister, Lee Hsien Loong, has characterized as "India's natural gateway to engage our region."[30] In 2005 Singapore–India trade (worth $7 billion) was nearly half of the total ASEAN–India trade (worth $15 billion).[31]

Singapore has further developed links with states along the western Indian Ocean littoral. With states such as Kenya or Kuwait, mutual trade and investment opportunities have been sealed by agreements and encouraged through the expansion of airline services, banking facilities, and professional training programs.[32] Singapore has even provided assistance in the management and upgrading of regional port facilities. The Port of Singapore Authority (PSA) acquired a stake in the management of several Indian ports, although it would probably be best remembered for somewhat controversial handling of multibillion-dollar operations at the Pakistani port of Gwadar (2007–11), which ran at a loss and would finally be managed by China.[33] But again, this development needs to be viewed against Singapore's wider business outreach in the western Indian Ocean; as Michael Leifer, emeritus professor of international relations at the London School of Economics, once commented: "Singapore is primarily about the business of business."[34] In 1998 PSA upgraded the Yemeni port of Aden, with hopes of transforming it into a regional transshipment center. Although PSA would pull out after the 2002 terrorist attack on French-registered tanker *Limburg* raised insurance premiums in regional waters, driving away shipping lines, this has not deterred Singapore's Overseas Port Management (OPM)—a private company run by several former PSA veterans—from taking over. True to Singapore's profit-maximizing entrepreneurial roots, OPM spearheaded a group of global investors in a $450 million project to upgrade and expand Aden. Successful management of Aden has since led to contract renewal and shortlisting for a similar project at the New Doha port.[35]

In 2004 Singapore's then senior minister Goh Chok Tong also initiated a series of high-level official visits to the Middle East. The following year, Singapore hosted the inaugural Asia-Middle East Dialogue, which has paved the way for several bilateral agreements. In 2007 the Singapore Business Federation launched the Middle East Business Group to synergize links between business chambers and companies from both sides and to provide consultations for local companies with business interests in Middle Eastern economies. The Gulf Cooperation Council states—Saudi Arabia, the United Arab Emirates, Kuwait, Qatar, Bahrain, and Oman—have been of particular interest to Singapore because the revenues generated by the energy industry have opened up avenues for investment in new economic sectors such as tourism, bioindustry, and real estate.[36]

Singapore, at the other end of the Indian Ocean, presents an ideal partner. Its port has evolved into the busiest container port in the world, handling nearly one-sixth of the world's total container transshipment throughput, linking shippers to two hundred shipping lines with connections to six hundred ports in 123 countries.[37] In addition to being one of the world's busiest cargo airports, its international airport at Changi is linked by more than one hundred passenger airlines to 210 cities in more than 60 countries and territories worldwide.[38] With its proven track record of stable public administration, sound finance, sophisticated infrastructures and strong industries—including oil refining, ship repairing, electronics, and, more recently, biochemicals—Singapore has realized if not surpassed the "Global City" of Rajaratnam's vision.

SINGAPORE'S EVOLVING STRATEGY: FROM GATEWAY TO GATEKEEPER?

Whereas Singapore has benefited immensely from its strategic geographical position on the India-China maritime route, the force of historical circumstance has also prevented it from developing an overarching "Indian Ocean strategy." Previously colonial Singapore had been factored into the commercial and strategic calculations of the Western great powers—and especially the British—with their policies of blue water expansion across the Indian Ocean. Port cities from Singapore to Bombay, Muscat, Mombasa, and Zanzibar reflected as much as reinforced the imperatives of the British Raj across this "British Lake," reaching their apotheosis in the strategic vision of British Indian viceroy Lord Curzon. Curzon envisaged a broader strategic space to defend the interests of Britain's "jewel in the crown," encompassing various buffer states and satellites extending from the Persian Gulf to Southeast Asia.[39] Even into the postcolonial era, Singapore would feature in intraregional maritime strategies of others, most notably India. Ironically, the strategic thinking of that visionary of Western global empire was echoed and elaborated decades later by nationalist pundits in independent India. In their neo-Curzonian grand design, they advocated Indian blue water naval expansion underpinned by a ring of Indian naval bases that could reclaim the "British Lake" to make it literally "India's ocean."[40]

There is a sense in which Kipling's earlier verse about Singapore's ability to "loose or bar" the "second gateway of the wide world's trade" could apply in that geostrategic context. If any great power were to control Singapore, its capacity to influence navigation along economically and strategically important straits—only some forty miles wide—would be considerable.[41] Paradoxically, the geostrategic significance of Singapore that made it intrinsically valuable to others would also account for its innate sense of vulnerability. As an independent yet vulnerable island republic, Singapore has had to evolve a host of balancing and developmental strategies to ensure its survival and safeguard its success in the region: first in relation to its immediate Southeast Asian neighbors, and then in the wider context of Indo-Pacific geopolitics.

Singapore's lack of a cohesive Indian Ocean strategy has much to do with the ebb and flow of post-1945 international history. From the end of the Pacific War in 1945 to the substantive withdrawal of British military forces from Singapore in 1971, Singapore was caught up in the politics of survival in a period of geopolitical flux and geostrategic uncertainty. Bipolar superpower rivalry and Britain's progressive decolonization "east of Suez" paved the way for significant ideological and geostrategic realignments around the world. These realignments would include indigenous nationalist attempts at some form of neutral "Afrasian" unity revolving around the Indian Ocean, in addition to American-led efforts to interweave strands of capitalist-economic and military-strategic partnership between the United States and its Pacific allies under the "San Francisco System." Post-1945 Singapore, having to survive politically and strategically torn between two divergent ocean-based systems, would be drawn increasingly to the Pacific.

In the decades after 1945 the cosmopolitan Indian Ocean of time and memory was gradually reduced to a "nonaligned" sea of forgetfulness. Jawaharlal Nehru, at an Asian Relations Conference held shortly before he became prime minister of independent India in 1947, was among the first to raise the possibility of a nonaligned IOR. But as autarkic India was increasingly sidetracked by its Cold War connection with the Soviet Union as part of a broader strategic alignment against China-US-Pakistan alliances, this idea got frozen until the Non-Aligned Meeting at Lusaka in 1970, when proposals for an Indian Ocean "Zone of Peace" were at last adopted. In 1971 the UN General Assembly declared the Indian Ocean a zone of peace, and it created an ad hoc committee to find ways to implement the declaration. Yet the zone of peace never really materialized, despite more than 450 meetings of the committee. India, perhaps hoping to become the dominant regional power, had succeeded in amending the initial proposal so that it circumscribed the activities of extraregional powers. While support was generally forthcoming from all the littoral states, including Singapore, neither the United States nor the Soviet Union was interested. Instead, the US Navy concentrated on maintaining key installations on the Anglo-American base at Diego Garcia (established 1966–73), which could prove useful for supporting a US-forward presence in the western Indian Ocean, thereby meeting any revived Soviet challenge or securing any threatened oil supply from the Persian Gulf region. In 1989 key Western members of the ad hoc committee withdrew altogether, arguing that superpower rivalry in the Indian Ocean had diminished with the end of the Cold War, rendering a zone of peace purposeless.[42] Diego Garcia, however, saw some of its finest moments as a staging point for military operations in the Persian Gulf War (1990–91) and the "global war on terror" (opening phases, 2001–6).

Some littoral states were nevertheless convinced of the need to band together for the purpose of regional economic cooperation, seeing the apparent triumph of global capitalism—including the reentry of both India and China—plus the advent of a new age of globalization. The Indian Ocean Rim Association for Regional Cooperation (IOR-ARC) was founded in Mauritius in March 1997, with Singapore as one of its founding members. Its aim has been to facilitate trade and investment between member states, which also include Australia, India, Indonesia, Kenya, Madagascar, Malaysia, Mauritius, Mozambique, Oman, South Africa, Sri Lanka, Tanzania, Yemen, Bangladesh, Iran, Thailand, and the United Arab Emirates. Dialogue partners include Britain, France, Egypt, Japan, and China. For its part, Singapore has been sending delegations led by a junior minister to IOR-ARC meetings on a regular basis; Masagos Zulkifli, Singapore's minister of state for foreign affairs, was in Bangalore, India, to attend the most recent Council of Ministers meeting in November 2011.[43] Given its regionalization strategy of investing in emerging economies over the past decade or so, Singapore is perhaps more keen than it has been in decades to support multilateral approaches that could advance economic and strategic cooperation in this arena.

All in all, however, IOR-ARC remains something of a backwater. Given the widely divergent national interests and political economies of its member states, there is difficulty in making headway toward regional cooperation or integration. Most member states already belong to other regional groupings that have possibly competing or conflicting interests, such as the South Asian Association for Regional Cooperation, Asia-Pacific Economic Cooperation, and ASEAN. Much economic activity in the IOR is also oriented externally. In contrast with the close economic ties of states around the North Atlantic, intra–Indian Ocean trade comprises less than one-quarter of its total trade. In the case of the Indian Ocean, the global dimension seems to have actually detracted from the idea of establishing effective multilateralism around the ocean.[44]

Conversely, the seaborne cycles of trade and politics after 1945 had the countervailing effect of shifting the balance of Singapore's economic and strategic interests toward the Asia-Pacific. Enmeshing defeated Japan in a network of US-centered relationships that protected Japan from the Soviet Union and China, and shielding the smaller states that had been victims of Japan's wartime aggression from the consequences of Japan's postwar economic rise, the San Francisco Peace Treaty process of 1950–51 contributed to the formation of an Asia-Pacific order from which Singapore could benefit.[45] For Singapore this new order would soon become essential rather than merely beneficial, as Britain began to draw down its military forces "east of Suez," withdrawing protection that had only been previously interrupted during the Japanese occupation.[46] Turning aside from the Indian Ocean, Singapore's balancing and developmental strategies would be initially geared toward survival in the immediate Southeast Asian and Asia-Pacific contexts.

As an island-state transitioning from colonial dependence to postcolonial independence, Singapore was often caught up in a tricky balancing act on a choppy sea of competing local nationalisms between the Indian and Pacific Oceans. Modern Singapore was not the archaic Indo-Islamic polity of Temasek-Singapura but rather an ethnically Chinese-majority island-state in a predominantly Muslim sea. Postcolonial Singapore was buffeted from the start by a full-blown confrontation with Indonesia (1963–66) and security challenges have arisen ever since, to a greater or lesser extent, in moments of contention with its Islamic neighbors. From the early 1960s through to the late 1970s, the communist insurgency in South Vietnam, Vietnam's invasion of Cambodia, and the Sino-Vietnamese War generated further waves of ideological complexity and insecurity.[47]

Singapore's political leadership and plural society coped with the pressures of transition by evolving a raft of equally pluralistic socioeconomic, foreign, and defense policies that together constituted a basic survival strategy. Goh Keng Swee was the architect of an export-oriented developmental strategy based upon the determination, initiative, enterprise, and self-reliance of a people under good governance: "These are human qualities that have helped to transform an island-swamp into a thriving metropolis."[48] S. Rajaratnam, taking into account the perception of Singapore by the world and by its neighbors as a "strategic key" in the region, articulated a combined diplomatic and deterrent approach: "We shall ensure that our foreign policy and our defense policy do not increase tensions and fears among our neighbors."[49] Singapore's current prime minister, Lee Hsien Loong, as political secretary (defense) in 1984, reiterated the approach of the republic's founding fathers by outlining four classes of strategy that could be applied to ensure the survival of small states such as Singapore: development, diplomacy, deterrence, and defense.[50]

In the area of foreign policy, Singapore's strategy has been to always cultivate "a maximum of friends" and ensure "a minimum of enemies," as Rajaratnam once put it.[51] From among those friends, Singapore would need to always have "overwhelming power on our side," in the words of Singapore's founding prime minister Lee Kuan Yew.[52] In Michael Leifer's analysis, such a strategic approach would mean avoiding entanglement in the conflicts of major states while also securing access to "benign external countervailing power" in the national interest; in other words, "a paradoxical combination of non-alignment and balance of power, with an emphasis on the latter."[53] With the disintegration of the British Empire and the rise of the United States as a global power, Singapore would come to rely on the latter's "overwhelming power" as the principal guarantor of its survival in the larger Asia-Pacific system. Postcolonial Singapore has sought to reconcile its friendship with the United States to the lasting development of intra-regional partnerships within ASEAN (founded in 1967) and a long-term strategy of encouraging the presence of all great powers, to "find it—if not in their interests to help us—at least in their interests not to have us go worse."[54]

In the area of defense policy, Singapore has embraced the concept of deterrence with an equally pluralistic approach. While the United States has played a far more significant role than any other power in those strategic calculations, Britain's military-strategic retreat from "east of Suez" would encourage Singapore's involvement with a host of other defense partners. For example, Singapore has participated since 1971 in alternative five-power defense arrangements with Malaysia, Australia, New Zealand, and Britain. In addition, Singapore would develop an indigenous defense establishment, initially with some assistance from Israeli military advisers who, it has to be said, shared the experience of being encircled by Islamic neighbors.[55]

Singapore's strategies in diplomacy and deterrence have evolved in tandem with Singapore's development as a global city. In the gradual transition from survival to success, Singapore's traditionally defensive strategic posture has progressed to one that is more proactive and expeditionary. Some earlier commentators likened Singapore to a "poisonous shrimp": a small creature, with bright warning colors, ultimately indigestible to predators. A fundamental problem with the "poisonous shrimp" concept, however, was its implication that Singapore would first have to be eaten alive: the Singapore Armed Forces would have to wage a finally unwinnable war on home territory.[56] Such a defensive strategic posture would prove eventually incompatible with Singapore's evolution from postcolonial independence to global interdependence. Over the years, Singapore's greater emphasis on technological sophistication along with mobility and firepower has propelled its defense establishment to a position of comparative primacy within Southeast Asia.[57] The island republic even inaugurated new naval bases at Tuas in 1994 and Changi in 2000. This "global" transition has entailed a broadening of maritime security partnerships that could protect Singapore's economic lifelines across the globalizing arena some have called the Indo-Pacific.

SINGAPORE'S MARITIME PARTNERSHIPS IN THE INDIAN OCEAN

The flows of "globalized" seaborne commerce and the fueling of global supply chains across the Indo-Pacific are perhaps more vital than ever. Oil from the Middle East continues to be transported by a host of multinational companies operating through the Indian Ocean and Malacca and Singapore Straits, to be refined in Singapore before being moved onward to fuel economic development in Northeast Asia. The Malacca and Singapore Straits alone carry more than 30 percent of the world's commerce and 50 percent of the world's oil.[58] Equally vital is the need for maritime partnerships capable of safeguarding the products of globalization, particularly against more insidious forms of asymmetric conflict.

How has the security of globalization led to the globalization of security in the IOR? What are Singapore's perceptions of America's "Cooperative Strategy for 21st Century Seapower," with its suggestion of a US-led "Global Maritime Partnership" that could enhance Indian Ocean security? What are Singapore's perceptions of the growing strategic presence of India and China in the Indo-Pacific? And finally, what is the extent of Singapore's participation, given the absence of a formal Indian Ocean strategy?

This study has shown how basic patterns of global interconnection and interdependence were already present in the long-term cycles and cosmopolitanism of life around the Indian Ocean. However, the sheer reach and rapidity of modern sea-based globalization have made the transoceanic milieu increasingly responsive as well as vulnerable to disruption. In 1902 American naval strategist Alfred Thayer Mahan observed, "This, with the vast increase in rapidity of communication, has multiplied and strengthened the bonds knitting together the bonds of nations to one another, till the whole now forms an articulated system not only of prodigious size and activity, but of excessive sensitiveness, unequalled in former ages."[59] Over a century later, following two world wars, one cold war, and the commencement of the global war on terror, America's latest maritime strategy—"A Cooperative Strategy for 21st Century Seapower"—seems to have come full circle in echoing the concerns of Mahan. As of 2007 this strategy acknowledges the importance of applying seapower to "protect and sustain the global, interconnected system through which we prosper"; it appreciates that American interests are best served by "fostering a peaceful global system comprised of interdependent networks of trade, finance, information, law, people, and governance."[60] Advocating integrated action by the "maritime services"—defined as the US Marine Corps, Navy, and Coast Guard—the strategy is geared especially to dealing with transnational threats against the global system in a new age of asymmetric operations. It recognizes the nature of modern sea-based globalization as much as the need to defend it against specific contemporary challenges.

The "cooperative strategy" encompasses more than a multipronged approach involving the maritime forces of one nation. It seeks to bring together many nations on a multilateral platform by way of its Global Maritime Partnership initiative.[61] In view of the sheer reach of globalization across many nations and oceans, the global system is not one that can be secured or defended successfully by any single nation, even a nation that is a global power. The finite pool of that nation's military-fiscal resources, drawn down by escalating international commitments, would end in a classic case of what the historian Paul Kennedy has termed "overstretch."[62] The defense of the global system must therefore derive from collaboration between local, regional, and global powers, involving a multiplicity of defense partners and a host of cooperative security mechanisms. In essence, the security of globalization requires the globalization of security in what should hopefully be a virtuous rather than vicious cycle.

Within the IOR itself, India has arrived at a similar strategy, recognizing the need for at least a regional form of maritime security partnership, the purpose of which would be to safeguard economic prosperity deriving from sea-based globalization. Modeled on the US-led Western Pacific Naval Symposium, of which Singapore is also an active member, the first meeting of the Indian Ocean Naval Symposium (IONS) in February 2008 announced its intention of promoting strategic cooperation between the navies and coast guards of the IOR. In so doing, the IONS aims to "deal with threats at or from the sea, including maritime natural hazards such as tsunamis and cyclones" and "foster a better understanding of the ocean through the application of marine science and technology."[63]

Both the American-led global approach and the Indian-sponsored regional approach have particular merits as well as vulnerabilities. The US cooperative strategy and its Global Maritime Partnership initiative have been critiqued elsewhere in some detail.[64] At least from an indigenous perspective within the Indian Ocean, the chief difficulties may lie in the area of technological interoperability and cross-cultural interaction. Echoing anticolonial sentiment from the days of European naval dominance, there may be underlying suspicion that extraregional powers would use the threat posed by trafficking in weapons (conventional or nuclear), drugs, and humans, as well as piracy and terrorism, to justify their longer-term naval presence in the region. Even in an age of acute global interdependence, many postcolonial Indian Ocean states retain cultural memories of an era when Western technologies served as "tools of empire."[65] The Indian-sponsored IONS, though largely intraregional in membership, may suffer from a similar problem. As a consequence of supplying most of the leadership and financial backing, India will probably seek to exercise firm control over IONS activities. This might resurrect fears of an Indian bid for regional hegemony, a latter-day attempt by neo-Curzonians among the Indian policy elite to transform the Indian Ocean into "India's ocean."[66]

Singapore, for its part, recognizes the value of maritime security partnerships at the global as well as regional level. If made to operate in complementary fashion, they could give extraregional and intraregional powers alike a greater stake in the stability of the region. Singapore has far fewer difficulties with both the American and Indian maritime strategies than perhaps many other Indian Ocean states.

Given its long history of collaboration with Western global powers such as Britain and the United States, Singapore is likely to remain an autonomous but willing partner of America when it comes to "globalizing" defense and security arrangements in the Indian Ocean. Singapore is strategically positioned to support America in engaging Islamic radicalism linked to terror, given that the regions of the Indian Ocean—including much of Singapore's neighborhood in Southeast Asia—are home to the majority of the world's Muslims. Singapore's Tuas and Changi bases have a geostrategic reach transcending Southeast Asia; the base at Changi has a pier designed specially to accommodate US aircraft carriers, and the countries signed an agreement in 2000 allowing America to use this base.[67] Singapore is already an active member of the US-led Proliferation Security Initiative (PSI) aimed at apprehending shipments of weapons of mass destruction and their delivery systems; in 2005 Singapore hosted the first PSI multilateral exercise in Southeast Asia, Exercise Deep Sabre I, and in 2009 followed through with another, Exercise Deep Sabre II.[68] Through Operation Blue Orchid (2003–8), Singapore played a supportive role in US-led coalition efforts to rebuild Iraq, contributing niche capabilities that ranged from air-to-air refueling of aircraft to the protection of key offshore installations and training of Iraqi armed forces.[69]

Singapore is also broadly supportive of India's regional maritime engagement. India's expansive view of maritime zones from East Africa to Southeast Asia as its natural strategic space has not deterred Singapore from strategic cooperation with India.[70] The "Lion King" (or SIMBEX) series of annual bilateral exercises has been held since 1993, in which Republic of Singapore Navy missile corvettes and antisubmarine warfare vessels have engaged in open ocean training with Indian Navy frigates and submarines across the Andaman Sea and Bay of Bengal.[71] In 2004 India granted Singapore's air force and army training facilities on Indian soil, raising speculation that India might "seek access to naval logistics/access facilities in Singapore as a *quid pro quo*."[72] Perhaps a sign of things to come, Exercise Malabar, a naval exercise held annually by the Indian Navy and the US Navy, was expanded in 2007 (then repeated in 2008 and 2011) to deepen multilateral naval cooperation with Australia, Japan, and Singapore.[73]

Singapore's participation in the five-nation "Malabar 07-02" naval exercise organized by India and America in September 2007 did raise concerns in Beijing. Yet Singapore's strategic cooperation with America and India need not necessarily clash with Singapore's "China Policy," not even with the evolution of China's "string of pearls" strategy. The string of pearls—a euphemism for China's Indian Ocean bases first used in an internal US Department of Defense report titled "Energy Futures in Asia"—forms the centerpiece of an interim maritime strategy to guarantee unimpeded access to trade as well as energy supplies in the Middle East and East Africa.[74] Recalling Leifer's statement that "Singapore is primarily about the business of business," it would not be averse to seeing China safeguard its own economic lifelines, given that Singapore's trade and investments with China are growing steadily. Such a view of China's "peaceful rise" toward the Indian Ocean is consonant with Singapore's long-term strategy to engage and facilitate the presence of all great powers in the region. Singapore's managerial handover of Gwadar to China, which had almost singlehandedly established the Pakistani port through heavy assistance, is indicative of the role that Singapore could play in facilitating China's legitimate entry as a responsible member of the greater Indian Ocean community.[75]

CONCLUSION

Faced with new transoceanic opportunities at this crossroads in time, Singapore's strategic calculations must surely have reached the following conclusions: (a) the stabilizing benefits of America's global presence in the Indo-Pacific significantly outweigh any potential Islamic extremist backlash against Singapore for its support of America; (b) the presence of all great (or rising) powers, such as India and China, must be encouraged in order to increase their stake in the prosperity and security of this globalizing arena; and (c) Singapore has its own immediate responsibility, along with the littoral states of Indonesia and Malaysia, to help safeguard the passage of shipping through the Malacca-Singapore Straits.[76]

The major challenges to Singapore's strategy of engaging all powers and stabilizing the regional balance would include (a) a deepening security dilemma between China and India; (b) the uncertainty in Sino-American relations; (c) the enthusiasm in the West to promote democracy in Asia; (d) Japan's quest for a larger maritime role; and (e) the difficulties of building a security community in the Indian Ocean. Singapore's current strategic approach is sustainable if great power relations remain comparatively benign or their competition is muted. The key question is how it might adjust to any significant deterioration in great power relations. To thrive in a highly fluid geostrategic environment, the "Merlion" must be ever mindful of ways in which it could if necessary reinvent its historically conditioned role—that of portal and pivot between East and West.

NOTES

1. See J. Bentley, "Sea and Ocean Basins as Frameworks of Historical Analysis," *Geographical Review* 89, no. 2 (April 1999): 215–25.
2. See, for instance, W. L. Dowdy and R. B. Trood, "The Indian Ocean: An Emerging Geostrategic Region," *International Journal* 38, no. 3 (1983): 432–58.
3. S. Bose, *A Hundred Horizons: The Indian Ocean in the Age of Global Empire* (Cambridge, MA: Harvard University Press, 2006), 1–71.
4. See R. D. Kaplan, "Center Stage for the 21st Century: Rivalry in the Indian Ocean," *Foreign Affairs* 88, no. 2 (March–April 2009); www.foreignaffairs.com/articles/64832/robert-d-kaplan/center-stage-for-the-21st-century; and R. D. Kaplan, *Monsoon: The Indian Ocean and the Future of American Power* (New York: Random House, 2010).

5. C. A. Bayly, "'Archaic' and 'Modern' Globalization in the Eurasian and African Arena," in *Globalization in World History*, edited by A. G. Hopkins, 47–73 (London: Pimlico, 2002); and P. Beaujard, "The Indian Ocean in Eurasian and African World-Systems before the Sixteenth Century," *Journal of World History* 16, no. 4 (2005): 411–65. Also see K. N. Chaudhuri, *Asia before Europe: Economy and Civilization of the Indian Ocean from the Rise of Islam to 1750* (Cambridge: Cambridge University Press, 1990). Historians have broadly applied the term "ancient" or "archaic" to the era before AD 1500, and the term "modern" to the era thereafter. Some scholars have been tempted to apply yet another term—"postmodern"—to the era starting to emerge after 2000. I have preferred to use the terms "colonial" and "postcolonial" when writing about "modern" Singapore from the nineteenth century to the present.
6. M. N. Pearson, *The Indian Ocean* (London: Routledge, 2003), 13–14.
7. S. Bateman, J. Chan, and E. Graham, eds., "ASEAN and the Indian Ocean: The Key Maritime Links," *RSIS Policy Paper* (November 2011), provides a useful strategic overview of historical and contemporary issues from a Southeast Asian perspective. Also see K. McPherson, *The Indian Ocean: A History of People and The Sea* (New Delhi: Oxford University Press, 1993), 4–75; and Pearson, *Indian Ocean*, 3–4, 281–88.
8. For more on "Merlion," see T. Koh, ed., *Singapore: The Encyclopedia* (Singapore: Editions Didier Millet and National Heritage Board, 2006), 349. A mythical creature with the body of a fish and the head of a lion, the Merlion features in various cultural traditions, of which the most ancient are found on Indian murals at Ajanta and Mathura, and on Etruscan coins of the Hellenistic period. The notion of adapting the Merlion to represent Singapore dates back to 1964—the year before national independence—when the newly established Singapore Tourist Promotion Board (precursor of the Singapore Tourism Board) unveiled a logo depicting a Merlion floating above stylized waves over a motto with the words "Lion City." Singapore's Merlion sculpture is a famous local landmark, situated at the mouth of the Singapore River.
9. Examining the broader historical canvas, the geography of the IOR was certainly capable of sustaining the evolution of large continental polities, such as the great land empires in Turkey and Iran (to the west), India (to the north), and China (to the east). Until the early modern period, such geopolitical evolution stemmed from a more complex symbiotic relationship between land caravans and transoceanic shipping, involving the agrarian economies of the hinterland, which controlled the centers of production, and the nodes and networks of long-distance seaborne commerce, which encompassed the circuits of exchange and redistribution. The nodes (typically port cities) would serve as bridgeheads or hinges connecting different maritime zones: those drawing goods from the hinterland have been tied more intimately to the affairs of the interior (e.g., Sofala, Kilwa, Zanzibar, Mombasa, Bombay, Surat, Colombo, Jakarta, Bangkok); others would draw little or nothing from the interior, functioning rather as redistribution centers dependent upon the ebb and flow of commercial traffic (e.g., Aden,

Hormuz, Malacca, Singapore). These emporia or entrepôt ports would typically be situated near the ocean's strategic choke points: the Bab el-Mandeb and the Strait of Hormuz in the western Indian Ocean, the gateways to the Mediterranean-Atlantic; and the Straits of Malacca and Singapore at the edge of the eastern Indian Ocean, the conduits opening out to the South China Sea and the Pacific Ocean. See Pearson, *Indian Ocean*, 30–45.

10. P. Wheatley, *The Golden Khersonese: Studies in the Historical Geography of the Malay Peninsula before AD 1500* (Kuala Lumpur: University of Malaya Press, 1961), 151–52. This thirteenth-century map incorporated data collected by an Alexandrian Greek named Claudius Ptolemaeus around AD 100 and compiled by a Byzantine monk around AD 1000.
11. R. Ptak, "Images of Maritime Asia in Two Yuan Texts: *Daoyi Zhilue* and *Yiyu Zhi*," in *China and the Asian Seas: Trade, Travel and Visions of the Other (1400–1750)* (Aldershot, UK: Variorum, 1998), especially 55; and M. Murfett, J. Miksic, B. Farrell, and M. S. Chiang, *Between Two Oceans: A Military History of Singapore from First Settlement to Final British Withdrawal* (Singapore: Oxford University Press, 1999), 20–22.
12. J. N. Miksic, *Archaeological Research on the 'Forbidden Hill' of Singapore: Excavations at Fort Canning, 1984* (Singapore: National Museum, 1985), 17. The word "*negara*" originally derives from Sanskrit and refers to a polity—city, state, or nation—within the Indo-Islamic or Malay world. The Ming admiral Zheng He, a Chinese Muslim, is credited with sailing his fleet through Singapore's Keppel Harbour while homeward bound from the Indian Ocean on his seventh voyage in 1433.
13. E. C. T. Chew and E. Lee, eds., *A History of Singapore* (Singapore: Oxford University Press, 1991), 4–6, 10–14. Also see C. G. Kwa, "Sailing Past Singapore," in *Early Singapore 1300s–1819: Evidence in Maps, Text and Artefacts*, edited by J. N. Miksic and C. M. G. Low, 95–105 (Singapore: Singapore History Museum, 2004); and C. G. Kwa, "From Temasek to Singapore: Locating a Global City-State in the Cycles of Melaka Straits History," in *Early Singapore 1300s–1819: Evidence in Maps, Text and Artefacts*, edited by J. N. Miksic and C. M. G. Low, 124–46 (Singapore: Singapore History Museum, 2004). Although the polity had disintegrated, the waterway itself remained a well-defined route in the sixteenth century when Portuguese mariners, in their caravels and carracks, traversed the Malacca–Singapore Straits and the South China Sea on voyages between Cochin (in India) and Macau. In the commentaries of Portuguese conqueror Afonso de Albuquerque, it was significantly referred to as the "gate to Singapura." This term recurred as "Strait of Sincapura" when described by Dutchman Jan Huyghen van Linschoten in 1595, and also as "gate of Tan-ma-his" (or Temasek) in a Chinese pilots' directory of the seventeenth century. The route through Singapore's Keppel channel would pass out of use, however, and had to be rediscovered by the British in the early nineteenth century.
14. F. Braudel, "Histoire et Sciences Sociales: La Longue Durée," *Annales Histoire, Sciences Sociales* 13, no. 4 (1958): 725–53.

15. T. S. Raffles, "The Founding of Singapore," in *Journal of the Straits Branch of the Royal Asiatic Society* 2:175–82, reprinted in M. Sheppard, ed., *Singapore 150 years* (Singapore: Times Books International, 1982), 87–93; and T. S. Raffles, "British Commercial Policy in the East Indies, 1819," in *British Colonial Developments 1774–1834*, edited by V. Harlow and F. Madden (Oxford: Clarendon, 1953), 73.
16. L. K. Wong, "The Trade of Singapore, 1819–69," *Journal of the Malayan Branch, Royal Asiatic Society* 33, no. 4 (1960): 11–204; T. R. Metcalf, "Imperial Towns and Cities," in *The Cambridge Illustrated History of the British Empire*, edited by P. J. Marshall, 224–53 (Cambridge: Cambridge University Press, 1996); and T. Harper, "Empire, Diaspora and the Languages of Globalism, 1850–1914," in *Globalization in World History*, edited by A. G. Hopkins, 141–66 (London: Pimlico, 2002). On defining the "plural society," see J. S. Furnivall, *Netherlands India: A Study of Plural Economy* (Cambridge: Cambridge University Press, 1939); and his other work, *Colonial Policy and Practice: A Comparative Study of Burma and Netherlands India* (New York: New York University Press, 1956), especially 304–5.
17. L. K. Wong, "Commercial Growth before the Second World War," in *A History of Singapore*, edited by E. C. T. Chew and E. Lee (Singapore: Oxford University Press, 1991), 52.
18. Ibid.
19. R. Kipling, *Selected Poems* (London: Folio Society, 2004), 50.
20. Trade figures derived from C. P. Holloway, *The Tabular Statements of the Commerce of Singapore during the Years 1823–1824 to 1839–1840 Inclusive* (Singapore: Mission Press, 1842); and *Annual Trade Returns, Singapore*, cited in Wong, "Commercial Growth before the Second World War," 42–54. Also see Wong, "Trade of Singapore, 1819–69," 205–301. "Southeast Asia" here refers to Burma, Malaya, and Northern Borneo (progressively integrated into the British colonial sphere); Indo-China (progressively annexed by France); the Philippines (at first a Spanish colony, then "liberated" by the United States after 1898); and the Dutch East Indies. Only Siam remained independent.
21. J. Baker, *The Eagle in the Lion City: America, Americans and Singapore* (Singapore: Landmark Books, 2005), 229–49.
22. Chew and Lee, *History of Singapore*, 182–215; cf. E. M. Chew and C. G. Kwa, ed., *Goh Keng Swee: A Legacy of Public Service* (Singapore: World Scientific, 2012). Goh identified six principle measures to facilitate industrialization for Singapore: the provision of infrastructure; tariff protection; fiscal incentives; supply of trained labor; maintenance of industrial peace and wage stability; and encouragement of saving. The essence of Goh's developmental strategy is captured in three volumes of his own writings—*The Economics of Modernization* (1971), *The Practice of Economic Growth* (1977), and *Wealth of East Asian Nations* (1995)—subsequently reissued with introductory prefaces by local scholars and proving to be influential in both academic and administrative circles.
23. S. Rajaratnam, "Singapore: Global City," in *The Prophetic and the Political*, edited by H. C. Chan and O. ul Haq, 225–27 (Singapore: G. Brash; New York: St.

Martin's Press, 1987). Rajaratnam was refuting comments by the British historian Arnold J. Toynbee, who observed that "in the World of 1969 the most important sovereign independent city-state is Singapore" although its future was uncertain because city-states represent an earlier stage in the evolution of "cities on the move." Toynbee, *Cities on the Move* (London: Oxford University Press, 1970). In Toynbee's analysis, Singapore was at the mercy of Malaysia, just as Gibraltar would be at the mercy of Spain or Hong Kong at the mercy of China should they opt for independence.

24. *Yearbook of Statistics, Singapore*, cited by S. H. Cheng in Chew and Lee, *History of Singapore*, 200–201.
25. For a discussion of the rationale behind Singapore's regionalization strategy of investment abroad and the concerns of Singaporeans at home, see K. M. Campbell, D. J. Campbell, and A. Chia, "Regionalization: Policy Issues for Singapore," in *Singapore Inc.: Public Policy Options in the Third Millennium*, edited by L. Low and D. M. Johnston, 113–30 (Singapore: Asia Pacific Press, 2001).
26. Koh, *Singapore*, 50. Also see "Joint Media Statement of the 10th ASEAN Telecommunications and Information Technology Ministers Meeting and Its Related Meetings with Dialogue Partners," Kuala Lumpur, January 13–14, 2011, *Association of Southeast Asian Nations*, www.aseansec.org/25748.htm; "Declaration of ASEAN Concord II (Bali Concord II)," October 7, 2003, *Association of Southeast Asian Nations*, www.aseansec.org/15159.htm; and "ASEAN Economic Community Blueprint" (2008), *Association of Southeast Asian Nations*, www.aseansec.org/5187-10.
27. Goh Chok Tong, then prime minister of Singapore, speech delivered at an official dinner hosted by Indian prime minister Manmohan Singh, July 9, 2004.
28. Ibid.
29. Koh, *Singapore*, 246; "India, Singapore Ink Pact," *Asia Times*, July 2, 2005; "India, Singapore Trade to Touch $50 Bn by 2010," *Hindu Business Line*, June 30, 2005; and V. Shekhar, "India-Singapore Relations: An Overview," *IPCS Special Report*, No. 41, June 2007; www.ipcs.org/IPCS-Special-Report-41.pdf.
30. Lee Hsien Loong, "Linking Up to a Rising Asia," *Singapore Government Press Release*, speech, June 30, 2005.
31. Ibid.
32. T. Koh and L. L. Chang, ed., *The Little Red Dot: Reflections by Singapore's Diplomats* (Singapore: World Scientific, 2005), 363–65. Through the Singapore Cooperation Programme, Singapore continues to share its experience of development with developing countries and emerging economies. Its training programs reflect Singapore's areas of expertise, which include public administration, civil service reform, urban development, civil aviation, port and customs management, information technology, and tourism.
33. Syed Fazl-e-Haider, "Singapore Takes Over Pakistani Port," *Asia Times Online*, February 8, 2007; www.atimes.com/atimes/South_Asia/IB08Df03.html; and Peter Lee, "China Drops the Gwadar Hot Potato," *Asia Times Online*, May 28, 2011; www.atimes.com/atimes/China/ME28Ad01.html. Gwadar Port,

complemented by an air defense unit, a garrison, and an international airport, has been largely developed with Chinese aid and has the potential to become a Chinese submarine base safeguarding China's energy supply lines across the Indian Ocean.

34. M. Leifer, *Singapore's Foreign Policy: Coping with Vulnerability* (London: Routledge, 2000), 14. Leifer was echoing US President Calvin Coolidge's "The business of America is business."
35. "Shipping: Arabian Fights," *Economist* (US), April 10, 1999; www.economist.com/node/320732; "Singapore Firm Spearheads Yemeni Port Expansion," *Portworld.com*, May 21, 2007; www.portworld.com/news/2007/05/67882?gsid=7834da94a45e0d3908e2501d44978ba2&asi=1; and "OPM Shortlisted for New Doha Port Project," April 21, 2011; www.ijonline.com/Project/22891.
36. B. Silm, "Reviving the Silk Road and the Role of Singapore," *Biblioasia* 4, no. 1 (April 2008); http://libguides.nl.sg/content.php?pid=103093&sid=775185. For an official summary of Singapore's revived interest in the Indian Ocean, including highlights of recent bilateral agreements and ministerial visits, refer to the sections on South Asia, the Middle East, and Africa in the "International Relations" chapter of *Singapore Yearbook* in the volumes for 2004 through 2009 (Singapore: Ministry of Information, Communications and the Arts, 2004 through 2009).
37. J. Tongzon, "The Future of the Port of Singapore as a Transshipment Hub," in *Singapore Inc.: Public Policy Options in the Third Millennium*, edited by L. Low and D. M. Johnston, 85–112 (Singapore: Asia Pacific Press, 2001); and the homepage of "PSA: The World's Port of Call"; www.internationalpsa.com/home/default.html.
38. Figures from Singapore Changi Airport website, accessed December 13, 2011; www.changiairport.com/our-business/about-changi-airport.
39. Murfett, Miksic, Farrell, and Chiang, *Between Two Oceans*, especially 87–117, 145–247; and McPherson, *Indian Ocean*, 252–60; cf. W. D. McIntyre, *The Rise and Fall of the Singapore Naval Base, 1919–1942* (London: Macmillan, 1979); and J. L. Neidpath, *The Singapore Naval Base and the Defense of Britain's Eastern Empire, 1918–1941* (Oxford: Clarendon, 1981). In a speech delivered on April 8, 2002, Singapore's then prime minister Goh Chok Tong made the observation that "during the British Raj, when India was the jewel in the Crown, Singapore was a small, semi-precious stone on the side."
40. See K. M. Panikkar, *India and the Indian Ocean: An Essay on the Influence of Sea Power on Indian History* (London: Allen & Unwin, 1951), 8, 14–16; and K. Vaidya, *The Naval Defense of India* (Bombay: Thacker, 1949), 1, 91, 101. "Even if we do not rule the waves of all the five oceans of the world," noted K. Vaidya, "we must at least rule the waves of the Indian Ocean. . . . The Indian Ocean must become an Indian Lake. That is to say India must become the supreme and undisputed power over the waters of the Indian Ocean . . . controlling the waves of the vast mass of water making the Indian Ocean and its two main offshoots, the Arabian Sea and the Bay of Bengal." Consequently, Vaidya argued for the

creation of three self-sufficient and fully fledged fleets to be stationed at the Andamans in the Bay of Bengal, at Trincomalee in Sri Lanka, and at Mauritius. Like K. M. Panikkar, he advocated a ring of Indian Ocean bases for India—from the Cape of Good Hope, Mozambique, Mombasa, Aden, Oman, and Muscat (on the western side), through Trincomalee, Rangoon, Penang, and Singapore (on the eastern side), and the Maldives, the Seychelles, Mauritius, and Madagascar (to the south)—which might stand India in good stead to face China as a potential future challenger and rival in the region. For excellent analysis of the historical challenges confronted by the British imperial defense system and independent India's growing naval involvement in the Indian Ocean, see P. J. Brobst, *The Future of the Great Game: Sir Olaf Caroe, India's Independence, and the Defense of Asia* (Akron, Ohio: University of Akron Press, 2004).

41. L. K. Wong, "The Strategic Significance of Singapore in Modern History," in *A History of Singapore*, edited by E. C. T. Chew and E. Lee (Singapore: Oxford University Press, 1991), 18.
42. Pearson, *Indian Ocean*, 286; cf. D. L. Berlin, "Neglected No Longer: Strategic Rivalry in the Indian Ocean," *Harvard International Review* 24, no. 2 (June 22, 2002). Also see R. B. Rais, *The Indian Ocean and the Superpowers: Economic, Political and Strategic Perspectives* (London: Croom Helm, 1986); S. S. Harrison and K. Subrahmanyam, ed., *Superpower Rivalry in the Indian Ocean: Indian and American Perspectives* (New York: Oxford University Press, 1989); and M. N. Pearson, "Indian Ocean: Regional Navies," in *The Oxford Encyclopedia of Maritime History*, vol. 2, edited by J. B. Hattendorf, 211–15 (Oxford; New York: Oxford University Press).
43. "Indian Ocean Rim Association for Regional Cooperation," *Indian Ocean Review* 13, no. 1 (March 2000), 3–7; and "Visit by Minister of State for Foreign Affairs Masagos Zulkifli to Bengaluru, India," *MFA Press Statement*, November 13, 2011; http://160.96.2.211/content/mfa/media_centre/press_room/pr/2011/201111/press_20111113.html.
44. S. Bateman, "The Indian Ocean Naval Symposium—Will the Navies of the Indian Ocean Region Unite?" *RSIS Commentaries*, March 17, 2008; http://dr.ntu.edu.sg/bitstream/handle/10220/6022/rsisc035-08.pdf?sequence=1; Pearson, *Indian Ocean*, 286.
45. A. I. Latif, *Between Rising Powers: China, Singapore and India* (Singapore: Institute of Southeast Asian Studies, 2007), 19–20; and K. E. Calder, "Securing Security through Prosperity: The San Francisco System in Comparative Perspective," *Pacific Review* 17, no. 1 (March 2004), 136.
46. Murfett, Miksic, Farrell, and Chiang, *Between Two Oceans*, 280–305.
47. Leifer, *Singapore's Foreign Policy*, presents a superb contemporary overview with incisive analysis. Areas of tension between Indonesia, Malaysia, and Singapore have ranged from religio-cultural affiliations and race relations through to creeping maritime jurisdiction and negotiations over the continuation of Singapore's water supply from Malaysia.

48. Goh Keng Swee, speech at the Chinese Chamber of Commerce, March 15, 1969; available on microfilm NA 1250, National Archives of Singapore.
49. S. Rajaratnam, "Framing Singapore's Foreign Policy," December 16, 1965, in *S. Rajaratnam on Singapore: From Ideas to Reality*, edited by C. G. Kwa (Singapore: World Scientific and Institute of Defense and Strategic Studies, 2006), 28.
50. Lee Hsien Loong, speech, in *Straits Times*, November 6, 1984.
51. C. G. Kwa, ed., *S. Rajaratnam on Singapore* (Singapore: World Scientific and Institute of Defense and Strategic Studies, 2006), xii.
52. Lee Kuan Yew, Singapore's founding prime minister, Speech, "We Want to Be Ourselves," October 9, 1966.
53. Leifer, *Singapore's Foreign Policy*, 5–6.
54. Lee, "We Want to Be Ourselves"; cf. O. ul Haq, "Foreign Policy," in *Government and Politics of Singapore*, edited by J. Quah, H. C. Chan, and C. M. Seah (Singapore: Oxford University Press, 1987), 667. Even during the Cold War, as ul Haq has observed, this included the development of some economic links with China and the Soviet Union, with the aim of giving these states in addition to the Western powers and Japan a "tangible stake in the prosperity, security and integrity of Singapore."
55. T. Huxley, *Defending the Lion City: The Armed Forces of Singapore* (St. Leonards, New South Wales: Allen and Unwin, 2000), 36–40.
56. Ibid., 56–57.
57. See A. Tan, "Force Modernization Trends in Southeast Asia," *RSIS Working Paper Series* No. 59 (January 2004).
58. Teo Chee Hean, Singapore's Minister for Defense, Remarks, "Setting National Security Priorities," delivered at the 5th Shangri-La Dialogue, June 4, 2006; www.mindef.gov.sg/imindef/news_and_events/nr/2006/jun/04jun06_nr.html.
59. A. T. Mahan, *Retrospect and Prospect: Studies in International Relations, Naval and Political* (London: Sampson, Low, Marston, 1902), 144.
60. US Navy, Marine Corps, and Coast Guard, *A Cooperative Strategy for 21st Century Seapower* (Washington, DC: Department of the Navy, October 2007), 1–2.
61. Ibid., 10–17.
62. P. Kennedy, "American Power Is on the Wane," *Wall Street Journal Online*, January 15, 2009; http://online.wsj.com/article/SB123189377673479433.html.
63. Bateman, "Indian Ocean Naval Symposium." The emphasis on maritime natural hazards is timely, not only on account of the Boxing Day Tsunami of 2004 but also Cyclone Nargis, which struck coastal Burma in May 2008.
64. See G. Till, "A Cooperative Strategy for 21st Century Seapower: A View from Outside," *Naval War College Review* (April 2008).
65. See D. R. Headrick, *The Tools of Empire: Technology and European Imperialism in the Nineteenth Century* (Oxford: Oxford University Press, 1981); and its companion volume by the same author, *The Tentacles of Progress: Technology Transfer in the Age of Imperialism* (Oxford: Oxford University Press, 1988).
66. Bateman, "Indian Ocean Naval Symposium"; D. Scott, "India's 'Grand Strategy'

for the Indian Ocean: Mahanian Visions," *Asia-Pacific Review* 13, no. 2 (2006): 97–129; doi:10.1080=13439000601029048; and D. L. Berlin, "India in the Indian Ocean," *Naval War College Review* (Spring 2006): 58–89.

67. D. L. Berlin, "The 'Great Base Race' in the Indian Ocean Littoral: Conflict Prevention or Stimulation?" *Contemporary South Asia* 13, no. 3 (September 2004): 248. The Indian Ocean strategic analyst Donald Berlin has pointed out that a key logistics hub for the US 7th Fleet, the Logistics Group Western Pacific, is located in Singapore. "Of course," writes Berlin, "it was precisely these US military links with Singapore that led terrorists linked to Osama bin Laden to try to target Singapore and Changi."
68. "Singapore Hosts Proliferation Security Initiative Exercise," *MINDEF Singapore*, August 15, 2005; www.mindef.gov.sg/imindef/news_and_events/nr/2005/aug/15aug05_nr2.html.
69. *Partnering to Rebuild: Operation Blue Orchid—The Singapore Armed Forces Experience in Iraq* (Singapore: Ministry of Defense, 2010).
70. See A. Vines and B. Oruitemeka, "India's Engagement with the African Indian Ocean Rim States," *Chatham House Papers*, AFP P1/08 (April 9, 2008).
71. Huxley, *Defending the Lion City*, 220–21. According to British defense analyst Tim Huxley, "Cooperation with India also allowed RSN personnel to train on board Indian Navy Foxtrot-Class submarines, providing valuable 'hands-on' experience before Singapore acquired its own submarines from Sweden in the late 1990s."
72. M. S. Pardesi, "Deepening Singapore-India Strategic Ties," *RSIS Commentaries*, March 22, 2005; www.rsis.edu.sg/publications/Perspective/IDSS132005.pdf.
73. "Reply to Media Queries on Ex Malabar 07-02," *MINDEF Singapore*, July 29, 2007; www.mindef.gov.sg/imindef/news_and_events/nr/2007/jul/29jul07_nr.html.
74. "China Builds Up Strategic Sea Lanes," *Washington Times*, January 17, 2005; C. J. Pehrson, "String of Pearls: Meeting the Challenge of China's Rising Power across the Asian Littoral," *SSI Carlisle Papers in Security Strategy*, July 2006; and A. Kumar, "A New Balance of Power Game in the Indian Ocean: India Gears Up to Tackle Chinese Influence in the Maldives and Sri Lanka," *IDSA Strategic Comments*, November 24, 2006.
75. Latif, *Between Rising Powers*, 34–43, 83–101, 261–89; cf. C. Kuik, "Rising Dragon, Crouching Tigers? Comparing the Foreign Policy Responses of Malaysia and Singapore Toward a Re-emerging China, 1990–2005," *Biblioasia* 3, no. 4 (January 2008).
76. On coordinated naval patrols as a means of promoting maritime security along the straits, see "Singapore and Indonesia Participate in Indo-Sin Coordinated Patrols (ISCP) and Joint Socio-Civic Activities," *MINDEF Singapore*, April 19, 2006; www.mindef.gov.sg/imindef/news_and_events/nr/2001/oct/09oct01_nr2.html; and Teo Chee Hean, Remarks, "Setting National Security Priorities." For details of the new "cooperative mechanism" to enhance navigational safety, see keynote address by S. Jayakumar, Singapore's deputy prime minister,

coordinating minister for national security, and minister for law, "Charting a New Framework for International Cooperation in the Straits of Malacca and Singapore," September 4, 2007, *Embassy of the Republic of Singapore*, www.mfa.gov.sg/content/mfa/overseasmission/jakarta/press_statements_speeches_archives/2007/200709/press_200709_01.html. Also see S. Ramesh, "Malaysia, Indonesia and Singapore Set Up Co-operative Mechanism," *Channel News Asia*, September 4, 2007; www.channelnewsasia.com/stories/singaporelocalnews/view/297801/1/.html; and "Milestone Agreement Reached over Co-operation in the Straits of Malacca and Singapore," *International Maritime Organization (IMO) Press Briefing*, September 18, 2007; www.imo.org/blast/mainframe.asp?topic_id=1472&doc_id=8471.

CHAPTER 11

THE INDIAN OCEAN AND US NATIONAL SECURITY INTERESTS

TIMOTHY D. HOYT

INTRODUCTION

The Indian Ocean is becoming an increasingly vital element in the global economy and in US national security planning. The US Navy, in its recent *Cooperative Strategy for 21st Century Seapower*, identified the Indian Ocean region (IOR) along with the Pacific Rim as areas of primary concern for the future.[1] This concern was further codified in the 2010 *Quadrennial Defense Review*.[2] This new focus reflects a simple truth: Asia is emerging as the hub of the global economy.[3] The economic rise of Japan, China, and India; the emergence of the "Tigers" in Southeast Asia; and the shift of the United States from a creditor to a debtor nation are crucial indicators of a potential shift in global power from Europe to Asia. This shift is matched, in fact, by the decline of Europe's navies and general military capabilities.[4] These emerging trends and the fact that the bulk of the fossil fuels that feed the globalized economy run across the Indian Ocean provided the initial impetus for the conference that spurred this book.[5]

Against this background of economic activity, however, is a growing arc of instability—the United States has been engaged in an ongoing conflict in the IOR since the tragic events of September 11, 2001. Each of the subregions of the Indian Ocean system—East Africa, the Middle East and Arabian Gulf, South Asia, and Southeast Asia—has also experienced threats to order and security from state and nonstate actors.

The United States, as a dominant world power and significant beneficiary of the global economic system, bears some responsibility for ensuring and maintaining freedom of commerce across the region. In addition, US military presence in the region remains a necessity at least until satisfactory outcomes to ongoing wars emerge and the threat of interstate conflict abates. Given these political realities, it is important to consider American (and broader Western) interests, the emerging threats to those interests over time, and the means by which the United States and its coalition partners might ensure those interests.

The United States and the international system face three key questions in this region in the twenty-first century. Do we fully understand the nature of current and emerging threats in this critical region? Do we have the mechanisms in place to manage the risk from them? What more needs to be done? This chapter analyzes current and future security threats in the region from the perspective of the United States and assesses current coalition and bilateral efforts to manage the risk from those threats. The following three sections examine each of these issues in turn—the nature of regional threats (transnational and state-centric), institutions and efforts to manage those threats, and recommendations for expanding security efforts across the region. The chapter concludes with three key recommendations for the United States and its IOR partners, at both the coalition and multilateral levels.

CURRENT AND EMERGING THREATS IN THE INDIAN OCEAN REGION

Threats to stability in the Indian Ocean come in two major varieties—transnational threats that cross multiple national borders and manifest themselves in both national and international waters, and more traditional interstate rivalries and the improving military capabilities available to emerging powers. For much of the past decade, transnational threats have occupied our attention. State-centric threats, however, pose significant challenges to regional stability. Since some of these challenges can be anticipated, appropriate policy responses can mitigate risk—but these responses may be difficult to coordinate given the weakness of security institutions throughout the region.

Transnational Threats to Regional Stability

TRANSNATIONAL TERRORISM. Since September 2011 the United States has been engaged in a protracted conflict with transnational terrorist organizations throughout the region. This conflict, which has taken many names, is waged by the United States and a range of coalition partners throughout the region against a variety of national and transnational threats.[6] The primary adversary is al-Qaeda ("The Base"), which launched successful terrorist operations against the United

States in East Africa and Yemen before the 9/11 catastrophe.[7] Al-Qaeda is also linked to a number of other radical Islamist militant groups from all over the IOR, including Indonesia, Pakistan, Afghanistan, Egypt, and Somalia.[8]

Although al-Qaeda has been unsuccessful in replicating its attack on the United States, its leadership remains active and engaged in organizing operations from the Federally Administered Tribal Areas in Pakistan.[9] The group and its adherents have carried out or attempted significant terrorist attacks in Indonesia, Spain, Morocco, the United Kingdom, Saudi Arabia, Jordan, Iraq (after the US invasion), Pakistan, and Afghanistan. In the latter two states, they are closely affiliated with Taliban movements that seek to overthrow the local government.[10] Al-Qaeda leadership has shifted its location rapidly in the past—from Afghanistan to Sudan and back, and from Afghanistan to Pakistan after the Taliban's defeat in Operation Enduring Freedom.[11] More recently, press reports suggested the emergence of new al-Qaeda strongholds in Iraq (prior to 2007), Somalia, and, most recently, Yemen. An effort to attack the United States over the Christmas holidays in 2009 appears to have originated in Yemen, and there are reports of other Yemeni links to terrorist efforts after 2010.[12] The proximity of reported al-Qaeda strongholds to the Indian Ocean periphery ensures a prolonged US and coalition maritime presence in the region. In addition, the suspected causal relationship between economic deprivation and nascent support for terrorism or insurgency creates an overlap between some forms of peacetime maritime activity and the agenda of the coalition. This overlap encompasses not only various forms of maritime criminal activity, which may be connected to terrorist financing or weapons acquisition, but also humanitarian relief and economic assistance. As a result, examination of other transnational trends is often difficult to separate from the terrorism issue.

PIRACY. The reemergence of piracy as a significant factor in the international system is discussed elsewhere in this volume. It is worth highlighting that piracy emerged as a problem on both ends of the Indian Ocean (Straits of Malacca and Horn of Africa) but appears to only be persistent in the western end—which suggests that coalition efforts (discussed later) may be an effective means of limiting the problem. As other authors have discussed in detail in previous chapters, pirates operating from Somalia have seized dozens of ships, received significant ransoms from commercial shipping agencies, and created a profitable entrepreneurial model that virtually guarantees a continuing problem in the region unless it is addressed at the source—the lack of governance and opportunity in Somalia proper.

Not all piracy is terrorist activity, obviously, but the link between piracy and terrorism is explored in chapter 2 in this volume. Moreover, the case of Somalia may be particularly affiliated with terrorist threats. First, Somalia is one of the most pertinent examples of failed states—a condition often associated with potential terrorist sanctuary and activity. Second, Somalia has been home to al-Qaeda activity in the past. Third, Somali governance remains threatened by the rise of the al-Shabaab movement, which some experts see as reflecting al-Qaeda-like ideology.[13] Finally, piracy is a lucrative entrepreneurial exercise in Somalia but requires some support from land—suggesting the possibility that, now or in the future, pirate activity could provide rents to support regimes or local strongmen who are affiliated with regional or transnational terrorism. This confluence of factors puts Somali piracy in a somewhat different category than piracy in the Bay of Bengal, for instance—and that unique concern is reflected by the coalition presence.

WEAPONS OF MASS DESTRUCTION AND OTHER PROLIFERATION EFFORTS. The Indian Ocean—defined in terms of the maritime periphery, including the Red Sea and the Persian Gulf—is both a regional center of proliferation activity and a primary transit route for illegal shipments. The region is currently the home of most of the states that have acquired nuclear weapons since 1965—Israel, India, Pakistan, South Africa, and potentially Iran. In addition, the other recent member of the nuclear club—North Korea—uses the Indian Ocean to supply components to nuclear programs in Syria, Iran, and possibly Burma. China has supplied both nuclear and delivery system technology to Pakistan. In particular, the A. Q. Khan proliferation ring, run from Pakistan with some level of official complicity, used firms throughout the IOR and provided industrial and scientific assistance to the regimes of Iran, Libya, North Korea, and several other as-yet-unidentified states. The region remains the focal point of nuclear and weapons of mass destruction (WMD) proliferation risks for the global community.

In addition, the IOR also continues to produce significant demand for both legal and illicit conventional arms transfers. India is expected to be one of the largest recipients of conventional arms transfers over the next few decades, due to the combination of increased defense budgets and demand for modernization of most weapons systems. Saudi Arabia is also a key player in the global arms market. The large number of internal conflicts in the region also create demand for illicit small arms by both states and nonstate groups.

ILLICIT TRAFFICKING. Criminal trafficking is pervasive in the region, and the sea provides a major transit route. Drugs are a major moneymaker for terrorist groups, criminal organizations, and even some governments. Opium from Afghanistan and Southeast Asia, methamphetamines from Burma, and khat in the Horn of Africa create significant profits for their growers and distributors. Smuggling and illegal fishing—often deliberately carried out by states outside the region—are major problems for maritime governance.

The A. Q. Khan network, mentioned earlier, was the focal point for illegal WMD technology transfer and transshipment, almost all of which crossed the Indian Ocean by sea or air.[14] Because of the size of the equipment transferred, passage by sea was the cheapest, most convenient, and least easily monitored method. In addition, Dubai—a free port—was a focal point of the Khan network's shipping efforts.[15] The passage of illegally transferred nuclear technology continues today; for example, the Syrian nuclear reactor complex, recently destroyed by the Israeli Air Force, consisted of components that could not easily be shipped by air from North Korea.[16] North Korean freighters carrying nuclear or missile technology have been intercepted in the Indian Ocean in the past and continue to be monitored at present.

HUMANITARIAN ASSISTANCE AND DISASTER RELIEF. The Indian Ocean is regularly victimized by natural disaster. The regional ecosystem is dominated by the monsoon—a roughly predictable change in weather that, while beneficial to regional agriculture, carries with it the seeds of catastrophe.[17] Climate change, man-made or otherwise, significantly threatens the region in the future, as island states may literally disappear and littoral states such as Bangladesh face significant threats to arable land through coastal flooding and salination.[18]

The geographic and climactic dangers of the region are exacerbated by poor governance, limited economic development, and population growth. Some estimates argue that there may be as many as 200 million "climate refugees" in the region by 2050.[19] Finally, the impact of climate change can also fuel regional tensions—India, Pakistan, China, and Bangladesh all rely heavily on water flows from the Himalayas. Competition over water resources, therefore, may lead to increased political confrontation and hostility.[20]

State-Centric Threats to Regional Stability

EMERGENCE OF CHINA. History demonstrates that, over time, emerging continental powers begin to move into the maritime domain.[21] China is no exception. China's integration with the global economy and its increasing need for energy from external sources create a powerful logic for concern about security in the Indian Ocean. Traditionally, as emerging powers improve their governance and resource extraction, and as they resolve or manage immediate security problems, they begin to build capabilities to assure their maritime interests. There is presently no indication that China is following a different path, or that it is willing to place substantial faith in the ability of international organizations or other coalitions to manage the stability that is crucial to its continued economic development. In addition, China is developing political relationships with regional states that may create incentives or obligations for support in crisis that contribute to instability.

China's economic role in the region is significant and growing. Often referred to as "neo-mercantilist," China is investing heavily in securing energy resources throughout the IOR.[22] It also has invested heavily in the west coast of Africa, and the products of those investments currently transit the Indian Ocean en route to Asia. If China's military presence in the region expands to mirror its economic presence, the US and regional states will face an additional set of complications in ensuring regional stability, and possibly an emerging threat to sea-lanes or to the international norms that govern sea traffic. Managing or shaping the emergence of Chinese military power in the region, therefore, is a major interest of the United States, the region, and the international community.

REGIONAL THREATS TO STABILITY: INDIA-CHINA, INDIA-PAKISTAN, IRAN, CHINA-ASEAN. Several historical interstate rivalries threaten to destabilize the IOR. Although China is not technically an Indian Ocean littoral state, its role in affecting regional security is quite significant. India and China have an unresolved border dispute in the Himalayas that led the two countries to war in 1962, and to a significant crisis in 1986–87. India named China as the primary threat justifying its testing of nuclear weapons in 1998.[23] The border dispute remains an irritant in Sino-Indian relations even as China has become India's leading trading partner.

China also plays a critical role in the Indo-Pakistani rivalry, which has led to four wars and a half-dozen crises since partition in 1947. Pakistan considers China an "all weather friend," and China is the major source of Pakistan's military equipment.[24] In addition, China is firmly implicated in Pakistan's nuclear weapons development, and is involved in the construction of major port facilities in Gwadar that may have long-term military implications.[25]

China's recent series of disputes in the western Pacific and South China Sea also suggest the possibility that problems could emerge with ASEAN states that might overlap into the IOR. India may be viewed increasingly as a potential balancer to Chinese interests in ASEAN. India's "Look East" policy and its joint military command on the Andaman-Nicobar Islands chain strongly suggest an Indian interest in improving its relations with ASEAN states and its presence at the eastern end of the Bay of Bengal.

In addition, the IOR is the scene of potential conflicts in the Arabian Gulf (Iran and its neighbors), and in the broader Middle East (Iran–Israel). As the United States downgrades its presence in Iraq, the Iran–Iraq rivalry may reemerge. Iran's support for militant groups in Palestine and Lebanon raises the possibility of Iranian–Israeli conflict at some point in the future. Shi'a–Sunni relations in the Arabian Gulf and the disputed status of Abu Musa and the Tunb islands also constitute possible initiators for regional conflict.

The fact that the IOR is also the intersection of so many nuclear powers creates additional threats to regional stability. The region has already seen conventional war between two nuclear powers (the multiple-month struggle in the Kargil region between India and Pakistan in 1999).[26] Pakistan and Iran use terrorist proxies to attack India and Israel, respectively. Israeli submarines have been reported in the Indian Ocean, potentially as a nuclear deterrent to Iran.[27] Both Pakistan and India have discussed nuclear triads that would put their own nuclear armed submarines into the Indian Ocean. War between any of the major regional powers, particularly as Iran's nuclear capabilities advance, raises the potential of nuclear weapons use for the first time since 1945—particularly given the vulnerability of these nuclear states to interruption of maritime commerce.[28]

SECURITY MANAGEMENT IN THE REGION: COOPERATION, COALITIONS, AND BILATERAL RELATIONS

Managing security in the region requires approaches that provide near-term stability while hedging against more serious emerging threats in the ten- to twenty-year time frame, particularly either the collapse of nuclear states (Iran, Pakistan) or an aggressive China. The United States remains, for the near term, both a dominant and a necessary power in the region. Stability and security, particularly in the long term, cannot rest purely on US military power, if only because of the inevitable pressure the current economic climate will put on US defense budgets and force posture.

In addition, the United States faces significant barriers to leadership in the region. Only five of the thirty-three littoral states in the region were independent before World War I: South Africa and Australia (both technically dominions), Ethiopia, Persia (Iran), and Thailand. Most of the littoral are postcolonial states, were members of the Non-Aligned Movement, and harbor significant suspicion of US power and intentions. Like many developing states, they are extraordinarily sensitive to threats to sovereignty and reluctant to follow a Western leader.[29] Unlike the Pacific Rim, where the United States has a long history of interaction with China, Japan, and Korea, in the Indian Ocean the United States faces a significant historical and cultural deficit—our traditional relationships in Europe and the Pacific are inadequate models for the security environment in the Indian Ocean.

Stability, however, can only be built on a multilateral basis. Collective security options are limited due to the uneven institutionalization of the region. This is particularly problematic in South Asia, where the South Asian Association for

Regional Cooperation lacks effectiveness because of the Indo-Pakistani rivalry. US efforts to create alliances in the Cold War also failed in this part of the world, with both the Central Treaty Organization (CENTO) and the South Asian Treaty Organization collapsing in the 1950s and 1960s, respectively. Cooperation, while essential to regional security, needs to be built from the ground up and in ways that do not threaten member sovereignty—which in turn will limit, at least initially, the effectiveness of new coalitions. Creating cooperative security organizations will be a long-term effort, but there are promising signs that multinational efforts are now emerging in the region, with and without US leadership.

In October 2007 Adm. Gary Roughead, chief of naval operations, formally released the new *Cooperative Strategy for 21st Century Seapower* at the International Seapower Symposium in Newport, Rhode Island.[30] The *Cooperative Strategy* is the product of more than a year of work, including a substantive contribution from the Naval War College, and represents a genuine effort to respond to the changing international environment. It reflects the proposal of Admiral Roughead's predecessor, Adm. Michael Mullen (later chairman of the Joint Chiefs of Staff) that the United States begin forming a "Thousand Ship Navy" based on cooperation with other navies to help deal with emerging maritime problems.[31] This proposal later became the Global Maritime Partnership, reflecting recognition by the US Navy that many maritime threats short of war could and should be managed through coalitions and cooperative activities.

The *Cooperative Strategy* is a sincere effort to reexamine, and in some cases rediscover, the unique role that the maritime services play in international affairs in both peace and war, particularly in a globalized economy that relies on maritime trade.[32] Moreover, the language and concepts imbedded in the *Cooperative Strategy* are shared by other nations as well. The strategy identifies the Indian Ocean as a core US interest, provides a framework for multinational cooperation on a range of issues, and may be the starting point for a changed US relationship with the region.

Coalition Operations with Direct US Involvement

COALITION TASK FORCES 150 AND 151 (CTF 150, CTF 151). Coalition Task Force 150 was established in 2001 in response to the trafficking of terrorist personnel and material and financial resources across the Arabian Gulf and the Horn of Africa. At least twenty-four states had participated in CTF 150's operations as of 2009. Command of the task force has been rotated among members, and Canada, the United Kingdom, France, Pakistan, Germany, Spain, Denmark, and the Netherlands have all had command on at least one occasion. CTF 150 is further empowered by operating under the aegis of the United Nations, reflecting UN Security Council Resolutions 1368, 1373, and 1378.[33]

CTF 150 conducts maritime security operations from the Arabian Gulf to the Horn of Africa and therefore has wide authority to monitor a range of illegal activities in the region. These include personnel flows, drugs, finances, smuggling, proliferation of WMD-related materials, and arms trafficking.

Until 2009 it also included a counterpiracy mission. The participation of more than two dozen nations in a naval mission intended to substantially constrain activities that support terrorism in the region clearly plays a role in the broader war on terror. The fact that command is rotated emphasizes the coalition element. Pakistan's participation has been particularly important diplomatically since many of the Gulf state navies send their future leaders to Pakistan's military institutions for staff and other training.

Created in 2009, Coalition Task Force 151 is a more focused task force established to manage piracy off the Horn of Africa (see chapter 2, this volume). CTF 151 includes ships from at least four nations (the United States, the United Kingdom, Denmark, and Turkey). The task force to date has been commanded by US and Turkish leaders. Although it is closely associated with operations off of Somalia, CTF 151 is remarkable in that it is mission focused. As a result, it is technically geographically unconstrained—including the peculiar US constraints imposed by combatant command boundaries.[34] As a result, at least in theory, CTF 151 could also be deployed against other centers of piracy as they emerge throughout the region.

CTF 151 acts in concert with other navies, including deployments by both India and China. China's squadron is viewed with particular interest because it demonstrates a capability for overseas power projection and logistic support that is relatively advanced. Preparations for India's naval deployments off the Horn reportedly began almost two months before their mission was officially approved in October 2008.[35]

COALITION OPERATIONS WITHOUT THE UNITED STATES. The US Navy is not a participant in all coalition operations in the IOR. Regional organizations and states play important roles in monitoring maritime activity, preventing disruption of sea-lanes and other criminality, and providing emergency disaster and humanitarian relief. Three important examples of this cooperation are the MALSINDO (Malaysia, Singapore, Indonesia) activities in the Straits of Malacca, the Indian Navy's decision to provide counterterrorism and antipiracy missions in the same region in 2002–3, and the Indian Ocean Naval Symposium (IONS).

On July 20, 2004, Singapore, Malaysia, and Indonesia launched the trilateral coordinated patrols, MALSINDO Malacca Straits Coordinated Patrol.[36] Codenamed MALSINDO, these patrols used cooperative efforts of all three navies to monitor the straits and combat piracy and seagoing terrorist activities. According to press reports, these patrols were motivated in part by international concern over piracy and terrorist activities in the Straits of Malacca, and a rumor that the US might intervene to ensure maritime security. While Singapore reportedly welcomed a cooperative American presence, both Malaysia and Indonesia vigorously rejected outside interference in their waters.[37]

Regardless of the rationale, however, the cooperation of these neighboring states in providing security for the straits is both a response to the unique emerging threats of the war on terror and an unusual act of multinational security cooperation within the region. In 2005 coordinated air patrols called "Eye in the Sky" were initiated as well. Although evidence of continued multinational coordination, the number of flights may suggest a more symbolic than substantive effort.[38] Piracy attacks in the straits dropped from thirty-eight in 2004 to twelve in 2005, evidence that modest cooperation can create significant results.[39] By September 2008 the number of pirate attacks had fallen to two—a massive decrease in a few short years.[40]

INDIAN NAVY COUNTERTERRORISM PATROLS (STRAITS OF MALACCA). In 2001, at US request, Indian naval vessels escorted US shipping through the Straits of Malacca and maintained a presence to deter possible terrorist acts at sea.[41] This operation indicated a significant shift in the Indo-US security relationship. During the Cold War, India reacted with suspicion to US naval presence in the Indian Ocean both during crisis (the "*Enterprise* Incident" in December 1971) and during peacetime (Indian calls for an Indian Ocean zone of peace and hostility toward the US base in Diego Garcia). Since 40 percent of India's trade passes through the Straits of Malacca, India has a strong national interest in this region.[42] Although this was a multinational mission in the sense that the United States requested Indian assistance, the presence of Indian naval vessels raised concerns in the region, and Indian forces remained for only a short time.

The first IONS was held in Mumbai in February 2008. IONS was an effort by the government of India to create an organization of Indian Ocean littoral states to discuss and address maritime concerns. The objectives of IONS were

- To promote a shared understanding of the maritime issues facing the littoral states of the Indian Ocean and the formulation of . . . common strategies to enhance regional maritime security;
- To strengthen the capability of all littoral nation states in the Indian Ocean to address the challenges to maritime stability [and] security;
- To establish [and] promote a maritime cooperative mechanism to mitigate maritime security concern among the members of IONS;
- To develop interoperability regarding effective humanitarian [assistance and] disaster relief throughout the region.[43]

IONS was deliberately focused on Indian Ocean states. As a result, the United States was not invited to some of the discussions, even though the US Navy plays such a major role in the region.[44] Indian leadership may be resisted by many of the states in the region, however. India's unique culture, size, and population—not to mention its historic difficulties with Pakistan—do not necessarily make it a natural leader for Middle Eastern, African, and Southeast Asian partners. IONS is reminiscent of India's efforts to create a "zone of peace" in the Cold War—a region free of external powers that the Indian Navy, in theory, could influence. As a result, IONS is likely to evolve slowly and deliberately—but the shared maritime and security concerns of many states in the region make it a natural forum for contributing to maritime cooperation. Members of the IONS include Australia, Bangladesh, Bahrain, Comoros, Djibouti, Egypt, Eritrea, France, Indonesia, India, Iran, Kenya, Kuwait, Malaysia, Madagascar, Myanmar, Mauritius, Mozambique, Maldives, Oman, Pakistan, Qatar, the Kingdom of Saudi Arabia (KSA), Seychelles, Singapore, Sri Lanka, South Africa, Sudan, Tanzania, Thailand, United Arab Emirates, and Yemen.

The second IONS meeting was held in Abu Dhabi, United Arab Emirates, in March 2010.[45] No significant outcomes emerged from the meeting, but a tradition has now been established. The 2012 IONS meeting was held in South Africa. IONS provides an institutional basis for multinational cooperation on maritime affairs. The fact that this organization has minimal US participation (mere observer status, along with other extraregional states) may be an important enabler for future efforts. Finding ways to enable this organization may be valuable in addressing the range of transnational threats that plague the region.

Overall, these coalition efforts—with and without direct US involvement—are providing some leverage over current regional security threats. Ad hoc coalitions are useful for dealing with immediate problems but also create institutional bases for more permanent institutions that may contribute to managing emerging problems. They may provide a basis for shaping the regional system in anticipation of Chinese entry, for example.

Bilateral Efforts

Another approach to long-term regional security could be the use of bilateral relationships to create allies or critical coalition partners. This concept was first tested in the Eisenhower administration, with the Baghdad Pact/CENTO (in opposition to both the Soviet Union and to Nasser and other Arab nationalist movements). It was tried again in the Nixon administration, when the "Twin Pillars" policy sought to ensure Persian Gulf security through the KSA and Iran (under the shah). More recently, then–secretary of state Condoleezza Rice suggested that the Bush administration would rely on bilateral relations with great powers to help ensure global stability—a concept (derailed by 9/11) that could be applied to the IOR.[46]

US bilateral relations within the region may hint at the possibility of using these relationships as a means of facilitating a more rapid response to both current and long-term threats—a kind of coalition "jump start." The US–Australia relationship, at the eastern end of the Indian Ocean, is extraordinarily close and has weathered democratic change in both states. Australia's recent white paper lays out a series of concerns regarding regional security as well as a range of options for addressing them.[47] All are strongly compatible both with US interests and with US force developments. At the eastern end of the Indian Ocean, therefore, the United States does have a very strong regional partner with significant capacity.

Other key players, however, have more mixed relations with the United States, complicated by regional rivalries, history, or differing interests. Indo-US relations are closer than they have ever been, and common interests in maritime security, counterterrorism, and regional stability provide a strong basis for future cooperation. Mutual concern about the entry of China into the Indian Ocean also provides a rationale for closer ties, although both states are careful not to assume that China will be an enemy. Nevertheless, this relationship is complicated by a history of distrust bred in the Cold War, and small steps in the relationship often take enormous (some might say disproportionate) effort.[48]

The US relationship with the Republic of South Africa, at the far end of the Indian Ocean, suffers similar limits. US official tolerance of the previous regime complicates bilateral relations. In addition, South Africa is wracked by domestic problems (crime, AIDS, population growth) and as yet does not appear poised to play an extended role even in East African affairs, much less the Indian Ocean writ large. Still, as one of the largest, wealthiest, and most militarily capable African states, South Africa could play an increasing role in the western Indian Ocean.

Intermediate pillars could include Kenya, Saudi Arabia (with whom the United States has a long-standing security relationship), Pakistan, and Indonesia. The latter two have been engaged in meaningful ways in the war on terror. Indonesia's cooperation on maritime terrorism and piracy indicates common interests on transnational issues, and recent Chinese belligerence in the South China Sea may provide a motive for engaging on longer-term security issues as well. Pakistan's role in the war on terror is more problematic and mixed—assistance in key areas but also provision of sanctuary and state support for both the Afghan Taliban and other militant groups that menace the region. Its close relationship with China also poses a potential obstacle to long-term cooperation; asked to choose between the United States and China, it is not clear what Pakistan's answer would be.

Emphasizing key states, therefore, is another approach that could emerge during the coming decade. Cooperation may be forthcoming on select transnational issues. Managing long-term threats, however, may be more complicated, particularly due to the likelihood of political instability in Pakistan and possibly other states.

US Unilateral Operations: Support for Conventional Operations/Counterinsurgency

Alfred Thayer Mahan noted that the seas are a global commons, and that utilization of the sea for national interest requires the maintenance of a capable navy.[49] Sir Julian Corbett demonstrated that a fundamental role of sea power in wars was the insertion, supply, and, if necessary, evacuation of ground forces, which often played the decisive role in winning wars through control of territory.[50] Commanding the commons, as Barry Posen has more recently noted, remains a critical element of American grand strategy, and the current massive effort in the Indian Ocean basin is only sustainable because of the presence of the US Navy.[51]

In addition to multinational security activity, the US Navy itself uses the Indian Ocean as a critical supply route. The opening of two major theaters of operation in Southwest Asia in a period of two years magnified the importance of the Indian Ocean in US grand strategy. The Indian Ocean is now a critical sea line of communication to support (until recently) two simultaneous operations in Iraq and Afghanistan that engage more than two hundred thousand American troops (and tens of thousands of coalition partners). In the 1990s the US regularly debated whether to plan on fighting two major regional wars or contingencies, and whether that was an achievable objective. From 2003 to 2010, the US fought two major operations (admittedly of a very different kind) in some of the most remote areas of the globe.

Supplies and reinforcements for operations in Afghanistan often require transiting the Straits of Hormuz and the Persian/Arabian Gulf—a scene of anti-shipping missions throughout the Iran-Iraq War. In addition, US Navy forces also protect critical nodes, including port facilities and offshore oil platforms, that are essential to the recovery of the Iraqi economy and the Iraqi state. The establishment of the Fifth Fleet in Bahrain and a continued presence of US Navy warships in the region helps maintain the viability of a supply line that extends nearly halfway around the globe.[52]

The logistics burden in landlocked Afghanistan is vastly greater and much more difficult. According to public reports, more than half of the US supplies to Afghanistan and more than 40 percent of the vehicle fuel must pass through Pakistan either by land or by air, and more than ten thousand cargo trucks transit the Afghan-Pakistan border every month.[53] Karachi is a critical port of entry for these goods but also remains a metropolitan area with extraordinary lawlessness, civic violence, and endemic crime.[54]

This precarious line of communication is also vulnerable to naval interdiction in periods of regional crisis. In 1999 the Indian Navy was mobilized and at sea in force during the Kargil Crisis. In 2001–2, after Pakistani terrorists attacked India's parliament house, Indian and Pakistani ships played hide and seek behind US forces engaged in Operation Enduring Freedom.[55] The November 2008 terrorist attack on Mumbai was launched by highly trained Pakistani terrorists from the sea, accentuating the vulnerability of the region to terrorist attack.[56]

In addition to using the seas for supply, the US Navy also provides military support for conventional and counterinsurgency operations in both Afghanistan and Iraq. US Navy aircraft fly up a special air corridor in Pakistan called "the Boulevard" to provide air support for international security assistance forces in southern Afghanistan. These missions could simply involve "showing the flag"—flying over a possible trouble spot to let Taliban and other irregular forces know that air power is in the neighborhood—to direct close air support of ground troops (subject to rules of engagement).[57] Flying close air support to a landlocked country from ships stationed hundreds of kilometers away in the Indian Ocean demonstrates the continuing flexibility of sea power, even as the character of modern war evolves.

In fighting transnational terrorism, the maritime domain remains an important asset for the United States in terms of support for unconventional operations as well. The USS *Kitty Hawk* was initially deployed to the Afghan theater in 2001 with a specially constituted air wing to support the rapid deployment of special forces and marines. Press reports suggest that more than one thousand special forces were deployed on the carrier, including both ground and air units.[58]

US Navy special warfare forces have played critical roles in both reconnaissance and direct action in both Afghanistan and Iraq. Most recently, US Navy SEAL forces were involved in the raid in Pakistan that ended with the death of Osama bin Laden. The first flag rank officer on the ground in Afghanistan was a US Navy SEAL in charge of Central Command's special operations. In Iraq, US Navy special forces have been critical in seizing and holding offshore oil platforms, in helping opening up the critical port of Umm Qasr, and in training and advising Iraqi special forces.

US Navy deployments also support a range of missions on the east coast of Africa.[59] Joint Task Force–Horn of Africa monitors Somalia for signs of al-Qaeda in addition to its other missions, and interdicting maritime terrorist movement in the Arabian Gulf and Gulf of Aden remains an important priority. Drone strikes on suspected terrorist leaders in Yemen and Somalia may have been assisted by US Navy surveillance.

RECOMMENDATIONS FOR US AND COALITION PARTNERS IN THE REGION

Given this context the coalition and bilateral cooperation discussed previously in this chapter, how might the United States and its coalition partners address problems at the policy, strategic, and operational levels?

Looking forward, the United States and the international community face significant challenges in dealing with security threats in the IOR. These can be expressed in a simple two-by-two matrix, dividing between state-centric and transnational on one axis, and short term and long term on the other (see figure 11.1.)

Some problems are both short term (already occurring) and long term (almost certain to persist into the more distant ten- to twenty-year future). These include transnational terrorism, piracy, Asian dependence on oil from the Arabian Gulf region, and increasing trade flows overall as Asian economic growth drives Indian Ocean maritime traffic. Some current state-centric challenges will remain—the Indo-Pakistani conflict, the threat of a radical Iran, and domestic political instability throughout the region are likely to be pervasive. In the longer term, however, the growth in economic and military power of both India and China will affect security dynamics throughout the region, and older regional hostilities may reemerge (Iran–Iraq, Ethiopia–Somalia).

The United States, as both the largest military power and a significant beneficiary of the current global economic system, bears a substantial stake in stability in the Indian Ocean—which at a minimum is the maritime highway that maintains that global economic system. The combination of the global economic recession, lack of US fiscal discipline, and the significant political, military, and economic costs of military interventions in the past ten years make it unlikely, in the long term, that the United States will be able to enforce stability alone. These trends suggest that building coalitions, in both the short and long term, are the most appropriate means of maintaining a US role in the region *and* providing for regional security.

Available templates for coalition building suggest challenges as well as opportunities. Collective security, either through the United Nations or through regional organizations, is simply not feasible in the short term. As it has demonstrated repeatedly in the past, the United Nations lacks the capacity to respond

FIGURE 11.1 Security Threats in the Indian Ocean

	Short-Term	Long-Term
State-Centric		
Transnational		

quickly and effectively to higher-order security threats. The United Nations may opt for operations that violate national sovereignty, constrain access to the global economy, or even create virtual pariah status for regional states—hardly a reassuring prospect for the majority of the states in the region. Furthermore, both China and the United States have UN Security Council vetoes, and recent US activities in the region may appear to be dangerously unilateral in the eyes of some regional actors.

Other collective security templates, such as regional alliance systems, are likely to fail due to general suspicions within the region—distrust of neighbors because of the multitude of unresolved territorial disputes and divided ethnic groups and distrust of the United States due to its power and history. In terms of local or regional organizations, institutionalization is uneven at best and unlikely to create the kinds of capabilities necessary to balance strong regional competitors (the Gulf Cooperation Council versus Iran, or ASEAN versus China).

There are, however, other options that give reason for optimism. The first is the emergence of local multinational efforts against transnational threats identified earlier. While these do not currently constitute the basis for the much broader coalitions that may be necessary for the long-term security of the region, they do indicate that progress is possible and that cooperation can occur in the face of common challenges.

A second positive sign is the mutual identification of common interests across the region more broadly, and the gradual erosion of previous barriers to US participation or leadership. It is this contemporary context that makes the new *Cooperative Strategy* so important in understanding affairs in the Indian Ocean. This document represents the cornerstone of official US Navy thinking on the unique set of problems in the region. On the one hand, the United States is engaged in supporting two ongoing military conflicts in the territory of substantial states—perhaps a matter of alarm for regional states. However, it is also involved in multinational counterterrorism operations on both land and sea, providing presence to deter or influence a number of possible crisis points in the region, providing security for sea-lanes, and battling pirates (see chapter 2, this volume).

One aspect of the *Cooperative Strategy* is particularly worthy of note. According to the new strategy, the United States remains a "Two Ocean Navy"—a status it has enjoyed since the landmark "Two Ocean Navy Bill" of 1940, the United States' response to the rising threats of Nazi Germany and Imperial Japan.[60] What is fundamentally different—tellingly so—is that the oceans in which the United States will focus its operational capability have changed. Rather than choosing between or focusing on the Atlantic and the Pacific, as it did throughout the twentieth century, the US Navy now deploys credible combat power in the Pacific Rim and the Indian Ocean/Arabian Gulf region.[61] The Indian Ocean and its littorals have replaced the Atlantic Ocean as a primary focus for the US Navy in the twenty-first century.

As discussed in a previous chapter, the Indian Navy's recently introduced *Indian Maritime Military Strategy*, for example, shows striking conceptual similarity with the *Cooperative Strategy* while still reflecting the particular concerns and requirements of the Indian Navy.[62] The emergence of organizations such as IONS adds to the institutionalization of the region but keeps leadership in the hands of regional states—addressing security fears of a dominant US role. Nevertheless, the United States and other interested powers have observer status, which suggests continued opportunities for cooperation on issues of common interest, particularly in the maritime sphere.

Institutionalization will be an uneven evolutionary process in the region. But these new efforts in the past decade suggest more promise for institutions across a broader expanse of the Indian Ocean littoral than has ever been possible. They also provide the basis for building patterns of cooperation and trust necessary for more productive and effective bilateral partnerships and "coalitions of the willing," as the need arises. This process will be slow and difficult—regional states have many historical and cultural reasons for mutual suspicion. But the relatively low level of imminent threat, the common interest in suppressing short-term challenges, and the importance of maritime commerce in the region all provide a basis for security cooperation that may, nurtured properly, eventually provide far more than the sum of its parts.

CONCLUSION

In the introduction, this chapter asked three questions: do we fully understand the nature of current and emerging threats; do we have the mechanisms in place to manage the risk from those threats; and what more needs to be done? This chapter suggests we have more to do in examining (and resolving) each of these questions.

The international community has a grasp on current threats in the region but still has important questions about resolution. This is particularly true for the issue of transnational terrorism, which is tied up with economic development, regime stability, schisms in the Islamic world, and overt and covert state support. These factors all suggest that this current problem will be a long-term problem—one amenable to management, perhaps, but not to resolution. Given this, the combination of US-led coalitions and unilateral operations appears necessary but insufficient. The emergence of regional antiterror coalitions, driven by unique local conditions but supported, perhaps, by US resources, would be a useful and important addition to the overall management of this security threat.

Many of the other transnational threats discussed in this volume (as well as more briefly in this chapter) are being managed successfully through a combination of local and regional initiatives as well as cooperation on bilateral or multilateral efforts that include the United States. Piracy is unlikely to go away unless managed on land, but the combination of efforts currently being taken appear sufficient to keep the problem at a level that will not have significant economic impact. Illicit trafficking can only be managed—and even when maritime suppression is successful, narcotics and other goods routinely find alternate routes on land.

The most troubling transnational problem remains WMD proliferation—a challenge the international community has trouble assessing and even more difficulty managing. It is not clear, for instance, whether the A. Q. Khan network is the precursor of things to come or a unique product of a combination of security concern, institutional weakness, and entrepreneurial acumen. Similarly, the fact that so much covert nuclear activity has its roots in Pakistan, that Pakistani soil is the base for so many different militant groups with ties to the security forces, and that Pakistan relies on mobile land-based missiles for nuclear deterrence raises very real concerns about command and control of nuclear weapons both in normal conditions and in crisis.[63] The possible combination of nuclear weapons in terrorist hands remains a critical security concern for the United States and the international community. It appears that current efforts, again, are necessary but utterly insufficient as reports continue to surface of the emergence of new nuclear weapons programs (Syria, Burma) and of persistent efforts by terrorist groups to acquire various forms of WMD. Finally, it is far from clear that the full story of the A. Q. Khan proliferation ring has been fully uncovered—the unclassified record shows significant gaps and uncertainties. State-centric problems also reflect a range of current and long-term problems, with some current problems showing no signs of abating. The Indian Ocean littoral is the home of many weak states, and internal conflicts and weak governance will continue to plague the region. This, in turn, will affect the resources available—from both those troubled states and the international community—that can be put to use countering larger, regional concerns.

Interstate rivalries will continue to create security challenges and may increase in intensity. These rivalries may include extraregional powers but still profoundly affect regional security—Iran and Israel, for example, or India and China. The India–Pakistan rivalry shows no real promise of resolution; Pakistani civilian politicians cannot carry out meaningful negotiations with the Indians without risking a coup, and the military has found reasons to back away every time a civilian or military government has gotten close to a deal. An optimist might argue that the US relationship with both states has been instrumental in managing the last three crises. A pessimist might note that if the two states rely on US intervention, it might allow them to step even closer to the escalation ladder in future crises. China's role in the region could be an ameliorating factor. It could also, however, become a complicating factor if, for example, it chooses to more actively align itself with Pakistan during a crisis.

Management mechanisms for interstate conflict in the region are utterly inadequate, even for current threats. India and Pakistan have experienced at least a half-dozen crises with nuclear implications since 1984. Iran and Iraq fought a massive eight-year war, Iraq and US-led coalitions fought two major wars, and Ethiopia's invasion of Somalia in 2006 was met with relief (at least initially). Regional institutions lack the security capacity to balance power or deter conflict. US military predominance plays some role in deterring conflicts, and US diplomatic intervention has played some role in defusing crisis, but the United States is unable to enforce or ensure regional peace or to resolve regional rivalries.

The interstate war puzzle becomes even more complicated in the future, with the growth of Asian reliance on Middle East energy and the rising military capabilities of China and India. China's military buildup has been driven in the past by Taiwan, but the growing capability of the Chinese military now provides it access and influence well beyond its immediate waters. China's heavy reliance on the Indian Ocean for energy and trade will act as a magnet, increasingly dominating Chinese policy and security considerations. As Robert Kaplan muses, the Indian Ocean may become the battlefield for a rising China and India.[64]

This is not a certainty. So long as the Taiwan issue remains contested, Chinese attention will be focused closer to home, and to the problem of deterring the United States in the event of a conflict. If Taiwan is resolved to China's satisfaction, the question then becomes, in the words of a colleague, whether Taiwan "is an appetizer or a dessert." If reunification with Taiwan sates Chinese ambition and it becomes a status quo power heavily invested in the global economic system, the threat to Indian Ocean stability will be relatively modest. If, however, Taiwan is simply a necessary step in a broader global ambition, the Indian Ocean is likely to become a realm of possible conflict.

Here again, existing mechanisms in the region are inadequate. In the case of China, however, the region has the advantage of time—time to create institutions, to evolve multinational coalitions, to build defenses, or to shape the region diplomatically. The ASEAN states, with US help, could create formidable obstacles to Chinese expansion. So, too, could an Indian Ocean coalition, although it would be complicated by China's close military, economic, and diplomatic relations with regional states. The concept of shaping the region over time so that when China emerges militarily in the region it does so in an environment that minimizes potential regional instability could be a driving force in US policy as well as the policy of other states. It is a powerful common bond against a real long-term threat but will also require overcoming large barriers of misunderstanding and mistrust that have marked the US experience in the region since the end of World War II.

NOTES

This article reflects the views of the author alone, and not the position of the US Naval War College, the US Navy, or any other organization of the US government.

1. See US Navy, Marine Corps, and Coast Guard, *A Cooperative Strategy for 21st Century Seapower* (Washington, DC: Department of the Navy, 2007); www.navy.mil/maritime/Maritimestrategy.pdf.
2. US Department of Defense, *Quadrennial Defense Review 2010* (Washington, DC: Department of Defense, February 2010); www.defense.gov/qdr/qdr%20as%20of%2029jan10%201600.PDF, 60–61.
3. National Intelligence Council, *Global Trends 2025: A Transformed World* (Washington, DC: National Intelligence Council, November 2008); www.dni.gov/files/documents/Global%20Trends_2025%20Report.pdf.
4. Robert D. Kaplan, *Monsoon: The Indian Ocean and the Future of American Power* (New York: Random House, 2010).
5. "The Indian Ocean: Security Challenges and Opportunities for Cooperation," The Jerome Levy Chair for Geo-Economics Conference, US Naval War College, Newport, RI, May 13–15, 2008.
6. At various times, it has been called "the war on terror," "the global war on terror," or, much more briefly, "the struggle against violent extremism" and "the long war."
7. Rohan Gunaratna, *Inside Al Qaeda: Global Network of Terror* (New York: Berkeley 2002).
8. The original list of al-Qaeda allies and partners can be found in the 1998 declaration against the United States. Groups continue to associate themselves formally with al-Qaeda, creating at least the appearance of a multitentacled terrorist organization with sympathizers in more than fifty countries and the ability to operate or find sanctuary in each.
9. National Intelligence Estimate, *The Terrorist Threat to the US Homeland* 2007 (Washington, DC: National Intelligence Council, July 2007); www.c-span.org/pdf/nie_071707.pdf. Osama bin Laden was killed by US military special forces in Abbottabad, Pakistan, on May 2, 2011. See Eric Schmitt and Thom Shanker, *Counterstrike: The Untold Story of America's Secret Campaign against Al Qaeda* (New York: Times Books, Henry Holt, 2011). Nevertheless, al-Qaeda continues to operate under the leadership of bin Laden's chief lieutenant, Ayman al-Zawahiri, and maintains working relations with a number of other groups in South Asia and the Horn of Africa.

10. See Jim Garamone, "McChrystal Delivers Afghan Assessment to US, NATO Leaders" *Army Times*, September 1, 2009; www.army.mil/article/26816/. Redacted copies of Gen. McChrystal's assessment have appeared in public sources. See also Bob Woodward, *Obama's Wars* (New York: Simon & Schuster, 2010).
11. Ahmed Rashid, *Descent into Chaos* (New York: Viking, 2008).
12. Anahad O'Connor and Eric Schmitt, "Terror Attempt Seen as Man Tries to Ignite Device on Jet," *New York Times*, December 25, 2009; www.nytimes .com/2009/12/26/us/26plane.html.
13. "Al Shabaab" Backgrounder, *Council on Foreign Relations*, August 10, 2011; www .cfr.org/somalia/al-shabaab/p18650.
14. See *Nuclear Black Markets: Pakistan, A. Q. Khan and the Rise of Proliferation Networks* (London: Institute of International and Strategic Studies, 2007); www.iiss .org/publications/strategic-dossiers/nbm/.
15. See Gordon Corera, *Shopping for Bombs* (Oxford: Oxford University Press, 2006); and William Langewiesche, *The Atomic Bazaar* (New York: Farrar, Straus and Giroux, 2007).
16. Paul Brannan, "ISIS Analysis of IAEA Report on Syria: IAEA Concludes Syria 'Very Likely' Built a Reactor," May 24, 2011 at http://isis-online.org/uploads/isis-reports/documents/ISIS_Analysis_IAEA_Report_Syria_24May2011.pdf.
17. See Kaplan, *Monsoon*, for a very poetic description of the impact of the monsoon on regional transport and the regional economy.
18. See David Michel and Amit Pandya, ed., *Coastal Zones and Climate Change* (Washington, DC: Stimson Center, 2010).
19. See Amit A. Pandya and Rupert Herbert-Burns with Junko Kobayashi, *Maritime Commerce and Security: The Indian Ocean* (Washington DC: Stimson Center, 2010).
20. Early stages of melt will produce flooding, which will increase silt levels in major rivers as well as affecting agricultural planning.
21. Andrew S. Erickson, Lyle J. Goldstein, and Carnes Lord, ed. *China Goes to Sea: Maritime Transformation in Comparative Historical Perspective* (Annapolis, MD: Naval Institute Press, 2009).
22. Gabriel B. Collins, Andrew S. Erickson, Lyle J. Goldstein, and William S. Murray, ed. *China's Energy Strategy: The Impact on Beijing's Maritime Policies* (Annapolis, MD: Naval Institute Press, 2008).
23. George Perkovich, *India's Nuclear Bomb* (Berkeley: University of California Press, 2002).
24. Evan A. Feigenbaum, "China's Pakistan Conundrum: The End of the All-Weather Friendship?" *Foreign Affairs.com*, December 4, 2011; www.foreignaffairs.com/articles/136718/evan-a-feigenbaum/chinas-pakistan-conundrum?page=show.
25. R. Jeffrey Smith and Joby Warrick, "A Nuclear Power's Act of Proliferation" *Washington Post*, November 13, 2009; www.washingtonpost.com/wp-dyn/content/article/2009/11/12/AR2009111211060_pf.html. For comments, see Joshua Pollack, "The Media, Generals, & Passion of A.Q. Khan," *Arms Control*

Wonk, March 23, 2010; http://pollack.armscontrolwonk.com/archive/2671/the-media-the-generals-and-the-passion-of-aq-khan. On port facilities in Gwadar, see Kaplan, *Monsoon*; and Peter Lee, "China Drops the Gwadar Hot Potato," *Asia Times*, May 28, 2011; http://theglobalrealm.com/2011/05/31/china-drops-the-gwadar-hot-potato/.

26. Peter R. Lavoy, ed. *Asymmetric Warfare in South Asia: The Causes and Consequences of the Kargil Conflict* (Cambridge: Cambridge University Press, 2009).
27. See Marsha B. Cohen, "London's Sunday Times: All the Nukes Unfit to Print?" *PBS.org*, May 31, 2010; www.pbs.org/wgbh/pages/frontline/tehranbureau/2010/05/londons-sunday-times-all-the-nukes-unfit-to-print.html. This refers to a May 30, 2010, report that Israel was moving nuclear-armed submarines to the Persian Gulf—a report denied by the Israelis and discredited in this account.
28. Specifically referred to in the "redlines" outlined by Pakistani head of Strategic Plans Division General Kidwai. See "Nuclear Safety, Nuclear Stability and Nuclear Strategy in Pakistan: A Concise Report of a Visit by Landau Network—Centro Volta," *Pugwash Online*, www.pugwash.org/september11/pakistan-nuclear.htm.
29. There is some risk of stereotyping the distrust of developing states. Nevertheless, the lack of contact and familiarity with many of the states in the region will limit both the level of trust and the rapidity with which trust is built. For a non-Western perspective on security concerns in developing regions, see Mohammed Ayoob, *The Third World Security Predicament* (Boulder, CO: Lynne Rienner, 1995).
30. *A Cooperative Strategy for 21st Century Seapower.*
31. Mike Mullen, "Commentary: We Can't Do It Alone," *Honolulu Advertiser*, October 29, 2006.
32. Colin Gray, *The Utility of Sea Power* (New York: Free Press, 1992).
33. UNSC resolutions are available at www.un.org/Docs/sc/unsc_resolutions.html.
34. The United States now has four combatant commands bordering the Indian Ocean periphery—Pacific Command (which extends to India), Central Command, Africa Command, and European Command (which includes the Israeli port of Eilat).
35. Conversations with Indian officials, New Delhi and Mumbai, November 2008.
36. "Launch of Trilateral Coordinated Patrols, MALSINDO Malacca Straits Coordinated Patrol," *MINDEF Singapore*, July 20, 2004; www.mindef.gov.sg/imindef/news_and_events/nr/2004/jul/20jul04_nr.html.
37. Anthony Tucker-Jones, "WEB Special—War on Terror Update," *Warships International Fleet Review*, October 2004; www.warshipsifr.com/terrorism_special12.html.
38. Carolin Liss, "The Challenges of Piracy in Southeast Asia and the Role of Australia," *Austral Policy Forum 07-19A*; http://nautilus.org/apsnet/the-challenges-of-piracy-in-southeast-asia-and-the-role-of-australia/.
39. Praveen Sawhney, "Redefining the Limits of the Straits: A Composite Malacca Straits Security System," *IDSS Commentaries* (37/2006), May18, 2006; www.rsis.edu.sg/publications/Perspective/IDSS0372006.pdf.

40. Jumaina Siddiqui, "Maritime Cooperation in the Indian Ocean, Success Stories," in "The Indian Ocean: A Critical Arena for 21st Century Threats and Challenges," by Ellen Laipson (Washington, DC: Henry L. Stimson Center, 2009), 75; www.stimson.org/images/uploads/research-pdfs/Indian_Ocean-Chapter_6_Laipson.pdf.
41. Tucker-Jones, "WEB Special—War on Terror Update."
42. Sawhney, "Redefining the Limits of the Straits."
43. See the IONS website at http://ions.gov.in/.
44. The president of the US Naval War College, Rear Adm. Jacob Shuford, was invited to make an address and attended some of the conference.
45. IONS website at http://ions.gov.in/.
46. Condoleezza Rice, "Campaign 2000: Promoting the National Interest," *Foreign Affairs* (January–February 2000); www.foreignaffairs.com/articles/55630/condoleezza-rice/campaign-2000-promoting-the-national-interest#.
47. "Defending Australia in the Asia-Pacific Century: Force 2030" *Defence White Paper 2009* (Canberra: Department of Defence, 2009).
48. For a short assessment of options and possibilities, see Timothy Hoyt and Andrew Winner, "Thinking about the Rimland: Responses to Chinese Power," *Force*, January 2011.
49. Alfred Thayer Mahan, *The Influence of Sea Power upon History, 1660–1783* (1890; reprint, Boston: Little, Brown, 1980).
50. Sir Julian Corbett, *Some Principles of Maritime Strategy* (London: Longmans, Green & Co., 1911).
51. Barry Posen, "Command of the Commons: The Military Foundations of US Hegemony," *International Security* 29, no. 1 (Summer 2003): 5–46.
52. See Commander, US Naval Forces Central Command, US Fifth Fleet Combined Maritime Forces, www.cusnc.navy.mil/.
53. See, for example, Imtiaz Gul, *The Most Dangerous Place: Pakistan's Lawless Frontier* (New York: Viking, 2010), 74.
54. Nicholas Shmidle, *To Live or to Perish Forever: Two Tumultuous Years in Pakistan* (New York: Henry Holt, 2009).
55. Conversations with US naval officers engaged in OEF, 2004, 2008.
56. Rajesh Basrur, Timothy Hoyt, Rifaat Hussain, Sujoyini Mandal, *The 2008 Mumbai Terrorist Attacks: Strategic Fallout*, RSIS Monograph No. 17 (Singapore: S. Rajaratnam School of International Studies, 2009); and Angel Rabasa, Robert D. Blackwill, Peter Chalk, Kim Craglin, C. Christine Fair, Brian A. Jackson, Brian Michael Jenkins, Seth G. Jones, Nathaniel Shestak, and Ashley Tellis, *The Lessons of Mumbai* (Santa Monica, CA: RAND, 2009).
57. The author was able to observe operations from the USS *Reagan* in October 2008 while visiting the IOR.
58. "Operation Enduring Freedom—Deployments," *GlobalSecurity.org*, www.globalsecurity.org/military/ops/enduring-freedom_deploy-usn-mc.htm.

59. "US Central Command History," *US Central Command*, www.centcom.mil/en/about-centcom/our-history/
60. George W. Baer, *One Hundred Years of Sea Power* (Stanford, CA: Stanford University Press), 135, 152.
61. *A Cooperative Strategy for 21st Century Seapower.*
62. *Freedom to Use the Seas: India's Maritime Military Strategy* (New Delhi: Integrated Headquarters, Ministry of Defence (Navy), November 2007).
63. A most alarming report is Jeffrey Goldberg and Marc Armbinder, "Pakistan: The Ally from Hell," *Atlantic Monthly* (December 2011); www.theatlantic.com/magazine/print/2011/12/the-ally-from-hell/8730/.
64. Kaplan, *Monsoon.*

CHAPTER 12

CONCLUSION

Access and Security in the Indian Ocean Region

JOHN GAROFANO AND ANDREA J. DEW

INTRODUCTION

In the introduction to this book, we discussed the broad themes that our contributing authors address in this volume: that conventional wisdom exaggerates the most commonly cited threats—energy transit and piracy—and insufficiently appreciates others, including terrorism; that great power confrontation in the Indian Ocean region is a persistent issue for concern, and some of the sources of friction include misunderstandings of India and China; and that the Indian Ocean provides a vast drawing board for international cooperation on lower-level threat issues while the great power challenges are significant and will require more imagination. The chapters looked at these challenges from a variety of perspectives including US, Japanese, Singaporean, Chinese, and Indian national perspectives, and identified the most pressing issues in the region for the twenty-first century.

If this is truly to be the Indian Ocean century, or at least a century in which the Indian Ocean comes into its own economically and politically, then some of the challenges discussed in this book must be faced: how to ensure that sea lines of communications remain open, how to ensure security and safety in the region from armed groups as well as states, and how to manage great power rivalries as they affect the region. This raises the questions, however, of how and by whom? In each case the options require careful assessment of what is at stake—the threats and the opportunities—and who the best actors are to deal with this problem.

COOPERATION AND ACCESS

The issue of access to, from, and across this vast swath of ocean is the most pressing daily challenge facing Indian Ocean countries and the states that have economy and security interests in the region. The challenges posed by piracy give us cause for cautious optimism. Consider, for example, the friction caused off the Horn of Africa by pirates. John Martin singles this area out for special attention, as do Clive Schofield and Robin Warner in their chapter. In this case, instability and insecurity on land and the ongoing crisis of governance in Somalia coupled with the willingness of commercial shipping carriers to pay ransoms have created a booming business model for pirates in the region. The question is, what can be done to minimize the threats and maximize the opportunities this challenge presents?

Without doubt, this issue of how to keep the sea lines of communication open is one in which interaction and adaptation at the operational level play an important role, and one in which legal institutions and addressing root causes are and will continue to be essential. In August 2009 NATO created its task force Operation Ocean Shield (OOS) based on lessons learned from Operation Allied Protector, NATO's previous counterpiracy mission. OOS works in conjunction with EU Naval Force and Combined Maritime Forces (CTF) 150 and 151 in the Arabian Sea on antipiracy missions. In a January 2011 news release, the OOS task force noted that there were twenty-three attacks on ships in the Arabian Sea by armed pirates, "with 5 of the attacks resulting in the ships being taken over and held by the pirates."[1] Despite these figures, OOS sounded a note of cautious optimism in the interaction game with pirates; the adoption of antipiracy best management practices such as traveling at high speed, placing barbed wire around the ship, and using water cannons to ward off an imminent attack have made it significantly more difficult for pirates to target larger vessels. The pirates have adapted, however, and small, slow vessels such as yachts have become more tempting targets and easier pickings.

In addition to the political issues at stake, the piracy issue presents opportunities for international cooperation that strengthens the legal frameworks for prosecuting and convicting them. Despite numerous complaints that pirates who are caught are simply released at sea or released on land (Kenya is a favorite dropping-off point for captured Somali pirates), the US Navy proved willing to intervene to save the US captain of the *Maersk Alabama*, and the surviving Somali pirate was sentenced to more than thirty years in a US jail as a result.[2] Another notorious pirate, Jama Idle Ibrahim, was sentenced "in a US District Court on three charges:

an attack to plunder a vessel, an act of violence against persons on a vessel, and use of a firearm during a crime of violence."[3] These and a handful of other successful prosecutions in the United States and in Europe barely make a dent in the hundreds of incidents of piracy in the region, however; nor do they seem to deter would-be pirates.

Moreover, as Schofield and Warner note, instability on the ocean around the Horn of Africa has its roots on land, and there are no easy solutions for the "seamy littorals." Although the OOS NATO task force is focusing on capacity building efforts "to assist regional states, upon their request, in developing their own ability to combat piracy activities," no country, including the United States, wants to become involved in a protracted stability operation in Somalia.[4] The challenge, of course, is the lack of political will to indulge in state building and the sheer complexity of the problems. Somalia remains a country in name only, with a weak interim government beset by challenges from militia and the al-Shabaab group, and instability across waters in Yemen only adds to Somalia's problems.[5]

Given US experiences in Somalia in the early 1990s, American reluctance to intervene on land is understandable, but as Somali pirates become more violent, there may be little choice. The violent deaths of four US citizens in February 2011 at the hands of Somali pirates may force a change in policy. Indeed, there are already demands that the US Navy treat the nests of pirates along the Somali coasts as it once did the Barbary Pirates: bombardment, blockade, and eventual destruction. As tempting as that sounds, however, the fact remains that as long as the insurance and shipping industries are willing to pay ransoms and the political vacuum in Somalia remains unfilled, the challenge will persist.

In this case, the shared responsibilities of the various counterpiracy task forces may seem like the best solution for a problem that flows from land to sea. Here, too, big power politics raises its ugly head. In December 2008, for example, the People's Republic of China sent ships from its navy (People's Republic Army Navy, or PLAN) to the region to protect Chinese, Hong Kong, and Taiwanese shipping from pirate attacks.[6] PLAN presence was greeted with cautious optimism by some analysts, who argue that this first international deployment of Chinese vessels is a positive development; having China work in the international area provides the opportunity to work together and develop norms. However, they are really working unilaterally and not cooperatively, so too much starry-eyed optimism may not be warranted.

Despite the headlines, piracy has had no discernible impact on the volume of international trade or trade security for the primary economies involved. Moreover, current cooperative initiatives such as CTF 151 suggest that it is possible to at least continue to contain the threat at this level, at least at sea. The challenges lie in addressing the persistent root causes of this problem, which are terrestrial. No country shows an appetite in becoming involved in addressing root causes in any meaningful way. Although the United States would seem the obvious choice to lead this effort, it is understandably wary of becoming enmeshed. Finally, as Richardson and Dew address in their chapter, there are core security challenges that are not being sufficiently discussed. These include the use of the Indian Ocean by terror groups to move supplies and launch terror attacks at sea and on land. There is some reason to be optimistic in this area because addressing these challenges requires cooperation among navies, coast guards, and law enforcement among a group of countries that have proven themselves already capable of cooperating on a global scale on challenges such as proliferation security and container security.

The cooperative approach that Singapore, Indonesia, and Malaysia have taken with their "Eyes in the Sky" has helped make the Straits of Malacca significantly more inhospitable to piracy and has helped to track the movement of other suspicious vessels through the Indian Ocean and into the Pacific. Cooperation between Singapore, Indonesia, and Malaysia and in the Maritime and Port Authority of Singapore, Singapore's regional maritime center, is driven as much from an acknowledgment of shared problems as a fierce independence. The countries recognize that if they fail to manage the problem of security in their own waters, China, Japan, and the United States are willing and capable of stepping into the breach with a robust maritime force of their own. For Singapore, Indonesia, and Malaysia, the key to preventing other powers from controlling access to the region is to find the resources to control it themselves.

COMPETITION AND DENIAL

It is important to consider how to manage the areas of competition, rivalries, and choke-point friction in the Indian Ocean, which extend into the Pacific through the South China Sea region. China's economic growth signals future peer competition for many for whom the United States and other powers may have to engage in warfare. However, the research in this book shows that the real medium-term challenge posed by China's rapid economic growth is the pressure this places on the thoroughfare between the Indian and Pacific Oceans. These challenges include concerns about choke points such as the Strait of Malacca, through which vital oil supplies flow, and competition over access to resources under the oceans. This nexus of access and resource concerns makes the thoroughfare a zone of competition, friction, and denial that China views as a key to strategic vulnerability.

As documented in this volume, several developments feed into this growing concern over access: energy demand; the challenges posed by terrorism, piracy, and organized crimes; and the resulting fear that something catastrophic could disrupt trade and flows of oil through and out of the region. These are challenges that the international community has begun to address using a cooperative approach. Cooperation along the littorals continues to increase, and some technological solutions are helping to ease fears, such as the Proliferation Security Initiative, the Container Security Initiative, and port security initiatives, which demonstrate the extent to which governments are taking concrete steps and using technological aids to advance maritime security.[7]

As Yuan argues in his chapter, China's maritime interests are looming ever larger as its economy continues to grow. While it is true that China is still debating whether to become a maritime superpower, it is unlikely that it can survive in its current incarnation without substantially increasing its maritime presence and power. China has not yet reached its maritime zenith, and its quest for resources is far from sated. It is unlikely that any international or regional cooperative initiative will completely remove China's competitive fixation on Malacca and other choke points. Given this context, the policy challenge for the United States and other regional powers is how to ensure that inevitable friction does not devolve into a situation that cannot be managed diplomatically.

Trying to manage these frictions becomes more difficult inside the Indian Ocean with the rise of two dynamic economic and aspiring maritime powers. India and China have great ambitions and historical chips on their shoulders. Moreover, they have also developed an approach to naval power that is strongly Mahanian in its emphasis on control of entire ocean realms and on traditional fleet-on-fleet engagement on the high seas. The expansion of Pakistan's maritime domain further complicates this relationship, as does the persistent belief in significant mineral reserves on the ocean bed in the South China Sea. As Holmes and Yoshihara make clear in their chapter, either country could realistically take steps that would threaten vital national interests and provoke a military response. These include China shutting India out of the South China Sea, India shutting China out of the Indian Ocean (both strategies that can be justified on Mahanian principles), or China significantly upgrading its littoral presence in the Indian Ocean.

There is an attitudinal asymmetry in the US approach to the two other major powers with growing interests and expanding capabilities in the region. Washington recognizes—indeed, perhaps overemphasizes—the game-changing nature of China's rise and has sought to complete the process begun in the late 1960s of integrating China fully into the globalized system as a responsible stakeholder. US policymakers have worked tirelessly to dampen potential conflicts, improve military-to-military relations, and craft what has become a vital economic relationship for both sides into a binding force for peace.

Yet, despite China's growing might and presence and the potential that could come out of a truly pacific US–China relationship, Washington inwardly tilts toward India. Its size and diversity, its experience and role in counterterrorism, its democratic form of government, its knowledge- and service-based economic model of entrepreneurship and growth, and its potential as a powerhouse of economic growth in South and Central Asia cause US leaders to envision a special future relationship with India. President Barack Obama and former Secretary of State Hillary Clinton refer to it as nothing short of a defining relationship of the twenty-first century. With the National Defense Strategy clearly shifting attention and resources to the Pacific, much rides on this burgeoning partnership. Can it achieve the same level of cooperation and impact as have, for example, US relationships with Japan, South Korea, Thailand, the Philippines, and Australia, and with such friends as Singapore? Thus far the trajectory is in the right direction but moving extremely slowly. Civil nuclear cooperation continues, military cooperation and sales have increased somewhat, and business initiatives have expanded. In terms of the value to the US economy, the impact of such progress remains small, and Washington would like key regional partners such as India to do more for international norms and regimes on nuclear power.

The realm of great powers competing over national interests may be one in which the United States is uniquely qualified to manage, given its maritime history. As Hoyt argues in his chapter, both multilateral and regional initiatives may be cause for cautious optimism. While they have had minimal success to date, institutions such as the Indian Ocean Naval Symposium provide a framework and foundation for potentially more robust cooperation in the future. These institutions and initiatives, however, must not be viewed as a substitution for US engagement. Rather, they can be parallel and complementary to US presence and engagement in the region; US engagement rather than isolationism must be its strategy. The United States has indentified more areas of common interest with all of the protagonists individually than any of them have established with each other. Notwithstanding the routine airing of dirty laundry between the United States and each of the regional protagonists, only the United States has the resources, experience, and strategic doctrine, including the US Navy's *A Cooperative Strategy for 21st Century Sea Power*, to play this vital role in the region. It is in American interests to continue to do so.

Finally, the bad news for competitive naval thinking may be good news for long-term management of the actual problems at sea level. As with China's mercantilist approach to the security of its energy supply, its atavistic Mahanian thinking is fundamentally a conceptual problem with conceptual solutions: the same goes for India's approach to the region. As the preamble to the UNESCO constitution reminds us: "Since wars begin in the minds of men, it is in the minds of men that the defence of peace must be constructed." Although current US policy about how to deal with the Indian Ocean is very much in its infancy, the United States is uniquely positioned to take a more active role in and serve as a hub for multilateral coordination, including accelerated military exchanges and more ambitious diplomatic symposiums. As conflicts in the Middle East and North East Asia have shown, a comprehensive approach by a major power is sometimes necessary to achieve what fragmented ad hoc incrementalism cannot. The challenge for the United States is that the US government must reconceive of the Indian Ocean region as a whole and construct a whole-of-government approach to dealing with the challenges outlined in this book. If the twenty-first century is at least partially an Indian Ocean century as well as a Pacific century, then the current piecemeal approach to the region will not be sufficient to manage disputes over access, competition for resources, and the challenges created by nonstate actors at sea.

NOTES

1. NATO Shipping Center, *Operation Ocean Shield Newsletter*, January 2011, available at www.shipping.nato.int/Pages/NscNewsletter.aspx.
2. Abduwali Muse was sentenced to thirty-three years and nine months in February 2011 after pleading guilty to two counts of hijacking maritime vessels, two of kidnapping, and two of hostage taking in 2009. See Chris Dolmetsch and Bob Van Voris, "Somali Pirate Muse Gets 34-Year Prison Sentence for Indian Ocean Hijacking," February 16, 2011; www.bloomberg.com/news/2011-02-16/somali-pirate-muse-gets-34-year-prison-sentence-for-indian-ocean-hijacking.html.
3. In November 2010 Jama Idle Ibrahim was "sentenced in a US District Court on three charges: an attack to plunder a vessel, an act of violence against persons on a vessel, and use of a firearm during a crime of violence." "Somali Pirate Gets 30 Years for US Ship Attack," *Telegraph*, November 29, 2010; www.telegraph.co.uk/news/worldnews/piracy/8169276/Somali-pirate-gets-30-years-for-US-ship-attack.html. See NATO's Operation Ocean Shield warning for the area: "NATO Warns of Clear and Present Danger from Pirate Attacks," January 31, 2011; www.manw.nato.int/pdf/Press%20Releases%202011/Press%20releases%20Jan-June%202011/SNMG2/31%2001%2011%20NATOWarnsoftheDangertoVesselsofPirateAttacks.pdf.
4. NATO Website for Operation Ocean Shield, available at www.manw.nato.int/page_operation_ocean_shield.aspx.
5. See, for example, "Al-Qaeda in Yemen and Somalia: A Ticking Time-Bomb," Report to the Committee on Foreign Relations, US Senate, January 21, 2010, available from www.foreign.senate.gov/imo/media/doc/Yemen.pdf.
6. You Ji and Lim Chee Kia, "Implications of China's Naval Deployments to Somalia," *East Asian Policy* 1, no. 3 (July–September 2009); www.eai.nus.edu.sg/Vol1No3_YouJiLimCheeKia.pdf.
7. For its part, there is evidence that Beijing is evolving toward a more market-oriented, cooperative, and multinational approach even as it hedges its bet by pursuing overland pipelines and alternative sea routes.

CONTRIBUTORS

Emrys Chew is assistant professor of history at the S. Rajaratnam School of International Studies (RSIS), Nanyang Technological University, Singapore, where he is currently coordinator of the Masters Program in Strategic Studies and coordinator of research assistants. He is the author of *Arming the Periphery: The Arms Trade in the Indian Ocean during the Age of Global Empire*. His edited works include *Goh Keng Swee: A Legacy of Public Service* and *Globalization and Defense in the Asia-Pacific: Arms across Asia.*

Chew read History at the University of Cambridge, where he obtained a PhD (2002) and BA with first-class honors (1995). His BA dissertation, "The Naning War, 1831–1832: Colonial Authority and Malay Resistance in the Early Period of British Expansion," was awarded the Alan Coulson Prize for Imperial and Commonwealth History and was later published in *Modern Asian Studies*, May 1998. While his academic supervision of undergraduates at Cambridge (2002–5) had focused on the themes of imperialism and nationalism, his current teaching at RSIS is conducted mainly at the postgraduate level, and his current research focuses on the interconnections between Asian and global history, with particular emphasis on the crosscultural networks and exchanges that transformed warfare and strategy.

Andrea J. Dew is the codirector of the Center on Irregular Warfare & Armed Groups, and an associate professor of strategy and policy at the US Naval War College. She holds a PhD and MALD in international relations from the Fletcher School of Law and Diplomacy, Tufts University, and a BA (Hons.) in history from Southampton University in the United Kingdom. Dew lived and worked in Japan for eight years and studied advanced Japanese at the Kyoto Japanese Language School. She has also served as a research fellow at the Belfer Center for Science in International Affairs at Harvard University, and senior counterterrorism fellow at the Jebsen Center for Counter Terrorism Studies at the Fletcher School. In addition to recently completing a study about risk management in US and international commercial space policy, she is the coauthor of a book on armed groups, *Insurgents, Terrorists, and Militias: The Warriors of Contemporary Combat*. Dew teaches workshops on armed groups for Naval Special Warfare, Marine Forces Special Operations Command, and the Kennedy School for Irregular Warfare at Fort Bragg. Her current research focuses on irregular warfare strategies on land and in the maritime environment.

Sarah A. Emerson is the president of Energy Security Analysis, Inc. (ESAI), an independent energy research and forecasting firm located near Boston, Massachusetts. Emerson joined ESAI in 1986. As managing principal of ESAI Energy, which is responsible for the petroleum and alternative fuels consulting practice, she has developed many of ESAI's proprietary analytical tools for assessing the liquid fuels markets and forecasting oil prices. In addition, she has supervised the development of an empirical source database of monthly oil data that cover the period of January 1978 to the present for every country in the world, with particular focus on non-OECD countries. More broadly, she has conducted industry studies on a diverse range of topics, such as the transfer of pollution in energy trade, the profitability of Asian refining, the future of the Asian bitumen market, petroleum product markets in the Indian Ocean, the outlook for global automotive fuel markets, the global market for heavy crude oil, and the future of the Russian refining industry. In 1992, she published the first description of the Russian refining sector ever available in the West.

In addition to her market analysis and forecasting activities, Emerson is an expert witness in energy sector arbitration and has been an adviser to the US, Japanese, and Indian governments on energy security issues. She regularly publishes articles in the energy trade press, and is frequently quoted in the daily press and interviewed on television. Emerson was a 2004 Key Women in Energy honoree. In 2004 and 2005, she was the Repsol-YPF Senior Fellow at the Center for Business and Government at Harvard University, where she conducted research on the oil markets and energy policy. She received her BA from Cornell University and her MA from the Johns Hopkins University Nitze School of Advanced International Studies.

John Garofano is dean of academic affairs at the US Naval War College. Previously, he was the Capt. Jerome Levy Chair of Economic Geography and professor in the college's strategy and policy and national security affairs departments. Garofano's research interests include military intervention, Asian security, and the making of US foreign policy. His writings include *The Intervention Debate: Towards a Posture of Principled Judgment*; *Clinton's Foreign Policy: A Documentary Record*; and articles in *International Security*, *Asian Survey*, *Contemporary Southeast*

Asia, *Orbis*, and the *Naval War College Review*. In 2011, he deployed to Camp Leatherneck to support I MEF in several areas of planning and red-teaming.

Prior to joining the War College's faculty, Garofano was a senior fellow at Harvard University's Kennedy School of Government. He has taught at the US Army War College, the Five Colleges of Western Massachusetts, and the University of Southern California. Garofano received his PhD in government from Cornell University, an MA in security studies from the Johns Hopkins School of Advanced International Studies (Bologna/Washington), and a BA in History from Bates College. He is a native of Lynn, Massachusetts.

James R. Holmes is a Phi Beta Kappa graduate of Vanderbilt University, and he earned graduate degrees at Salve Regina University, Providence College, and the Fletcher School of Law and Diplomacy at Tufts University. He earned the 1994 Naval War College Foundation Award, signifying the top graduate in his Naval War College class. He previously served on the faculty of the University of Georgia School of Public and International Affairs and as a research associate at the Institute for Foreign Policy Analysis in Cambridge, Massachusetts. A former US Navy surface warfare officer, he served on board the battleship *Wisconsin*, directed an engineering course at the Surface Warfare Officers School Command, and served as military professor at the Naval War College, College of Distance Education. He is coauthor of *Indian Naval Strategy in the 21st Century* and *Red Star Over the Pacific: China's Rise and the Challenge to US Maritime Strategy*, an *Atlantic Monthly* Best Book of 2010.

Timothy D. Hoyt is professor of strategy and policy and the John Nicholas Brown Chair of Counterterrorism Studies at the US Naval War College in Newport, Rhode Island, where he has taught for ten years. Hoyt earned his undergraduate degrees from Swarthmore College and his PhD in international relations and strategic studies from The Johns Hopkins University's Paul H. Nitze School of Advanced International Studies in 1997. Before joining the Naval War College, he taught at Georgetown University's School of Foreign Service. Hoyt is the author of *Military Industries and Regional Defense Policy: India, Iraq and Israel* and more than forty articles and chapters on international security and military affairs.

Recent publications include chapters and articles on the war on terrorism in South Asia, the limits of military force in the global war on terrorism, the impact of culture on military doctrine and strategy, military innovation and warfare in the developing world, US–Pakistan relations, the impact of nuclear weapons on recent crises in South Asia, and the strategic effectiveness of terrorism. Hoyt served previously as cochairman of the Indian Ocean Regional Studies Group at the Naval War College. He is currently working on a multivolume study of the strategy of the Irish Republican Army from 1913 to 2005, a series of projects examining US relations with India and Pakistan, and analyses of irregular warfare and terrorism in South Asia.

James Kraska is the Howard S. Levie Chair of Operational Law, member of the faculty of the international law department, and senior associate in the Center for Irregular Warfare and Armed Groups at the US Naval War College in Newport, Rhode Island. He also holds appointments as senior fellow at the Foreign Policy Research Institute and as guest investigator at the Marine Policy Center, Woods Hole Oceanographic Institution.

Kraska served as legal adviser to joint and naval task force commanders in the Asia-Pacific, for two tours in Japan, and in four Pentagon major staff assignments, including as oceans law and policy adviser as well as chief of international treaty negotiations, both on the Joint Staff. He has taught and lectured at numerous academic institutions, including The Hague Academy of International Law, Stanford Law School, National Defense University, and the International Institute of Humanitarian Law in San Remo, Italy. He has consulted on oceans law and policy issues for international organizations, research institutions, and private companies in the United States, Europe, and Asia.

Kraska has published more than eighty articles and book chapters, including articles in *Yale Journal of International Law*, *Stanford Journal of International Law*, *Georgetown Journal of International Law*, *The American Interest*, *Journal of International Affairs*, *Comparative Strategy*, *Current History*, and *Orbis*. His books include *Maritime Power and the Law of the Sea* and *Contemporary Maritime Piracy*.

He earned a doctor of juridical science and master of laws from University of Virginia School of Law and a doctor of jurisprudence from Indiana University Maurer School of Law, Bloomington. Kraska also received a master of arts in foreign affairs from the School of Politics and Economics, Claremont Graduate School. In 2010, he was selected for the Alfred Thayer Mahan Award for Literary Achievement by the Navy League of the United States.

John Martin graduated from Exeter University in the United Kingdom with combined honors in history and archaeology. He then served in the Royal Hong Kong Police until 1983, resigning from the Commercial Crime Bureau to establish, operate, and sell two trading companies there. Returning to the United Kingdom to study and graduate to the Institute of Chartered Secretaries and Administrators in 1994, he then researched and wrote *No Catch, No Con, No Work, No Limits*, an analysis of multilevel marketing schemes in the United Kingdom that was used by the junior minister for consumer affairs in Parliament. In 1995, he was appointed as Far East regional director of the International Maritime Bureau. According to "Trends in Organised Crime" 3, no. 4 (1998), his "brief but intense tenure at the RPC's [Regional Piracy Centre] helm has made him the premier authority on piracy." Since 1998, Martin has recruited and led a multidisciplinary team to investigate and recover ships and cargoes stolen by hijack, fraud, and nonperforming loan in the Asia-Pacific region, and has recovered more than $100 million in assets for his clients. In 2000, Martin began compiling a database of all reported pirate attacks in the world from 1983 to the present day. Since then, he has repeatedly addressed students at the US Naval War College and delegates to the 2009 International Conference on Piracy in Kuala Lumpur, where he also acted as a moderator. He has also written articles on piracy for shipping magazines, such as *The Sea* and *Fairplay*.

Vivek S. Mathur is an associate at ESAI Energy LLC, where he specializes in Asian oil and petrochemical feedstock markets. He also leads ESAI's analysis of the Indian energy market. Mathur graduated with an MA from the Fletcher School, Tufts University, specializing in energy studies and strategic business management, and received an MA in politics from the School of International Studies, Jawaharlal Nehru University, India.

Michael Richardson is a visiting senior research fellow at the Institute of Southeast Asian Studies (ISEAS), in Singapore. Part of his recent research has focused on maritime security. His book *A Time Bomb for Global Trade: Maritime-Related Terrorism in an Age of Weapons of Mass Destruction* was published by ISEAS in May 2004 and was recently reprinted. He is currently researching energy and sea-lane security and counterproliferation in the Asia-Pacific region. He has spoken on these subjects at conferences organized by the CNA Corporation, the Johns Hopkins University Applied Physics Laboratory, the US Pacific Command, and the Australian Navy. Based in Singapore, he was the Asia editor of the *International Herald Tribune* (IHT) from 1987 until 2001, with broad responsibility for writing Asia-Pacific news and analysis and coordinating the IHT's reporting from the region. He was a journalist and political correspondent for the *Age* newspaper from 1966 to 1971, working from Melbourne and Canberra, Australia. Until 1985, he was the Southeast Asia and South Asia correspondent, based in Singapore, for the *Age* and the *Sydney Morning Herald*. Born in 1943, he was educated at schools in Australia and at Oxford University, where he graduated with honors in Modern History.

Clive Schofield is professor and director of research at the Australian Centre for Ocean Resource and Security (ANCORS), University of Wollongong, Australia. He is a political geographer and international legal scholar. ANCORS is Australia's sole academic center devoted to multidisciplinary research on national and international ocean law, policy, management, and maritime security. Schofield currently holds an Australian Research Council (ARC) Future Fellowship. He previously served as director of research at the International Boundaries Research Unit (IBRU), University of Durham, United Kingdom. Schofield holds a PhD (geography) from the University of Durham and an LLM from the University of British Columbia, Canada. He has researched and published primarily on issues related to the delimitation of maritime boundaries; geotechnical issues in the law of the sea; maritime security, notably in relation to piracy and armed robbery against ships; and maritime boundary disputes, including disputes over islands and their resolution. He has been involved in the peaceful settlement of boundary and territory disputes, for example, through the provision of technical advice and research support to governments engaged in boundary negotiations and in dispute settlement cases before the International Court of Justice. He has published more than one hundred book chapters and scholarly articles. He is also coauthor (with Victor Prescott) of the book *The Maritime Political Boundaries of the World* and editor of recent volumes, including *Maritime Energy Resources in Asia* (two volumes, National Bureau of Asian Research, December 2011 and January 2012), *Beijing's Power and China's Borders: Twenty Neighbors in Asia* (with Bruce Elleman and Stephen Kotkin, M. E. Sharpe, 2012), and *Climate Change and the Oceans: Gauging the Legal and Policy Currents in the Asia Pacific* (with Robin Warner, Edward Elgar Publishers, 2012).

Robin Warner is an associate professor at the Australian National Centre for Ocean Resources and Security, University of Wollongong. She holds a BA (Honors) and LLB from the University of Sydney, a Master of International Law from the Australian National University, a PhD from the University of Sydney, and a graduate diploma in strategic studies from the Joint Services Staff College in Canberra. She was formerly the assistant secretary of the International Crime Branch in the Commonwealth Attorney General's Department from 2002 to 2007 and director of International Law for the Australian Defence Force from 1997 to 2001. Prior to that, she held many prominent positions in the Australian Defence Force Legal Service, including deputy director of Naval Legal Services and fleet legal officer during a twenty-two-year career in the Permanent Navy, achieving the rank of captain. She also spent time on exchange service with the US Navy and the New Zealand Defence Legal Services. From 2002 to 2008, she was head of the ACT Reserve Legal Panel.

Warner's current research interests include law of the sea, oceans governance, marine environmental law, climate law, ocean energy regulation, and transnational criminal law. She is an Australian Research Council postdoctoral fellow and lead researcher on a project titled "Harnessing the Oceans to Combat Climate Change." She has published widely in oceans law and policy and is the author of *Protecting the Oceans beyond National Jurisdiction: Strengthening the International Law Framework* (Martinus Nijhoff Publishers, 2009), editor (with Simon Marsden) of

Transboundary Environmental Governance: Inland Coastal and Marine Perspectives (Ashgate Publishers, 2012), and editor (with Clive Schofield) of *Climate Change and the Oceans: Gauging the Legal and Policy Currents in the Asia Pacific* (Edward Elgar Publishers, 2012), as well as many book chapters and journal articles.

Warner is Australian vice president of the New Zealand and Australian Armed Forces Law Association, a member of the Reference Group of the Institute of Marine and Antarctic Studies, University of Tasmania, and a member of the World Conservation Union (IUCN) Commission on Environmental Law, Oceans, Coasts, and Coral Reefs Specialist Group. She has undertaken consultancies for a wide range of international organizations including IUCN, the Convention on Biological Diversity, and the International Seabed Authority, and for Australian government departments including the Department of Defence, prime minister, and cabinet, and the Department of Sustainability, Environment, Water, Population, and Communities.

Andrew C. Winner is a professor of strategic studies in the strategic research department at the Naval War College, Newport, Rhode Island. His areas of focus are South Asia, the Middle East, nonproliferation, maritime partnerships, maritime strategy, and US national security. He is director of the Indian Ocean Studies Group at the Naval War College. In June 2007, he was awarded the Navy Meritorious Civilian Service Award for his work on the navy's new maritime strategy. Prior to his current appointment, he was a senior staff member at the Institute for Foreign Policy Analysis. Prior to joining the institute, he held various positions at the US Department of State on the staff of the undersecretary of state for arms control and international security affairs and in the Bureau of Political-Military Affairs, where he worked on nonproliferation, security in the Persian Gulf including negotiating access and prepositioning agreements, arms transfer policy, NATO enlargement, and security assistance. He is the coauthor of *Indian Naval Strategy in the 21st Century*. He holds a PhD from the University of Maryland, College Park, an MA from the Johns Hopkins University Paul H. Nitze School of Advanced International Studies (SAIS), and an AB from Hamilton College.

Toshi Yoshihara is professor of strategy and John A. van Beuren Chair of Asia-Pacific Studies at the US Naval War College in Newport, Rhode Island. He is an affiliate member of the China Maritime Studies Institute at the War College. Previously, he was a visiting professor in the strategy department at the Air War College. He is coauthor of *Red Star Over the Pacific: China's Rise and the Challenge to US Maritime Strategy*, *Indian Naval Strategy in the Twenty-First Century,* and *Chinese Naval Strategy in the Twenty-First Century: The Turn to Mahan*. He is also coeditor of *Strategy in the Second Nuclear Age: Power, Ambition, and the Ultimate*

Weapon and *Asia Looks Seaward: Power and Maritime Strategy*. Yoshihara holds a PhD from the Fletcher School of Law and Diplomacy, Tufts University.

Jingdong Yuan is acting director of the Centre for International Security Studies and an associate professor with the department of government and international relations at the University of Sydney. Yuan specializes in Asia-Pacific security, Chinese defense and foreign policy, and global and regional arms control and nonproliferation issues. A graduate of the Xi'an Foreign Language University, People's Republic of China (1982), he received his PhD in political science from Queen's University in 1995 and has had research and teaching appointments at Queen's University, York University, the University of Toronto, and the University of British Columbia, where he was a recipient of the prestigious Iaazk Killam Postdoctoral Research Fellowship. Between 1999 and 2010, he held various appointments at the Monterey Institute of International Studies, including as director of East Asia Nonproliferation Program, James Martin Center for Nonproliferation Studies. He is the coeditor of *Australia and China at 40* (Sydney: University of New South Wales Press, 2012), the author of *The Dragon's Will: The Exercise and Limitation of China's Power from Pyongyang to Khartoum* (in press), and the coauthor of *China and India: Cooperation or Conflict?* His publications have also appeared in *Asian Survey*, *Far Eastern Economic Review*, *Contemporary Security Policy*, *International Herald Tribune*, *International Journal*, *Journal of International Affairs*, *Nonproliferation Review*, and *Washington Quarterly*, among others.

Moeed Yusuf is the South Asia adviser at the United States Institute of Peace (USIP) and is responsible for managing the institute's Pakistan program. Yusuf is engaged in expanding USIP's work on Pakistan to cover aspects that remain critical for the United States and Pakistan to better understand the other's interests and priorities. His current research focuses on the Pakistan–US relationship, South Asian regional conflict dynamics, youth and democratic institutions in Pakistan, and policy options to mitigate militancy in the country. Yusuf is a native of Pakistan. In his training as a political scientist, he has worked extensively on issues relating to South Asian politics, Pakistan's foreign policy, the US–Pakistan relationship, nuclear deterrence and nonproliferation, and human security and development in South Asia.

Before joining USIP, Yusuf was a fellow at the Frederick S. Pardee Center for the Study of the Longer-Range Future at Boston University, and concurrently a research fellow at the Mossavar-Rahmani Center at Harvard's Kennedy School. He has also been affiliated with the Brookings Institution as a special guest. In 2007, he cofounded Strategic and Economic Policy Research, a private sector consultancy firm in Pakistan. Yusuf has also consulted for a number of Pakistani and international organizations. From 2004 to 2007, he was a full-time consultant with the Sustainable Development Policy Institute, Pakistan's premier development sector think tank. He has also consulted for a number of national and international organizations. Yusuf taught in Boston University's political science and international relations departments as a senior teaching fellow in 2009. He had previously taught at the defense and strategic studies department at Quaid-e-Azam University, Pakistan. Yusuf has published widely in books, national and international journals, professional publications, and magazines.

He is currently finalizing two edited volumes, one on South Asia's long-term future and the other on insurgencies and counterinsurgencies in South Asia. He writes a regular column for *Dawn*, Pakistan's leading English daily. He has also appeared as an expert on US and Pakistani media including CNN, Al Jazeera English, Voice of America, BBC, NPR, Dawn News, AAJ TV, Geo News, Express News, SAMAA TV, Dunya TV (Pakistan), and ND TV (India).

INDEX

Surnames beginning with al are alphabetized by the following part of the name.